Vorwort / Foreword

Liebe Leserinnen und Leser,

alles was sich geändert hat – ist Alles.

Mit dieser Botschaft kündigte der Apple-Konzern 2015 sein neues iphone 6s an. Und auch wenn die Botschaft mehr hintergründig daherkommt, so passt sie doch wie maßgeschneidert auf die neue Ausgabe des Portbook & Island Guide.

Denn es ist die Summe der Verbesserungen in allen Details, die am Ende den Unterschied macht. Das Format, das Gehäuse, ist geblieben, wie beim iphone 6s, aber drinnen hat sich fast alles geändert – oder ist schlicht umfassender geworden. Im Einzelnen:

328 Seiten – das ist ein dickes Plus von 116 Seiten! Die meisten davon entfallen auf die wunderschönen Buchten der Inseln, die wir jetzt in aller Ausführlichkeit vorstellen.

Pläne – die fünf Handelshäfen auf den Balearen – Palma, Alcúdia, Mahón, Ibiza und La Savina auf Formentera – zeigen wir jetzt auch im aktuellen Kartenbild. Unser Dank gilt der Hafenverwaltung Autoridad Portuaria Baleares. Dazu gibt es Details der schwierigen Ansteuerung von Addaya/Menorca und zu den Bojenfeldern im Naturhafen Portocolom.

Luftaufnahmen – zirka 500 Fotos waren zuletzt im Buch, jetzt sind es 750. Sie zeigen alle Anlegestellen und Buchten und wo dort Sand oder Seegras den Boden bedecken. Auch gefährliche Untiefen werden sichtbar.

Schneller Finden – auf den Übersichtsseiten gibt es jetzt direkte Seitenverweise zu den ausführlichen Beschreibungen von Häfen und Buchten.

Neue Symbole – Wir haben die Kennzeichnung in den (Luft)-bildern verbessert. Alles ist jetzt leichter, freundlicher und auch genauer!

Last but not least möchten wir Ihnen unsere Webseite zum Buch an Herz legen – www.portbook-mallorca.com

Hier erfahren Sie alle Veränderungen nach Drucklegung. Den Wechsel von Hafenbetreibern, Neues zu Bojenfeldern und, und, und …

Auf schöne Erlebnisse mit dem Boot und auf den Balearen!

Ihr

Martin Muth

Herausgeber & Autor

Dear Readers,

the only thing that's changed is everything.

With this message, in 2015 the Apple Group announced its new iphone 6s. And even if this message is more cryptic than striking, it fits perfectly to this new edition of our Portbook & Island Guide.

In this latest edition, we have concentrated on improving the details. The format and the cover have remained unchanged, but like with the iPhone 6s, what you will find on the inside has been improved and updated:

328 pages – that is an additional 116 pages! Most of these pages have been dedicated to the gorgeous bays of the Balearic islands. You will find beautiful pictures and indepth descriptions that will make you want to set sail!

Plans – we now present you with detailed, up-to-date maps the five commercial harbours in the Balearic Islands – Palma, Alcudia, Mahón, Ibiza and La Savina on Formentera – thanks to Autoridad Portuaria de Baleares (APB). In addition, you will find detailed plans for the difficult approach of Port Addaya / Menorca laid out in two small scale plans, and a drawing of the various buoy fields in the natural harbour of Portocolom for easy orientation.

Aerial pictures – about 500 photographs were included in the last edition. Now we have a total of about 750 pictures. They show all piers and coves and with their help one can easily identify where sand or weed cover the ground – as well as dangerous shoals and washed rocks.

Quickfinder – now the overview pages refer directly to the pages with the detailed descriptions.

New symbols – we have improved all markers in the aerial pictures, making it easier and more accurate to navigate.

Last but not least we would like to recommend our website www.portbook-mallorca.com

Here we provide you with continuously updated information including new port operators, changes made to bouy fields and so on.

We wish you good winds and wonderful experiences as you explore the Balearic Islands!

Yours sincerely

Martin Muth

Editor & Author

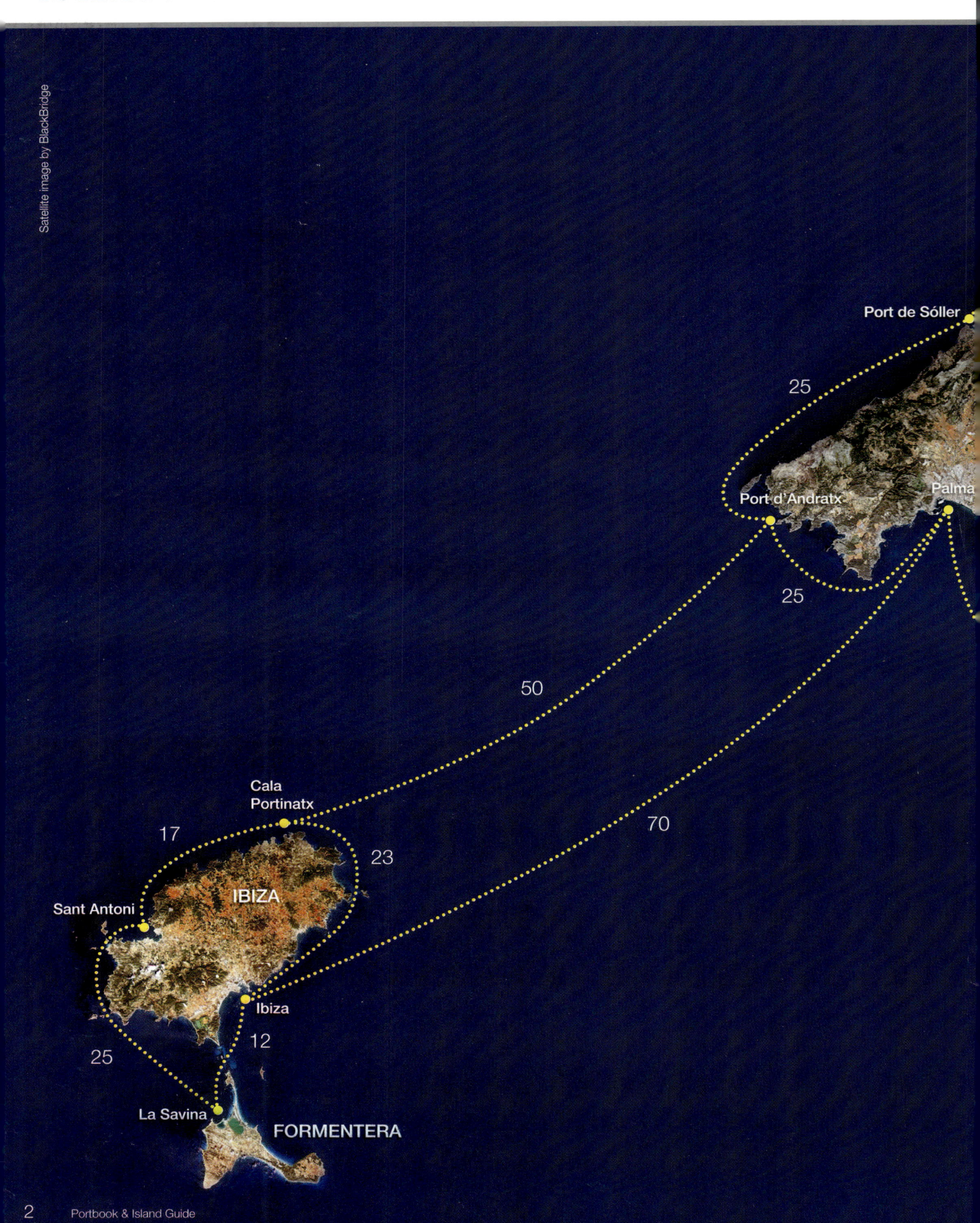

Die Balearen / The Balearic Islands

Satellite image by BlackBridge

Port de Sóller

25

Port d'Andratx   Palma

25

50

70

Cala Portinatx

17   23

Sant Antoni   IBIZA

Ibiza

12

25

La Savina

FORMENTERA

Distanzen / Distances

Alle Angaben in sm
All distances in nmi

- Pollença — 35 — (north route)
- Pollença — Alcúdia — 13
- Alcúdia — Ciutadella — 33
- Alcúdia — Cala Rajada — 21
- Cala Rajada — Ciutadella — 25
- Cala Rajada — Porto Cristo — 15
- Porto Cristo — Sa Rapita — 30
- Sa Rapita — Cabrera — 23
- Cabrera — 13
- Ciutadella — Fornells — 23
- Fornells — Addaya — 9
- Addaya — 17
- Mahón — 26
- Ciutadella — Cala Macarella — 11

MALLORCA

- Pollença
- Alcúdia
- Cala Rajada
- Porto Cristo
- Portocolom
- Sa Rapita
- Cabrera

MENORCA

- Ciutadella
- Fornells
- Addaya
- Mahón
- Cala Macarella

Die Balearen / The Balearic Islands

Detaillierte Übersichtskarten im Buch: / Detailed page overview:

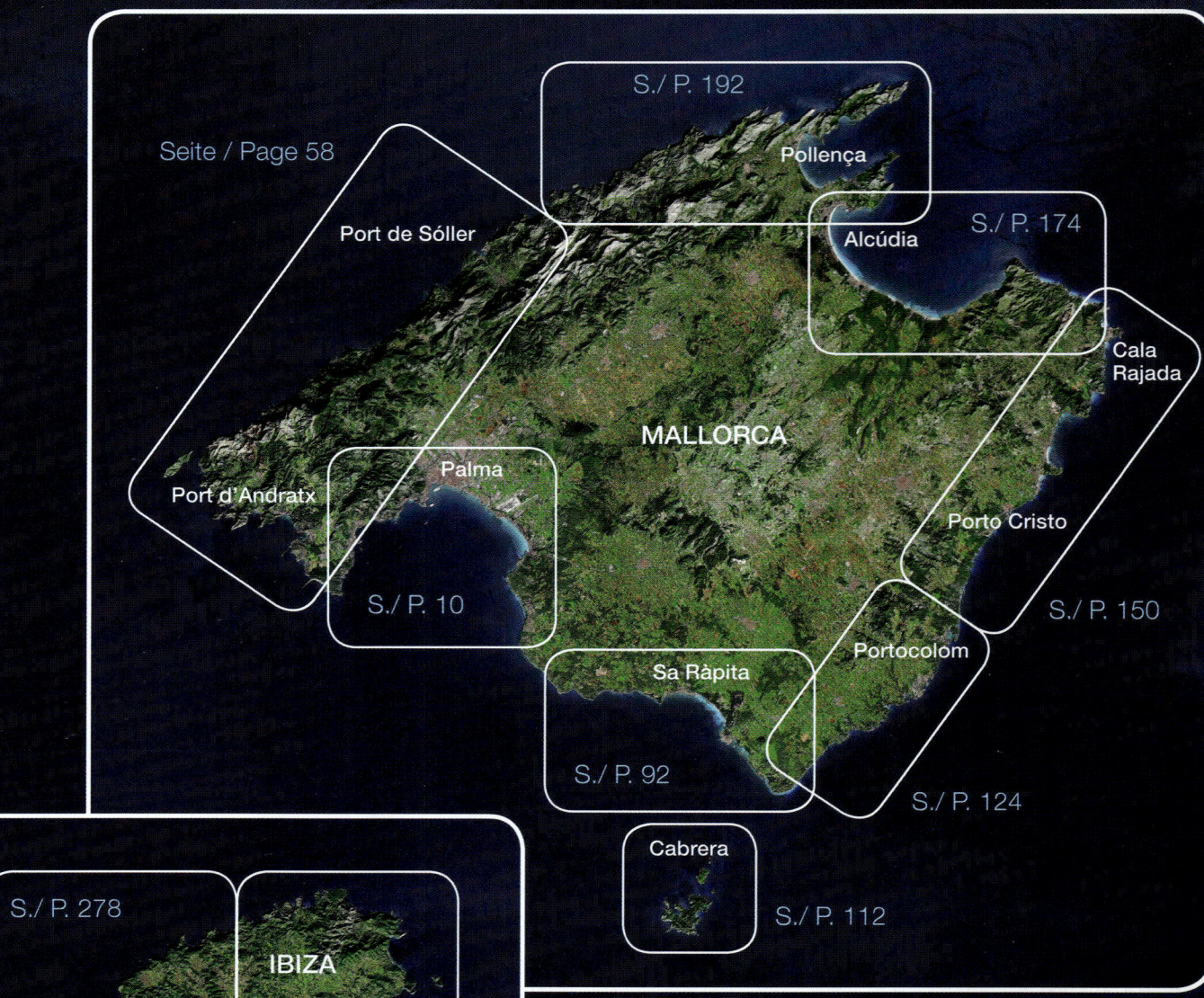

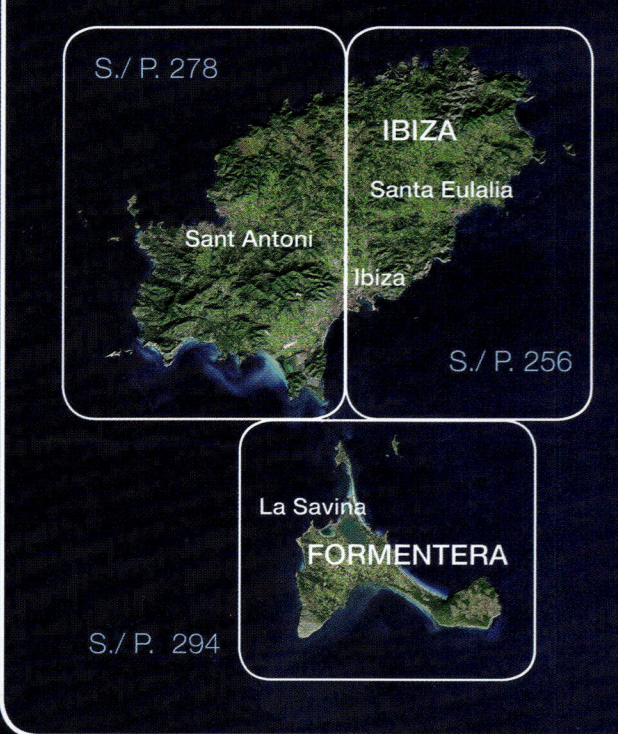

S./ P. 192 — Pollença
Seite / Page 58
Port de Sóller
S./ P. 174 — Alcúdia
Cala Rajada
Port d'Andratx
Palma
MALLORCA
Porto Cristo
S./ P. 10
S./ P. 150
Sa Ràpita
Portocolom
S./ P. 92
S./ P. 124
Cabrera
S./ P. 112

S./ P. 278
IBIZA
Santa Eulalia
Sant Antoni
Ibiza
S./ P. 256

La Savina
FORMENTERA
S./ P. 294

Die Balearen-Inseln aus dem Weltall gesehen: Die Abstände zwischen den hier abgebildeten Inseln und die Größenverhältnisse zueinander sind zum Teil nicht maßstabsgerecht.

Balearic Islands seen from space:
The distances between the islands displayed here and their respective sizes in proportion to each other are not always true to scale.

Hinweis zu den Satelliten-Bildern:
Die Balearen und viele andere Mittelmeerinseln sind als hochwertiger Satellitenbildkunstdruck erhältlich bei der albedo39 Satellitenbildwerkstatt, Köln, www.albedo39.de

Note on satellite images:
High-quality satellite image art prints of the Balearic Islands and many more islands of the Mediterranean are available at albedo39 Satellitenbildwerkstatt in Cologne, Germany.
See www.albedo39.de

Inhalt / Content

Die Balearen
Balearic Islands

MALLORCA 6
Die Bucht von Palma / The Bay of Palma 8
Mallorcas Westen / The West of Mallorca 56
Mallorcas Süden / The South of Mallorca 90
Cabrera-Archipel / The Cabrera Islands 110
Mallorcas Osten / The East of Mallorca 122
Mallorcas Norden / The North of Mallorca 172
MENORCA 208
IBIZA 254
FORMENTERA 292

TÖRN-TIPPS / FAVOURITE CRUISES
Mallorcas Süden / The South of Mallorca 306
Mallorcas Ostküste / Mallorcas East Coast 308
Mallorcas umrunden / Cruising around Mallorca 310
Ibiza & Formentera 312
Menorca 314

Wissenswertes / Facts 316
Register 324
Foto- und Inserentenverzeichnis /
Photo credits & Advertisers 326
Vielen Dank / Acknowledgements 327
Impressum / Imprint 328

Magic Mallorca

Mallorca

Kleine Schwester: Cala Molto ist nur ein Anhängsel der Cala Guya – aber so verlockend ...

Little Sister: Cala Molto is often overlooked next to Cala Guya – but so tempting ...

Mallorcas Zauber entspringt ihren vielen Facetten. Vom alten Fischerhafen bis zur Mega-Marina, von den hohen Bergen der Tramuntana bis hin zu langen Stränden und kleinen Buchten – es ist alles darunter.

Mallorca's magic lies in the huge variety that the island offers. From old fishing harbours to mega-sized marinas, from the towering Tramuntana mountain range down to long beaches and small bays – it simply has everything.

Bay of Palma

Ein Spielplatz für Yachten und eines der attraktivsten Ziele in Europa zum Bootfahren – das und nicht weniger ist die Bucht von Palma.

A playground for yachts and one of the most attractive sailing destinations in Europe – the Bay of Palma.

Die Bucht von Palma / The Bay of Palma

- Mehr als 5000 Yachtliegeplätze
- Zentrum nautischer Fachbetriebe
- Die Regatta-Bucht Mallorcas

More than 5000 berths for yachts
Centre for nautical companies
The place for sailing events

Mallorca

Portals Vells – Cala Veya

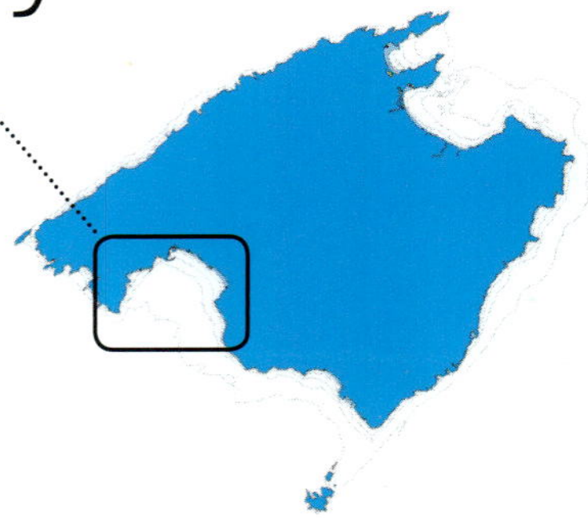

🇩🇪 Die Bahia de Palma ist eines der sonnenreichsten Fleckchen der Insel und mit ihren zirka 10 mal 10 sm perfekt, um Bootfahren einfach zu genießen..

🇬🇧 *The bay of Palma is one of the sunniest places on Mallorca and measures about 10 by 10nm. The perfect spot to enjoy cruising or racing.*

1 Cala Portals Vells - 39° 28,3' N 002° 31,6' E → page 12
Viel besuchte Bucht mit kleinen Stränden. Strandbars und eine Höhle.
Much frequented bay with three small beaches & beach restaurants.

2 Ensenada de la Porrasa - 39° 30,2' N 002° 32,5' E → page 13
Markiert durch die kleine Isla de la Porrasa. An Land der Nikki Beach Club.
Fringed by the islet de la Porrasa. Close to exclusive Nikki Beach Club.

3 Palmanova - 39° 31,1' N 002° 32,6' E → page 13
Sicherer Platz bei Westwind. Viele Hotels, dennoch schöne Atmosphäre.
Well protected with westerly winds. Many hotels, though nice atmosphere.

4 Puerto Portals - 39° 31,6' N 002° 33,8' E → page 14
Weiterhin Mallorcas Nr.-1-Marina zum Sehen und Gesehen werden.
After many years still Mallorca No.-1-Marina to see and to be seen.

5 Illetas - 39°31,7' N 002° 35,0' E → page 18
Für Yachten aus Palma der nächstgelegener Ankerplatz. Im Sommer voll.
Yachts from Palma find here their first anchorage. During summer crowded.

6 Port Calanova - 39° 32,9' N 002° 36,1' E → page 20
Nach Umbau jetzt mehr Platz für Gastyachten. Tankstelle. 75-t-Travellift.
After reconstruction now more berths for yachts in transit. 75t travel lift.

7 Palma de Mallorca - 39° 33,0' N 002 38,8' E → page 24
Mallorcas Hauptstadt wird immer mehr zum Zentrum der Superyachten.
Mallorca's capital increasingly turns into a key destination for super yachts.

8 Portixol - 39° 33,4' N 002 40,1' E → page 47
Gastyachten fragen selten nach einem Liegeplatz. Geringe Wassertiefen.
Yachts in transit rarely ask for a berth here. Shallow water depths.

9 Cala Gamba - 39° 32,6' N 002 41,6' E → page 47
Nur von Booten mit wenig Tiefgang zu nutzen. Gastplätze werden vermietet.
Only boats with shallow depths can use this port. Guest berths are available.

10 C'an Pastilla - 39° 31,8' N 002° 43,0' E → page 48
Nah am Flughafen. Geführt durch den Club Marítimo San Antonio de la Playa.
Close to the airport. Managed by Club Marítimo San Antonio de la Playa.

11 Club Nàutic S'Arenal - 39° 30,2' N 002° 44,6' E → page 52
Professionell geführte Clubmarina mit einem beliebten Werftgelände.
Professional managed club marina that also runs a popular boatyard.

12 Cala Blava - 39° 29,1' N 002° 43,9' E → page 55
Vor der ruhigen Ortschaft befindet sich ein kostenpflichtiges Bojenfeld.
Beneath this quiet small village there is a buoy field. Subject to charges.

13 Cala Veya / Illots de Can Climent - 39° 26,4' N 002° 44,6' E → page 55
Ankerplatz vor Steilküste. Zum Meer hin offen, aber türkise Wasserfarbe.
Anchorage below the cliffs. Open to the sea, but turquoise water colour.

Portbook & Island Guide

Die Bucht von Palma / The Bay of Palma

BAHIA DE PALMA

- 1 Portals Vells
- 2 Ensenada de la Porrasa
- 3 Palmanova
- 4 Puerto Portals
- 5 Illetas
- 6 Port Calanova
- 7 PALMA
- 8 Portixol
- 9 Cala Gamba
- 10 C'an Pastilla
- 11 Club Nàutic S'Arenal
- 12 Cala Blava
- 13 Cala Veya / Illots de Can Climent

Mallorca

Cala Portals Vells – Palmanova

ANKERPLÄTZE
ANCHORAGE AREAS

A **Cala Portals Vells**
39° 28,3' N 002° 31,6' E

🇩🇪 Viel besuchte „Dreifingerbucht" mit kleinen Stränden. Es gibt zwei Strandbars resp. Restaurants und eine Höhle. Dazu die Mini-Marina eines örtlichen Yachtclubs, der freie Liegeplätze vermietet.

Es gibt in der direkten Einfahrt zur Bucht keine Untiefen. Der Ankergrund besteht aus Sand mit vielen Seegrasflecken, die Wassertiefen liegen zwischen knapp 10 m kurz hinter der Einfahrt und 5 m. Portals Vells ist nach Osten offen und nur bei westlichen Wind oder ruhigen Bedingungen als Nachtankerplatz tauglich. Auch steht oft erheblicher Schwell in die Bucht. Mit gut einem Dutzend Yachten ist die Bucht eigentlich belegt, im Sommer sind es jedoch deutlich mehr.

Die Bucht liegt in etwa in der Verlängerung der Start- und Landbahnen des Flughafens von Palma, so dass Fluglärm mal mehr Mal weniger eine Rolle spielt. Die südliche Bucht und ihr Strand sind familientauglich, während die mittlere vornehmlich von Anhängern der gleichgeschlechtlichen Liebe aufgesucht wird. Man ist hier unbekleidet. Die nördlichste Einbuchtung ist gleich hinter der Einfahrt zum Clubhafen für Yachten gesperrt. Die eingangs erwähnte Höhle entstand im 15. Jahrhundert durch den Abbau von Steinblöcken für Bauwerke in Palma. Drinnen gibt es einen Altar mit rätselhaften, eingeritzten Symbolen.

Hier die Details zum Hafen:
Asociación Club Náutico Portals Vells
Einfahrtsfeuer: Fl G 3s
Wassertiefen 3,5-3 m, auf den innersten Liegeplätzen weniger. Es empfiehlt sich, an einigen Stellen mit dem Bug voran anzulegen (unter Wasser Steine). 55 Liegeplätze für Yachten bis 13 m Länge von Mitgliedern des Club Náutico, freie Liegeplätze werden vermietet, sind allerdings nicht preiswert. Anfragen unter: T 971 13 43 74, M 627 945 313 (Angel, Marinero), UKW-Kanal 09

🇬🇧 *Frequently visited bay with small beaches. There are two beach bars/restaurants and a cave. Furthermore, a small-marina of a local yacht club that even accommodates yachts in transit if berths are available.*
No shallow areas aound the entrance of the bay. The sea floor consists of sand with weed, water depths range from less than 10m just past the entrance and 5m. Portals Vells is open to the east and is suitable as a night anchorage only with westerly winds or in calm conditions. Also often significant swell occurs. With a dozen yachts the bay could be full, during high season you can count on considerably more yachts. The southern bay and its beach are suitable for families, while the middle is mostly frequented by nudist

B — Isla de la Porrasa

C — Fl(4)G 11s — Playa de Palmanova

Portbook & Island Guide

Cala Portals Vells – Palmanova

Palma
Isla de la Porrasa

A Cala Portals Vells

bathers. The northern most cala is blocked just past the entrance to the club harbour.

The aforementioned cave was formed in the 14th and 15th century by the mining of limestone for buildings in Palma. Inside there is an altar with enigmatic, incised symbols.

Marinas details are as follows:

Asociación Club Náutico Portals Vells

Entrance light: FLG 3s

Water depths from 3.5 to 3m. Some berths better approach with bow to (underwater rocks). 55 berths for yachts up to 13m in length for members of the Club Náutico, free berths are rented, but are quite expensive. Inquiries: T 971 134 374, M 627 945 313 (Angel, Marinero), VHF 09

B Ensenada de la Porrasa
39° 30,2'N 002° 32,5' E

Vergleichsweise wenig besuchte Bucht, eingerahmt durch die kleine Isla de la Porrasa, die landseitig passiert werden kann (min. 3.5 m Wassertiefe). An Land der Nikki Beach Club.

Less visited than calas in the vicinity. Fringed by the islet de la Porrasa, which can be passed on its north side (min. 3.5m depth). Sea floor more weed than sand. Nikki Beach Club ashore.

Reservations: M 697 150 392

C Palmanova
39° 31,1'N 002° 32,6' E

Ankergrund überwiegend Seegras, viele Hotels entlang des Strandes. Dennoch ein beliebter Platz und sehr sicher bei westlichen Winden. Die hinter dem Strand gelegene Ortschaft Palmanova bietet alles, von Supermärkten, über Restaurants bis zur ärztlichen Versorgung. Im Nordwesten der Bucht der Minihafen des Club Náutico Palmanova. Hier sind üblicherweise alle Liegeplätze belegt. Einfahrt nur mit Booten mit max. 1,50 m Tiefgang.

Seafloor mostly weed, many hotels along the beach, nevertheless popular. A safe place with westerly winds. The touristy and lively village of Palmanova offers supermarkets, restaurants, doctors and many more. In the bays northwest corner lies the small marina of Club Náutico Palmanova. All berths are occupied and only boats with max. 1,50m depth can enter.

T 971 681 055

Mallorca

Puerto Portals

🇩🇪 Puerto Portals bleibt mit dem umfassenden Angebot an Land und einem gewissen Promi-Faktor eine der attraktivsten Marinas auf Mallorca. Verschiedene Veranstaltungen über das Jahr locken auch Landurlauber. Das Ambiente von Puerto Portals wird bestimmt von Motoryachten zwischen 20 und 35 m Länge, hinzukommen ein paar beeindruckende Segelyachten. Das Angebot an Land ist entsprechend: Es gibt zahlreiche Bars und Restaurants, Boutiquen und Juweliergeschäfte, Yachtverkauf- und Vermietung und sogar Immobilienmakler sind her vertreten. Diese Mischung zieht auch Besucher an, die zum Schauen kommen oder zum Essen oder nur auf einen Drink. Wer die Marina Richtung Werftgelände verlässt, kommt nach wenigen Metern zu einem schönen Sandstrand mit Gaststätten und Segelschule. Oberhalb des Strandes liegt die Ortschaft Portals Nous mit einem ebenfalls breiten Angebot an Geschäften und Restaurants.

🇬🇧 *Even after decades Puerto Portals represents on Mallorca the exalted yacht tourism. You will not miss anything on the marina's premises and the chance to meet celebrities here is still quite high. Recurring events all year round also attract many tourists.*
The ambiance of Puerto Portals is determined by motor yachts between 20 and 35m in length, completed by a couple of impressive sailing yachts. The harbour is lined with shops and a wide variety of quality complementary services: restaurants, bars, fashion boutiques, nautical firms, watchmakers, hairdresses, supermarket, beauty center, perfumeries and estate agents, among others. This mixture also attracts many visitors who just come to stroll, have a drink or dining out. Upon leaving the marina towards the yard premises, you will arrive at a small, beautiful sandy beach with restaurants and a sailing school. Above the beach lies the town Portals Nous, which also offers an extensive choice of shops and restaurants.

- Eine angesagte Top-Marina
- Viele große Motoryachten
- Gastronomie mit Anspruch
- *Hip & High-Class Marina*
- *Many large motor yachts*
- *Selected gastronomic choice*

39° 31,6' N 002° 33,8' E

Fl(3)G 14s

ANSTEUERUNG
APPROACHING

Frei von Untiefen. Wassertiefen in der Einfahrt über 5 m. Der weiße Turm mit der Hafenmeisterei ist markant.
No shallow areas. Over 5m deep at the entrance. The harbour master's white tower catches the eye.

FESTMACHEN
FIND A BERTH

A 670 Liegeplätze von 8–60 m. Anmeldung empfohlen. Wartekai bei der Tankstelle, einlaufend an Backbord. Das Hafenbecken ist überall mindestens 3 m tief.
670 berths ranging from 8 to 60 m. Registration required. Waiting pier and petrol station when entering on portside. The harbour basin is at least 3m deep everywhere.

€ 12x4 m
132 EUR (01/06-15/09)

Puerto Portals

43 EUR (16/09-31/05)
Plus 2,20 EUR V./s.f.
3,276 EUR/m³ für Wasser / *water*
Plus Hafengebühren / *Plus harbour taxes*, plus 21% MwSt. / *IVA*
Alle Tarife auf der Webseite:
All Prices listed on the website:
www.puertoportals.com

T 971 171 100, UKW/VHF 09
info@puertoportals.com
M 608 186 189, Marineros, 24 h
(Wenn UKW oder Büro nicht erreichbar sind / *If VHF or office are not available*)
 Marina Office
Summer season daily 9-21 h
Winter season daily 9-17 h
Sicherheitsdienst / *Security* (24 h)
www.puertoportals.com

ANKERPLÄTZE
ANCHORAGE AREAS

B Ankerplatz vor der Marina. Wassertiefe 7-4 m. Grund: überwiegend Seegras. Es gibt hier auch viele von privat gelegte Muringbojen.

Anchorage in front of the marina, depth 7-4m, sea floor mostly weed. **Note:** *Some mooring bouys are private.*

TANKEN / *FUEL*

D+B, Jan-Dec.: daily 9-18 h

TECHNISCHER SERVICE
TECHNICAL SERVICES

1 **Varadero Mundimar Portals**
90-t-Travellift für Yachten bis 27 m Länge, 6,70 m Breite und ca. 4 m Tiefgang, alle Arbeiten und Motorenservice. Ganzjährig rund um die Uhr zu erreichen.
90t Travellift for yachts up to 27m length, 6,70m width and ca. 4m depth. All kind of works and engine service

Mallorca

Puerto Portals

available. All year round 24/7 service
www.mundimarportals.net
mundimar@mundimarportals.com
T 971 676 369, M 660 173 487

YACHTAUSRÜSTER
CHANDLERIES

2 **Ferreteria „Kompas"**
In der Ortschaft Portals Nous oberhalb von Marina und Strand
In Portal Nous village, above the marina.
Mon-Fri 8.30-19.30 h, Sat 9-13 h
www.kompas.es, T 971 675 447

EINKAUFEN / SHOPPING

Die Anwesenheit von einem Dutzend Yachtbrokern und einigen Immobilienmaklern unterstreicht die Bedeutung dieser Marina. Modeläden für angesagte Marken, Schmuckgeschäfte. Bank mit Geldautomat.
A dozen yacht brokers and several real estate agents symbolise the importance of this marina. Shops with fashionable clothing brands, jewellers. Bank and ATM.

3 **Corte Inglés Yacht Provisioning**
Beim Werftgelände / *at the yard premises*, daily 8-19.30 h
T 648 688 949
puertoportals@elcorteingles.es

Kleiner Supermarkt in der Marina, neben Corte Inglés / *Supermarket in marina adjacent to Corte Inglés*
Außerhalb der Marina in Richtung Palmanova: / *Outside of marina towards Palmanova:* Mercadona, Lidl, Eroski...

RESTAURANTS & BARS

4 Ein Dutzend Restaurants mit z. T. anspruchsvoller Küche. Auswahl:
A dozen restaurants, some with upscale cuisine. A choice:
Tristan Portals
T 971 675 5 47
booking@tristanportals.com
www.tristanportals.com

Flanigan
Mediterrane Küche, gehobenes Niveau. Spezielle Weinkarte.
Mediterranean kitchen with high standard. Very special wine list.
T 971 679 191, www.flanigan.es

Wellies
Mit Blick auf den Hauptsteg; von Frühstück bis Dinner, kreativ, große Weinkarte / *Overlooking the main pier. Everything from breakfast to dinner, creative, extensive wine list*
T 971 676 444, www.wellies.es

Puerto Portals

Playa de S'Oratori

Mahal Tandoori, T 971 283 410
Indische Küche mit mediterranem Einschlag / *Indian cuisine with a Mediterranean touch.* www.mahaltandoori.com

Cappucino Grand Café
Café/Bar/Snacks
Der zentrale Platz zum Sehen und gesehen werden mit Blick auf große Yachten. / *The central place to see and be seen, with great views of large yachts.*

Tahini, T 971 676 025
Sushi & mehr/ *more*
tahini@grupocappuccino.com

Ritzi Restaurant & Lounge Bar
T 971 684 104

Lollo Rosso, Italian, T 971 675 186
Local 40, Puerto Portals

Diablito, T 971 676 503
www.diablitofoodandmusic.com
diablito@diablitofoodandmusic.com

Spoon Restaurant, T 971 677 225
La Concha, T 971 677 772

Reeves, Café & Bar
T 971 677 774, M 696 062 831
www.reeves-portals.com

5 Beach Alm
Mit Meer-Blick: zwischen Werft und sich anschließendem Strand, österreichische Küche. / *Nice sea view: between shipyard and adjacent beach, Austrian cuisine.*
www.beach-alm.com
M 680 258 532

6 Roxy Beach Bar
Zum Sonnenuntergang; Chiringuito am östlichen Ende des Strandes *Great for watching the sunset, beach bar at the east end of the beach*

AUSFLÜGE / *EXCURSIONS*

Außerhalb der Marina Richtung Palmanova drei Ziele, die sich lohnen:
Three destinations outside of the marina in Palmanova direction which are worth visiting:

Marineland, Für Kinder / *for children*
www.marineland.es/mallorca

Sporting tenis & padel,
Für Sportler; Tennisplätze und mehr
for sports enthusiasts; tennis courts and more, T 971 675 887
www.sportingtenispadel.com

Mood Beach Club, Bar & Restaurant
Für Genießer / *for gourmets*
T 971 676 456
www.moodbeach.com

Illa d'en Sales

6 Roxy Beach

Mallorca

Illetas

ANKERPLÄTZE
ANCHORAGE AREAS

Illetas / The Anchorage
39°31,7' N 002° 35,0' E

🇩🇪 Für Yachten aus Palma der nächstgelegene Ankerplatz. Im Sommer voll, besonders an den Wochenenden. Herrlich türkisfarbenes Wasser lockt. Man ankert auf 10–4 m Wassertiefe vor einer abgetrennten Badezone und über Sand, z. T. mit Seegras. **Achtung:** Es gibt eine einzelne Untiefe südwestlich der vorgelagerten Insel Illeta/Isla de sa Torre mit ca. 2 m Wassertiefe.

🇬🇧 *Sailors coming from Palma will find their first fine anchorage here. During high season crowded, espacially on weekends. Gorgeous turquoise water lures. Anchorage on 10-4m water depth in front of a separate bathing area. Sea floor sand, further out also weed.*
Caution: There is a single shoal southwest of Isla de sa Torre with appr. 2m water depth, not displayed in any chart.

An Land / Ashore

1 Anlanden mit dem Beiboot auf der Isla de sa Torre (oder hinschwimmen). Der beste Blick auf den Ankerplatz bietet sich dort vom alten Wachturm aus, der sich mit etwas Mühe und Risikobereitschaft besteigen lässt. / *Landing with the dinghy in the Isla de sa Torre (or swim up). Climb the ancient watchtower for the best views over the anchorage.*

2 **Weyler Beach Bar**
Nicht auf VIP-Publikum ausgelegt. Am Am kleinen Strand. Zuletzt noch akzeptable Preise. Am besten zum Sonnenuntergang. / *Not pretentious. At the small beach. Recently still acceptable prices. Best for sunset.*

3 Club-Anlage und Restaurant, das nach Anmeldung besucht werden kann, Ausnahme der Monat August. / *Club facility and restaurant, which can be visited by appointment, except for the month of August.*
T 971 400 890
anchorage@theanchorage.es
www.theanchorage.es

4 Die Einbuchtung westlich der Isla Caleta, die unmittelbar östlich anschließt, eignet sich wegen überspülter Untiefen nicht zum Ankern. Zudem gibt es hier goßzügig abgetrennte Badezonen rund um die Cala Comtessa. / *The bay west of Isla Caleta, which adjoins immediately to the east, is no place to anchor because of shoals. In addition there are generous marked bathing areas here around Cala Comtessa.*

5 Erst vor der Playa de Illetas kann man wieder ankern, auf ca. 10 m Wassertiefe. An Land hier zwei Beachclubs. / *In front of Playa de Illetas one can drop anchor again, at approximately 10m water depth. Ashore you will find two Beach Clubs.*

Virtual Beach Club
T 971 703 235
www.virtualclub.es
Balneario Illetas - Beach Club
T 971 401 031
comercial@balnearioilletas.com

Illetas / The Anchorage

Cala Burgit
Isla Caleta
Playa de Illetas
Cala Comtessa
Isla de sa Torre

Isla de sa Torre, Illetas

Portbook & Island Guide 19

Port Calanova

Mallorca

- Marina-Alternative zu Palma
- Liegeplätze bis 25 m Länge
- Großer Travellift für Mallorca

The alternative to Palma marinas
Berths now up to 25m length
A new large travel lift for Mallorca

🇩🇪 Kleine Marina unmittelbar westlich von Palma. Seit 2012 neuer Konzessionär mit Vertrag bis 2042. Die wesentlichen Umbaumaßnahmen sind abgeschlossen. Die Molenköpfe wurden so verändert, dass der Schwell im Hafenbecken spürbar nachgelassen hat. Es gibt einen Steg weniger, dafür mehr Liegeplätze für größere Yachten. Auch für Gastyachten steht nun mehr Platz zur Verfügung.

Die Marina liegt direkt an einer stark befahrenen Uferstraße. Davon bekommt man jedoch im Hafen nichts mit. Die Verbindungen nach Palma sind sehr gut, die Versorgungsmöglichkeiten und das Angebot an Restaurant etc. rund um die Marina ebenfalls. Mit dem angekündigten 75-t-Travellift wird kleine Werft (mit Volvo-Penta-Service) interessant für Eigner und Service-Betriebe. Yachten bis zu 4 m Tiefgang sollen hier gekrant werden können. Eine Tankstelle ist vorhanden. Es gibt ein Club-Restaurant und ein Schwimmbad und weiterhin das Sportangebot einer bekannten Yachtschule. Man kann hier auch Dinghies leihen, Strandkatamarane und Stand-up-Paddle-Boards. Die Liegeplatzpreise sind etwas günstiger als in Palma im Durchschnitt.

🇬🇧 *Newly upgraded marina just west of Palma. Since 2012 new concessionaire with contract until 2042. The main modifications have been completed. The pier heads were changed so that the swell inside the harbour basin has subsided noticeably. One pier has been removed to establish more berths for larger yachts. Also for boats in transit there is now more space available.*

The marina is located right close to a busy coastal road but that does not affect the berths. Connections to Palma are very good, the supply facilities and the number of restaurant etc. around the marina as well. With the announced 75-t travel lift the shipyard (with Volvo Penta Service) becomes more interesting for owners and service companies. Yachts up to 4m depth can now be lifted and launched. A petrol station is located at the marinas entrance. There is a club-restaurant, a swimming pool and the National Sailing School. Here one can also rent dinghies, beach catamarans and stand-up paddle boards. The mooring rates are slightly cheaper than in Palma, on average.

ANSTEUERUNG
APPROACHING

Keine Untiefen, aber bei starkem auflandigem Wind laufen die Wellen quer zur Einfahrtsrichtung.

No shoals, but with strong onshore winds, waves can run across the steered course in front of the marinas entrance.

FESTMACHEN
FIND A BERTH

A Die Marina kann Yachten bis 25 m Länge und 7 m Breite aufnehmen. Die Wassertiefen liegen zwischen

Calanova

Blick in die nahe Zukunft: Der Umbau der Molen ist schon passiert, mehr folgt.
Architect impression of Port Calanova: The new breakwater heads are already realized, more works have to follow.

39° 32,9' 002° 36,1'
Fl(2)R 7s

7 und 2,5 m. Die Gastplätze und die Wartemole befinden sich am Anfang der Außenmole. Es gibt Muringleinen, Strom und Wasser. Die Sanitäreinrichtungen wurden renoviert.
The marina can shelter yachts up to 25m in length and 7m width. Water depths are 7-2.5m. Guest berths and waiting dock are located inside the breakwater. There are mooring lines, electricity and water supply. The sanitary facilities have been renovated.

T 971 402 512, VHF/UKW 09
Office: (Jan.-Dec.): Mon-Fri 9-19 h, Sat 9-14 h, Sun closed
€ Bis 12 m/up to 12m:
53,09 (01/05-31/10),
49,31 (01/11-30/04), incl. water + electr., plus 21% MwSt./IVA; plus G-5 + T-0
Kurzeittarif für max. 4 Stunden:
Special rate for max. 4 hours:
Max. 12m: 22 EUR; max. 15m: 30 EUR

info@portcalanova.com
www.portcalanova.com
WiFi Kostenlos, mit Passwort
Free of charge. With password & log in.

ANKERPLÄTZE
ANCHORAGE AREAS

B Direkt vor der Marinaeinfahrt in der Nähe eines kleinen Strandes. Guter Schutz gegen Westwind. Weitere Ankerplätze 1 sm südwestlich Richtung Illetas und bei ruhigen Bedingungen vor der abgetrennten Badezone der Cala Mayor.

Situated immediately in front of marina entrance near a small beach. Well protected against western winds. Additional anchorages 1nmi to the southwest, Illetas, and in calm conditions in front of the separated bathing area of Cala Mayor nearby.

Mallorca

Illetas

Calanova ist ein Stützpunkt für Dingi-Segeln.
The National Sailing School has its base in Calanova.

TANKEN / *FUEL*

Täglich, 24 Std., D+B; am Kopf der Innenmole. Max. Tiefgang: 4 m / *Daily, 24 h, D+B; Situated at the head of the inner breakwater. Max. depth: 4 m.*
Contact: M 603 603 897

TECHNISCHER SERVICE / *TECHNICAL SERVICES*

C Travellift 75 t; Bootsslip / *slipway*; Werft / *Shipyard*: 9-17 h; nach Anmeldung / *by appointment*

YACHTAUSRÜSTER / *CHANDLERIES*

→ „Palma de Mallorca", p. 37

EINKAUFEN / *SHOPPING*

1 Supermarkt Eroski nach Verlassen der Marina ca. 200 entfernt Richtung Palma. Weitere kleine Geschäfte, Obst- und Gemüseladen. *Supermarket Eroski outside of the marina, some 200m towards Palma. Many additional smaller shops.*

2 Bäckerei, Zeitschriften, Eisdiele, Wäscherei, Apotheke, Bank. *Bread and pastry shop, magazines, ice cream parlour, laundry, pharmacy, bank.*

RESTAURANTS & BARS

3 Restaurant in der Marina, *Marina restaurant*, T 971 700 238, restaurantecalanova@hotmail.com
🕒 May-Oct: 9-11 h, daily;

Calanova

Port Calanova

Cala Mayor

Nov-April: Mon-Thu: 9.30-18 h, Fri-Sat

1 Nach Verlassen der Marina Richtung Palma: / *Outside of marina, located towards Palma:*
Nawaab, Indian Restaurant, Terrasse mit Meerblick, *terrace with sea view* T 971 401 691

La Trattoria, Restaurant./Pizzeria; Terrasse mit Meerblick, *terrace with sea view* 🕐 13-16 + 19.30-23.45 h, T 971 401 755

Zhero Beach Club
Lounge Music, Healthy Food & Pool
T 971 917 917

DANCING / DISCOS

→ „Palma de Mallorca", p. 41

AUSFLÜGE / *EXCURSIONS*

→ „Palma de Mallorca", p. 42

Bushaltestelle, Linie 3, 20 & 46.
Bus stop, line 3, 20 & 46.

4 Motorrad- und Fahrradverleih nach Verlassen der Marina ca. 200 m entfernt Richtung Palma.
Motorcycle & bicycle rental outside of marina some 200 m towards Palma.

Calanova beherbergt auch Charteryachten, u. a. von Dream Yacht Charter
Calanova houses also charter boats, e.g.. Dream Yacht Charter

Portbook & Island Guide 23

Mallorca

PUERTO DE PALMA
PORT OF PALMA

Palma de Mallorca

Hafenplan / Harbour map – Palma de Mallorca

| | Zona Portuaria / Port area | | Zona ajardinada / Gardens | | Edificios / Buildings | | Accesos / Access |

| | Casco urbano / Urban area | | Viales / Roads | | Límite zona servicio del puerto / Limits of the port service area |

	Faro / Lighthouse		Destellos aislados verdes / Isolated green flashes		Grupo 3 destellos verdes / Group of 3 green flashes		Destellos aislados amarillos / Isolated yellow flashes
	Baliza / Landing beacon		Grupo 2 destellos rojos / Group of 2 red flashes		Grupo 4 destellos rojos / Group of 4 red flashes		Cardinal S
	Sirena / Siren		Grupo 2 destellos verdes / Group of 2 green flashes		Grupo 4 destellos verdes / Group of 4 green flashes		Cardinal E
	Destellos aislados rojos / Isolated red flashes		Grupo 3 destellos rojos / Group of 3 red flashes		Grupo (2+1) destellos rojos / Group of (2+1) red flashes		

Portbook & Island Guide

Mallorca

Palma de Mallorca

39° 33,0' N 002 38,8' E

Zwischen dem Blau des Meeres und Ausläufern der Tramuntana:
Mallorcas Hauptstadt-Häfen in bester Lage.

*Embedded between the blue sea and the foothills of the Tramuntana:
The harbours of Mallorca's capital are a prime location.*

Palma de Mallorca

- Metropole mit Idealmaßen
- Attraktive Altstadt & Gastronomie
- Marinas für jeden Anspruch
- Zahlreiche Charterbasen

A perfectly dimensioned metropolis
Attractive Old Town & gastronomy
Marinas for all requirements
Numerous charter bases

Mallorca

Marinas in Palma de Mallorca

Palma de Mallorca ist eine geschäftige und hoch attraktive Metropole. Mit traditionellen und modernen Bars und zahlreichen guten Restaurants. Auch zum Shopping findet man hier die richtigen Adressen. Dazu viel Kultur, Feste und Veranstaltungen.
In der Balearen-Hauptstadt ist der nautische Tourismus zuhause – mehr als ein halbes Dutzend Marinas entlang des Paseo Marítimo beherbergen Eigner- und Charterschiffe gleichermaßen, spezialisierte Werften kümmern sich um Superyachten. Dazu liegen hier berühmte Klassiker, die man sonst nur aus Zeitschriften kennt. Bordwand an Bordwand mit rassigen Rennyachten, die hier bei vielen Regatten starten können, auch beim Jahreshöhepunkt Anfang August: der Copa del Rey. Wenn Königscup und Sommer vorüber sind, schlägt die Stunde der nautischen Fachbetriebe, von denen Palma voll ist. Dann verschwinden viele Yachten zur Überholung unter weißen Planen.

Palma de Mallorca is a busy and attractive Metropolis offering many traditional and modern bars and a great variety of restaurants. It's a great shopping destination as well, and hosts a large variety of cultural events and festivals.
The capital Palma is also the hotspot of all nautical activities in the Balearic Islands - half a dozen marinas along the Paseo Marítimo offer berths for private and charter yachts alike, specialised shipyards care of superyachts.
Many classical yachts usually only seen in magazines lay side by side, next to fast racing boats, ready to participate in one of the many regattas. Their highlight is the Copa del Rey, taking place around the 1st of August.
When summer and regattas have gone, the nautical business starts booming, while white becomes the colour of choice as many yachts disappear under plastic covers for maintenance.

ANSTEUERUNG
APPROACHING

Anstelle von Untiefen zu beachten:
- Fähren und Kreuzfahrtschiffe, manchmal auch Frachter, nutzen Palmas Hafen regelmäßig, vor allem in den Morgen- und Abendstunden.
- Frachter oder Marineschiffe können vor dem Hafen auf Reede liegen.
- Gelbe Schilder mit symbolisierten Flugzeugen an einigen Molenköpfen weisen darauf hin: Die Wasserfläche innerhalb der Südwestmole ist im Notfall frei zu halten für Löschflugzeuge, die hier Wasser aufnehmen.

Shoals are less of a problem, but:
- *Ferries, cruise ships and sometimes freighters use the port, especially during morning and evening hours.*
- *Freighters and naval vessels may be anchored in front of the port.*
- ***Note:*** *yellow warning signs on the pier heads indicate that the channel inside the southeasterly breakwater must be kept free to allow fire-fighting planes to pick up water.*

Moll Vell + La Lonja Marina

Palma de Mallorca

FESTMACHEN
FIND A BERTH

A **STP Shipyard Palma**
Bedeutende Schiffswerft mit eigenen Wasserliegeplätzen für Yachten von 53 bis 120 m Länge. Travellifte bis 700 t, Yachten bis 60 m können an Land gestellt werden. Sehr viele Service-Betriebe sind auf dem 105.000 m² großen Gelände ansässig. STP bietet Kunden einen Concierge-Service und je nach Größe der Yacht und Verweildauer Sonderkonditionen in der Marina Palma und in der Marina Port de Mallorca. Angebote auf Anfrage.

This important shipyard meets all necessary services for a perfect maintenance or refit, where clients have freedom to choose their own contractors. Specialised in sailing boats, more than 1500 vessels worldwide trust for a job well done and convenience of concentrating the necessary services under one roof. Travellifts up to 700t, 6 pits grounding 60m LOA, moorings for boats up to 120m LOA and 7.5m depth, diesel fuel station with 6 jets to supply 300l/minute. STP Shipyard Palma also offers a Concierge Service for clients and discounts on services at Marina Port de Mallorca and Marina Palma Cuarentena, depending on yacht size and duration of the stay.

www.stp-palma.com
info@stp-palma.com
T 971 214 747 (Reception)
UKW/VHF 09
€ Upon request, WiFi free

B **Amarres Deportivos, Moll Vell**
Nach der Fertigstellung im Frühjahr 2014 der neueste Hafenteil und eine Zierde der Hauptstadt. Die 205 m lange Wasserfront wurde modernisiert und kann 26 Yachten von 15 bis 40 m Länge aufnehmen. Landseitig gibt es ein modernes Gebäude mit Freitreppe zum Zentrum hin. Darin unter anderem Restaurants und die britische Yachtwerft Oyster. Auf dem Dach befindet sich eine Aussichtsterrasse und einem sehr schönen Blick über den Hafen, zum Castell Bellver und auf die nahen Berge.

Newest part of Palma harbour when finished in spring 2014. The 205m

Moll commercial / STP Shipyard

Travel lift, STP Shipyard

Portbook & Island Guide 29

Mallorca

waterfront was modernised and can shelter up to 26 yachts from 15 to 40m length. Modern building with outside staircase leading towards the city. An adornment to the capital. Houses restaurants and the office of the british boatbuilder Oyster. Patio on the roof with a very nice view over the harbour and to the Bellver Castle and the nearby mountains.
T 971 716 332, M 618 526 931
UKW/VHF 09, palma@mollvell.com
€ 0,85/m²/day; 0,95/m²/day (July/August), plus VAT + electr. (0,29/kWh, incl. VAT), plus taxes G 5 + T 0
Water 2,5 € m³; Long term discount 8%
www.mollvell.com

C La Lonja Marina (Charter)
Die Marina liegt vis à vis der alten Seehandelsbörse. Überwiegend belegt durch Charteryachten verschiedener Anbieter. Von Sonntag bis Donnerstag Vermietung von nicht genutzten Liegeplätzen. Die Liegeplatzpreise sind je nach Saisonzeit, Yachtgröße und Verfügbarkeit unterschiedlich. Anfragen werden über die Webseite erwünscht.

Marina is located vis-à-vis of the old Maritime Exchange building. Mainly charter yachts from various companies. Free berths rented to visitors from Sunday to Thursday. Berth prices vary depending on season, yacht size and availability. Inquiries via website.
T 971 100 446, M 634 279 890
Contact: Luis Márquez
UKW/VHF 09
info@lalonjamarinacharter.com
www.lalonjamarinacharter.com
WiFi kostenlos / free of charge

D Real Club Náutico Palma (RCNP)
Mit fast 1000 Liegeplätzen die größte Marina im Hafen von Palma. Zirka 600 sind von Mitgliedern belegt. Nah zur Altstadt gelegen. **Achtung:** Es gibt keine Gastliegeplätze während der Regatten Palmavela (1. Maiwoche) und Copa del Rey (1. Augustwoche)

*With up to 1000 berths it's the biggest Marina in the Port of Palma. Approx. 600 of those belong to members. Close to the old city centre. **Caution:** There are no vacant berths for boats in transit during these regattas: Palmavela (1st week of May) and Copa del Rey (1st week of August)*

T 971 726 848, UKW/VHF 09 +77
capitania@rcnp.es, secretaria@rcnp.es
www.rcnp.es
Marina-Office, Jan–Dec
Mon-Fri 8-20 h, Sat+Su 8-14 +15-20 h
Closing days: 1st of January and 25th of December
€ 12x4 m:
38,78 EUR (1/10-Easter),
51,42 EUR (Easter-14/06 + 01-30/09),
98,06 EUR (15/06-14/07 + 16-31/08),
122,09 EUR (15/07-15/08)
Alle Preise werden nach qm berechnet (Länge x Breite des Bootes) und beinhalten Wasser, Strom, Gebühren und MwSt.; über 20 m Länge: Wasser und Strom extra. Plus Gebühren T-0 und G-5 / *All prices per exact sqm; incl. water, electricity, showers, fees + VAT; over 20 m length: water + electr. extra.; Plus harbour taxes T-0 und G-5.*
WiFi Kostenlos; Kennwort im Marinabüro / *free of charge; Password through the marina office*

Palma de Mallorca

E Marina Naviera Balear
Die Marina vergibt auch Dauerliegeplätze, ist aber zum überwiegenden Teil mit Charteryachten belegt. Gastplätze sind von daher zwischen Frühjahr und Herbst m. E. nur von Sonntag bis Donnerstag verfügbar. Reservierung empfohlen. Strom und Wasser an allen Liegeplätzen. **Achtung:** Wenige Meter vor der östlichen Pier gehen die Wassertiefen auf unter 2 zurück (Grund ist Sand und Schlamm). Kleine gelbe Bojen markieren diesen Bereich!

Marina offers annual berths but is mostly occupied by charter boats from various companies. Therefore guest berths are usually available only from Sunday to Thursday between spring and fall.

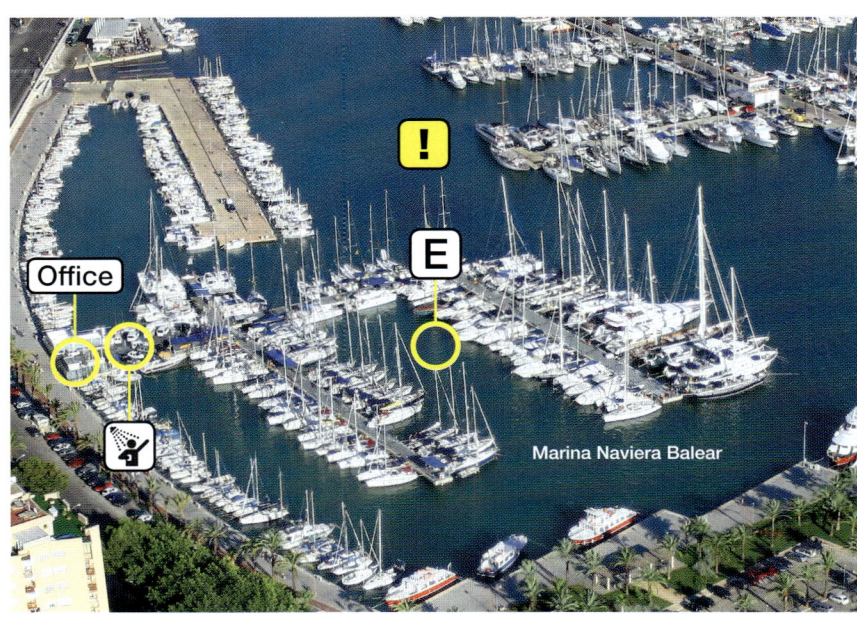

Marina Naviera Balear

SAILACTIVE
ACTIVE TRAVELLING WITH FRIENDS

MALLORCA
Palma d.M.
Portocolom

IHR MALLORCA-SPEZIALIST
YACHTCHARTER 15 Yachten ab Palma und Portocolom
MITSEGELN Wöchentliche Segeltörns
HOTEL Orange Colom Seaside Appartements

www.sailactive.com | mallorca@sailactive.com

Portbook & Island Guide 31

Mallorca

Advance booking recommended. Electricity and water supply on every berth. Caution: Close to the easterly pier there are shallow areas with only 2 m depth, Small yellow bouys mark this area.
T 971 45 44 55
UKW/VHF 08, Naviera Balear
24 h erreichbar; *opening hours* 24 h
marina@navierabalear.com
www.navierabalear.com

€ Tagesliegeplatz auf Anfrage / *Daily rates on request,*
Jahresliegeplatz ab 10.000 EUR
Annual berths from 10.000 EUR

WiFi Kostenlos, Password wird vergeben / *free of charge; password will be provided*

Es gibt eine Absauganlage für Rückhaltetanks. Max. Tiefgang: 2,5 m
Wastewater removal in place. max. depth: 2.5m
kostenlos / free of charge
🕐 9-21 h (Fri 9-16 h)
Boote unter 12m ohne Anmeldung *boats under 12m without appointment*
Boote über 12m Anmeldung:
Boats over 12m, appointment:
T 971 454 455

F · Marina Port de Mallorca
Bietet Liegeplätze von 12 bis 50 m Länge, einen Consierge Service für Kunden und Rabatte auf Dienstleistungen in der STP-Werft in der Marina

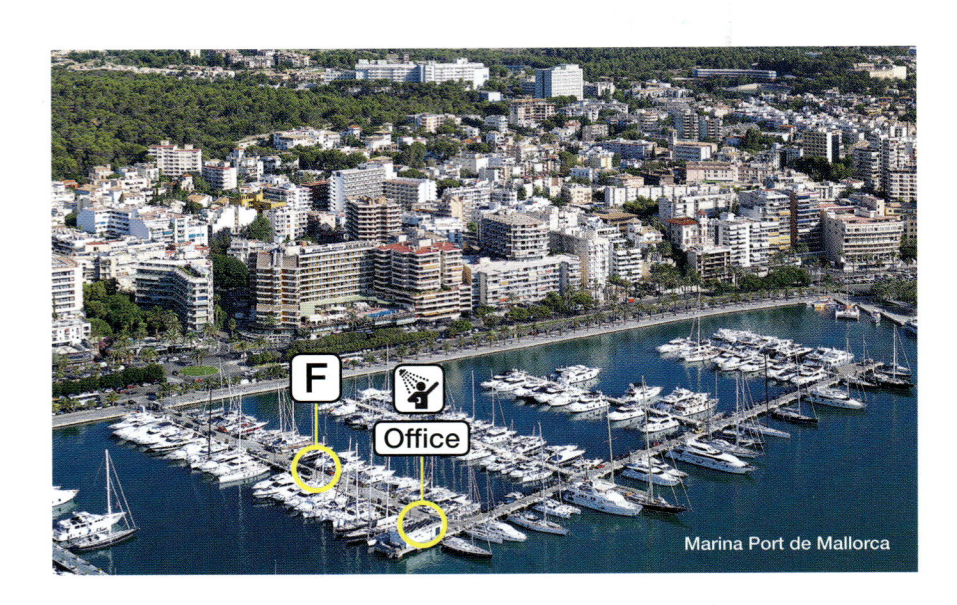

Marina Port de Mallorca

PALMAWATCH

yacht maintenance
haul-out works
antifouling applications
seacock / thruhull service
propeller / shaft service
marine plumbing systems
shipwright / carpentry
material supplies

www.palmawatch.com, Palma de Mallorca - office/workshop in STP,
tel: (+34) 871 932 249 or at *info@palmawatch.com*

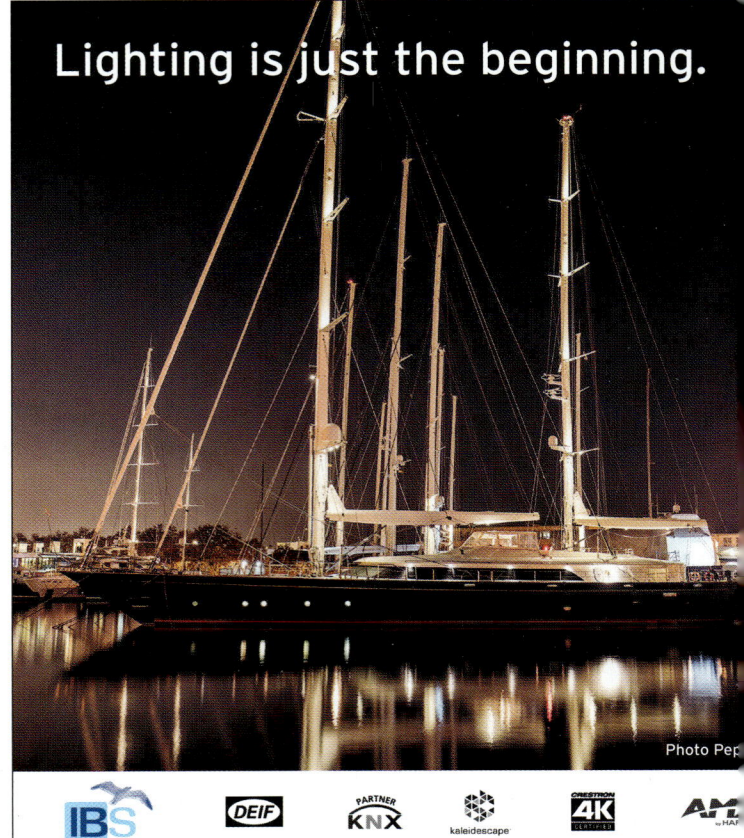

Lighting is just the beginning.

Photo Pep

Marine Electric s.l. · Muelle Viejo Espigón de la Consigna s/n
07012 Palma de Mallorca (STP) · +34 971 72 90 76
info@MarineElectric.es · www.MarineElectric.es

Palma de Mallorca

Palma Cuarentena, die Höhe variiert in Abhängigkeit von der Größe der Yacht und der Dauer des Aufenthalts.

Marina Port de Mallorca offers berths from 12-50m LOA, a Concierge Service for clients and discounts on services at STP Shipyard Palma and Marina Palma Cuarentena, depending on yacht size and duration of the stay.

Reception:
T 971 289 693 / 971 289 698
Headoffice: T 971 739 030
M 664 002 269 📱 UKW/VHF 09
🕐 Reception
01/04-31/10 Mon-Sunday 9-21 h,
01/11-31/03 Mon-Fri 9-20 h,
Sat-Sun 9-14 h.
€ upon request **WiFi** kostenlcs / *free*
comercial@group-ipm.com
www.portdemallorca.com

G **Pantalán del Mediterráneo**
Zur Saison 2014 wurde die Anlage komplett modernisiert und der T-Steg um 68 m verlängert. Nun können hier Einheiten bis zu 130 m längsseits festmachen. Es wird um Anmeldung gebeten. Liegeplätze ab 20 m Länge.

Facilities were completely modernised for the 2014 season, and the T-shaped pier was extended by 68m. Ships up to 130m can now dock here alongside. Reservation recommended. 61 berths from 20m.

➤ Pantalán del Mediterráneo + Marina Palma Cuarentena

WE ARE BAVARIA IN SPAIN.

BAVARIA YACHTS

SAILING YACHTS
MOTOR BOATS
CATAMARANS
SALE
CHARTER
BROKERAGE
SERVICE

BAVARIA SPAIN
BAVARIA SPAIN PALMA DE MALLORCA
Official Distributor for Bavaria Yachts in Spain
Tel: (+34) 971 707 774 · info@bavaria-spain.com
WWW.BAVARIA-SPAIN.COM

Sales Office and Services in Club de Mar · Charter Base in Marina La Lonja

Mallorca

T 971 458 211
UKW/VHF 09
M 656 272 396 (Marinero, 24 h)
€ 0,55€/m²/day; 0,85€/m²/day (July/August), plus VAT + electr. (0,29/kWh, incl. VAT), plus T-0 + G-5 (Hafengebühren, s. S. 319 / *harbour taxes, see p. 319*)
Water 2,5€/m³;
Long term discount 8%
WiFi kostenlos / *free*
Office 9-15 h daily
info@pantalanmediterraneo.com
www.pantalanmediterraneo.com

Marina Palma Cuarentena
Bietet Liegeplätze bis 60 m Länge, einen Consierge Service für Kunden und Rabatte auf Dienstleistungen in der STP-Werft in der Marina Port de Mallorca, die Höhe variiert in Abhängigkeit von der Größe der Yacht und der Dauer des Aufenthalts.
Offers berths up to 60m LoA, a Concierge Service for clients and discounts on services at STP Shipyard Palma and Marina Port de Mallorca, depending on yacht size and duration of the stay.

T 971 45 43 95 (Reception)
UKW/VHF 09
info@marinapalma.com
www.marinapalma.com
Reception:
01/04-31/10 Mon-Fri 10-17 h,
Sat 9-14 h, Sun closed.
01/11-31/03 Mon-Fri 9-17 h,
Sat + Sun closed.
€ upon request
WiFi kostenlos / *free*

Club de Mar
Bietet an der äußeren Pier einige Liegeplätze für Megayachten. Reservierung obligatorisch, keine Wartemole, Platz wird zugewiesen. Schwimmbadnutzung gegen Gebühr. Concierge Service.
Some berths alongside the outer pier for big boats. Advance bookings are mandatory, no waiting pier, place will be assigned. Entrance fee for pool. Consierge Service.

T 971 403 611, UKW/VHF 09
secretaria@clubdemar-mallorca.com
www.clubdemar-mallorca.com

Mon–Fri 8–18 h, Sat 9–13, Sun closed € 12–15 m, max. Breite / beam bis 4,30 m: 63 EUR (Jun–Sept), 30 EUR (Oct–May); plus MwSt./VAT, water, electricity and T-0 on a daily base.
WiFi Drahtlos nutzbar für Mitglieder und in der Bar des Clubs; freier Netzzugang nach Passwort-Erteilung; Verschiedene Tarife im Marinabüro buchbar.
Several rates available in Marina office, access after obtaining password. Wireless access free of charge inside bar.

ANKERPLÄTZE
ANCHORAGE AREAS

Guter Ankergrund, Wassertiefen 8–4 m, direkt vor der Kathedrale und nahe einer alten Betonmole beim Club Anima Beach, in Richtung Yachthafen Portixol. Hier ist Anlegen mit dem Dingi gut möglich, so lange der Seegang moderat ist. Bei stärkerem Wind vom Meer besteht der beste Schutz nahe der Bar „Varadero", gelegen in Höhe der Kathedrale auf der

Palma de Mallorca

CHARTER del mar

Quality Yacht Charter Mallorca

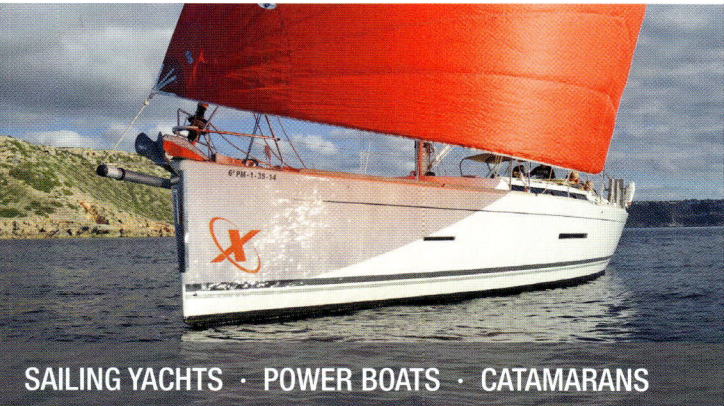

SAILING YACHTS · POWER BOATS · CATAMARANS

CHARTER DEL MAR
Real Club Náutico Palma · Mallorca
Tel:+34 606 591 784
info@charterdelmar.com   www.charterdelmar.com

Near Club de Mar, Palma de Mallorca

Centro Médico Porto Pi

Internationales Facharztzentrum
International Medical Centre

Terminvereinbarung / Appointments:

☎ **971 70 70 35** ☎ **971 70 70 55**
Avda. Gabriel Roca, 47   Calle Porto Pi, 8

Dr. Gessner · HNO-Arzt / *ENT Specialist*	....	607 55 90 84
Dr. Terrasa · Frauenheilkunde / *Gynaecologist*	...	607 55 90 85
Dr. v. Dessel · Urologe / *Urologist*	....	600 74 62 22
Dr. Rittweiler · Kinderärztin / *Pediatrician*	....	607 55 90 81
Dr. M. Springer · Internist / *Internal Medicine*	....	607 55 90 82
Prof. Dr. A. Dietz · Internist / *Internal Medicine*	..	670 30 40 80
Dr. C. Springer · Frauenärztin / *Gynaecologist*	..	607 55 90 88
Dr. Löhnert · Hautarzt / *Dermatologist*	....	627 08 60 92
Dr. Pötzsch · Augenarzt / *Eye Specialist*	....	607 55 90 87
Dr. Linnenbecker · Orthopäde / *Traumatologist*		600 44 40 00
Dr. Poblotzki & L. Antic · Zahnärzte / *Dentists*		607 55 90 80

Notfall Telefon / Emergency numbers

www.centromedicoportopi.es

Mallorca

Außenmole des Hafens von Palma. Beim Ankern immer Rohrleitungen beachten, die vom Land kommen.

Good holding ground, depths 8–4m, directly in from of the Cathedral. At a concrete pier at Anima Beach club towards Portixol, good dinghi landing with moderate sea conditions.
With stronger onshore winds the best protection can be found near the „Varadero" bar, in front of the Cathedral at the outer pier the Muelles Comerciales of the port of Palma. When anchoring always look out for (old) piping coming from landside.

TANKEN / *FUEL*

Real Club Náutico Palma (RCNP)
July+August 8–20 h (daily), April, May, June + Sept. 8–18 h (daily), Oct-March: 8–14 h (daily)
T 971 716 709, UKW/VHF 09 / 77

STP Shipyard
Auf 100 m Kailänge Muringleinen für Großyachten, zwei Zapfsäulen mit hohem Durchfluss von 300 l/Min.
100m of moorings for large ships, two petrol pumps with filling rate 300l/min.
T 971 214 747; info@stp-palma.com
8.30-21 h (daily)

Club de Mar
9-20 h (daily), T 971 403 611
Wassertiefe / *Depth* 6–5m

TECHNISCHER SERVICE
TECHNICAL SERVICES

Auswahl / *Choice*
REAL CLUB NÁUTICO:

Audax Marina
Varadero Real Club Náutico, 100-t-Travellift, AWL-Grip-Painting, Osmosis Treatment, Hull repair, Gel Coats …
T 971 720 474, M 639 303 943
info@audaxmarina.com
www.audaxmarina.com

Astilleros de Mallorca
Werft für sehr große Yachten, mit langer Geschichte. Unterhält eine Dependance bei STP Shipyard.
Shipyard for superyachts, can review on a long history. Runs a branch at STP, Global Building.
T 971 710 645
info@astillerosdemallorca.com

STP SHIPYARD:

Kontakt-Details / *Contact details* p. 29
Bedeutendes Werftgelände, die hier ansässigen Firmen sind überwiegend spezialisiert auf Großyachten. U. a.
Major shipyard, the companies established here are mostly specialised in large yachts, i. a.

Palmawatch S.L.
Gut etabliertes Yacht-Service-Unternehmen mit eigenem Team von Technikern, die viele Eigenleistungen anbieten: Heraus- und hineinheben von Yachten, Reparatur von Wasseranlagen, Stahl und Aluminium, Anker und Decksbeschlägen, Reinigung von Kraftstofftanks. Enge Zusammenarbeit mit Spezialisten aller benötigten Fachbereiche.
Well established yacht service company with it's own team of technicians, covering an expanding offer of in-house services – haul out works, water systems, steel/alu works, windlass & deck gear systems, cleaning of fuel tanks. Working in close collaboration with specialists of all necessary expertise areas.
T 871 932 249, M 627 451 358
pierre@palmawatch.com
www.palmawatch.com

Marine Electric S. L.
T 971 729 076; M 649 708 708
info@MarineElectric.es
www.MarineElectric.es
Eine der besten Firmen im Fachgebiet Marine Elektrik auf den Balearen. Man investiert in den neuesten Stand der

Palma de Mallorca

Viel Platz für Kreuzfahrtschiffe / *A long pier for cruise ships*

Technik, so dass fachlich gesehen jede Art von Arbeit ausgeführt werden kann. *One of the best Marine Electric companies in the Balearic Islands has invested in a new state of the art technology, to make sure that the team is capable of carrying out any type of work.*

CLUB DE MAR:

Motonautica Vert S.A.
Spezialisiert auf Motorboote
Specialized in power boats
T 971 404 604
UKW / VHF 09
www.motonauticavert.com

YACHTAUSRÜSTER
CHANDLERIES

Auswahl / *Choice*

Mercanautic
Mon-Fri 9-14 + 16-19 h, Sat 10-14 h
Paseo Marítimo, 38, T 971 281 011
www.mercanautic.com

Yachtcenter Palma
www.yachtcenterpalma.net
T 971 715 612 + 971 690 684

Nautipaints, T 971 213 366
www.nautipaints.com

Ferreteria La Central, T 971 731 838
Carrer de Sant Magí, 37 (Sta Catalina)
www.ferreterialacentral.com

Pinmar, www.pinmar.com
T 971 713 744 + 971 720 672

Rolling Stock, www.rollingstock.es
T 971 713 744 + 971 711 728

REGATTEN & EVENTS
REGATTAS & EVENTS

Eine Auswahl / *Selected Events* 2016

04/05-08/05:
Gaastra Palma Vela
www.palmavela.com

22/06-25/06:
The Superyacht Cup Palma
www.thesuperyachtcup.com

30/07-06/08: **Copa del Rey**
www.regatacopadelrey.com

10/08-13/08: **Regata Illes Balears Classics**
www.clubdemar-mallorca.com

25/05-02/04 2016:
Trofeo S.A.R. Princesa Sofía
www.trofeoprincesasofia.org

28/04-02/15 2016:
XXXIII Salón Náutico de Palma + IV Palma Superyacht Show

The Superyacht Cup Palma

Mallorca

RESTAURANTS & BARS

🇩🇪 Die Aufzählung der Bars und Restaurants selbst in Hafennähe könnte ein Buch füllen.

🇬🇧 *The names of just those bars and restaurants close to the port could fill a book. So here's merely a subjective but select choice...*

ALTSTADT & LONJA-VIERTEL / OLD TOWN & LA LONJA QUARTER:

1 Celler sa Premsa
Am Ende der Ramblas, am kleinen Plaça Obispo Berenguer de Palou. 1958 gegründet. Zeichnet sich durch seine traditionelle und rustikale Innengestaltung aus. Weitläufige Räume und beeindruckende Weinfässer. Gutes Preis-Leistungsverhältnis.
Towards the end of the Ramblas, near small Plaça Obispo Berenguer de Palou. Founded in 1958. Characterised by traditional, simple interior décor. Large rooms and impressive wine barrels. Very good value for money.
www.cellersapremsa.com
Tel. 971 723 529

2 Simply Fosh / Misa Brasseria
Zwei Restaurants mit unterschiedlichen kulinarischen Angeboten von Marc Fosh. / *Two restaurants with different culinary offers by chef Marc Fosh.* www.marcfosh.com

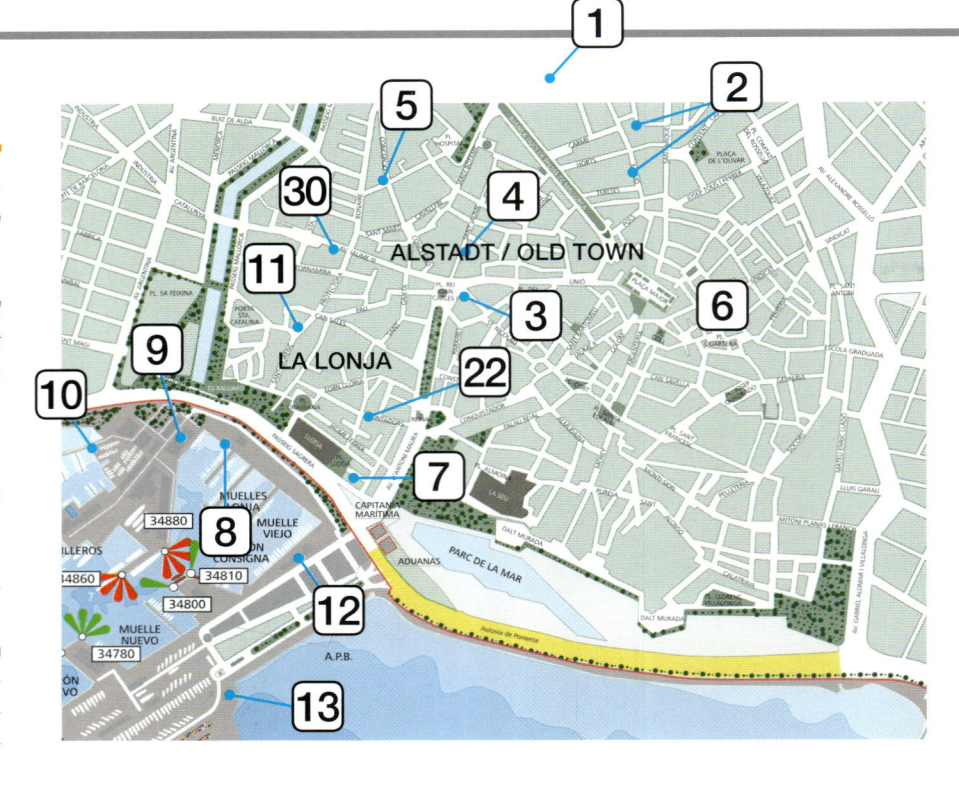

Tapas Bar, La Boveda

3 Bar Bosch
Seit Jahrzehnten der Treffpunkt Nr. 1, zwischen Paseo Borne und Altstadt.
For decades the No. 1 place to be, between Paseo Borne and Old Town.
Plaça Rei Joan Carles I,
Mon-Sat: 07-02, Sun 07-02 h

4 Tast
Bekannte Tapasbar, in der man zu vernünftigen Konditionen auf angenehme Weise satt werden kann. Keine 50 m entfernt von der Bar Bosch in Richtung Theater, rechterhand.
Well-known tapas bar, good value for money, 50 m from Bar Bosch, towards the theatre, on the right-hand side.
C./ de la Unión, 2
www.tast.com, T 971 729 878

5 Emilio Innobar
„Fine Fusion Food". Feine hochpreisige Gerichte des Küchenchefs Emilio mit mexikanischen, asiatischen und mediterranen Einflüssen in modern renoviertem, edlem Stadtpalast.
„Fine Fusion Food". Exquisite, pricey dishes by chef Emilio with Mexican, Asian and Mediterranean influences served in a modern, renovated and upscale palazzo.
T 657 50 72 94, Calle Concepcion, 9
www.emilioinnobar.com

6 Ruta Martiana
Ein Häppchen oder ein Spießchen, dazu ein Gläschen Bier oder Wein – dazu laden nahe der Plaça Mayor in der Altstadt immer dienstags ein Dutzend Bars ein. Beides zusammen zum Festpreis von 2 EUR. Das ist vor allem bei jungen Leuten beliebt.
It's the "tapas" route. An attractive idea really: every Tuesday in Palma old quarter, many pubs and bars (more than 12) offer a small dish ("tapas" or brochettes) with a drink (wine or beer) for only 2 EUR from 19.30 h to midnight.
http://rutamartiana.wordpress.com/los-bares-de-la-ruta2/

Palma de Mallorca

Paseo Marítimo + Lonja

Zwischen C./Apuntadors und Paseo Marítimo, auf Höhe der Seehandelsbörse La Lonja. Viele Gaststätten, aber wenige Tische unter freiem Himmel.
Between C./Apuntadors and Paseo Marítimo, situated around the antique fish market. Many restaurants, but few offer outside seating.

7 La Bóveda + Taberna de La Bóveda
Spanische Tapas und baskisch-kastellanisch angehauchte Küche; Große Weinfässer im Schankraum, uriges Gewölbe; Gruppen sollten reservieren. Auch am Platz vor der La Llonja.
Spanish tapas and Basque–Castilian cuisine, antique wine barrels and arched ceilings. Groups should make advance reservation. Also at the square in front of La Llonja.
C./Botería + Paseo Sagrera, 3
T 971 720 026 + 971 714 863
Mon-Sat 13.30-16 h + 20-24 h;
Sun closed
www.restaurantelaboveda.com

8 Pesquero
Beim Fischereihafen, Abendsonne auf der Terrasse. / *Near fishing harbour, terrace is lighted by evening sun.*
T 971 715 220, M 628 529 981,
08 - 01 h, daily
www.restaurantpesquero.com

9 Ca N'Eduardo
Einst urig und „angestaubt", jetzt feines Fischrestaurant in direkter Nachbarschaft der Fischhandelsbörse; 1. OG, zum Teil mit Blick auf den Fischerhafen.
Formerly cozy and old fashioned, this is now a high-class fish restaurant next door to the fish market. Located on first floor, some tables offer a view over the fishing harbour.
www.caneduardo.com
T 971 721 182, M 608 396 100

10 La Cantina
Am Eingang zur Steganlage des RCNP, hinter der Schranke rechts. Gute Küche, auch Mittagstisch.
Situated at the entrance to the RCNP piers, behind the gate to the right-hand side. Also lunch.
T 971 422 880

11 Restaurant Café Bar Ca'n Toni
Spanferkel bzw. Lamm aus dem Holzofen und phantastisch gute Caracoles (Schnecken) zu recht normalen Preisen. Gutbürgerlich mit Lokalkolorit.
Suckling pig or lamb from the wood stove and fantastic good 'caracoles' (snails) fair priced. Home cooking with local flavor.
T 871 716 661, cafecantoni@hotmail.es
www.cafecantoni.com

22 Bar Día
Treffpunkt der Berufssegler
Where captains and crew meet
C/. Apuntadores, 18
T 971 716 264

12 Mar de Nudos
Übersetzt „Meer der Knoten". Eines der beiden Restaurants im modernen Gebäude an der neu gestalteten Alten Mole.
Translated "Sea of knots". One of the two restaurants in the modern building on the redesigned old pier.
reservas@mardenudos.com
T 971 214 722
T 971 727 240
hotelsaratoga@hotelsaratoga.com

12 Restaurant Port Blanc
Ebenfalls an der Moll Vell gelegen. / *Also located at the Moll Vell.*
T 971 255 422
www.portblancmallorca.com

13 Varadero
Man sitzt wahlweise drinnen oder auf der Terrasse mit Blick auf die Kathedrale. / *One sits either indoors or on the terrace with a great view of the cathedral.*
T 971 726 428, M 675 973 638
info@varaderomallorca.com

Mallorca

SANTA CATALINA

Stadtteil oberhalb der Club Náutico außerhalb der Altstadtmauern. Verschiedene gute Restaurants, Cafes und Bars rund um die Markhalle, für fast jeden Geschmack, darunter das…

Quarter hovering above Club Náutico outside of Old Town walls. Many good restaurants and bars for all tastes, such as…

[14] Monolisto
Frische bodenständige Küche zu zivilen Preisen; große Portionen, lockere Atmosphäre. Wenige Plätze vor dem Lokal entlang der Straße, innen urig.
Fresh, local food at reasonable prices, big portions, relaxed atmosphere. A few outside tables along the pavement, cosy inside.
T 971 916 699, Mon-Sat 12 h-22.45 h, Plaça Navegació, 18

[15] Duke
Leichte, multikulturelle Speisen in Surfer-Atmosphäre. Selbst der Hamburger wird gelobt.
Light, multinational food in easy surfer atmosphere. Even their hamburgers are recommended.
C. Soler, 36; T 971 071 738
http://dukepalma.blogspot.de
13-15.30 + 19.30 - 23.30 h,
Closed: Sat noon + Sun

[15] Bunker
Ähnliches Angebot wie das Nachbarlokal „Duke" mit italienischer Note des Küchenchefs Luigi. Auch hier fühlen sich Surfer und Yachties zuhause.
Similar offerings as in neighbouring restaurant „Duke", with Italian flair by chef Luigi. A home from home for all surfers and yachties.
C. Soler, (corner C. Pursiana)
Telefon: 971 220 504

[16] Patrón Lunares Cantina
Ein Muss für jeden „Seefahrer". Eine ehemalige Kantinenbar für Arbeiter und Fischer des Viertels beherbergt das Szenelokal. In dieser alten Halle mit hohen Decken ist Platz für viele Gäste. Die Dekoration erinnert an alte Zeiten und ist liebevoll zusammengesucht. Die Karte ist international mit lokalen Einschlägen. / *A must for every „sailor". A former cantina bar for workers and fishermen of the quarter now houses this trendy location. The old hall with its high ceilings offers space for many guests. Nostalgically decorated, with carefully selected details. International menu with local character.*
C/ de la Fábrica 30
Reservas: 971 577 154
daily 19-24 h, www.patronlunares.com

[17] Kho, Thai Restaurant
Klein, aber fein. Vor allem im Innenhof nur wenige Plätze. Reservieren!
Small is beautiful here! Few seats, especially in the courtyard. Advance bookings recommended!
Carrer de Servet, 15, T 971 287 039
Mon-Sat 19-23 h & lunch
www.kohmallorca.com

[18] Calle de la Fabrica
Eine ganze Straße voll mit Bars und Restaurant / *An entire street teeming with bars and restaurants.*

PASEO MARÍTIMO / EL TERRENO

[19] Cappuccino
Nett, aber teuer Café trinken: Das geht am Paseo Marítimo, 1, und noch mehrmals in Palma: in der Altstadt, am Passeig Born, nahe des Almundaina-Palastes und, und, und…
Good but expensive coffee on Paseo Marítimo, on the Passeig Born, in the Old Town, near the Almudaina Palace and many more locations.
www.grupocappuccino.com
T 971 282 162
Direkt nebenan / *Directly next door*

[19] Hard Rock Cafe Mallorca
T 971 281 872
Bar: Sun-Thu 12-01 h, Fri-Sat 12-02 h
www.hardrock.com

[20] Dàrsena
Café mit kleiner Speisekarte gleich vis à vis des Hard Rock. Blick auf den Real Club Náutico und die Kathedrale.
Café with a short menu, situated on the waterfront opposite Hard Rock Cafe, overlooking the port and the Cathedral.
T 971 180 504

[21] Boutique del Gelato
Gleich neben dem Tanztempel Tito's. Hört sich teuer an, ist aber nur gut. Große Portionen, den Preis mehr als wert. / *Right next to dance venue Tito's. Sounds expensive, but is merely delicious. Large servings, more than good value for money.*

[21] Bahia Mediterraneo
Gediegenes Restaurant, etwas teurer, für einen besonderen Abend, Terrasse im 5. Stock mit Blick über die

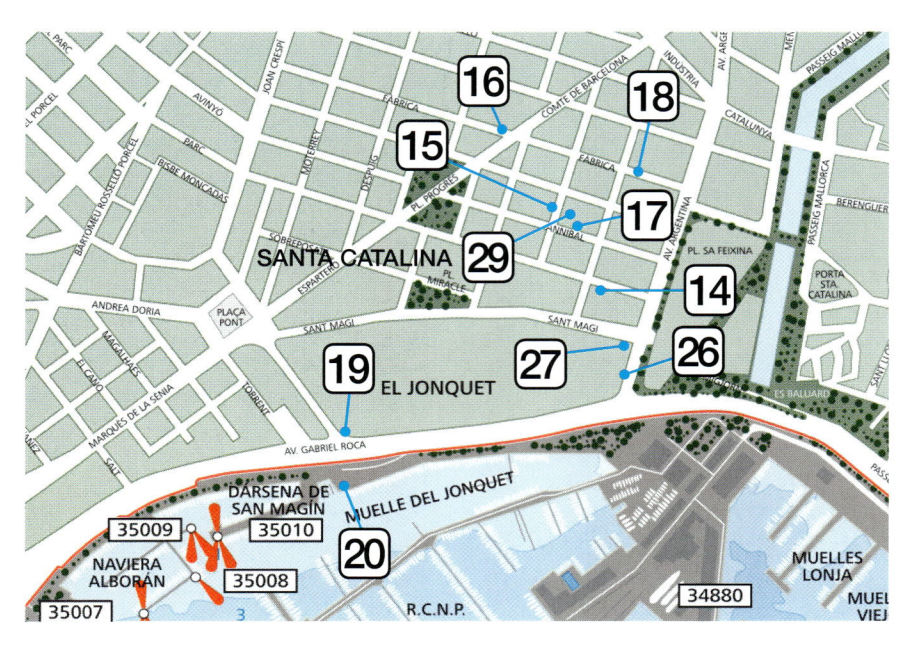

Palma de Mallorca

Häfen / *Dignified restaurant, slightly expensive, suitable for special occasions, terrace on 5th floor with harbour view*
Paseo Marítimo, 33,
T 971 457 653
www.restaurantebahiamediterraneo.com

DANCING / DISCOS

PASEO MARÍTIMO / EL TERRENO

22 Jazz Voyeur Club
C/ Apuntadores, 5, La Lonja,
T 971 720 780
info@jazzvoyeurfestival.com
Wed/Thu/Sun: 20:30-01h; Fri/Sat/Hol. 20:30-03h
Eintritt frei. Täglich wechselndes Programm, einzusehen unter / *Free entry. Programme changes daily – check at* www.jazzvoyeurfestival.com

21 Tito's
Disco-Tempel mit Außenfahrstuhl; nicht vor 24 h besuchen
Huge disco with outside elevator: only gets interesting after midnight.
Paseo Marítimo, s/n
www.titosmallorca.com

23 Pacha
Gegenüber vom Club de Mar. Große Disco mit Bars und Lounges auch im Aussenbereich und einem integrierten Club. / *Across from Club de Mar. Large disco with bars and lounges in- and outside, and an integrated club.*
Paseo Maritimo, 42
www.pachamallorca.es

24 Club de Mar Club
Im Tiefparterre des Clubhauses im Club de Mar, Nachfolger des „Marsalada". / *In the basement of the club house within the Club de Mar.*

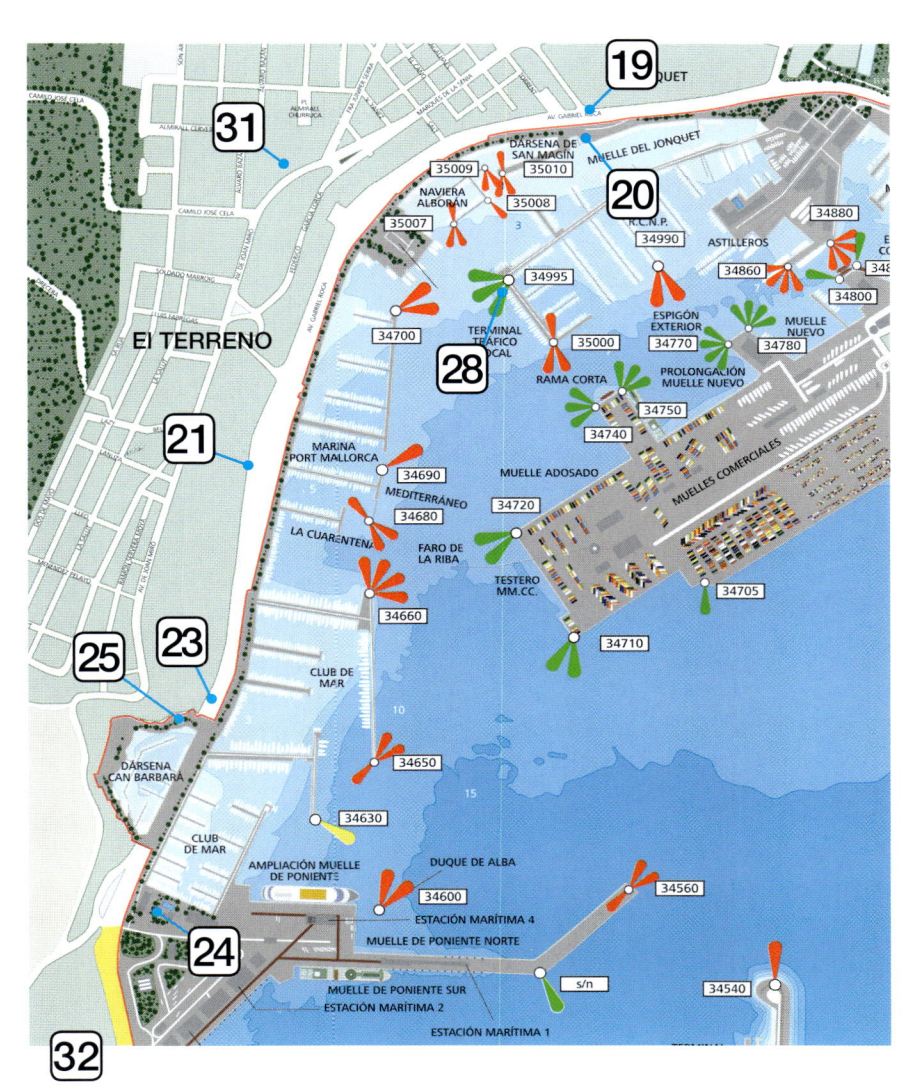

25 Garitos Café
Cafe, Bar, Club
Etablierter Club an der Dàrsena Can Barbara mit Aussenterasse am Wasser, auch zum Essen. Ausgewählte DJs zu später Stunde.
Long established club at Dàrsena Can Barbara with terrace towards the water. Selected DJs at late hours.
Agenda: www.garitocafe.com

SANTA CATALINA

26 Kaelum Klub
Bar und Club in Gewölbe-Keller
Bar and club in vaulted cellar
Avda. Argentina, 1

27 Hostal Cuba
Bar, Sky-Bar, Restaurant & Night Club, C/ San Magín, 1

EINKAUFEN / SHOPPING

28 Corb Marí
Bar mit kleiner Karte am Ende der Hauptmole des Club Náutico. Kleiner Supermarkt angeschlossen.
Small bar with a short menu situated at the end of the main pier in Club Nautico. Small supermarket next door.
www.corbmaricnp.com, T 971 105 850

29 Mercat de Santa Catalina
Mitten im Szene-Viertel gelegen: Besser als hier kann man Fleisch, Fisch, Brot, Obst und Gemüse sicher nicht einkaufen. Es gibt auch Bars, die Bocadillos und Häppchen servieren. Direkt am Markt ist auch ein „Eroski"-Supermarkt (C./ San Magí) für Getränke und Sonstiges. In den Strassen rund um die Markthalle viele kleine individuelle Läden mit ausgewähltem Angebot an Mode, Einrichtungen, Wellness & Massagen, Frisöre, etc.
Embedded in the trendy quarter: The best place for buying fresh fish, meat, bread, fruit and vegetables. Small bars serve sandwiches and tapas. Adjacent to the market there's also an "Eroski" supermarket (C./ San Magí) selling beverages and much more. In the streets surrounding the market there are many small, individual shops with a good selection of fashion, furniture, wellness & massage services, hairdressers etc.

Portbook & Island Guide

Mallorca

Kathedrale und Almundaina-Palast (l.)
Cathedral with Almundaina-Palace (left)

30 **Corté Ingles,**
Kaufhaus mit gut sortierter Lebensmittelabteilung.
Department store with a very well-assorted supermarket.
Avda. Jaume III, (Altstadt, *City centre*)

Kleiner Ableger / *branch in*
Club de Mar
Belieferung von Yachten
Yachts provisioning
clubdemar@elcorteingles.es

NAHE / *NEAR* MARINA NAVIERA BALEAR, PORT DE MALLORCA

31 Im Stadtteil Terreno oberhalb der genannten Marinas ein großer, sehr gut sortierter und preiswerter Mercadona-Supermarkt und ein kleiner aus der Eroski-Kette. Kleinere Supermärkte mit eingeschränkter Auswahl auch am Paseo Marítimo.

Supermarkets of the Eroski and Mercadona chains can be found above the aforementioned marinas in the Terreno quarter. Several smaller supermarkets along the Paseo Maritimo.

NAHE / *NEAR* CLUB DEL MAR

32 **Centro Commercial Porto Pí**
Im Einkaufszentrum Porto Pí gibt es u. a. einen großen Carrefour Supermarkt mit Lieferservice an Bord (Servicio a domicilio) für gerade 4 EUR Aufpreis. Das soll auch für „barcos" gelten. Zur Sicherheit vor dem Einkauf bestätigen lassen. Ausserdem alle möglichen Arten von Läden, Mode, Kosmetik, etc.
In Porto Pi's shopping mall there is a huge Carrefour hypermarket offering home delivery at an additional charge of only 4 EUR. This should also include yachts, but better check to make sure. In addition all kinds of shops, fashion, cosmetics, etc.

ALTSTADT / OLD TOWN

Zahlreiche Geschäfte zum Bummeln und Shoppen in den Gassen Altstadt bis hin zur Plaça Major und auf den Prachtboulevards der Stadt, Paseo Borne und Av. Jaime III

There are many shops to look at while strolling through the alleys of the Old Town, all the way down to Plaça Major and town boulevards Paseo Borne and Av. Jaime III

AUSFLÜGE / *EXCURSIONS*

Kathedrale / *cathedral* **La Seu**
Einmalige Lage am Meer, 13. Jahrhundert, gotisch; auf der alten Stadtmauer von Palma de Mallorca errichtet.
Unique sea front location, built in gothic style in the 13th century upon the remnants of the old city wall.
4 EUR. Kinder bis 10 Jahre frei - *Children aged up to 10 free of charge*
Mon-Fri 10-17.15 h; Sat 10-14.15 h
www.catedraldemallorca.org

Palacio Reial de la Almundaina
Unmittelbar neben der Kathedrale.
Right next to the cathedral
www.patrimonionacional.es, T 971 719 145 + 214 134
Oct.-March: 10-17 h (daily), April-Sept.: 10-19 h (daily), Mon closed
7 EUR; Ermäßig: 4 EUR; Kinder bis 5 Jahre frei: Führung: 6 EUR
7 EUR; children 4 EUR, aged up to 5 years free of charge: guided tour 6 EUR
Free of charge on Wed+Thu, Oct-March, 15-18; April-Sept, 17-20 h.
Für Bürger der Europäischen Gemeinschaft / *For EU citizens*

Sa Llotja
Stromern Sie durch die Gassen der Altstadt. Dort finden Sie auch die alte die

Palma de Mallorca

Paseo Borne

alte Warenbörse von Palma de Mallorca hat einen rechteckigen Grundriss. Der Innenbereich besteht aus einer einzigen Decke mit Kreuzbogengewölbe, das auf Säulen ruht. Mit dem Bau wurde 1426 begonnen.
Stroll through the Old Town alleyways. There, you'll also find the old rectangular-based Palma commodity market. The interior is covered by an arched, groyned vault ceiling supported on pillars. Construction started in 1426.
Eintritt frei, wechselnde Ausstellungen.
Free entry, changing exhibitions
T 971 71 17 05
Tue-Sat: 11-14 + 17-21 h, Sun: 11-14 h (only for exhibitions)

9 Fischversteigerung
Fish Auction

Jeden Morgen kommt der frisch angelandete Fisch unter dem Hammer. Romantisch muss man sich das nicht vorstellen, aber interessant. Ab 6 h.
Every morning, freshly caught fish is auctioned off here. Though less than romantic, it is quite interesting. Begins 6 a.m.
Contramuelle near Club Nautico

Hop-On-Hop-Off Bus

Rot, bunt bemalt und oben offen: So sieht ein Sightseeing-Bus in Palma aus (www.city-sightseeing.com), dort bei der Suche „Palma de Mallorca" auswählen. Die Fahrkarte über die Webseite oder im Bus: 15 EUR, ermäßigt 7,50 EUR. 24 Stunden gültig. Beliebig oft ein- und aussteigen. 16 Haltestellen, davon einige in Hafennähe.
Painted in red and colourful patterns, sightseeing busses with their open top are easy to spot in Palma. Select Palma de Mallorca on www.city-sightseeing.com. Tickets on the bus or on website: adults 15 EUR / children 7.50 EUR, valid for 24 hours. Hop on and off as you like at one of 6 stops, with several near the port.

Palma – mit dem Rad / *by bike*

Neben dem Auditorium Vermietung von Fahrrädern, Rollerblades, Seekajaks etc. Es werden verschiedene Touren angeboten. / *Rent a bicycle, rollerblade, sea kayak etc. next to the Auditorium. Different tours on offer by:*

www.palmaonbike.com,
palmaonbike@palmaonbike.com
T 971 718 062 + 918 988,
Mon-Son: 9.30-14 h + 16-18 h
Av. Gabriel Roca, 15 (Zweite Filiale / *2nd branch*: Av. Antoni Maura 10)

La Lonja z. Z. der Ausstellung „Faces"
during the exhibition „Faces"

Mallorca

Castell Bellver
Eine der wenigen rund gebauten europäischen Burgen, Baubeginn im 14. Jhd. 112 m über dem Hafen. Blick auf die Bucht von Palma und auf einen großen Teil der Insel. Im Kastell das historische Museum Palmas mit archäologischen Funden und Kunstsammlungen. Es werden Rundgänge angeboten.
One of the few rotund fortresses in Europe; construction started in the 14th century at 112 m above sea level. Fortress overlooks the bay of Palma and a large part of the island. It houses Palma's historic museum with archaeological specimens and art collections. Guided tours available.

Veranstaltungen, Zeiten etc.
Events, dates and times etc:
T 971 735 065
www.tacostamlacultura.cat
Entrance: 4 EUR, reduced 2 EUR, minus 14: free
Sun: Freier Eintritt / *free entry* (Ausstellungsräume und Museum geschlossen / *Exhibitions and museum closed*)
01/04-30/09: Mon: 8.30-13 h, Thu-Sat: 8.30-20 h, Sun + hol.: 10-20 h
01/10-31/03: Mon: 8.30-13 h, Thu-Sat: 8.30-18 h, Sun + hol.: 10-18 h

Die Arabischen Bäder
The Arabian Baths
Eines der wenigen noch erhaltenen Gebäude aus arabischer Zeit in Palma (10. bis 12. Jhd.). 8 hufeisenförmige Säulen tragen eine Kuppel, durch die Licht einfällt. / *One of the few intact Arabic buildings, dating from the 10th to 12th century; 8 pillars in horseshoe shape support a vaulted roof which lets through the sunlight.*
Can Serra, 7, T 971 721 549
Entrance: 2 EUR, Daily 9:30-18 h

Patios & Altstadt / *Old Town* Calatrava
Palma ist bekannt für seine prächtigen Stadthäuser mit großzügigen Innenhöfen, den so genannten Patios. Die Stadtverwaltung empfiehlt eine Besichtigungstour in der Altstadt Palmas, rund um Kathedrale und Pfarrkirche Santa Eulàlia unter:
Palma is renown for its beautiful city houses with their generous large courtyards, so-called patios. Guided tours around the old city, the cathedral and church of Santa Eulalia organised by the city council on:
www.conselldemallorca.net/altramallorca/index.htm

El Faro de Porto Pí
Eines der ältesten Leuchtfeuer weltweit in Betrieb. Angegliedertes Museum. Besichtigung nach Anmeldung montags, mittwochs und Freitags.
The lighthouse of Porto Pi: One of the world's oldest operating lighthouses, with museum. Visits by appointment on Mondays, Wednesdays and Fridays.
T 971 402 175
fardeportopi@portsdebalears.com
www.farsdebalears.org

Portixol & Es Molinar
Spaziergang oder Radtour an der schönen Promenade an den kleinen Fischerhäfen vorbei. Viele Cafes und Restaurants. Kurz vor Portixol am Stadtstrand Palmas gelegen zwei Beachclubs.
Take a walk or bike ride along the beautiful promenade passing fishing harbours. Lots of cafés and restaurants. Near Portixol, situated on Palma's city beach, two beach clubs.

Anima Beach
www.animabeachpalma.com

Nassau Beach Club
www.nassaubeach-palma.com

Castell Bellver

Palma de Mallorca

MUSEEN / *MUSEUMS*

Fundació La Caixa

Hier ist schon die Fassade des Gebäudes Kunst, weil einst im Modernisme-Stil errichtet, dem nordeuropäischen Jugendstil vergleichbar. Im ehemaligen Gran Hotel, nahe dem Theater von Palma, eröffnete die Bank „La Caixa" 1993 ein Kulturzentrum mit wechselnden Ausstellungen. Eintritt frei.

The modernist style facade is itself a piece of art, comparable to north European Art Noveau style. This former grand hotel near the Theatre was transformed in 1993 by the Caixa bank in to a cultural centre with changing exhibitions. Free entry.

Mon-Sat 10-21, Sun + hol: 10-14 h
Placa de Weyler, 3, T 971 178 500
www.obrasocial.lacaixa.es/nuestroscentros/caixaforumpalma/caixaforum-palma_es.html

Es Baluard

Museum für zeitgenössische Kunst in einem Teil der alten Stadtmauer gegenüber vom Haupteingang zum Real Club Náutico. Gut zu erkennen an der schwarzen Skulptur von Calatrava, die über die Stadtmauer hinausragt. Museumsladen mit schöner Auswahl. Café mit Blick über den Hafen.

Contemporary art museum built into a part of the old city wall, opposite the entrance to Real Club Náutico. Easy to find thanks to the black Calatrava sculpture towering above the city wall. Museum shop with nice range of goods. Café provides nice harbour view.

museu@esbaluard.org, T 971 908 200
Thu-Sat 10-20, Sun 10-15; Mon + 25.12. + 1. 1. closed
6 EUR (ganzes Museum), 4 EUR f. zeitweilige Ausstellungen
Entrance: 6 EUR (entire museum), 4 EUR for temporary exhibitions

Fundació Pilar i Joan Miró

Joan Miró lebte und arbeitete von 1956 bis zu seinem Tod 1983 in Palma. Seine bekannteste Skulptur im öffentlichen Raum in Palma steht nahe der Kathedrale in der C./Conquistador, „Femme", Bronze, 2,50 m hoch. Ein Video auf der Webseite gibt einen sehr schönen Überblick über Stiftung und Ausstellung in der C. de Saridakis, 29, Stadtteil Palma Nova.

Joan Miró lived and worked in Palma from 1956 till his death in 1983. His most famous sculpture in Palma's public space, "Femme" bronze and 2.5 m high, stands near the cathedral in the C./ Conquistador. The video on the website gives a wonderful insight into the Miró foundation and its exhibition.

in Cala Major, C./Saridakis 29
16 May - 15 Sept.: Thu-Sat 10-19 h;
Sun + hol. 10-15 h, Mon closed
16 Sept. - 15 May: Thu-Sat 10-18 h;
Sun + hol. 10-15 h, Mon closed
Entrance: 5 EUR; Bus 3 + 46,
T 971 701 420
www.miro.palmademallorca.es

Museo Palau March

In unmittelbarer Nachbarschaft von Kathedrale und Almundaina-Palast. Zeitgenössische Skulpturensammlung mit Werken von Rodin, Moore und Chillida. Im Büchersaal eine einzigartige Seekartensammlung vom 15. bis 17. Jahrhundert, die berühmten Portolane.

In the vicinity of the Almudaina Palace. Collection of contemporary sculptures from Rodin, Moore and Chillada. A unique collection of 15th to 17th century nautical maps is on show in the library, known as the Portolan charts.

T 971 711 122, Entrance: 4,50 EUR, younger than 12 years free
1/4 - 31/10.: Mon-Fri 10-18:30 h,
1/11 - 31/03.: Mon-Fri 10-14 h
www.fundacionbmarch.es

Dalí in Palma

Dauerausstellung im Museo Can Morey de Santmartí in unmittelbarer Nähe der Kathedrale mit 200 Originalgrafiken des katalanischen Surrealisten.

Permanent exhibition in Museo Can Morey de Santmartí in the vicinity of the Cathedral, boasting 200 original drawings of the great Catalan surrealist.

www.museo-santmarti.es

Museo Militar Palma

Auf der Westmole des Hafens, im Castillo de San Carlos. Ein Video, auch auf Deutsch, zeigt die verschiedenen Wehranlagen entlang der Inselküsten. Ein Saal über die Geschichte der Wehrtürme Mallorcas. Ein weiterer Saal widmet sich den Steinschleuderern der Balearen. Seit 2013 ein Café auf der Festungsmauer mit Meerblick während der Öffnungszeiten.

Situated on the west pier of the harbour in San Carlos castle. A video shows the fortifications alongside the island's coast. There is also a room treating the antique use of catapults for military defense on the Balearic islands. Since 2013 the museum houses a Café with sea view on the fortification ramparts.

www.museomilitarsancarlos.com
T 971 402 145
Buslinie 1 (Haltestelle Estacíon Marítima) / *Bus no. 1 (get off at Estacíon Marítima)*
Thu-Sun 10-14 h, Mon + hol. closed
Eintritt frei / free
Kontakt / *contact* Café:
T 971 702 987, M 622 408 488

Mallorca — Palma de Mallorca

Palmas Sóller-Bahnhof, Plaça Espana
The train to Sóller departs at Placa Espana.

TAGESAUSFLUG / DAY TRIP

Zugfahrt nach Sollér –
Train Trip to Sollér

Historische Eisenbahn auf der Linie Palma-Sóller, 2012 war der 100. Jahrestag der Ferrocarril de Sóller. Die Schienen führen durch verschiedene Tunnel des Tramuntana-Gebirgszuges. In Sóller schöner Bahnhof nahe des Zentrums. Weiterfahrt mit einer kaum minder betagten Straßenbahn nach Puerto Sóller möglich.

Historic train from Palma to Sollér which celebrated its 100th anniversary in 2012. The railway takes visitors through various tunnels of the Tramuntana mountains to the pretty station near the centre of Sollér. From there an almost equally historic tramway will take you down you to the port of Sollér.

Preise für beide Verkehrsmittel unter / *Find prices for both on:*
www.trendesoller.com
Station in Palma, Plaça España, 2
T 971 752 051

Valldemossa

Von keinem anderen Küstenort kommt man so schnell in dieses Bergdorf, das durch einen einzigen Roman zu Ruhm gekommen ist: „Ein Winter auf Mallorca" von George Sand. Die französische Schriftstellerin verbrachte 1838/39 keine 100 Tage und einen Winter mit dem Komponisten Frédéric Chopin und ihren Kindern dort und bis heute Pilgern Touristen zu Tausenden dorthin, um deren Wohnstatt in Augenschein zu nehmen. Das muss man nicht tun, es reicht der Ort an sich.

No other place on the coast lets you get more quickly to this mountain village, made famous by a single novel: „A Winter In Mallorca" by George Sand. The French writer spent not quite 100 days during the winter 1838/39 there, accompanied by composer Frédéric Chopin and their children. To this day, thousands of tourists travel there to visit their dwelling. But for those not interested in historic sightseeing, the village itself is sufficiently interesting.

SERVICE

MIETWAGEN / CAR RENTAL

Damit kommt man überall hin. Ob in die Berge, zu verträumten Orten oder zu Stränden, vor denen man nicht ankern konnte. Die besten Preise gibt es fast immer ab Flughafen oder Ca'n Pastilla. Einige größere Vermieter haben auch Zweigbüros am Paseo Marítimo. Gute Buchungsplattform, die zu sehr günstigen Preisen führt:

A good way to get around; into the mountains, to dreamy little villages or beaches where anchoring is impossible. Best prices at the airport or in Ca'n Pastilla. Some of the larger companies also have branches on the Paseo Marítimo. Good booking platform, guides user to best prices:
www.billiger-mietwagen.de

BUSVERBINDUNGEN
BUS CONNECTIONS

Öffentliche Verkehrsmittel sind preiswert, 1,50 EUR pro Fahrt im Gebiet von Palma. Busse verkehren über die ganze Insel, in Palma zentral ab dem unterirdischen Busbahnhof an der Plaça d'Espanya. In unmittelbarer Nähe befindet sich auch der unterirdische Bahnhof für die S-Bahnen, die u. a. über Inca bis nach Manacor fahren. Alle Verbindungen über:

Public transport is reasonably cheap, with 1.50 EUR per ticket around Palma. www.emtpalma.es (in English and German as well) Buses cover the entire island; from Palma they leave from the underground bus station on the Placa d'Espanya. From the train station next door, commuter trains go to Inca and Manacor, among others. For connections see:
www.tib.org

Valldemossa

Portixol – Cala Gamba

Portixol
39° 33,4' N 002 40,1' E

🇩🇪 Ingesamt geringe Wassertiefen, mehr als 2,50 m sollte man im Einfahrtsbereich nicht erwarten. Danach weiter abnehmend, vorsichtig navigieren. Der ansässige Club Nàutic Portixol hat die Konzession für die Liegeplätze im östlichen Teil des Hafens, bis ungefähr zum weißen Kran. Gastyachten haben nur eine geringe Chance auf einen Liegeplatz.
T 971 242 424, cnportitxol@gmail.com, www.cnportitxol.com

Der westliche Teil des Hafens ist in der Zuständigkeit der regionalen Hafenbehörde Autoridad Portuaria, Service-T. 971 228 487.

Der Stadtteil Portixol und das angrenzende Molinar sind Szene-Viertel mit zahlreichen Restaurants und Bars. Wer nicht so weit gehen möchte, kann auch die Speisekarte der Club-Gaststätte ins Auge fassen. T 971 273 868

🇬🇧 *Shallow water depths, more than 2.5m should not be expected in the entrance area. Continuously decreasing, navigate with caution. Berths in the eastern part of the harbour belong to Club Nàutic Portixol, limited more or less by the white painted crane. Yachts in transit have a small chance of getting a free berth.*
T 971 242 424, cnportitxol@gmail.com, www.cnportitxol.com
The western part of the port is organised by Autoridad Portuaria, service tel. 971 228 487.
The Portixol district and the adjoining Molinar are trendy with many restaurants and bars. Also the club-restaurant is well visited. T 971 273 868

Cala Gamba
39° 32,6' N 002 41,6' E

Von Booten mit mehr als 1,40 m Tiefgang nicht anzulaufen. Freie Liegeplätze werden vermietet. An Land gibt es technischen Service, einen 12,5-t-Kran, eine Tankstelle und eine Club-Gaststätte mit Terrasse im Obergeschoss (hier wird mittags ein preiswertes Menu del día serviert), möbliert im kühlen spanischen Stil früherer Jahre. Ebenerdig ein Meeresfrüchte-Restaurant.

Boats with a draft that exceeds 1.40m cannot enter. Vacant berths are rented. Around this small marina, run by a sailing club, there are technical services, a petrol station and a 12.5-ton crane and a club-restaurant with terrace on the top floor (here an inexpensive menu del día is served at noon), furnished in a previous Spanish interior style. At ground level a seafood restaurant.

Club Nàutic Cala Gamba
T 971 261 849
www.cncg.es, info@cncg.es

Tankstelle / *Fuel station*
Mon-Fri 9.30–18 h, Sat: 7.30 h–18 h; Sun + hol.: 8.30–13 h
Kreditkartenzahlung
pay with credit card

Cafetería-Restaurante, T 971 262 372
🕐 Tue-Thu: 8–20 h, Fri-Sat: 7.30 h–open end, Sun: 7.30–20 h, Mon: closed
Restaurante-Marisquería
T 971 494 289
www.marisqueriacalagamba.es

Nauta Marine Services
Spezialisiert auf Bootsmotoren. Dazu alle anderen Arbeiten rund ums Schiff.
Specialised in marine engines. All crafts needed for boat maintenance.
M 689 603 587 + 697 707 235
www.nautamarineservices.es
info@nautamarineservices.es

Portixol

Cala Gamba

Mallorca

C'an Pastilla

🇩🇪 Die Marina wird geführt vom „Club Marítimo San Antonio de la Playa". Sie liegt ungefähr auf halber Strecke zwischen Palma de Mallorca und S'Arenal.
Südöstlich der Marina erstreckt sich über 4 km bis nach S'Arenal die Playa de Palma, eine bei Deutschen sehr beliebte touristische Hochburg mit dem einschlägigen Vergnügungsangebot.
Wegen der Nähe zum stark frequentierten Flughafen können Flugzeuge, die zum Meer hin starten, eine Lärmbeeinträchtigung mit sich bringen.
Technisch gute Ausstattung mit Travellift (50 t) und Werkstatt.

🇬🇧 *This marina is run by „Club Marítimo San Antonio de la Playa". It's located half way between Palma de Mallorca and S'Arenal. Southeast of this marina Playa de Palma stretches across 3mi to S'Arenal. Very popular amongst German tourists with the relevant public entertainment. May be quite noisy due the busy airport nearby. Technically well equipped with travel lift (50t) and workshops.*

ANSTEUERUNG
APPROACHING

Dem Inselchen Isla Galera 0,5 sm westlich des Hafens sind weitere Untiefen vorgelagert. Diese sind ernst zu nehmen, immer wieder kommt es hier zu Grundberührungen, selbst durch Motoryachten. Eine weitere, unbezeichnete Untiefe mit weniger als 2 m Wasser befindet sich auf Höhe des Balenario 6.

Additional shallows situated in front of islet Isla Galera 0.5nm west of the harbour. These must be taken seriously since many boats and even motor yachts tend to touch ground. Another unmarked shoal with not more than 2 m of water is located around 1nmi northwest of the marina of S'Arenal.

Vorsicht: Bei auflandigem Wind von mehr als 25 kn sollten Skipper nicht mehr auslaufen. Und besser auch nicht einlaufen. Die Hafeneinfahrt liegt im Brandungsbereich. Nach dem Winter Vorsicht auch innerhalb des Hafens: Wegen Versandung kann die Wassertiefe hinter dem äußeren Wellenbrecher und hinter der Tankstelle auf unter 2 m zurückgehen. Einlaufend an Steuerbord markieren kleine grüne Tonnen vor der Innenmole flache Bereiche.

Caution: with onshore winds exceeding 25kn, skippers shouldn't try to leave the port. And they should better not enter, since the entrance is located in between the breaking wave zone. After the winter period shoaled areas with less than 2m water depths are likely within the outer breakwater and close to the the petrol station. Green bouys mark shoals in front of the inner breakwater.

FESTMACHEN
FIND A BERTH

A Wartekai und Liegeplätze für durchreisende Yachten befinden sich an der Innenseite der Außenmole einlaufend an Backbord. Wasser und Strom am Steg.
Wassertiefe ca. 3 m

Waiting pier and berths for visiting yachts are on the inside of the breakwater, i.e. on portside when entering. Water and electric supply on the pier. Depth: ca. 3m

🕐 ganzjährig / all year: Mon-Fri 8-20 h, Sat 8-18 h, Sun closed
T 971 745 076, UKW / VHF 09
www.cmsap.com
cmsap@cmsap.com
€ Bis/up to 12 m: 76,80 EUR
Bis/up to 15 m: 96,80 EUR
ganzjährig ohne saisonale Unterschiede, 21% MwSt. & WiFi inkl.
All year prices, 21% VAT + Wifi included

ANKERPLÄTZE
ANCHORAGE AREAS

B Nahe der Hafeneinfahrt auf 3-5 m Wassertiefe. Grund überwiegend Sand. Geringer Schutz und bei stärkerem thermischem Wind tagsüber sehr unruhig. Dann sind hier ohnehin zu viele Kite-Surfer unterwegs …

Near the harbour entrance with 3-5m water depth. Bottom predominantly sand. Less protection even with stronger onshore winds. In which case too many kite surfers make this a busy place …

C'an Pastilla

- Sehr nah am Flughafen
- Touristische Umgebung
- Charter-Ausgangshafen
- *Close to the airport*
- *Touristy place*
- *Charter base*

39° 31,8' N 002° 43,0' E

Fl (4) R 13s

TANKEN / *FUEL*

D+B; Year round, 24 h
Bezahlung nur per Automat und kompliziert; besser vorher einen Marina-Angestellten oder die Charterbasis K.P. Winter (T 971 490 900) befragen.

Automatic cash machine, no service; rather complicated, better ask Marinero or charter base K.P. Winter (T 971 490 900) beforehand
Wassertiefe / *depth* 2,5 m

TECHNISCHER SERVICE
TECHNICAL SERVICES

Mecanáutica y Servicios Asensio
Motorenservice für Volvo Penta u. a.
Engine service for Volvo Penta etc.
Tel 971 908 282
asensio@mecanautica.com
www.mecanautica.com

YACHTAUSRÜSTER
CHANDLERIES

Mecanáutica
siehe oben / *see above*

EINKAUFEN / *SHOPPING*

Lebensmittel lassen sich in verschiedenen Geschäften in Hafennähe besorgen. Für Großeinkäufe mehr Supermärkte in größerer Entfernung bis hin zum Carrefour-Supermarkt in Coll d'en Rebassa. Bankautomaten, Post, Ärzte und Apotheke im Ort.

Provisioning is possible in several shops near the harbour. For large-scale supplies several supermarkets available including Carrefour hypermarket near Coll d'en Rebassa. Town offers ATMs, post office, doctors and pharmacies.

Portbook & Island Guide

Mallorca

Purobeach

RESTAURANTS & BARS

1 **El Club** Restaurant + Cafe
im zentralen Marina-Gebäude im Obergeschoss, Café mit Sonnenterrasse. / *In the marina's central building on the top floor, bar with sun terrace.*
T 971 261 025

Weitere Bars und Gaststätten am Eingang zum Hafen und im Ort. / *More bars and restaurants close to the marina's entrance and in the surroundings.*

2 **La Mejillonera**
An der Einfahrt zur Marina
At the marina entrance
T 971 490 703

La Payesita
Gleich nebenan / right next door
T 971 263 367

Sa Farinera
Fleisch vom Grill, urig. An einer Parallelstraße zur Autobahn zwischen Abfahrt Flughafen u. Abfahrt Manacor gelegen. *Barbecued meat, very authentic. Located on a street parallel to the highway between exit airport and exit Manacor.*
daily 19-02 h, T 971 262 011
reservas@safarinera.com
www.safarinera.com

3 **Purobeach**
Exklusiver Beachclub, chic & teuer, zirka 500 m entfernt, Richtung Palma / *Exclusive Beach club, chic & pricy, at ca. 500m distance towards Palma.* T 971 744 744
www.purobeach.com
info.palma@purobeach.com
11/05-23/09 11-01 h

Palma Aquarium

DANCING / DISCOS

In Richtung Arenal (ab ca. 2 km von der Marina entfernt am Strand entlang) ein umfassendes Angebot an Nachtleben. *Towards S'Arenal (approx. 2km from the marina along the beach) there is a huge entertainment variety on offer.*
u.a. / *amongst others:*
Pabisa Beach Club
www.pabisabeachclub.com
T 971 743 334

AUSFLÜGE / *EXCURSIONS*

Direkt in Hafennähe: Hotspot für Kite-Surfer, wenn Wind ist. Ansonsten ein Stand-Up-Padel Board leihen und zur kleinen Insel am Puro Beach paddeln. Oder einen Kurs belegen:
Close to the harbour: a hot spot for kite surfers when the wind blows. Otherwise just rent a stand-up paddle boat and proceed to the small island at Puro Beach. Or take a course:

El Niño Surf Centre
Windsurf, Surf, SUP, Kite Surf & Kayaks
C/ Vaixell, 2; T 971 490 811
www.mallorcapaddlesurf.com

Cafe Bona Ona
Stand Up Paddle, Wind Surf & Kite Surf & Café Bar
Boards for Rent, Classes, Excursions
T 619 749 271 / 971 261 261
www.bonaona.com

4 **Palma Aquarium**
Haie, Rochen und mehr.
Sharks, rays, etc.
T 902 702 902
www.palmaaquarium.com
1 km entfernt / *1mi away*
C/ Manuela de los Herreros 21
€ 21,50 EUR + 14 EUR (4-12)
🕘 09.30-17 h

Radtour entlang der Playa oder in Richtung Palma. Es gibt mehrere Verleiher, u. a. / *Bicycle rides along the beach or in Palma direction. Several bike rentals, including:*

M 634 373 786
Rollerking, M 672 805 449
www.ebike-point-mallorca.com

C'an Pastilla

Palma besuchen
Gut mit dem Bus zu erreichen, Linie 15 und 30 ab Ca'n Pastilla bis zur Plaça Espanya in Palma
Vorsicht vor Taschendiebstählen, vor allen in voll besetzten Bussen.
Good bus connections, bus no. 15 and 30 from Ca'n Pastilla to Plaça Espanya in Palma. Watch out for pickpocketers, especially on crowded busses.

MIETWAGEN / *CAR RENTAL*

Wegen der Nähe zum Flughafen große Zahl von Autovermietern, u. a.
Big choice of car rentals due to airport nearby, including:

Hiper
T 971 269 911 + 262 223
08-22 h, www.hiperrentacar.com

Hasso Rent a car
T 902 203 012
www.hasso-rentacar.com

Autos Roig
T 971 648 118
www.autosroig.com

Satt sparen Mit uns!
- Vorteile beim Seewetter
- Vorzugspreise in Marinas
- Spezielle Yacht-Kasko-Versicherungen
- Bücher günstiger kaufen u.v.m.

Mitglied werden! Ab 18 Euro/Jahr
Tel.: 040 - 632009-0

www.kreuzer-abteilung.org

S'Arenal

🇩🇪 Durch den Club Nàutic S'Arenal professionell geführte Marina im östlichen Zipfel der Bucht von Palma mit einigen Gastplätzen und einem beliebten Werftgelände. Wer sich in das Nachtleben an der Playa de Palma stürzen möchte, findet hier die ideale Ausgangsbasis. Kaum hat man die Marina verlassen, ist man mitten drin.

🇬🇧 *Established marina, professionally managed by a yacht club, in the eastern tip of the Bay of Palma. Offers a few visitor's berths and a popular shipyard. If you want to launch yourself into a turbulent nightlife, you have come to the right place; it's a few steps away from the marina.*

ANSTEUERUNG
APPROACHING

Durch ihre Lage neben einem langen Sandstrand neigt die Hafeneinfahrt zur Versandung. Unbezeichnete Untiefe mit weniger als 1,5 m Wasser vor dem Balneario 6, zirka 1 sm nordwestlich der Marina. / *The harbour entrance situated at the end of the long sandy beach tends to sand up. Unmarked shallow with less than 1.5m depth in front of the Balneario 6, ca. 1nm to the northwest of the marina.*

FESTMACHEN
FIND A BERTH

A Club Nàutic S'Arenal
Wenige Gästeplätze für Yachten bis 22 m Länge. Anmeldung notwendig. Freie Plätze werden zugewiesen. Der Club hat eine eigene Webseite zur Reservierung von Liegeplätzen eingerichtet, dort sind auch alle Preislisten einsehbar.
Few berths for yachts up to 22m. Registration required. Free moorings will be assigned. The club has set up a seperate website for online booking of moorings with complete price lists.
www.cnamoorings.com

€ Bis 13 m / up to 13m, inkl. 21% MwSt. / incl. 21% IVA
July-Sept.: 100,73, April-Juni + Okt.: 91,83, Jan-March + Nov./Dec.: 68,87
T 971 440 142, F 971 440 568

📱 UKW/VHF 09, info@cnarenal.com
www.cnarenal.com

🕐 01/05-31/10: Mon-Fri: 08.30 – 21 h, Sat, Sun + hol.: 09.00-13.30 + 16.30-21.00 h
01/11-30/04: Mon-Fri: 08.30 – 20 h, Sat, 09.00 - 14.00 h, Sun + hol.: closed
Marineros: 08-22 h

WiFi kostenlos / free
Benutzung des Swimming-Pools kostenlos für Gäste, / *Use of pool free of charge for guests*

ANKERPLÄTZE
ANCHORAGE AREAS

B Südlich der Außenmole vor einem kleinen Sandstrand auf zirka 4m Wassertiefe. Grund: Sand mit Seegras. / *South of the breakwater in front of a small sandy beach at about 4m water depth. Bottom: sand with weed.*

TANKEN / *FUEL*

🕐 08-20 h (summer); 08-19 h (winter)
24h: mit Kreditkarte / with creditcard

TECHNISCHER SERVICE
TECHNICAL SERVICES

70-t-Travellift
70-t-Travellift auf dem Werftgelände, Betriebzeiten der Werft 08-21 h. Preise für Landstellplatz auf Anfrage im Marinabüro. Dort empfiehlt man auch externe Service-Betriebe.
70-t travel lift at the shipyard, uptime shipyard 08-21 h. Prices for land parking space on request at the Marina Office. There you will also get recommendations to external service companies.

Bert Penning de Vries
Alle Yacht-Reparaturen inkl. Arbeiten am Teakdeck. Guter Berater für das stehende und aufende Gut. Spricht viele Sprachen, auch fließend Deutsch. Oft sehr ausgebucht.
All kinds of yacht repairs incl. teak

39° 30,3' N   002° 44,6' E

Mallorca

S'Arenal

- Beliebte Marina und Werft
- Einfahrt neigt zur Versandung
- Partymeile fußläufig erreichbar
- *Popular marina and boatyard*
- *Entrance tends to silt*
- *Bars & nightlife nearby*

Fl (3) G 9s

Calò de Sant Antoni

Mallorca

deck work. Give good advice on standing rigging and running rigging. Multilingual, also speak German fluently. Frequently booked up.
M 627 958 788

Jörg Hagedorn
Kompetent bei Elektrik, Elektronik und Computer-Problemen.
Competent support for all issues concerning electrics, electronics and IT.
M 600 507 118

YACHTAUSRÜSTER / *CHANDLERIES*

Mar Blau, am Eingang zur Marina, *at marina entrance.*
T+F 971 440 440, M 619 789 884
www.mar-blau.com

EINKAUFEN / *SHOPPING*

Ordentliche Supermärkte, Ärzte, Post etc. im nahegelegenen Stadtzentrum.
Well-assorted supermarkets, doctors, post office etc. in nearby town centre.

RESTAURANTS & BARS

1 Restaurant **Club Nàutic S'Arenal**
Neben dem Schwimmbad, auch Mittagsmenü, *Next to the pool, special lunch menu,* T 971 440 427, 13-23 h

2 **Restaurant Las Sirenas**
vor Hafeneingang; kleine Terrasse, gute Küche zu fairen Preisen. Reservierung empfohlen.
At harbour entrance with a small terrace, good value for money. Reservations recommended.
T 971 440 039

3 **Varadero Beach**
Antiguo Club Nautico Arenal
Ebenfalls auf dem Gelände des Club Náutico, am alten Hafenteil, wo die Playa de Palma beginnt. Terrasse.
Located on the premises of the Club Náutico, at the old port part of the marina, adjacent to Playa de Palma. Terrace.
T 971 442 745

4 Das Amüsierviertel von S'Arenal an der Playa de Palma beginnt fußläufig keine Viertelstunde vom Yachtclub entfernt. Neben bekannten Vergnügungsstätten (Megapark, Oberbayern etc.) gibt es immer mehr Szenelokale wie den Pabisa Beach Club, Ctra Arenal 56

The Arenal entertainment quarter begins at 15 min's walk off the marina. Besides well-known establishments (e.g.: Megapark, Oberbayern), new trendy places keep opening such as the Pabisa Beach Club on Ctra Arenal 56
www.pabisabeachclub.com
T 971 743 334

Cap Rocat
Das Besondere: Dinieren in einer ehemaligen Militärfestung, im Gourmet-Restaurant „La Fortaleza" des Hotels Cap Rocat, am Cabo Enderrocat, keine 4 km südwestlich der Marina.
A very Special place! Dining in a former military stronghold at gourmet restaurant "La Fortaleza" in Cap Rocat hotel, at Cabo Enderrocat some 4 km to the southwest of the marina.
Ctra. d'Enderrocat, s/n, 07609 Cala Blava, T 971 747 878
www.caprocat.com

AUSFLÜGE / *EXCURSIONS*

Palma de Mallorca ist von Arenal nicht aus der Welt. Wenn nicht mit dem Taxi (Station an der Zufahrtsstraße zum Yachtclub), dann gut mit dem Bus zu erreichen, Linie 15, 23 und 25 ab S'Arenal bis zur Plaça Espanya. Vorsicht vor Taschendiebstählen, vor allen in voll besetzten Bussen.
Wer einen schönen Blick über die Insel zu schätzen weiß, könnte auch den Klosterberg von Randa bei Llucmajor ins Visier nehmen.

It is not far to Palma de Malllorca from Arenal. One can take a taxi from the access road to the yacht club. Also good bus connection by no. 15, 23 and 25 from S'Arenal to Plaça Espanya in Palma. Watch out for pickpockets, especially in crowded busses.
To enjoy a beautiful island view try visiting the Cura monastery mountain of Randa near Llucmajor.

Möglich z. B. per Taxi / *e.g. by taxi*
www.taxillucmajor.com
T 971 442 256

www.emtpalma.es

Cala Blava – Illots de Can Climent

Illots de Can Climent

ANKERPLÄTZE
ANCHORAGE AREAS

Ⓐ Cala Blava
39° 29,1' N 002° 43,9' E

🇩🇪 Ein ausgedehntes, kostenpflichtiges Bojenfeld vor einer kleinen Ortschaft, die vor allem zur Ferienzeit erblüht. Das Bojenfeld wird auslegt zwischen dem 1.6.-30.9. Keine Tarife für kurzzeitiges Festmachen. Reservierung notwendig. An Land das Restaurant „Panoramica Playa" mit großer Terrasse zum Meer, T 971 740 211.

🇬🇧 *Extensive buoy field beneath a quiet residential area which comes to life during summer holidays. Subject to charges. The buoy field is laid out between June 1st and September 30th. No short-term mooring fees. Ashore the restaurant „Panoramica Playa" with large terrace overlooking the sea, T 971 740 211*

Reservierung / *Reservation*
www.balearslifeposidonia.eu

€ (2015)
Max. 8 m: EUR 13,34
Max. 14 m: EUR 29,10
Max. 16 m: EUR 48,50

Ⓑ Cala Veya
Illots de Can Climent
39° 26,4' N 002° 44,6' E

Ein ausgedehnter und landschaftlich außergewöhnlicher Ankerplatz unterhalb der 100 m hohen Steilküste, der sich über zirka 1 sm erstreckt und nur bei ruhigen Bedingungen genutzt werden kann. Wassertiefen 15-5 m, man findet ausreichend sandigen Grund. Es kommen auch ein paar wenige Besucher von Land, die hier ein vergleichsweise einsames Plätzchen suchen. Sie finden es auf vielen Felsflächen, die noch von Abbau des Sandsteins stammen, der unter anderem für die Kathedrale in Palma benutzt worden sein soll. Besucher nutzen eine Straße, die vom bebauten Hochplateau zum Mhares Sea Club hinunterführt.

An extensive and exceptional scenic anchorage underneath the high cliff which extends over about 1nmi and should be used only in calm conditions. Water depths 15–5m, one finds sufficient sandy spots. There are also a few visitors looking for an isolated place for swimming, snorkeling and sun bathing. They find it on many flat slabs of limestone, where centuries ago pieces were cut out, probably also used for the Cathedral in Palma. Visitors use a road that leads down from the plateau to Mhares Sea Club.

T 971 213 691, M 616 705 102
reservas@mharesseaclub.com
www.mharesseaclub.com

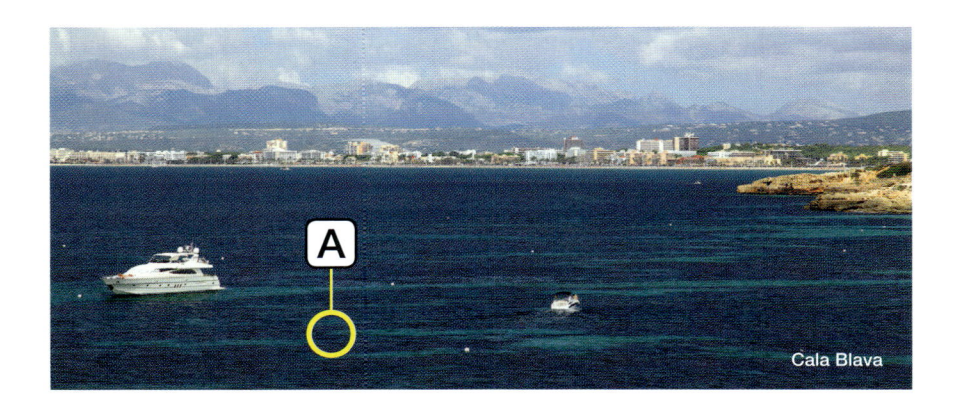

Cala Blava

Mallorca

Sail West!

Mallorcas Westen wird markiert von der langen Isla Dragonera, ein Ausläufer der Gebirgskette Tramuntana. Diese Berge begleiten einen Törn bis zum Naturhafen Port de Sóller. Wichtige Marinas sind Richtung Palma zu finden.

Mallorca western part is marked by the long Isla Dragonera, an offshoot of the Tramuntana mountain range. These mountains accompany a trip to the natural harbour of Port de Sóller. Important marinas can be found towards Palma.

Der Westen Mallorcas / The West of Mallorca

Wie ein überdimensionaler Wellenbrecher liegt die Isla Dragonera vor der Ortschaft Sant Elm. Sie markiert Mallorcas Westspitze.

Like a giant breakwater Isla Dragonera provides shelter to the village of Sant Elm. The long streched islands marks Mallorca's western tip.

- 35 sm Kontrastprogramm
- Lebhafte Orte und stille Natur
- Dazu ein gewaltiges Küstengebirge

- *35nmi of great variety*
- *Busy villages – peaceful nature*
- *In addition huge coastal mountains*

Mallorca

Port Adriano – Port de Sóller

🇩🇪 Mallorcas Westzipfel gehört den hohen Bergen der Tramuntana. Sie bekränzen auch den fast perfekten Naturhafen Port de Sóller. Wichtige Marinas sind Richtung Palma zu finden.

🇬🇧 *The Tramuntana mountain range covers Mallorca's western part and surrounds the almost perfect natural harbour Port de Sóller. Important marinas can be found in the direction of Palma.*

1 **Port Adriano** - 39° 29,4' N 002° 28,5' E → page 60
Megayacht-Marina mit Shops & Restaurants; von Star-Designer Philippe Starck.
Mega-yacht marina with shops & restaurants; by star designer Philippe Starck

2 **Santa Ponsa** - 39° 30,9' N 002° 27,9' E → page 66
Marina mit wenig Gastplätzen; davor eine sehr stark frequentierte Ankerbucht.
Marina offers few visitors berths; but there's a much frequented anchorage

3 **Cala Fornells / Ens. Sta. Ponsa** - 39° 31,8' N 002° 26,4' E → page 69
Guter Schutz bei westlichen Winden. Nachts genutzt von Ausflugsboote.
Well protected with westerly winds. Cruise boats use this place at nighttime.

4 **Camp de Mar / Cala Blanca** - 39° 32,1' N 002° 25,2' E → page 70
Weiträumiger Ankerplatz. In Camp de Mar volle Versorgung eines Ortes.
Wide anchorage space: close to Camp de Mar, village offers everything.

5 **Cala Llamp** - 39° 32,9' N 002° 23,2' E → page 71
Ankerplatz mit Sandgrund vor Beachclub Gran Follies. Stark bebaute Küste.
Anchorage with sandy sea floor in front of beach club. Built-up cliff coast.

6 **Port d'Andratx** - 39° 32,5' N 002° 22,6' E → page 72
Einer der landschaftlich schönsten Häfen. Ideal für eine Überfahrt nach Ibiza.
One of the most beautiful ports on Mallorca. Perfect for a passage to Ibiza.

7 **Sant Elm** - 39° 34,5' N 002° 21,0' E → page 76
Mallorcas westlichste Ortschaft. Viele Restaurants; Bojenfeld und Ankerplatz.
Mallorca's westernmost village. Many restaurants; buoy field and anchorage.

8 **Isla Dragonera** - 39° 35,0' N 002° 19,2' E → page 76
Naturgeschützt und bekannt für ihre Eidechsen; zum Besuchen ankern.
A nature reserve and famous for its lizards; anchorage and small harbour.

9 **Cala Banyalbufar** - 39° 35,0' N 002° 19,2' E → page 81
Einzigartig: Banyalbufar inmitten einer terrassierten Berglandschaft
Unique: Banyalbufar in the middle of terraced mountain scenery

10 **Cala & Port Valldemossa** - 39° 43,2' N 002° 35,2' E → page 81
Mini-Hafen für kleine Boote. Anker vor Berglandschaft, Restaurant im Ort.
Only small boats can find shelter here. Scenic view. Restaurant availabe.

11 **Na Foradada** - 39° 45,3' N 002° 37,2' E → page 82
Eine Felsnase im Meer. Beim Ankerplatz ein Tages-Restaurant.
A beak of rock juts into the sea. A restaurant lies above the anchorage.

12 **Cala Deia** - 39° 45,8' N 002° 38,45' E → page 82
Bucht mit Restauration unterhalb des bekannten Künstler-Dorfs.
Bay with restaurants ashore. Deia is well known as a village of artists.

13 **Port de Sóller** - 39° 48,0' N 002° 41,2' E → page 84
Der einzige Hafen auf 50 sm Bergküste; tolle Kulisse; Marinas und Ankerfeld.
The only port along the 50nmi coastline; great scenery & anchorage.

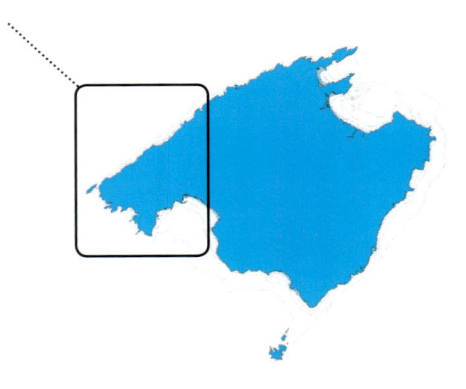

Der Westen Mallorcas / The West of Mallorca

- 13 Port de Sóller
- 12 Cala Deia
- 11 Na Foradada
- 10 Port de Valldemossa
- 9 Cala Banyalbufar
- 8 Isla Dragonera
- 7 Sant Elm
- 6 Port Andratx
- 5 Cala Llamp
- 4 Camp de Mar
- 3 Cala Fornells
- 2 Santa Ponsa
- 1 Port Adriano

Sóller
Valldemossa
MALLORCA
Andratx
Calvià
Palma

Portbook & Island Guide   59

Mallorca

- Mallorcas Superyacht-Marina
- Beste nautische Infrastruktur
- Viele Shops, Bars & Restaurants

- *Mallorca's Super Yacht Marina*
- *Perfect range of nautical services*
- *Great for wining, dining & shopping*

Port Adriano

Eine Marina in diesen Dimensionen ist auf Mallorca einmalig, die Atmosphäre auf der neuen Mittelmole mit ihren luxuriösen Läden, Bars und Restaurants ebenfalls. Der französische Star-Designer Philippe Starck hat mit seinem Entwurf einen bemerkenswerten Fußabdruck hinterlassen.

Zwischen Frühjahr und Herbst lebt die Marina so richtig auf, dann werden Events veranstaltet, kommen auch viele Besucher von Land und füllen die Restaurants und Bars. Innerhalb der gewaltigen Aussenmole liegen die größten Motoryachten in beachtlichen Dimensionen. Das „alte" Hafenbecken innerhalb der Mittelmole ist weiterhin die Heimat für Yachten mit relativ normalen Abmessungen.

A marina on this scale is unique in Mallorca, as is the atmosphere on the new middle pier teeming with luxury shops and restaurants. French star designer Philippe Starck left behind a remarkable masterpiece.

Between spring and autumn, the marina becomes very busy, special events are held and many visitors come to crowd the restaurants and bars. Impressive super yachts dock at the outer breakwater and even on the opposite side. The inner part of the marina is the part for hundreds of mid-size yachts.

ANSTEUERUNG
APPROACHING

Vor dem Hafen keinerlei Untiefen. Bei stärkerem auflandigem Wind ist aber ausreichend Abstand zur steilen Molenmauer wichtig, da Wellen zurückgeworfen und dabei unberechenbar werden. Befeuerte, rote Fahrwassertonnen markieren die Nordseite der Einfahrt. Wassertiefe im Außenhafen und in der Zufahrt 7 m, im alten Hafenbecken 4-2 m.

No shallow areas in front of the harbour. But in case of strong inshore wind be careful to keep a good distance from the steep breakwater which causes unpredictable waves. Four lighted red buoys mark the north side of the marina's entrance.

The marine management indicates a depth of 7m at the outer harbour and entrance, and 4-2m for the inner basin.

FESTMACHEN
FIND A BERTH

A Im neuen Hafenteil Liegeplätze für Yachten bis zu 80 m Länge und 15 m Breite. Modernste technische Ausstattung. Garantierte Wassertiefe 6,5 m. Wartekai vor Kopf der Außenmole, bis max. 100 m Länge.

The outer part of the harbour houses berths for yachts up to 80m length and 15m width. State-of-the-art technical facilities. 6.5m water depth guaran-

Port Adriano

Fl5s
Islote El Toro

Fl(2)G 5s

6,5

7,0   39° 29,4' N   002° 28,5' E   9,0

teed. Waiting pier in front of breakwater head, up to 100m length.

B Liegeplätze für Yachten von 6–16 m an Muringleinen. Wartekai einlaufend an Backbord.
Berths for yachts sized 6-16m, for use with mooring lines. Waiting pier portside when entering.
€ 13x4,15 m
70,50 (June-Sept), 51,30 (April+May), 22,60 (Oct.-March)
Wasser, Strom, Hafensteuern und 21% MwSt. nicht eingeschlossen.
Water, electricity, harbour tax and 21% VAT not included.
T 971 232 494, M 678 788 072 (24 h)

UKW/VHF 09, info@portadriano.com
www.portadriano.com
Office: June-Sept: Mon-Fr: 09–21 h; Sat+Sun: 09–14 h + 17–21 h
April-May + Oct.: Mon-Fr: 09–20 h; Sat+Sun: 09–14 h + 16–20 h, Nov-March: Mon-Sun: 09–14 h & 17–20 h
Hinweis: Crews, die über Mittag einlaufen wollen, um in einem der Restaurants zum Essen zu gehen, können sich

Fl5s

Islote El Toro

Portbook & Island Guide

Mallorca

nach einem kostenlosen Liegeplatz für diesen Zeitraum erkundigen.
Note: Crews who want to arrive at noon to visit one of the restaurants for dinner, can inquire about a free berth for this period.

WiFi Schnell, frei & kostenlos / *High transfer rate, free of charge & codefree*

ANKERPLÄTZE
ANCHORAGE AREAS

C Zwischen der roten Tonnenreihe und der abgeteilten Badezone vor dem Strand auf 4-5 m.
Between the row of red buoys and separate bathing area, in front of the beach near the entrance, 4-5m depth.

D Beim Inselchen Islote El Toro 2nmi südlich der Marina.
At islet Islote El Toro some 2nm south of the marina.

TANKEN / *FUEL*

D+B, June-Sept: 09-20 h
April-May + Oct.: 09-19 h
Nov-March: 09-18 h

TECHNISCHER SERVICE
TECHNICAL SERVICES

E Yates Adriano
Varadero Port Adriano
Die ansässige Schiffswert; immer gut gebucht. 250-t-Travellift
Nautical repairs in general; nautical transports, wintering.
T 971 237 006
www.yatesadriano.net

Marlin Marine Services
Reparaturen am Rumpf, an Antrieben, Hydraulik-Systemen etc.

Port Adriano

A marina designed by Philippe Starck

Hull repairs, hydraulic systems and antifouling application.
T 971 232 896
www.marlinmarinemallorca.com

PSB Marine Service Baleares
Yachtbetreuung und technische Wartung. / *Maintenance, repair and complete renovation services for boats.*
M 619 18 95 59
www.psb-marine.com

YACHTAUSRÜSTER
CHANNDLERIES

E Mercanautic Acastillaje
Breites Angebot an Ausrüstung und Ersatzteilen für Yachten. / *Sale of nautical products and accessories.*
www.mercanauticonline.com

NAUTIK-FIRMEN
NAUTICAL COMPANIES

Nautor's Swan Mallorca International
Vertretung einer der renommiertesten Segelyacht-Marken weltweit durch Swan Germany-Austria and Swan Benelux. Modernes Büro auf der oberen Etage der Mittelmole.
Representative of one of the most prestigious sailing yacht brands through Swan Germany-Austria and Swan Benelux. Modern style office on the middle pier overlooking the berths for big boats.

T 971 232 578
info@nautorswan-mallorca.com
www.nautorswan-mallorca.com

FYS Baleares
Die balearische Vertretung des renommierten Flensburger Yacht-Service vertritt hier die Marken Delta Powerboats, Italia Yachts und Frauscher. Gemeinsam mit Nautor's Swan in einem Büro auf der oberen Etage.
The balearic representation of the well known german Flensburger Yacht-Service. Sales and Service for Delta Powerboats, Italia Yachts and Frauscher. In the same office with Nautor's Swan on the top floor of the new harbour. T 971 232 578
info@fys-baleares.com
www.fys-baleares.com

Sunseeker Mallorca
Einer der wichtigen Motorboot-Hersteller hat hier eine Niederlassung.
Local branch of one of the main motor boat manufacturers.
T 971 676, info@sunseeker-mallorca.es
www.sunseeker-mallorca.es

Fahrschule Kaden /
Adriano Yacht Charter
Namhafte Yacht-Fahrschule. Theorie, praktische Ausbildung und Yacht-Charter. / *Well-known yachting school focused on theoretical & practical training and yacht charter.* T 971 237 093
www.fahrschule-kaden.com

Frauscher
Design-Motorboote aus Österreich.
Design motor boats from Austria.
M 648 423 036
spain@frauscherboats.com
www.frauscherboats.com

FYS BALEARES
Your competent partner for nautic brands in Port Adriano:
FYS Baleares SL · Tel: +34 971 232 578 · www.fys-baleares.com

Frauscher · ITALIA YACHTS venezia · delta POWERBOATS · NAUTOR'S SWAN MALLORCA INTERNATIONAL

Portbook & Island Guide

Mallorca

Yacht Moments
Verkauf und Service, Yachtmanagement und Charter für Motoryacht-Hersteller wie Baglietto und Leopard Yachts. / *Sales and services, yacht management and charters for big boat brands such as Baglietto and Leopard Yachts.* T 971 679 406
www.yachtmoments.com

BWA Yachting
Führende Service-Agentur für Planung und Betreuung von Seereisen mit Superyachten. / *Leader in concierge and marine agency services to the super yacht industry.*
T 686 146 138
www.bwayachting.com

Burgess
Spezialisiert auf Verkauf, Vermietung und Management von Großyachten. *Specialises in yachts larger than 40 meters – sale, rental and management.*
www.burgessyachts.com

Lamprell Marine
Vermietung von Motoryachten
Motor yachts for hire
T 971 232 025
www.lamprellmarine.com

Marina Balear, T 971 232 204
Yachtcharter & Brokerage
www.marina-balear.com

Ponent Yates
Yachtverkauf und -service für verschiedene Motorboot-Marken. / *Sales and maintenance for different power boat brands.* T 971 234 486
www.ponent-yates.es

Princess Motor Yacht and Sales
T 971 234 140, www.princess.eu.com

Mar Balear Dive Center
Tauchspezialist mit Laden und Schulungsräumen. / *Diving specialist with shop and training rooms.*
T 971 699 799, www.marbalear.com

RESTAURANTS & BARS

Coast By East & Sansibar Wine
Auf der Spitze der Mittelmole. Das Hamburg Hotel East und Sansibar von Sylt sind hier eine Partnerschaft eingegangen. Seit 2014 mit eigenem Pool. *At the end of the middle pier. Hamburg's top hotel East teams up with the well know Sansibar brand, born on the island Sylt. Since 2014 with an own pool.* T 971 576 757
www.coast-mallorca.es

Bruno & Bar El Tandem
Auf Meeresfrüchte spezialisiert, umfangreiche Weinkarte. / *Specialises in seafood, extensive wine list.*
T 971 232 498
www.restaurantebruno.com

Crew Bar
Treffpunkt für die Besatzungen der Schiffe. / *Meeting point of ship crews.*
www.crewbar.es, M 630 436 527

Port Adriano

250t travel lift

Harbour Grill
Leichte Grillküche im mittleren Preissegment. / *Light barbecue food, mid-level prices.* T 971 232 492
www.harbour-grill-mallorca.com

La Terraza
Beim landseitigen Zugang zur Marina gelegen, bietet das Restaurant von der Terrasse einen sehr schönen Blick auf das innere Hafenbecken und die moderne Mittelmole. / *Restaurant is situated near marina's land entrance and offers a beautiful view from the terrace.*
T 971 232 728
www.laterrazadeportadriano.com

Trattoria Vino del Mar
Speisekarte mit italienischem Einschlag. Man liefert auch an Bord. *Menu with predominantly Italian flavour. Catering service for boats.*
T 971 237 360
www.vinodelmar.com

La Cantina del Puerto
Die Adresse für zivile Preise, mit schöner Sonnenterrasse. / *Set in a privileged location within the port, good value for money, daily specials.*
T 971 232 411
www.sacantinacafe.es

Pizzería La Oca
Treffpunkt zum Frühstück und für ein unaufgeregtes Mittagessen. / *A good choice for informal lunch and breakfast.*
T 971 232 816
www.facebook.com/laoca.portadriano

El Faro Restaurant
Nautisches Ambiente. Spezialisiert auf Fisch und Meeresfrüchte.
Sailing décor, seasonal fish and fresh seafood are the main ingredients.
T 971 232 676
www.elfaro-deltoro.com

Gleich oberhalb der Marina
above marina:

Aroma Restaurant
Mehr als eine beliebte Speisegaststätte. Es gibt regelmäßig Musikabende. *More than a popular restaurant. During evenings scheduled concerts.*
T 971 232 842
info@aromaeltoro.com
www.aromaeltoro.com

EINKAUFEN / *SHOPPING*

Größere Supermärkte in Santa Ponsa und Palmanova, jeweils gut 5 km entfernt. / *Larger supermarkets to be found in Santa Ponsa and Palmanova, about 5 km distance.*

In der Marina/Inside the Marina:
Mehrere edle Shops für Mode, Uhren Sonnenbrillen etc / *other shops for fashion, watches etc*

Corte Inglés Yacht-Provisioning
M 630 045 218
portadriano@elcorteingles.es
www.elcorteingles.com

Nauti-Parts
Wassersport-Ausrüstung. Vermietung von Jet skis, deren Reparatur und Ersatzteile. / *Equipment for practicing watersports. Rental, repair service and sale of spare parts for jetski.*
T 610 708 167, www.nauti-parts.com

Ahoy! Port Gallery
Galerie von Renate & Michael Pentzien, u. a. mit Bildern von Udo Lindenberg und Gunter Sachs. / *First art gallery in Port Adriano. Contemporary art shown. Exhibitions change regularly.*
www.ahoygallery.com

Banco Popular Es Credit
Bankautomat / ATM, T 971 699 239
www.grupobancopopular.es

EVENTS

Die Marinaleitung organsiert ganzjährig eigene Veranstaltungen, von der eigenen Bootsausstellung im Mai (Best of Yachting, www.bestofyachtingportadriano.com) über Konzerte bis zur Silver Bollard Regatta Ende August mit dem Yachtclub Santa Ponsa. Details jeweils unter: www.portadriano.com, Menüpunkt „Events"

The marina management organises events the whole year round. An annual boat show in May called "Best of Yachting" (www.bestofyachtingportadriano.com), a competition for classic boats, the Silver Bollard Regatta end of August in cooperation with Yacht Club Santa Ponsa. More details about the annual events on the Port Adriano premises are published on: www.portadriano.com -> „Events"

Golf
Drei Golfplätze unter einem Dach und ganz in der Nähe / *Three golf courses under the same roof and nearby*
www.golf-santaponsa.com

Sixt Autovermietung / *car rental*
(neben / *next to* Sunseeker)
Mon–Fri, 09–17.30 h
Sat, Sun + hol., 09–13 h
T 902 491 616

Portbook & Island Guide

Mallorca

Santa Ponsa

- Wenig Platz für Gastyachten
- Großes Ankerfeld vor Marina
- Untiefen inmitten der Bucht

- Few berths for guests
- Large anchoring site in front
- Marked shoals in bay centre

🇩🇪 Dem Ankerplatz vor der kleinen und gepflegten Marina kommt einige Bedeutung zu, denn Gastplätze sind rar. 30 Yachten auf Reede sind an einem normalen Sommerabend keine Seltenheit.

Der Ort Santa Ponsa ist in weniger als einer Viertelstunde fußläufig erreicht. Er ist touristisch geprägt mit einem ordentlichen, aber in großen Teilen durchschnittlichen Angebot an Restaurants.

🇬🇧 *The anchorage area in front of the small, neat marina is rather important since there are few guest berths; up to 30 yachts may be anchoring there on any summer evening. The town centre of Santo Ponsa can be reached within 15 min walk. Great variety of restaurants and bars on many levels.*

ANSTEUERUNG
APPROACHING

Der Seeraum vor Santa Ponsa ist tief. Aus südlicher Richtung lässt sich die Isla Malgrats auf allen Seiten passieren. **Achtung:** Östlich der Isla Conills gibt es eine Flachstelle mit weniger als 2 m. Auf dem Ankerplatz fallen die Kardinalzeichen inmitten der Bucht auf. Sie markieren eine Untiefe zwischen ihnen, oft zu erkennen an einer Welle, die sich darüber bricht.

Die Westtonne ist befeuert. Kennung: Fkl (9) 10s. Die Osttonne ist unbefeuert.

From the south, Isla Malgrats can be passed on all sides. **But caution,** *there is one exemption: east of Isla Conills is a shallow spot with less than 2m.*
The striking cardinal buoys in the anchoring area clearly mark the shallow in-between; this can be seen every now and then as a wave rolls over. The west buoy is lighted. Character: VQ(9)W 10s. The east buoy is unlit.

FESTMACHEN
FIND A BERTH

A Club Náutico Santa Ponça
Anmeldung erwünscht. Einlaufende Yachten machen einlaufend an der Backbordseite fest und lassen sich einen Liegeplatz zuweisen.

39° 30,9' N   002° 27,9' E

Isla Conills

Reservations recommended. Entering yachts dock on portside, and then wait to be assigned a berth.

T 971 694 950   UKW/VHF 09
cnsp@cnsp.es, www.cnsp.es

🕐 15/06-15/09: Mon-Fri 9-19 h, Sat 9-14 h, Sun closed

16/09-14/06: Mon-Fri 9-18 h, Sat 9-14 h, Sun closed

€ 12,50 m
97,36 EUR (01/05-31/10)
47,70 EUR (01/11-30/04)
Inkl. Wasser / Strom und 21% MwSt.
incl. water & elec. + 21% IVA

Santa Ponsa

ANKERPLÄTZE
ANCHORAGE AREAS

B Die beliebtesten Plätze finden sich gleich östlich der Hafeneinfahrt. Man ankert auf ca. 9-5 m Wassertiefe und gut haltendem Sandgrund, mit Seegras durchmischt. Anlegen mit dem Dingi an der Südseite der Bucht.
The most popular places lie to the east of the harbour entrance. Anchoring at ca. 5-9m depth, anchor-friendly sandy bottom mixed with weed. There are dinghy landings on the south side of the bay.

TANKEN / *FUEL*

Diesel, Super Plus, Gasoline 95
Verkauf von Öl, Eis, Trinkwasser, Bier
Station sells oil, ice, drinking water, beer
Ohne ausdrückliche Erlaubnis ist es verboten, über Nacht an der Tankstellenpier festzumachen. / *Overnight mooring is forbidden at the fuel quay without express permission of the captain of the port.*

🕒 1/06-15/09: Mon 9.30-14.30 h, Tue-Sun 9.30-20 h
16/09-31/05: Mon closed, Tue-Sat 9.30-15 h, Sun+hol. 10-14 h

TECHNISCHER SERVICE
TECHNICAL SERVICES

1 Servicios Nauticos Integrados
Betreibt die Bootswerft der Marina / *Operates the marina's boat yard*
T 971 694415, S.N.I@telefonica.net

Cor Marine
T 971 694 704 + M 619 518 001
info@cormarine.es

Balearic Marine Engineering
T 971 696 613
info@balearicmarineengineering.es

PSB Marine Service
T 971 676 465, M 619 189 559
luis@psb-marine.com
www.psb-marine.com

2 Zahlreiche nautische Servicebetriebe im Industriegebiet (Poligono) Son Bugadelles, zirka 4 km entfernt von der Marina

Many nautical services in industrial zone (Poligono) Son Bugadelles at some 4km distance from the marina.

Hier begann die Rückeroberung Mallorcas 1229.
The place Jaume I. started the reconquest of Mallorca.

RESTAURANTS & BARS

Innerhalb / *Inside of marina*

1 Restaurante Classico,
Italian Food. T 971 693 641
classicoristopizza@yahoo.es
www.restauranteclassico.com
🕐 12.30-15.30 + 19-23 h; Tue closed

Siete Fuegos
Argentinische Küche / *Argentine cuisine*. T 971 694 380 + 971 695 405
🕐 13-16 + 19-23 h; Wed closed

Eolo Bar
Live-Musik, Grill, Pizza etc. …
Live music, barbecue, pizza etc.
T 971 695 405, info@eolobar.com
www.eolobar.com

3 Sehr große und qualitativ sehr unterschiedliche Auswahl an Restaurants und Bars; einige mit Blick auf die Bucht in der Nähe des Strandes.
Very broad variety of bars and restaurants; quality also varies. Some offer a view to the bay near the beach.

EINKAUFEN / SHOPPING

In der Marina Bankautomat und Geschäft für Bootszubehör. Kleinere Supermärkte auf dem Weg von der Marina zum Ort, größere im Ort.
ATMs and ship stores inside marina. Some small supermarkets situated en route from the marina to town, bigger ones in town.

AUSFLÜGE / EXCURSIONS

4 Kurzer Fußweg zur Hafeneinfahrt. Dort steht ein Kreuz, das zum Gedenken an die Landung Jaumes des Eroberers (1229) errichtet wurde und an die Befreiung Mallorcas von den Mauren erinnern soll. In der Bucht von Santa Ponsa ging das spanische Heer damals an Land.
Immer in der Woche vor dem 9. September wird die Rückeroberung Mallorcas, die in der Bucht von Santa Ponsa vor fast 800 Jahren ihren Anfang nahm, mit einer Festwoche begangen. Details unter: www.calvia.com

There is a short footpath to the harbour entrance, where a cross stands in commemoration of the landing on Mallorca of James I the conqueror, and its liberation from Moorish rule (1229).
Every year in the week leading up to Sept. 9th the re-conquest of Mallorca, which began almost 800 years ago in Santa Ponsa bay, is celebrated for a week. For details see: www.calvia.com

Abendessen am Ankerplatz / Dining near the anchorage

Cala Fornells

ANKERPLÄTZE
ANCHORAGE AREAS

A Cala Fornells / Ensenada de Santa Ponsa
39° 31,8' N   002° 26,4' E

Die fast 2 sm breite Bucht Ensenada de Santa Ponsa bietet bei ruhigen Bedingungen verschiedene Ankerplätze, zumeist vor abgeteilten Badezonen. In ihrem nördlichen Teil finden wir die beliebte Cala Fornells. Eingerahmt von Felsen, Hotels, Wohnanlagen und Einzelhäusern findet man hier Schutz auch bei westlichen Winden, den die Cala de Santa Ponsa vor der Marina des Ortes nicht bieten kann.
Auch in der Cala Fornells sind gelbe Bojen ausgelegt und markieren die Schwimmbereiche von Land. Davor liegt die Wassertiefe zum Ankern bei 7 m und mehr. Der Ankergrund besteht überwiegend aus Seegras mit einzelnen Sandflecken. Nachts bekommt man Gesellschaft durch Ausflugsboote, die hier bis zum nächsten Tag an Bojen vertäut werden. An Land Restaurants und kleine Supermärkte. Größere Supermärkte in der Ortschaft Peguera, gut 1 km nördlich.

Ensenada de Santa Ponsa, which is almost 2nmi wide, offers different anchorages for calm conditions, mostly in front of seperated bathing areas. In its northern part we find the popular Cala Fornells. Surrounded by rocks, hotels, apartment blocks and houses this bay provides shelter even with westerly winds that Cala de Santa Ponsa (in front of the marina) cannot offer.

Also in Cala Fornels yellow buoys mark a swimming area. Where anchoring is possible, the water depths start from 7m. The sea floor consists mainly of weed with only few sandy spots. At night you get company by excursion boats which are moored here until the next day. Ashore one will find restaurants and a small supermarket. Larger supermarkets are around 1mi away to the north in Peguera.

Playa de Paguera

Mallorca

Cabo Andritxol

Camp de Mar & Cabo Andritxol (rechts / right)

Camp de Mar – Cala Llamp

B Camp de Mar / Cala Blanca
39° 32,1' N 002° 25,2' E

🇩🇪 Am nördlichen Ende einer fast 1 sm tiefen Einbuchtung findet man zwischen der Cala Blanca im Nordwesten und der touristischen Ortschaft Camp de Mar verschiedene Möglichkeiten zum Ankern. Die Wassertiefen liegen zwischen 5 und 10 m, überwiegend sandigen Grund gibt es an den meisten Stellen. Cala Blanca und Camp de Mar werden tagsüber von Ausflugsbooten angefahren. In Camp de Mar findet man verschiedene Restaurants (auch auf der kleinen Insel) und Bars, kleine Supermärkte, Apotheke etc. Schutz gegen südliche Winde gibt es hier auf keinem Ankerplatz.

🇬🇧 *In the northern part of a bay that is nearly 1nmi deep there are different anchorage areas between Cala*

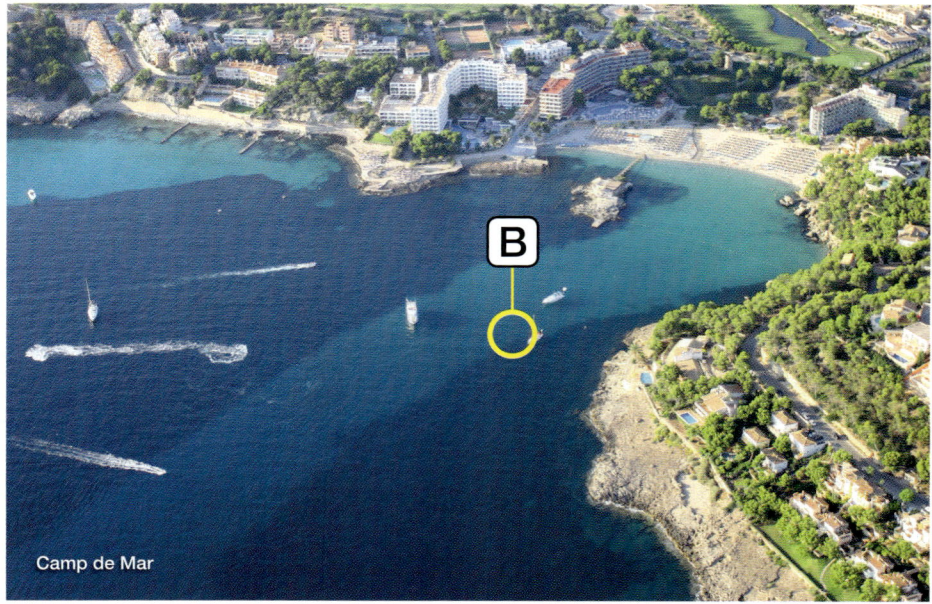

Camp de Mar

Cala Llamp & Cabo Llamp (rechts / right)

70 Portbook & Island Guide

Camp de Mar – Cala Llamp

Blanca in the northwestern tip and the tourist resort of Camp de Mar opposite. Water depths are between 5-10m, predominantly sandy bottom can be found. Cala Blanca and Camp de Mar are visited during daytime by excursion boats. In Camp de Mar one can find numerous restaurants (also on the small island, that is linked to the mainland by a small bridge) and bars, a small supermarket, pharmacy and so on. Not to be found is shelter against southerly winds.

C Cala Llamp
39° 31,9' N 002° 23,2' E

Hier liegt man eingerahmt von stark bebauten Kliffs. Ankerplatz mit Sandgrund vor dem Beachclub Gran Follies, wo man gleich daneben mit dem Dinghy anlanden kann. An Land keine Versorgungsmöglichkeiten. Aber: Der Beachclub bietet auch Service an Bord an.

Covered cliff coast to both sides. Anchorage with mostly sandy seafloor in front of beach club Gran Follies. One can land by dinghy. Ashore no supplies available, but the beach club will also service yacht crews …

T 971 671 094
www.beachclubgranfolies.com
www.granfolies.net

Cala Llamp, oben im Bild Port d'Andratx
Cala Llamp, at the head Port d'Andratx

Mallorca

Port d'Andratx

- Beliebter, touristischer Hafen
- Marina, Bojenfeld und Stadtpier
- Kürzeste Distanz nach Ibiza

- Popular yacht harbour
- Marina, buoy field, local pier
- Shortest distance to Ibiza

🇩🇪 Eingerahmt von Hügeln und Bergen ist Port d'Andratx einer der landschaftlich schönsten Anlegemöglichkeiten rund Mallorca. Allein die intensive Bebauung rund um die Hafenbucht schmälert den Gesamteindruck ein wenig. Sehr großes Angebot an Bars & Restaurants, nicht nur direkt am Wasser. Schöne Urlaubsatmosphäre.

🇬🇧 *Surrounded by hills and mountains, the Port d'Andratx landscape remains one of the most beautiful places to berth in Mallorca, which is only disturbed by intensive building around the harbour bay. Wide range of restaurants and bars, along the waterfront and behind. Relaxing holiday atmosphere.*

ANSTEUERUNG
APPROACHING

Die Südseite der Zufahrt markiert das erkennbar stark bebaute Cabo de la Mola. An dessen Spitze steht ein Leuchtfeuer, Fl(1+3)W 12s, das aus 128 m Höhe bis zu 12 sm weit zu sehen ist. Seine Bebauung unterscheidet Cabo de la Mola vom nahen und ähnlich mächtigen Cabo Llamp.
Untiefen sind nicht zu beachten, aber ein- und auslaufende Fischer. Befeuerte Fahrwassertonnen leiten in den inneren Teil der Hafenbucht. Außerhalb der Tonnenreihen liegen Festmachebojen aus. Das Ankern im Fahrwasser ist nicht erlaubt auch nicht im inneren Teil der Bucht.
Intensively built-over Cabo de Mola marks the southern part of the bay entrance. On its summit we see a lighthouse Fl (1+3) W 12s, 128m high, whose signal is visible for some 12nmi around. Its many buildings clearly distinguish Cabo de la Mola from nearby and similarly impressive Cabo Llamp.
No shallow areas to look out for, but fishing boats keep entering and leaving the bay. Lighted bouys lead to the interior part of the harbour bay. On both sides of this channel several mooring bouys. Anchoring is not permitted inside the channel and also not in the inner part of the bay.

FESTMACHEN
FIND A BERTH

A **Im Club de Vela**
Für den Hochsommer empfiehlt das Marina-Büro eine Anmeldung. Die meisten Liegeplätze für Yachten auf der Durchreise befinden sich nahe des Travellifts an einem Schwimmsteg, der nur zur Saison ausgelegt wird. Zur Saison 2016 hat der Club de Vela sieben neue Liegeplätze für Yachten von 26-30 m Länge fertiggestellt.
Marina office recommends making reservations in midsummer season. Most berths for boats in transit are located on a floating pontoon laid out during summer, close to the travel lift. For season 2016 Club de Vela has completed seven new berths for yachts of 26-30m in length.
T 971 671 721 + 971 672 337

📱 UKW/VHF 09
info@cvpa.es, www.cvpa.es
🕘 Office
9-22 h (June-Aug); 9-20 h (Sept-May)
🚿 01/05-14/10: 8-12 + 17-22 h
15/10-30/04: 9-12 + 17-20 h
Schwimmbad / *Pool*
01/05-14/10: 9-19 h
€ 12-14 m:
100,62 EUR (01/06-30/09); 61,59 (01/10-31/05) inkl. Wasser, Strom, Dusche, Pool-Benutzung und 21% MwSt. Es gibt eine Absauganlage für Rückhaltetanks.
Incl. water, electricity, showers, pool and 21% VAT. There is an evacuation system for holding tanks.

B Festmachebojen zwischen der Außenmole und der Marina-Mole des Club de Vela und auf der gegenüberliegenden Seite der Zufahrt. Wassertiefen 6-3 m; Zuständigkeit Club de Vela. Dingi-Shuttle-Service für den Skipper (nicht die Crew), Benutzung der Sanitäranlagen, Wi-Fi, und Müllentsorgung (am Abend) im Preis enthalten.
Mooring buoys between the outer breakwater and the breakwater of the marina and on the opposite side of the entrance channel. Club de Vela is charging the fees. Depth 6-3m. Dinghy shuttle service (for the captain, not the whole crew), use of sanitary facilities, Wi-Fi and refuse collection (in the evening) included in fee.

€ 12-14 m: May-Oct: 42,37 EUR; Nov.-April: 22,43 EUR inkl. 21% MwSt., + Wasser; Duschen extra (8,14 EUR

Port d'Andratx

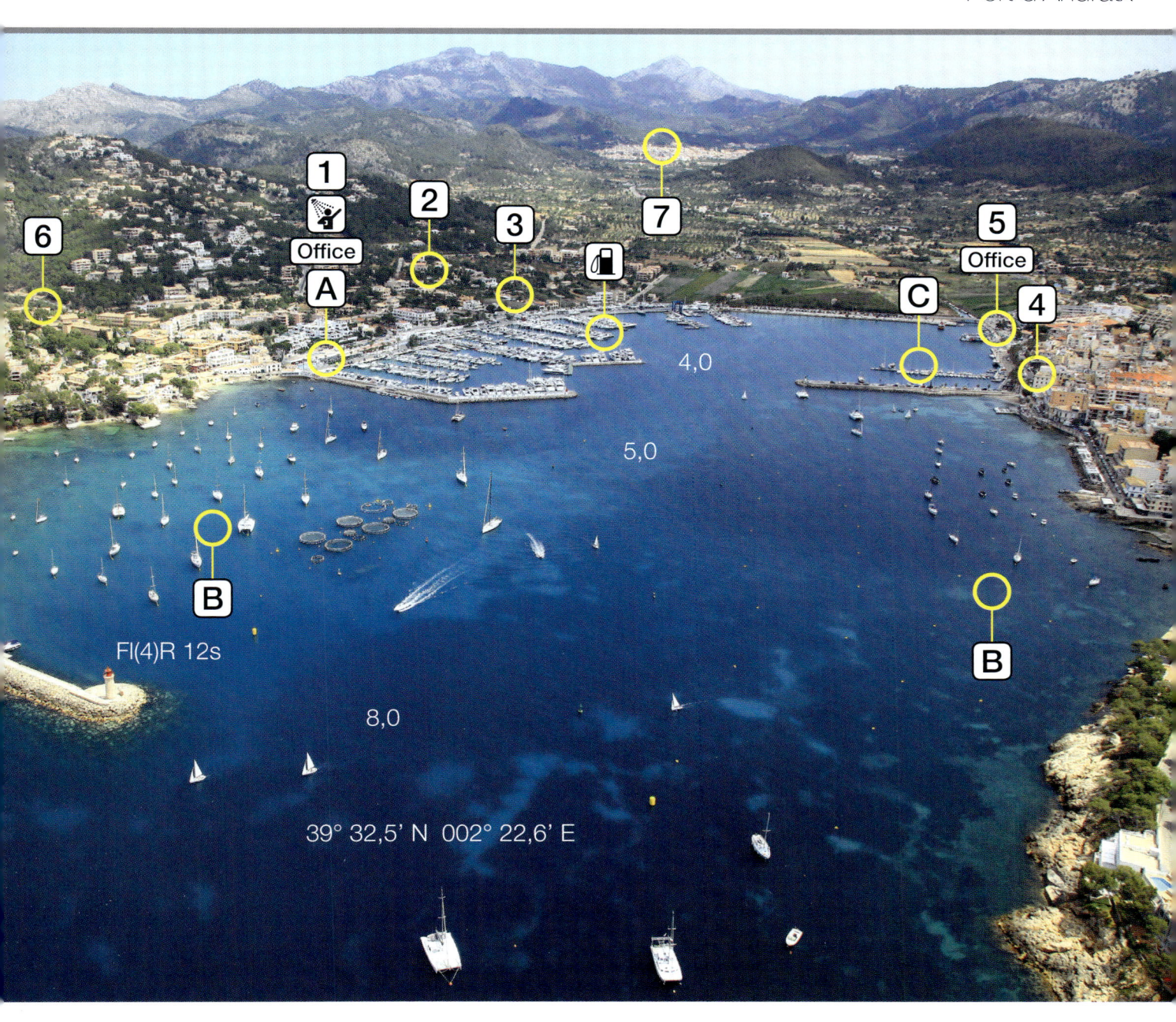

Fl(4)R 12s

8,0

39° 32,5' N   002° 22,6' E

5,0

4,0

pauschal für alle Crewmitglieder) / *incl. 21% VAT + water; showers extra (8,14 EUR flat-rate for all crew members)*

C Liegeplätze von Ports Islas Baleares

Auf der Innenseite der Südmole: Anlegen mit dem eigenen Anker, wo die Pier als Moll Transit gekennzeichnet ist. Wasser und Strom vorhanden. Die Plätze hier können nicht reserviert werden – first come, first serve.

Achtung: Unterwasservorsprung beachten. Mit dem Heck größeren Abstand zur Pier wahren.

Am folgenden Schwimmsteg Muringleinen. Wassertiefen 6-3 m. Strom und Wasser. 6 Plätze können hier reserviert werden. Reservierung notwendig: mindestens drei Tag im Voraus über www.portsib.es. Bezahlung per Kreditkarte. Stornierung oder Umbuchung über die Webseite www.portsib.es.

Berths managed by Ports Islas Baleares

On the inside of the southerly breakwater: Docking by using the own anchor. Water and electricity at the pier. These berths cannot be reserved – first come, first serve.

Caution: *There is an underwater ledge. Keep major distance to avoid damages to the rudder.*

Mooring lines on the subsequent floating pontoon: water depth ca. 6-3m. Water and electricity. Reservation required (for max. 6 berths) at least 3 days in advance at www.portsib.es Payment by credit card. For cancellation or modifications please use the web site.

T 971 674 216, 📱 UKW/VHF 08
port.andratx@portsib.es
🕐 01/06-30/09 08-21 h;
01/10-31/05 08-18 h
€ EUR/m2: 0,60 (01/06-30/09); 0,20 (01/10-31/05) - Water: 5,50 EUR; Electricity: 5,50 EUR - Alle Preise / *All prices* plus 21% MwSt. / *VAT*

Mallorca

Einfache Sanitäreinrichtungen beim Hafenbüro, 200 m entfernt.
Simple sanitary facilities at the harbour office some 200m away.
🕐 08-20.30 h

ANKERPLÄTZE
ANCHORAGE AREAS

Tagesankerplatz in der kleinen **Cala Egos** 1 sm nw-lich des Hafens. Pure Natur. Es gibt einen Kiesstrand, ein Weg führt zur Bucht. Wassertiefen 10-5 m, der Grund ist überwiegend sandig.
Anchor during the daytime at small Cala Egos 1nmi northwest of the harbour. Pure, unadulterated nature. There is a pebble beach, a path leads to the bay. Water depths 10-5 m, the sea floor consists mostly of sand.

TANKEN / *FUEL*

Im Club de Vela
D+B, Tiefe/ depth: 3m
🕐 Jan-Dec: Mon-Sat 08-20 h; Sun closed

TECHNISCHER SERVICE
TECHNICAL SERVICES

Travellift (100 t, max. 25 x 5,80 m) und Kran (3 t) in der Marina / *Travel lift (100 t, max. 25x5.80m) and crane (3t) within marina.*
🕐 Mon-Fri: 09-13 + 15-18 h, Sa: 09-14 h

Atlas Marine, Yacht Service
T 971 672 677. M 686 204 590
www.atlasmallorca.com
Braun Yachtservice
T 971 137 667, M 609 444 707
www.braun-yachtservice.com
Tot Nautic
T 971 235460, M 625 662 980
www.tot-nautic.com

YACHTAUSRÜSTER
CHANDLERIES

Ferreteria Seguina
C. Rodriguez Acosta, 31
T 971 672 490
Auch Tausch von Gasflaschen
Gas container exchange here
Náutica Casa Vera
Geschäft für Sportfischen, Tauchen und Boote. Wenige Meter entfernt vom Büro von PortsIB. / *Shop for sport fishing, diving and boats. Only a few meters away from the office of PortsIB.*
Av. Mateo Bosch, 10, T 971 671 619, www.nauticacasavera.com

RESTAURANTS & BARS

[1] Restaurant Club de Vela
8-24 h, T 971 674 164
Cantina, 8-20 h; Frühstück ab / *Breakfast from* 8.30 h
Restaurant Barlovento
Unmittelbar neben dem Clubgelände
Immediately next to the club grounds
T 971 671 049

[2] Restaurante Vent de Tramuntana
Gehobene mallorquinische Küche, Gartenlokal, Hauptgerichte um 20 EUR, Reservierung notwendig. Vom Club de Vela beim Trockenplatz in die C, de Can Perot gehen. / *Exalted Mallorcan cuisine, garden restaurant. Main courses around 20 EUR. Reservation recommended. From Club de Vela towards the centre turn left into C. de Can Perot.*
T 971 671 756

[3] Ristorante Media Luna
Italienische Küche; vom Club de Vela Richtung Ort linker Hand nach 250 m / *Italienische Küche; vom Club de Vela Richtung Ort linker Hand nach 250 m*, T 971 672 716
www.media-luna.biz

[4] Im Ort und an der Wasserfront wird der Besucher mit einer kaum überschaubaren Zahl von Bars und Restaurants konfrontiert. Deshalb hier die u. a. die Tipps eines Seglers und Residenten nach mehr als 20 Jahren in Port d'Andratx.
The town's waterfront welcomes visitors with an overwhelming number of bars and restaurants. So here's the personal selection of a yachtsman and resident who's been around the area for more than 20 years.

Cala Egos

Port d'Andratx

Erste Reihe: / *On the waterfront:*
Can Pep, mallorquinisches Restaurant/ *Mallorcan restaurant*, T 971 671 648
Bar Central, gutes und preiswertes Frühstück / *good value for money breakfast*, T 971 673 692
Forn la Consigna
am kleinen Marktplatz, feiner, hausgemachter Kuchen / *at market square, tasty, homemade cakes*
T 971 671 604, www.laconsigna.es
Ristorante Don Giovanni, italienische Küche/ *Italian*, T 971 673 359
Layn Fisch in Salzkruste/ *Try their fish in salt crust*, T. 971 671 855; restaurant@layn.net

Zweite Reihe: / *Second row:*
Urbano
Aus El Patio wurde Urbano, jetzt in Hafennähe. Ein gastronomisches Highlight im Südwesten Mallorcas.
El Patio turned into Urbano and moved into the port. A gourmet highlight in this part of Mallorca.
Plaza Patrons Cristino, 4
T 971 671 703
info@restaurante-urbano.com
Daily 13-15 + 18-23 h, Tue closed.
Made in Italy, beste Pizza im Ort/ *best pizzas in town*, T 971 671 474
Osteria da Sandro
preiswerter Italiener / *inexpensive Italian*, T 971 671 038

Tres Paises
T 971 672 814, M 608 419 436
www.trespais-mallorca.com

EINKAUFEN / *SHOPPING*

5 Supermarkt (Eroski) in der Nähe des PortsIB-Hafenbüros und im Ort der gut bestückte Supermarkt APROB
Eroski supermarket near the PortsIB harbour office, and well-stocked APROB supermarket in town
Weitere kleine Läden im Ort. In Hafennähe Banken (Sa Nostra, Credito Balear, Targo) mit Geldautomat und Apotheke / *More small shops in town. Near the harbour: various banks (Sa Nostra, Credito Balear, Targo) with ATMs and a pharmacy.*
Kleiner Supermarkt 100 m entfernt vom Club de Vela Richtung Zentrum.
Minimarket 100m from Club de Vela towards the centre.
Corte Inglés, Lieferservice im Club de Vela / *delivery service in the Club de Vela*, M 650 934 251

AUSFLÜGE / *EXCURSIONS*

6 Fußweg nach Sant Elm
Von der Marina über die C./ Aldea Blanca. Nach 200 m links in die C./ Cala d'Egos, die in eine unvollendetes Baugebiet führt (Holzschild „S. Elm"). Hier immer bergan und auf der ersten Kuppe rechts halten. Der weitere Weg führt vorbei an weithin sichtbaren Funkmasten. Schöne Ausblicke auf das Meer und Dragonera. Man erreicht Sant Elm bei der Cala Conills. Pro Weg 1,5 Std.
Footpath to Sant Elm
Starts at the marina along C./ Aldea Blanca. After 200m turn left into C./ Cala d'Egos which leads into an unfinished construction area (wooden sign "S. Elm"). The route then passes some aerial masts visible from far. Great view over the sea and Dragonera. You'll reach Sant Elm at Cala Conills. Duration 1.5h one way.

7 Besuch der Stadt Andraitx, zum Beispiel zum Markttag am Mittwoch, 8-13 h. / *A visit to the town of Andratx, for example during market on Wednesdays, 8-13h*
Nits a la Fresca
Juli/August: Veranstaltungsreihe (Nächte der Frische); Theater, Konzerte, Feuerwerk *July/August: event series (Fresh Nights); theatre, concerts, fireworks*

Mietwagen / Car rental
Autocares Pujol, T 971 136 219
Taxi - Radio Taxi Andraitx
T 971 235 544 + 971 136 398

Mallorca

Sant Elm & Isla Dragonera

- Ein Idyll für Naturfreunde
- Viele Ausflüge möglich …
- … auch auf Dragonera

- *Nature Lover's Paradise*
- *Many excursion options …*
- *… also on Isla Dragonera*

🇩🇪 Der Naturpark Dragonera markiert den kleinen Urlaubsort Sant Elm, der nur im Sommer auflebt. Hoch aufragend und langgestreckt ist die Insel Dragonera für Sant Elm wie ein überdimensionaler Wellenbrecher, schützt den Ankerplatz und das Bojenfeld beim Inselchen Es Pantaleu, das ebenfalls zum Naturpark gehört.

🇬🇧 *Nature reserve Dragonera marks the small town of Sant Elm, which only comes alive in summer. Towering and elongated, Dragonera Island looks like an oversized breakwater next to Sant Elm, protecting the anchorage site and buoy field near Es Pantaleu islet which is also part of the nature reserve.*

ANSTEUERUNG
APPROACHING

Südlich der Ortschaft Sant Elm, vor dem Bojenfeld und Ankerplatz, sind keine Untiefen zu beachten. Überspülte Untiefen und Felsen liegen in der Passage Freu de Dragonera auf der Seite der Insel Dragonera, sind bei normaler Sicht aber gut zu erkennen.
Zwischen dem Inselchen Pantaleu und dem Ort Sant Elm sollte man mit mehr als 1,50 m Tiefgang nicht passieren und auch nur auf der Mallorca-Seite. Richtung Isla de Pantaleu liegen zahlreiche kleine Fischerboote an Bojen.

South of the village of Sant Elm, in front of the buoy field and anchorage, no shallows must be observed. Few rocks, partly washed, can be found in the passage Freu de Dragonera on the side of island Dragonera, but are clearly visible under normal conditions.
Between the islet Pantaleu and the village Sant Elm boats with more than 1.50m draft should not pass and if, closer to the Mallorca coast. Direction Isla de Pantaleu numerous small fishing boats are moored on buoys.

BOJENFELD & ANKERN
BOUY FIELD & ANCHORAGE

Man kann vor Sant Elm frei ankern oder kostenpflichtig eine Muringboje aufnehmen. Einen Hafen gibt es nicht.

One can drop anchor in front of Sant Elm or reserve and pay for a mooring bouy. A port does not exist.

A Bojenfeld
Bouy field

Das Bojenfeld wird auslegt zwischen dem 1.6.-30.9. Seit 2013 ist es kostenpflichtig. Für Yachten bis 14 m Länge wurden zuletzt 29,10 EUR kassiert, für Yachten bis 16 m Länge sogar 48,50 EUR. Es gibt keine Tarife für kurzzeitiges Festmachen. Reservierung notwendig über www.balearslifeposidonia.eu. Ankern neben dem Bojenfeld auf Sandgrund ist erlaubt. **Achtung:** Berichten zufolge wurden 2015 hohe Geldstrafen verhängt, wenn innerhalb des ausgelegten Bojenfeldes geankert wurde.

The buoy field remains in place between June 1st and September 30th. Rates vary. Recent charges for yachts up to 14m in length 29.10 EUR, and for yachts up to 16m even 48.50 EUR. No short-term mooring fees. Reservations required, on: www.balearslifeposidonia.eu. Anchorage permitted next to buoy field above sandy bottom. **Caution:** *According to reports, in 2015 heavy fines were imposed when yachts dropped anchor within the buoy field.*

B Ankern
Anchorage

Außerhalb des Bojenfelds ankern auf zirka 3 bis 8 m gut haltendem Sandgrund mit einigen Seegrasflecken.

Outside of the buoy field anchorage at 3-8m depth, good sand bottom with patches of seaweed.

C Anlanden mit dem Dingi
Dinghy landing options

- im Nordteil der Bucht, an einer Pier für Ausflugschiffe und Fischerboote / *In the north of the bay, at the pier for excursion and fishing boats*
- am südöstlichen Strandende – die Bojenreihe lässt einen Weg zum Strand frei / *On the southeastern beach end – the row of buoys leaves a passage to the beach*
- beim Restaurant Cala Conillls / *at the restaurant Cala Conills*

Sant Elm & Isla Dragonera

|D| Weitere Ankerplätze eine halbe Seemeile nördlich vor Punta Blanca. An dieser Stelle ist auch die Tauchschule Scuba Activa beheimatet, Inh. Mathias Günther (Betrieb 01/04-31/10). Bei Ankerproblemen haben Taucher der Schule schon mehrfach geholfen.

Another anchorage area can be found 0.5nmi north at Punta Blanca. The diving school Scuba Activa (Operating 01/04-31/10) is also situated here. In case of problems one may ask here for assistance.

T 971 239 102, M 653 917 284
www.scuba-activa.com

RESTAURANTS & BARS

|1| **Na Caragola**
Sonnenuntergangs-Restaurant mit Terrasse Richtung Isla Dragonera.
Sunset restaurant with a terrace facing Isla Dragonera. T 971 239 006

|2| Entlang der verkehrsberuhigten Hauptstraße viele Restaurants und Bars.

Many bars and restaurants along the main street, several pedestrian-only areas.

|3| Hotels und Restaurants an der Straße, die vom Strand Richtung Cala Conills führt. Eine Empfehlung ist hier das Xaloc, gegenüber vom Hotel Aquamarin.

Hotels and restaurants on the street leading from the beach to Cala Conills. "Xaloc" is recommended, situated opposite of Hotel Aquamarin.

Portbook & Island Guide

Mallorca

Sant Elm & Dragonera — *Isla Es Pantaleu* — *Isla Mitjana* — VQ(9) 10s

[4] Restaurant Cala Conills
Im Südostteil der Bucht, gelegen auf einer felsigen Landzunge. Sonnenuntergang mit Blick auf die Insel Dragonera. Pool und Sonnenliegen für Gäste. Reservierung empfehlenswert. Gehobenes Preisniveau. Im Sommer 2015 wurde dem Restaurant nach einem Nachbarschaftsstreit die Lizenz entzogen. Zu einer möglichen Wiedereröffnung war bei Drucklegung nichts bekannt. Aktuelles unter: www.portbook-mallorca.com

In the southeast part of the bay, situated on a rocky headland. Perfect during sunset, overlooking the island of Dragonera, with pool and deck chairs for guests. Reservation recommended. Elevated prices. In summer 2015 the restaurant lost the licence after a neighbourhood dispute. For a possible reopening nothing was known when going to press. Updates at: www.portbook-mallorca.com

www.calaconills.com

calaconills@calaconills.com
T 971 239 186
12-23 h, Mon closed
Closed: 01/11-30/04

EINKAUFEN / *SHOPPING*

[1] Entlang der teilweise verkehrsberuhigten Hauptstraße kleine Supermärkte, Bank, Apotheke, Bäcker usw. / *Along the main street there are small supermarkets, bank, pharmacy, bakeries etc.*

AUSFLÜGE / *EXCURSIONS*

Wanderungen ab Sant Elm
Hikes from Sant Elm

Zum / *to* Torre Cala Basset
Vom nördlichen Ortsende entlang der Küste oder weiter landeinwärts parallel in Richtung Norden. Zirka 45 Minuten, ein Weg. Vom Wachturm aus schöner Blick auf Dragoneras Nordwestspitze.

Starting from the northern part of Sant Elm, walk along the coastline or further inland towards north. One way ca. 45 min. Beautiful view from the watchtower to the northwest point of Dragonera.

Nach Sa Trapa und zum Mirador Joseph Sastre / *To Sa Trapa and Mirador Joseph Sastre*
Von der Placa Monseñor Sebastian Grau im Norden von Sant Elm weg von der Küste und in den Wald hinein. Nach ca. 20 Minuten ist ein Gehöft erreicht. Zum ehemaligen Kloster Sa Trapa muss man gut 300 m aufsteigen, von dort beeindruckender Blick auf Dragonera. Der lässt sich noch steigern, wenn man ca. 1 Stunde weiter geht entlang der Küstenlinie nach Nordwesten zum Mirador Joseph Sastre, 447 m.

All walks start at Placa Monseñor Sebastian Grau in the north of Sant Elm, away from the coast into the woods. After 20 min. you reach a farmstead. To reach former monastery Sa Trapa

Sant Elm & Isla Dragonera

Fl(2) 12s

Mirador Joseph Sastre

you need to ascend a couple of hundred metres, and can enjoy the impressive view of Dragonera. For even more beauty proceed along the coastline for another hour towards the northwest, finally reaching Mirador Joseph Sastre at 447 m.

Anlanden auf Isla Dragonera
Landing on Isla Dragonera

Ankern ist an verschiedenen Stellen möglich: / *Anchoring is possible at various places:*

In kleinen, offenen Buchten an der Südostseite Dragoneras, darunter die Cala Cocó. Anlanden mit dem Beiboot. / *Try the small open bays on the southeast side of Dragonera nature reserve, such as Cala Cocó; landing with a dinghy.*

E Vor dem kleinen Hafen der Cala Lladó, dann mit dem Beiboot hinein fahren.
Try in front of small Cala Lladó harbour, and then enter with a dinghy.

! Abstand halten und ein- und auslaufende Ausflugsboote nicht behindern. Auch ist eine Untiefe zu beachten (ca. 2 m Wasser!). Zusätzlich gibt es auf dem Grund einen Edelstahlbügel, in den sich Anker verfangen können. Ankergrund felsig und verkrautet, wenige Sandflecken.

Take care to keep your distance without obstructing entering and leaving excursion boats. There is also a shallow area (ca. 2m depth!) to keep an eye on, and a piece of stainless steel lurks at the bay bottom where an anchor might be caught. The bottom consists of weed and rocks, only few sandy patches.

Cala Lladó

Portbook & Island Guide   79

Mallorca — Sant Elm & Isla Dragonera

F **Anlanden mit dem Beiboot**
Landing with a dinghy

Auch diese Buchten auf der Südostseite von Dragonera dürfen zum Ankern und Anlanden aufgesucht werden:
These bays on the southeast side of Dragonera may also be visited for anchoring and landing:
Cala Llebeig, Cala Cucó, Cala Bubú

Wanderungen auf Dragonera
Hikes on Dragonera

Am Hafen eine kleine Ausstellung zum Naturpark Dragonera. Hier zahlreiche Eidechsen, die auch gefüttert werden. Eine Wanderung zur höchsten Stelle dauert ungefähr 1,5 Stunden (ein Weg). Von den Ruinen des alten Leuchtfeuers Sa Popi aus 376 m Höhe blickt man in das tiefblaue Meer und auf lotrechten Fels. Die aktiven Leuchttürme an beiden Enden Dragoneras lassen sich weniger schweißtreibend erreichen. Den Zeitangaben auf den Schildern darf man Glauben schenken.

There is a small exhibition on Dragonera nature reserve in the harbour. Many lizards live here which like being fed. Walking up to the highest point takes some 1.5 hours (one way). From the ruins of the old lighthouse Sa Popi at 376m, look down upon steep cliffs and deep blue water. The active lighthouses at both ends of Dragonera can be reached with less effort. Time information on the signs is quite reliable.
Cala Lladó-Far de Tramuntana: 1h,
Cala Lladó-Far de Llebeig: 2 h 40 min
jeweils Hin- und Rückweg / *round trip*

Alles über Dragonera und die zum Naturpark gehörenden Inselchen unter:
Find more information on Dragonera and the islets of the nature reserve here:
www.conselldemallorca.net/dragonera/

Cabo Llebeig, die Südwestspitze von Dragonera. Oben Sa Popi.
Cabo Llebeig, southwestern tip pf Dragonera. On top: Sa Popi

Cala Banyalbufar – Cala Deia

ANKERPLÄTZE
ANCHORAGE AREAS

A Cala Banyalbufar
39° 41,6' N 002° 30,9' E

🇩🇪 Nirgendwo an der bergigen Nordwestküste kann man seeseitig so schön eine terrassierte Landschaft bewundern wie bei der Ortschaft Banyalbufar. Sie wurde in der Zeit der maurischen Herrschaft angelegt, die 1291 endete.
Fischer haben Ihre Boote hinter einer kleinen Mole, daneben kann man mit dem Beiboot anlanden. Ankern vor der Bucht auf ca. 10 m Wassertiefe.

🇬🇧 *Banyalbufar is the perfect place at Mallorcas Tramuntana coast to admire a gorgeous terraced landscape from the seaside. It was created during the period of Moorish rule, which ended 1229.*
Local fishermen have their boats behind a small rounded breakwater, next to this one can land with a dinghy. Anchor off the bay to approximately 10m water depth.

B Cala & Port Valldemossa
39° 43,2' N 002° 35,2' E

Ankern vor Berglandschaft bei Wassertiefen zwischen 10-5 m (aber ohne Blick auf Valldemossa …). Überwiegend felsiger und krautiger Grund. Mini-Hafen hinter kurzer Mole zum Anlanden mit dem Dingi. Bootsslip, viele Trailerboote werden hier im Sommer zu Wasser gelassen. Gaststätte am Hafen.
Anchorage in front of the Tramuntana mountain range with water depths between 10-5 m (but the town of Valldemossa is not visible). Sea floor mostly rocky with weed. Small port behind a short breakwater where landing by dinghy is possible. Boat slip, many trailer boats are launched here in summer. Restaurant available.

Restaurante Es Port
T 971 616 194
www.restaurantesport.es

Cala Banyalbufar: viele Felsen im inneren Teil der Bucht.
Many rocks in the inner part of the bay.

Port Valldemossa

Mallorca

Na Foradada

C Na Foradada
39° 45,3' N 002° 37,2' E
Ankerplatz auf der Südseite einer riesigen Felsnase mit Loch, keine 5 sm sw-lich von Port de Sóller. Wassertiefen über 10 m. Unterhalb eines Restaurants Anlanden mit dem Beiboot. Empfehlenswert: Aufstieg zum 250 m hoch gelegenen Anwesen Son Marroig, in dem der österreichische Erzherzog Ludwig Salvator Ende des 19. Jahrhunderts viele Jahre verbrachte. Dauer ca. 1 h. Schöner Altan über dem Meer und Pavillon im Garten. Eintritt: 3 EUR
Das Restaurant „Sa Foradada" ist bekannt für seine Paella-Gerichte, die Atmosphäre auf der einfachen Holzterrasse über dem Meer einzigartig. Reservierung empfohlen.

Anchorage area is located on the south side of a huge crag with a hole, less than 5nm south west of Port de Sóller. Depths exceed 10m. Dinghy landing below a small restaurant. Recommended: Ascent to the residence Son Marroig at altitude 250m, where Austrian Archduke Ludwig Salvator spent many years at the end of the 19th century. Duration ca. 1 h. There is a beautiful balcony above the sea and a pavilion in the garden. Entrance fee 3 EUR
Restaurant „Sa Foradada" is famous for its Paella dishes; dine on a simple wooden terrace above the sea for the unique atmosphere. Reservations recommended. March-Oct.: 12-18 h, Thu closed. M 616 087 499
www.saforadada.com

D Cala Deia
39° 45,9' N 002° 38,5' E
Port de Sóller ist jetzt nur noch 3 sm entfernt. Mit einem halben Dutzend Yachten ist die Bucht belegt. Wassertiefen unter 10 m, Ankergrund auch Sand. Sommerrestaurants am Ufer. Vom Ankerplatz Blick in die Berge, aber nicht auf den malerischen Ort.
The bay next to Sóller is fully booked by half a dozen yachts. Water depths less than 10m, the sea floor consists also of sand. Restaurants ashore open during summer. The anchorage overlooks the mountains but not the picturesque village.
Ca's Patró March
12.30-20 h (July + Aug:12.30-22.15 h), Nov-April: closed. T 971 639 137

Cala Banyalbufar – Cala Deia

Na Foradada

Cala Deia

Mallorca

Port de Sóller

- Wichtiger Schutzhafen
- Im Herz der Tramuntana
- Besondere Atmosphäre

- *Important safe harbour*
- *Enjoy the special ambience*
- *Tramuntana mountain range*

🇩🇪 Der einzige Hafen inmitten der gebirgigen Nordwestküste Mallorcas. Diese perfekte Naturbucht verspricht gegen fast alle Windrichtungen Schutz.
Auch bei Landtouristen ist Port de Sóller sehr beliebt. An den kleinen Stränden liegt das sicher nicht, sondern an der gewaltigen Berglandschaft und den Ausflugsschiffen, die von hier zur Bucht Sa Calobra fahren, wo die Schlucht Torrent de Pareis spektakulär zum Meer durchbricht. Nicht zu vergessen, die historische Straßenbahn zwischen Sóller und seinem Hafen.

🇬🇧 *The only harbour in the middle of the mountainous northwest coast of Mallorca. This perfect natural bay provides shelter against almost all wind and wave directions. Port de Sóller is also very popular with land tourists, less for its beaches but because of the impressive Tramuntana*

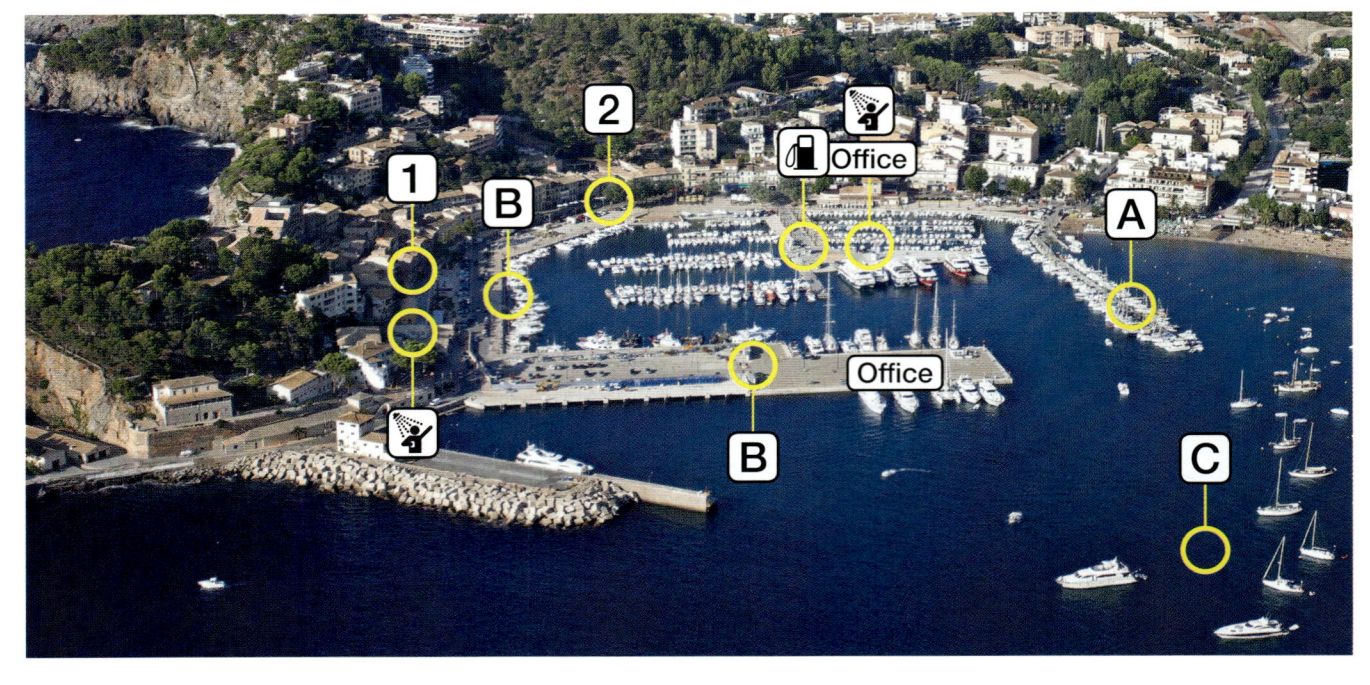

84 Portbook & Island Guide

Port de Sóller

39° 48,0' N 002° 41,2' E

Fl W 2.5s

mountains in the backdrop and the many excursion boats leaving for the bay of Sa Calobra, where the spectacular Torrent de Pareis gorge cuts into the sea. And of course there's the historical tram from Sóller to its port, a popular attraction.

ANSTEUERUNG
APPROACHING

Bei starkem auflandigem Wind reflektiert die Steilküste die anlaufenden Wellen. Die Folge: ein konfuser und unberechenbarer Seegang. Die Einfahrt zur Bucht ist tief und bis an ihre Ränder frei von Untiefen. Mehrere starke Leuchttürme und ein Richtfeuer (Peilung 126°).

Note: With strong onshore winds the steep coastline repels the waves, causing irritating and unpredictable swell. No shallow areas in the bays entrance up to its very border. There are various bright lighthouses and leading lights (bearing 126°)

FESTMACHEN
FIND A BERTH

A Am Schwimmsteg im Sommer
Floating pier during summer
Vom Mai bis Oktober wird ein Schwimmsteg verankert, an dem Yachten mit Bug oder Heck an Muringleinen festmachen. 25 Liegeplätze bis 15 m stehen zur Verfügung. Reservierung notwendig, mindestens drei Tage im Voraus über www.portsib.es. Bezahlung per Kreditkarte. Stornierung oder Umbuchung über die Webseite.

A floating pontoon is mounted from May through October. Yachts berth bow or stern to, using available mooring lines. 25 berths up to 15m are available. Reservation recommended at least 3 days in advance at www.portsib.es. Payment by credit card. For cancelation or changes please use the web site.

Hafenbüro portsIB
(beim Yachtclub / *at yacht club*,
www.clubnauticsóller.es)
T 971 186 129, UKW/VHF 09
port.soller@portsib.es

€ EUR/m2: 0,60 (01/06-30/09); 0,18 (01/10-31/05), Water: 5,50 EUR; Electr.: 5,50 EUR, Alle Preise / All prices plus 21% MwSt. /VAT

🕐 May-Sept: Mon-Sun 08-21 h
Oct.-April: Mon-Fri 08-18 h,
Sat 08-15 h, Sun closed

Mallorca

Einfache Sanitäreinrichtungen neben dem Gebäude des Hafenbüros. / *Simple Sanitary facilities next to the harbour office.*

🕐 Neben dem Büro zu den Öffnungszeiten. An der Westmole durchgängig, auch während der Nacht.
Beside the office during opening hours. At the western pier throughout the day, even during the night.

B Marina Tramontana

Eine Marina auch für große Yachten. Die Preisliste reicht bis 40 m Länge, aber auch 60 m und mehr sind möglich. Entlang der Westpier des Hafens sind die Liegeplätze für Yachten von 12-20 m, alle anderen machen an der großen Außenmole fest, die auf ihrer Innenseite auch von Fischern genutzt wird. Duschen und Toiletten gegen Kaution. Von 19 bis 01 Uhr öffnet auf der Außenmole die Chill-out- und Musik-Bar „La Base". Jeden Samstagabend werden die Marinagäste hier zu einem leichten Dinner eingeladen.

Neben dem Hafenbüro gibt es das Marina Tramontana Diving Center.

Marina Tramontana offers more than 60 berths for yachts from 12-20 m at the western pier and up to 60 m at the outer mole. Water and electricity up to 125 Amp-hour. Changing rooms with showers (key upon deposit payment). On the outer mole the chill-out and music bar „La Base" opens from 19-01 h. Every Saturday night the Marina guests are invited here for a light dinner.

Next to the harbour office there is the Marina Tramontana Diving Center.

WiFi

T 971 631 188, T 671 037 671 (24 h)
M 667 637 161 (Harbourmaster)
VHF/UKW 09
info@marinatramontana-portdesoller.com
www.marinatramontana-portdesoller.es
www.marinatramontanadivingcenter.com

🕐 Office
June–Sept.: Mon-Sun 09.30-21.30 h
Oct.-May: Mon-Fri 09-15 h

Port de Sóller

€ 14m (inkl. 21% MwSt./incl. 21% IVA) Aug: 102, July 86, June+Sept. 75, Oct. 58, Nov. 47 EUR
Plus: 10 EUR water; 10 EUR Elec.; >16m: 16 EUR water, 36 EUR Elec.
Alle Preise auf der Webseite
All prices: see website

ANKERPLÄTZE
ANCHORAGE AREAS

C Im Sommer ankern auf ca. 8-4 m gut haltendem Schlickgrund vor markierten Badezonen. Wenig Schutz gegen Seegang. / *In the summer, anchorage is at 8-4m depth on muddy but stable bottom in front of the designated bathing zone. Almost no protection against swell.*

TANKEN / *FUEL*

July-Sept.: Mon-Sun 09-13 + 16-19 h
Oct-June: Mon-Fri 09-13 + 16-19 h,
Sat 09-13 h, Sun: Closed

TECHNISCHER SERVICE
TECHNICAL SERVICES

Marina Sóller, Serveis Nautics
20-t-Kran für Boote bis 15 m Länge, Reparaturen / *20t davit for vessels up to 15m length, repairs*, M 609 141 836
marinasóller@gmail.com
www.marinasóller.es

Diesel Doc
Palma, T 971 253 576
info@diesel-doc.com
www.diesel-doc.com

YACHTAUSRÜSTER
CHANDLERIES

Bootsausrüster an der Ostseite der Bucht in der Calle de l'Esglesia. *Ship chandlers are on the east side of the bay in C/ de l'Eglesia.*

RESTAURANTS & BARS

Das Treiben in Puerto de Sóller wird von Tagesausflüglern bestimmt. Deshalb gibt es eine Fülle von Bars und Restaurants. Hier eine kleine subjektive Auswahl. / *Puerto de Sóller is much frequented by day trippers, hence the wide range of bars and restaurants. Here's a small personal choice.*

1 Só Caprichos
Serviert angeblich die besten Fleischgerichte. Vom Grill und auf dem heißen Stein (nur auf der Terrasse). *Best meat in town is reported. From the grill and hot stone (only on the terrace).*
T 971 630 095
socaprichos@socaprichos.com
www.socaprichos.com

Cantina Marinera
Spezialisiert auf Fisch und Meeresfrüchte. / *Specialised in seafood*
T 971 635 193

Lua Restaurant, T 971 634 745
Am Treppenaufgang / *On the stairs*
www.restaurantelua.es

2 El Pirata
In der Nähe des Bootskrans. Küche mit Anspruch zu zivilen Preisen. *Cuisine with good standard & reasonable prices.* T 971 631 497
elpiratasóller@hotmail.com

Restaurante Balear
Traditionelle Küche. Spezialisiert auf Paella und Fisch. Aber auch Rind darf nicht fehlen ... / *Traditional cuisine. Specialised in paella and fish. But beef*

Die historische Straßenbahn nach Sóller
A historic tram links the port and Sóller

Mallorca

Lake Cuber & Puig Mayor

Der alte Wachturm nordöstlich der Hafenbucht.
The ancient watchtower northeast of the harbour bay.

should not be missed ...
www.restaurantebalear.es
12.30-22 h

Ca's Mariner, T 971 834 727
Preis-Leistung gut, familiär / *good value for money, friendly atmosphere*

3 Randemar
In einem typisch mallorquinischen Haus. Gartenterrasse mit dem Blick auf die Bucht. Innen Loungebereich. Anspruchsvolle mediterrane Küche, aber auch Pastagerichte, Paellas, Pizzen und vegetarische vegetarische Gerichte. / *Housed in a typical Mallorcan building. Garden terrace with view of the bay. Lounge area inside. High-standard Mediterranean cuisine,* rounded off *by pasta dishes, paella and pizza. Many vegetarian dishes, too.*
12.30-24 h (summer),
T 971 634 578
oficina@randemar.com
www.randemar.com

Nautilus, Bar/Restaurant
(neben / *next to* Jumeira Hotel)
Für den perfekten Sonnenuntergang über dem Meer / *The Sunset Place.*
Daily: Mon-Fri 9.30-23 h,
Sat/Sun 11-24 h. T 971 638 186
C/ Llebeig 1, www.nautilus-soller.com

EINKAUFEN / *SHOPPING*

Kleine Supermärkte in den Seitenstraßen der Uferstraße, vor allem in der C./ Jaume Torrens. Banken und Geldautomaten in Höhe der Mittelmole, an deren Kopf die Ausflugsschiffe nach Sa Calobra ablegen.
Spezialität, – ob zum selber zubereiten oder im Lokal: Die roten Gambas von Sóller.
There are small supermarkets in side streets along the seafront, especially in C/Jaume Torrens. Banks and ATMs are near the middle pier, where the excursion boats dock to Calobra.
Try red shrimps, the local specialty of Sóller, either prepared by yourself or when dining out.

AUSFLÜGE / *EXCURSIONS*

4 Mit der alten Straßenbahn
Zum Zentrum von Sóller, wenn auch teuer. Zuletzt 5,50 EUR pro Person für die kurze Fahrt. Immer samstags ist dort Markt. Von dort könnte es weiter gehen bis ins Herz von Palma, mit dem historischen Orangenexpress, der 2012 sein 100jähriges Jubiläum feiert.
A lovely ancient tram
(5,50€ p/p) connects the Port with Sóller centre only two miles away. There's a market on Saturday there. An option to continue to Palma is by historic train, whose 100th anniversary was celebrated in 2012. Check prices for both at:
www.trendesóller.com

5 Museu de la Mar
Neben der Ermita Santa Catalina. Leider geschlossen. Dennoch besuchen, denn daneben liegt ein schöner Aussichtspunkt über einer lotrecht stürzenden Steilküste.
Next to Ermita Santa Catalina. Unfortunately closed. But nevertheless one should make the short hike because there is a viewpoint on top of the cliffs.
C./ Sta. Caterina d'Alexandria, 50

Fet a Soller
Regionale Produkte sind das Markenzeichen. Fast am Ende der Hafen-Promenade gibt es neben Delikatessen Getränke, Torten und hausgemachte Eiscreme. Ein weiterer Laden liegt neben dem Hotel Esplendido, ebenfalls am Paseo Maritimo.

Port de Sóller

Regional products are the hallmark. Almost at the end of the Paseo Maritimo one will find a shop that offers Feta-Sóller-products, drinks, cakes and homemade ice cream. Another shop is located next to hotel Esplendido, also on the Paseo Maritimo.
Avinguda de Cristòfol Colom, 15

Feste / *Festivals*

Mai, 2. Woche / *May, 2nd week*
Traditionelles Fest, bei dem der Kampf zwischen Mauren und Christen dargestellt wird, die Rückeroberung Mallorcas. Tänze, Ausstellungen, Konzerte.
A traditional celebration takes place with a replay of the battle between Moors and Christians during the conquest of Mallorca. Dances, exhibitions, concerts.

End of June
San Juan (mit Lichtern am Strand) und San Pedro / *Festival of Saint John (with bonfires and lights on the beach) and Saint Peter*

Mitte Juli / *Mid-July*
Señora del Carmen, Bootscorso/Pilgerfahrt durch die Hafenbucht
Celebration of Our Lady of Mount Carmel with a small-boats procession in the bay

Wanderungen / *Hikes*

Küstenwanderung zum Wachturm
und weiter Richtung Nordosten bis zu Toni, eine Bar mit kleiner Speisekarte und Ausblick auf die Küste. Schließt gegen 16 Uhr. Der Weg beginnt an der C. de Belgica, unweit des Hotels Jumeira. Dauer Hinweg ca. 1 Stunde.

Coastal walk to the old watchtower and continue towards the northeast up to Toni, a bar which also offers snacks. Scenic views! Closes around 4 o' clock. The trail starts at the C. de Belgica, not far from the Jumeira hotel. Duration: one way about 1 hour.

Von 0 auf 1000 Meter
Das geht hier in einem Tag, wenn man früh anfängt. Wer es sich etwas leichter machen will, nimmt den Bus (Linie 212) nach Biniaraix, zum Beispiel um 9 Uhr und wäre schon eine Viertelstunde später am Anfang des Aufstiegs (Wanderweg GR 221) durch den Barranc de Biniaraix und schon 100 m höher.
Bis zum Pass Coll d'Ofre sind es nun gut 800 Höhenmeter. Weitere gut 100m mehr und man steht auf dem fast bis zur Spitze grün bewachsenen und kegeligen Ofre, 1090 m über dem Meer. Dauer ab Biniaraix: ca. drei Stunden.
Blick auf den Hafen und zwei weitere Tausender, die sich nordöstlich anschließen, auch auf den höchsten Berg Mallorcas, den Puig Major, und den Cuber-Stausee. Besser geht es nicht.

From 0 to 1000m
Can be done in a day when starting early. For an easy start take bus 212 to Biniaraix e.g. at nine a.m., to arrive at the beginning of the footpath (No. GR 221) after 15min, at an altitude of 100m. From there continue 900m upwards to the Coll d'Ofre. Another 100m up, and you have almost arrived at the top of lush, cone-shaped Ofre, 1090m above sea level. Duration ca. 3 hours from Biniaraix. Grandiose view of the harbour and two 1000m-high connecting mountains to the northeast, followed by Mallorca's highest mountain Puig Major and Cuber water reservoir... simply amazing.

www.tib.org/portal/de/web/ctm/autobus/linia/212

Modernistische Fassade: die Pfarrkirche Sant Bartomeu im Zentrum von Sóller.
Modernistic front: church of Sant Bartomeu in the center of Sóller.

Mallorca

Sunny South

Wenn sich über Mallorca Wolkenberge türmen, ist der Südzipfel oft unbedeckt. Und das ist gut so, denn hier finden sich einige der schönsten Ankerbuchten, mit Sandstrand und Dünen.

Whenever mountains of clouds pile up over Mallorca, the southern tip quite often remains uncovered. And that's all the better, as it boasts some of the most beautiful bays with sandy beaches and dunes.

Sehnsuchtsziel für Viele: Wassersportler und Strandliebhaber teilen sich den Sandkasten von Es Trenc.

Dream destination for many: water sports enthusiasts and beach lovers share the sandpit of Es Trenc.

Der Süden Mallorcas / The South of Mallorca

- Keine Region zum Hetzen
- Kleine Orte und viel Natur
- Zentrale Marina Sa Rápita

- *No place for bustle*
- *Only small villages and nature*
- *Central Marina Sa Rápita*

Cabo Blanco – Cabo Salinas

🇩🇪 Die Steilküste der Bucht von Palma wird jetzt abgelöst von herrlichen Sandstränden. Die Ankerplätze rund um Colònia Sant Jordi zählen zu den schönsten Mallorcas.

🇬🇧 *The steep cliffs of Palma Bay level out and long sandy beaches are to follow. The bays around Cólonia de Sant Jordi are among the most beautiful Mallorca has to offer.*

1 Cabo Blanco - 39° 21,8' N 002° 47,2' E
Aus 95 m Höhe sendet der weiße Leuchtturm seine Blinks.
Towering at 95 m, the lighthouse emits its character, LFl 10s

2 Cala Pí - 39° 21,5' N 002° 50,1' E → page 94
Kleine Ankerbucht, aber sehr beliebt; Restaurants und Supermarkt.
Small inlet, but quite popular; ashore restaurants and supermarket.

3 Punta Plana - 39° 21,5' N 002° 55,3' E
Flaches Kap mit Leuchtturm unweit der Marina S'Estanyol, Fl(1+3)W 12s
Flat headland with small lighthouse, situated close to S'Estanyol.

4 S'Estanyol - 39° 21,5' N 002° 55,3' E → page 96
Clubhafen mit wenig en Gastplätzen und Mini-Ortschaft dahinter.
Club Marina with few visitor's berths and small village in the backdrop.

5 Sa Ràpita - 39° 21,5' N 002° 57,3' E → page 98
Wichtige Marina mit vielen Gastplätzen. Angrenzend langer Sandstrand.
Important marina with numerous visitor's berths. Borders on long beach.

6 Playa de Sa Ràpita - 39° 21,5' N 002° 57,6' E → page 102
Über 0,5 sm schöner, aber offener Ankerplatz. An Land zwei Strandbars.
A fine but open anchorage stretches over 0.5nmi. Ashore two beach bars.

7 Ses Covetes / Es Trenc 39° 20,8' N 002° 58,5' E → page 102
Ankern südlich der kleinen Ortschaft Ses Covetes; über 1sm möglich.
Anchorage close to the small village Ses Covetes; Level sandy bottom.

8 Isla Gabina / Isla Redonda - 39° 20,8' N 002° 58,5' E → page 102
Inselchen beim Südende des Es Trenc; Ankergrund manchmal felsig.
Islets at the southern tip of Es Trenc beach; the bottom can be rocky.

9 Colònia de Sant Jordi - 39° 18,9' N 003° 00,0' E → page 104
Gastplätze für Yachten bis 1,80 m Tiefgang; Ankerplatz vor dem Hafen.
Berths for yacht with max. 1.8m depth; anchorage in front of the port.

10 Playa Es Carbó - 39° 18,2' N 003° 00,2' E → page 108
Nördlich und südlich des Inselchens. Mit Dünen und feinem Sandstrand.
Anchorage north and south of the islet, dunes and fine sandy beach.

11 Cala en Tugores - 39° 17,2' N 003° 01,5' E → page 109
Eine Bucht voll von Algen. Selten verirren sich Yachten hierhin.
A small bay full of weed. Yachts rarely drop anchor here.

12 Cala Es Caragol - 39° 16,6' N 003° 02,3' E → page 109
Rechte offene Ankerbucht. Umgebung pure Natur, keinerlei Versorgung.
Little protection. Surrounded by nature, no supplies or facilities nearby.

13 Cabo Salinas - 39° 15,9' N 003° 03,2' E → page 109
Mallorcas südlichster Punkt, Fl(2+1) 20s. Nationalpark Cabrera 8 sm entfernt.
Southernmost point of Mallorca, Fl(2+1) 20s. At 8nmi distance to Cabrera.

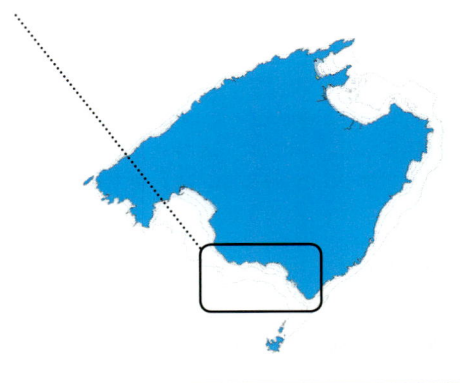

Der Süden Mallorcas / The South of Mallorca

- 1 Cabo Blanco
- 2 Cala Pí
- 3 Punta Plana
- 4 S'Estanyol
- 5 Sa Ràpita
- 6 Playa de Sa Ràpita
- 7 Ses Covetes Es Trenc
- 8 Isla Gabina
- 9 Colònia de Sant Jordi
- 10 Isla Moltana
- 11 Cala en Tugores
- 12 Cala Es Caragol
- 13 Cabo Salinas

MALLORCA

Ses Salines

Mallorca

Cala Pí

- Kleine, aber beliebte Ankerbucht
- Schnell belegt, wenig Schwojraum
- Nahe Siedlung mit Vollversorgung

• Small but popular anchoring bay
• Occupied quickly, little swing space
• Nearby village, full range of supplies

🇩🇪 Gelegen gut 2 sm östlich von Cabo Blanco, dessen Leuchtfeuer das Südostende der Bucht von Palma markiert, schneidet die schmale Cala Pí fjordartig in die Küstenlinie hinein. Man landet mit dem Beiboot an, am besten bei den alten Fischerhäusern vor dem Sandstrand. Ankern mit Heckleine.

🇬🇧 *Located at 2nmi east of Cabo Blanco, whose lighthouse marks the southeastern end of Palma's bay, narrow, fjord-like Cala Pí cuts into the coastline. You can land by dinghy, preferably at the old fishing houses in front of the beach. When the anchor is set, attach a land line.*

HINWEIS ZUM EINLAUFEN
WHEN ENTERING

Ein alter Wachturm markiert die Ostseite des Felseinschnitts. Keine Untiefen. Grund: Sand, wenig Seegras; Tiefe: In der Einfahrt elf, bei den Ankerplätzen zirka 5-3 m. Vor der benachbarten, kleineren Cala Beltran können Fischernetze und -bojen bis in die Ansteuerung hinein ausgelegt sein.

An old watchtower marks the east side of the cala. No shallow spots. Sea floor: sand, little weed. Depth: at the entrance 11m and in anchoring site 5-3m. Watch out for fishing nets and buoys in the entrance to the neighboring Cala Beltran.

RESTAURANTS & BARS

[1] Ein halbes Dutzend Restaurants in einer Ortschaft, die außerhalb der Sommermonate recht ausgestorben sein kann. Da und dort besteht sogar die Möglichkeit, Speisen zum Mitnehmen zu ordern, sollte man an Bord essen wollen, sogar Paella in der Pfanne ist möglich.

Half a dozen restaurants can be found in a small touristic village. Take-away food can be ordered if you prefer to eat on board, even paella in the pan.

Aufzählung vom Treppenaufgang und dann weiter rechter Hand:
Listing begins at stairways exit and continues to the right:

El Mirador de Cala Pí
Cafeteria / Restaurante
T 971 123 010, 8-24 h

Ca'l Reiet Restaurant
T 971 123 170

La Paleta Taverna
griechisch-italienische Speisekarte
Greek-Italian menu
18-22 h, Thu closed

Miguel Bar Restaurante
große Südterrasse, weitere Plätze unter Ranken, gute Qualität, etwas teurer
Large terrace on the south, more seating beneath branches, good quality, slightly expensive
+ Snack Bar „Miquelet"

Cala Pí

39° 21,5' N 002° 50,1' E

MIRADOR DE CABRERA
Restaurant mit Anspruch zu nicht überzogenen Preisen; auf der Steilküste mit Blick auf Cabrera.
4 km in Richtung Osten am Ende der Urbanisation im Teil Vallgonera

Ambitious restaurant on cliff location; Cabrera view; 2mi by foot along the coast towards the East, at the end of the settlement.

Reservierung / *reservation*:
M 647 988 970
joergklausmann@yahoo.de
www.mirador-de-cabrera.com

EINKAUFEN / *SHOPPING*

2 Supermercado beim Treppen-Aufgang von Strand kommend links im Cala-Pí-Club. Dort auch Bankautomat. Ein weiterer, kleinerer Supermarkt vom Aufgang nach rechts nach ca. 20 m

Supermarket situated at stairway going up from beach, on the left in Cala Pí Club. ATM.
Another smaller supermarket 20m to the right of stairway.

AUSFLÜGE / *EXCURSIONS*

3 Eine kurze Wanderung führt von der Bucht in Richtung Cabo Blanco. Umkehren jederzeit möglich. Dazu bei den Fischerhäusern die Steilküste erklimmen (z. T. Treppenstufen) und dem Küstenverlauf folgen.

A short hike leads from the bay towards Cabo Blanco. Climb the cliffs at the fishermen houses (with stairs in parts) and follow the shoreline. You can turn back any time.

Mallorca

S'Estanyol

- Ruhiger Yachthafen
- Geringe Wassertiefen
- Gastplätze ungeschützt
- *Quiet marina*
- *Little water depths*
- *Unsheltered visitors berths*

🇩🇪 Die kleine Ortschaft S'Estanyol ist verschlafen wie immer. Es gibt ein paar Restaurants und Bars und wer einen kleinen Fußmarsch am Meer entlang nicht scheut, kann die Restaurants aufsuchen, die näher bei Sa Rápita liegen. Oder er wählt die Gegenrichtung, zum kleinen Leuchtturm Punta Plana für eine kurze Wanderung – die sich natürlich auch weiter ausdehnen lässt.

🇬🇧 *The small village of S'Estanyol remains as sleepy as always. There are a few restaurants and bars and visitors who like taking a short stroll along the sea may try the restaurants situated closer to Sa Rápita. Or take the opposite direction towards Punta Plana lighthouse for a hike.*

HINWEIS ZUM EINLAUFEN
WHEN ENTERING

Die Punta Plana (flaches Kap, mit Leuchtfeuer 0,5 sm südwestlich der Marina) mit Abstand runden. Vor der Hafeneinfahrt nur 3,50 m, in der Einfahrt auf 2,60 m abnehmend. Deshalb ist bei starkem auflandigen Wind das Anlaufen von S'Estanyol nicht ratsam.
Keep sufficient distance when rounding Punta Plana (flat promontory with beacon 0.5nmi southeast of the marina). At merely 3.50m before port entrance, water depth decreases to 2.60m in the entrance itself. We therefore recommend not trying to call at S'Estanyol during strong inshore winds.

FESTMACHEN FÜR GÄSTE
BERTHS FOR VISITORS

A Zirka 12 Gastplätze mit Muringleinen auf der Außenseite der kurzen Außenmole. Es besteht hier kein Schutz gegen Schwell vom Meer oder durch vorbeifahrende Boote. Max. Bootslänge hier 15 m; Wassertiefe 3-2 m. Innen besser mit dem Bug voraus anlegen. Wasser und Strom vorhanden. Manchmal werden auch freie Plätze im Hafenbecken vergeben.
Some 12 visitor berths with moorings at the outside of the short outer jetty. There is no protection against swell from the sea or passing vessels. Max. vessel length is 15m; water depth 3-2m. Docking bow to can be an option at the inner berths. Water supply and electricity available. Sometimes vacant berths within the port can also be rented.

T 971 640 085
gerencia@@cnestanyol.es
www.cnestanyol.es

🕐 Summer: Mon-Sat 9-20 h, Sun 9-13; Winter: Mon-Fri 9-17 h, Sat 9-13, Sun : closed

€ 12.50 m
80 EUR (June-Sept), 49 EUR (Oct.-May) inkl. Strom, Wasser und MwSt.
incl. electricity, water supply and VAT.
Neue Duschen und Toiletten am Fuß der Außenmole. / *New shower and toilet facilities at the end of the outer jetty.*

WiFi
Kostenlos, Kennwortvergabe
Free of charge, password assigned

TANKEN / *FUEL*

D+B; in der Einfahrt an Steuerbord
D+G/P; in entrance on starboard
08-20 h

RESTAURANTS & BARS

1 Restaurant Club Nàutic
Empfehlenswert; mittags wird ein preiswertes und gutes Menu del Dia serviert.
Recommended; a cheap, tasty Menu del Dia is offered at lunchtime.
T 971 640 036

2 Restaurant Es Mollet
vom Hafen keine 100 m entfernt; direkt an der Küstenstraße gelegen. Immer gut besucht.
Less than 100 m distance from the port; situated directly at the coastal road. Well attended.
T 971 641 022

3 An der Straße Richtung Llucmajor / *at the road to Llucmajor*
- Bar "Can Marola"
- Cafeteria Gelateria "Migjorn"
- Tapas Bar "S'Estany"

EINKAUFEN / *SHOPPING*

3 An der Straße Richtung Llucmajor im Mini-Supermarkt „Sa Botigueta" neben der „Bar Ca na Marola" Markt am Marktplatz Richtung Llucmajor, von Juni bis September immer Montagnachmittag.
Farmer's market takes place every Monday afternoon from June to September on the market place situated in Llucmajor direction.

S'Estanyol

Fl(2)R6s

39° 21,5' N 002° 55,3' E

At the road towards Llucmajor there's the Mini Supermarket „Sa Botigueta" next to „Bar Ca na Marola"

TECHNISCHER SERVICE
TECHNICAL SERVICES

12,5-t-Kran; für Yachten bis 1,80 m Tiefgang zu erreichen
12.5t davit; accessible for yachts with up to 1.80m draught

SHARK NAUTIC, TONI VADELL
Ausrüstung, Reparatur, Tauchen, Fischen / *Equipment, repair, diving, fishing*, M 666 865395

YACHTAUSRÜSTER
MARINE SUPPLIERS

s.o. / *see Technical Services*

AUSFLÜGE / *EXCURSIONS*

🚌 Bus nach Palma und Campos
Bus to Palma and Campos
Die Linie 515 verkehrt zweimal am Tag nach Campos bzw. Llucmajor; Bushaltestelle in der Nähe der Marina. Fahrpläne unter / *No. 515 bus runs twice daily to Campos and to Llucmajor; bus stops near the marina. Timetables see* www.tib.org/portal/de/web/ctm/autobus/seccio/500

Portbook & Island Guide 97

Sa Rápita

Mallorca

🇩🇪 Feine Lage der Marina im Nordwesten des geschützten Naturstrands Es Trenc/Playa de Sa Rápita. Der Ort Sa Rápita zieht sich entlang der Straße nach S'Estanyol. Die ersten Restaurants und Bars sind nach 500 m erreicht, wenn man die Marina neben dem Mini-Supermarkt verlässt. Schon die Gaststätte des Yachtclubs ist nicht zu verachten. Davor als Ergänzung eine schöne Terrasse am Meer mit Blick auf Cabrera und den fast karibischen Mix aus weißem Strand und türkis leuchtendem Meer.

🇬🇧 *Marina snugly located at Es Trenc natural beach. Sa Rápita town extends along the road to S'Estanyol. The first bars and restaurants appear some 0.5mi after leaving the marina next to the mini supermarket. The yacht club's restaurant is quite nice, too; it's nicely rounded off by a pretty terrace on the waterfront overlooking Cabrera and the almost Caribbean-like turquoise waters and white sands of Es Trenc.*

HINWEIS ZUM EINLAUFEN
WHEN ENTERING

Keine Untiefen. Es sind aber oft viele Surfer, Kiter und Jollen unterwegs, die unter Segeln allemal Vorfahrt haben, was hier oft genug missachtet wird. Starker auflandiger Wind kann das Einlaufen erschweren, denn die aufgeworfene Welle kann wegen Wassertiefen unter 5 m im Bereich der Einfahrt steil oder brechend werden.

No shoals. But often many windsurfers, kite surfers and skiffs travel along who all have right of way when sailing, although they're frequently ignored here. Strong inshore wind may complicate entering; the rising waves may become very steep or break due to water depths of less than 5 m.

FESTMACHEN FÜR GÄSTE
BERTHS FOR VISITORS

A **Club Náutico Sa Rápita**
Ein Verein hat hier die Konzession für die Marina. Bis zu 30 Gastplätze auf der Innenseite des Wellenbrechers vor der Tankstelle. Im Sommer weitere 40-50 verteilt im Hafenbecken. Anlegen mit Bug oder Heck an Muringleinen; Reservierung empfehlenswert. Die Plätze an der Mole sind leichtem Schwell ausgesetzt. Wassertiefen hier gut 3 m.

The marina is run by a yacht club. Up to 30 guest berths available inside of the breakwater near the petrol station. During summer, another 40-50 berths are spread out over the harbour basin. Anchor stern or bow to mooring lines. Reservations recommended. Slight swell at berths inside the breakwater. Depth: 3m.
T 971 640 001, (24 h)
UKW/VHF 09
administracion@cnrapita.es
www.cnrapita.com

Sa Rápita

- Wichtige Marina bei Chartertörns
- Nur 12 sm bis nach Cabrera
- Direkt neben Strand Es Trenc

• Important charter tour marina
• Only 13nmi to Cabrera
• Right next to the beach of Es Trenc

39° 21,5' N 002° 57,3' E

🕐 Mon-Sat 8-13 + 16-19 h (June-Sept), Mon-Sat 8-13 + 16-18 h (Oct.-May)

€ 12,50 m
85,50 EUR (June-Sept), 70,50 EUR (Oct, March, April, May), 45,50 EUR (Nov, Dec, Jan, Feb);
inkl. MwSt., Wasser, Strom
incl. IVA, water and electricity
Landstellplatz / *Hardstanding*:
Ab dem 1. Tag / *Starting from*:
0,68 EUR/m²/day

B Es gibt ein Hochregellager für Boote bis 9 m Länge (Marina Seca) / *The Club also runs a storage system for boats up to 9m length (Marina Seca)*

🚿 Toiletten und Duschen verteilt über das Hafengelände.
Toilets and showers on various locations in the marine area.

📶 kostenlos im Hafenbereich, Kennwortvergabe im Marinabüro.
Free of charge inside harbour area, password provided by the marina office.

TANKEN / *FUEL*

An der Südmole; Diesel und Benzin. Dort auch Absaugung von Grau- und Schwarzwasser; Frischwasser-Zapfstelle.
On the south pier: diesel and gasoline. Disposal facility for grey and black water, fresh water filling station.

Daily: 8-20 h (June-Sept),
8-18 h (Oct.-May)

Mallorca

TECHNISCHER SERVICE
TECHNICAL SERVICES

1 50-t-Travellift, 12-t-Kran, Slipbahn
50 t travel lift, 12-t-crane, slipway

In der Marina ansässig:
Within the marina:

Nautica 180°
Ausrüster u. techn. Dienstleistung
equipment & technical services
T 971 640 266
nautica180@nautica180.com
www.nautica180.com

Nautica Tramuntana;
Ausrüster u. techn. Dienstleistung
equipment & technical services
T 971 640 002
M 678 735 666
info@nauticatramuntana.com
www.nauticatramuntana.com
Mon-Fri 8.30-13 + 15.30-18 h
Sat 8.30-13 h

YACHTAUSRÜSTER
MARINE SUPPLIERS

→ Siehe 1 / *see 1*

RESTAURANTS & BARS

2 **Club Náutico Sa Rápita**
Mit Blick auf Hafen, den Naturstrand Es Trenc und die Insel Cabrera – ein empfehlenswertes Restaurant; auf der Terrasse eine abgespeckte Speisekarte. Kann in Vor- und Nachsaison abends geschlossen sein. / *Recommended restaurant overlooking harbour, Es Trenc beach and Cabrera Island – reduced menu on the terrace. May be closed in off-season evenings.*
T 971 640 413
restaurantcnr@gmail.com
www.restaurantclubnauticsarapita.com

3 **La Cantina**
Kleines Hafen-Restaurant mit Mittagstisch / *Small harbour restaurant.*

4 Ein halbes Dutzend Restaurants und Bars, alle mit Blick auf die naturgeschützte Inselgruppe Cabrera am Horizont. Am bekanntesten unter Wassersportlern ist das C'an Pep, aber auch den anderen sollte man durchaus eine Chance geben. Für den Abschluss

Ankerplatz neben der Marina und vor Badebereich. Im Hintergrund Ses Covetes.
Anchorage east of the marina and in front of a marked bathing area. In the background, Ses Covetes.

Sa Rapíta

des Abendessens könnte man eine Eisdiele aufsuchen, ebenfalls an der Uferstraße gelegen.
Half a dozen restaurants and bars, all offering a view of nature reserve Cabrera archipelago on the horizon. Water sports enthusiasts are most familiar with C'an Pep, but the others are also worth a try. To round off dinner there's the ice cream parlour which is also situated along the promenade.

EINKAUFEN / SHOPPING

3 Marina Supermarket
8-13 + 16.30-20 h (March-Oct)

4 Spar-Supermarkt „Brisas"
An der Küstenstraße (neben Rest. Voramar). Bäckerei Forn Sa Rápita (von der Hauptstraße zirka 100 m ortseinwärts) zwischen den Restaurants S'Amarador und C'an Vila. Es gibt einen Fußweg, beginnend in der Westecke des Hafens. Mittwoch Markt in Sa Ràpita, auf dem Platz hinter der Filiale der Banca March (Geldautomat).

Spar supermarket „Brisas" on the coastal road (adjacent to rest. Voramar). Bakery Forn Sa Rapita (from the main street, 100m into town) between restaurants S'Amarador and C'an Vila. There is a footpath starting at the harbour's western corner. Market on Saturday in Sa Rapita, on the square behind the Banca March branch (ATM).

Apotheke / *Pharmacist*
Av. Miramar, 62, T 971 640 677

AUSFLÜGE / EXCURSIONS

Es Trenc
Für einen ausgedehnten Spaziergang oder einen Strandlauf drängt sich der nahe Strand geradezu auf. / *Visit the long beach for a hike, a walk or jogging.*

🚌 **Bus nach Palma und Campos**
Bus to Palma and Campos
Die Linie 515 verkehrt zweimal am Tag nach Campos bzw. Llucmajor; Bushaltestelle in der Nähe der Marina. Fahrpläne unter: *Bus 515 goes twice daily to Campos and Llucmayor. There's a bus stop near the marina.*

Timetables please see:
www.tib.org/portal/de/web/ctm/autobus/seccio/500

Tankstelle und Gastliegeplätze
Filling station and visitor's berths

Club-Restaurant neben dem Strand
Club restaurant with terrace

Mallorca

Playa de Sa Rápita – Playa d'es Trenc

ANKERPLÄTZE
ANCHORING SITES

A Playa de la Rápita
39° 21,5' N 002° 57,6' E

🇩🇪 Auf 0,5 sm zwischen der Marina von Sa Rápita und der kleinen Ortschaft Ses Covetes ankern vor flach auslaufendem Sandstrand. Bei starker Thermik ungemütlich durch Seegang. Grund: Fast reiner Sand, kaum Seegras. Tiefe: ca. 5 m vor gelben Bojen, die im Sommer einen Badebereich markieren. Versorgung: eine Strandbar in der Mitte, eine weitere am Westrand von Ses Covetes. **Achtung:** Es können einige unmotorisierte Wasserfahrzeuge unterwegs sein, die Wegerecht haben!

🇬🇧 *Anchorages stretch along 0.5nmi from marina Sa Rápita to the small coastal settlement of Ses Covetes. Slowly leveling sandy seafloor in front of beaches. During strong thermical winds there's an uncomfortable swell. Depths ca. 5m. Yellow buoys seperate a bathing area in summer. One beach bar in the middle of the long beach, another close to Ses Covetes. Caution: surfers, kiters and dinghy sailors have right of way!*

B Playa de es Trenc
39° 20,8' N 002° 58,5' E

Südöstlich der Ansiedlung Ses Covetes, wo 2014 nach jahrzehntelangem Rechtsstreit Bauruinen abgerissen wurden, kann man bei passenden Bedingungen über gut 1 sm Distanz bis zur Isla Gabina über türkis leuchtendem Sandgrund und feinem Sandgrund ankern. Über die gesamte Strecke ist ein Badebereich mit gelben Tonnen markiert, so dass man mindestens auf 5 m Wassertiefe antreffen wird. Es gibt markierte Dinghy-Passagen und an Land zwei Beach Bars, die auch Gerichte servieren.

Southeast of the small settlement Ses Covetes, where in 2014 the relics of a formerly planned holiday resort were finally demolished, one can drop anchor above turquoise waters. The sea floor is pure sand for about 1nmi and along the whole distance a bathing area is marked with yellow bouys including dinghy passages to be used for landing. The depths in front of the bouys are min. 5m. Two beach bars are also serving some meals.

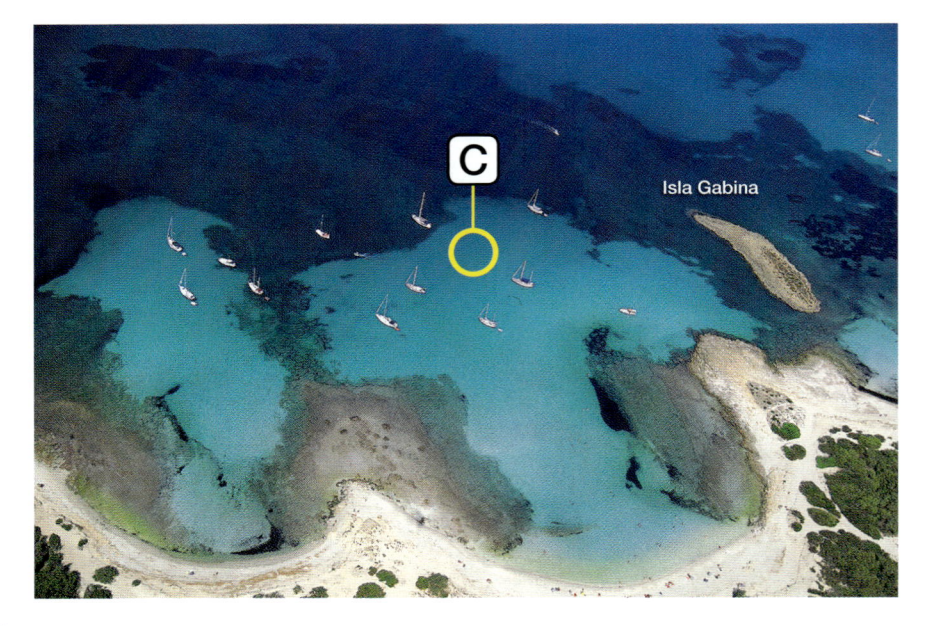

C Isla Gabina – Isla Redonda
39° 19,9' N 002° 59,3' E

Auf den 0,5 sm zwischen den Inselchen ist der Ankergrund deutlich weniger sandig. Es mischen sich Felsplatten und Seegras dazwischen. Hier befinden sich die am besten geschützten Ankerplätze bei westlichen Winden zwischen Cabo Salinas und der Bucht von Palma. Wassertiefen: 6-3 m.

Achtung: Es gibt zwischen Isla Gabina und Isla Redonda eine felsige Untiefe, die zumindest nicht in allen Seekarten vermerkt ist. An Land gibt es einen Ver-

102 Portbook & Island Guide

Playa de Sa Rápita – Playa d'es Trenc

leih von Strandkatamaranen und eine Strandbar. Mehr Restaurants und Bars in Colònia de Sant Jordi.

Between these islets, on a distance of 0.5nmi, the seafloor becomes more rocky. Also weed occurs more frequently. Best of all: One can find the most sheltered anchorage here during stronger easterly and southeasterly winds on the whole distance between the Bay of Palma and Cabo Salinas, Mallorca's southernmost point. Water depths are 6-3m.

Caution: *there is a rocky shoal between Isla Gabina and Isla Redonda, which is not displayed in any chart. Ashore one will find a rental of beach catamarans and a beach bar. More restaurants and bars in Colònia de Sant Jordi.*

Mallorca

Colònia de Sant Jordi

🇩🇪 Früher Verladehafen für die Salinen im Hinterland, heute prägt Bade-Tourismus den Ort. Inseln des Cabreras Nationalparks verzieren den Horizont, Ausflugsboote dorthin verkehren von hier. Ankerplätze vor dem Hafen und in den südöstlich anschließenden Buchten. Sie zählen zu den schönsten Mallorcas, haben Sandstrand und Dünen.
Bei stärkerem Wind aus Süd bis West sind die Ankerplätze keine gute Wahl. Die nächstgelegenen Alternativen:
• Cabo Salinas runden, um ins Lee der Ostküste zu gelangen
• Puerto de Cabrera anlaufen. Dieser mit einem Bojenfeld ausgerüstete Naturhafen im Nationalpark verspricht exzellenten Schutz. Detail S. 80
• Marina Sa Rápita anlaufen

🇬🇧 *A former lading port for the salines, this place is today teeming with seaside tourism, with a backdrop of Cabreras national park islands and day trip boats coming and leaving. There are anchorages close to the harbour and in the southeasterly bays. These are among Mallorca's most beautiful bays, with fine sandy beaches and dunes.*
With stronger south to west winds, these anchorage sites are not a good choice. Nearby alternatives are:
• Rounding Cabo Salinas to reach the more sheltered east coast
• Advance to the natural harbour of Cabrera's nature reserve, which offers excellent protection. Details p. 80
• Sail on to marina Sa Rápita

HINWEIS ZUM EINLAUFEN
WHEN ENTERING

Die Isla de Guardia kann von Yachten bis 2 m Tiefgang landseitig passiert werden. Die Passage verläuft ungefähr auf einer Linie zwischen dem Feuer auf der Außenmole des Hafens und einer Steinsäule auf der Isla Moltona.
Achtung: In der Zufahrt aus Südwesten liegt die kleine Isla Corberana. Sie ist nicht durch Feuer gekennzeichnet und ein einer dunklen Nacht kaum zu erkennen. Ähnliches gilt für die Islote Cabot Richtung Es Trenc.

Yachts with a max. depth of 2m may sail northeast of Isla de Guardia. The passage follows a line marked by the entrance light of the harbour's outer breakwater and a stone column on Isla Moltona.
Caution: *Approaching the harbour from the southwest you will pass Isla Corberana. This small island has no lighthouse or similar and can easily be overseen during a dark night. This can also happen with Islote Cabot in direction Es Trenc beach.*

FESTMACHEN FÜR GÄSTE
BERTHS FOR VISITORS

A Die Innenseite des Wellenbrechers ist belegt durch Ausflugsboote. Hier maximal 1,50 m Wassertiefe. Große versandete Bereiche.
20 Gastplätze mit Muringsleinen für Yachten bis 1,80 m Tiefgang und 12 m Länge befinden sich auf der Außenseite der ersten Pier. Wasser und Strom vorhanden.

All berths inside the breakwater are occupied by Cabrera cruise boats etc. In this area the max. depth will not exceed 1.50m.
The outer part of the first pier is designated to yachts in transit. Max. 1.80m depth and 12m length. Mooring lines, water and power available.

Reservierung notwendig, mindestens drei Tag im Voraus über www.portsib.es. Bezahlung per Kreditkarte. Stornierung oder Umbuchung über die Webseite.
Reservation recommended at least 3 days in advance at www.portsib.es. Payment by credit card. For cancelation or changes please go to the webpage.
T 971 656 224, M 629 484 014
port.coloniasantjordi@portsib.es

🕐 01/06-31/10:
Mon-Sun, 09-14.40 + 15.30-20 h
01/11-31/05:
Mon-Fri, 09-14.40 + 15.30-20 h,
Sat 09-14.40 h, Sun closed

€ EUR/m2: 0,60 (01/06-30/09); 0,18 (01/10-31/05) Water: 5,50 EUR; Electr.: 5,50 EUR Alle Preise / All prices plus

Colònia de Sant Jordi

- Schöne Strände locken Landurlauber
- Gastplätze in Zahl und Größe limitiert
- Besucherzentrum Cabrera-Nationalpark

• Beautiful beaches attract many tourists
• Guest berths limited by size and numbers
• Visitor Centre Cabrera NP

Isla de la Guardia
2,0
39° 18,6' N 002° 59,8'E
Fl(4)R12s

21% MwSt. /VAT

Einfache Sanitäreinrichtungen neben dem Hafenbüro.
Simple sanitary facilities next to the harbour office.

ANKERPLÄTZE
ANCHORING SITES

B Direkt vor dem Hafen über einem Ankergrund aus Sands, Fels und Seegras, Tiefe 3-2 m. Bei südlichen und südwestlichen Winden dringt viel Schwell zu den Liegeplätzen. / *Directly in front of harbour above anchoring ground made up of sand, rock and seaweed, depth 3-2m*

TECHNISCHER SERVICE
TECHNICAL SERVICES

Náutica Colonia,
Neben dem Hafenbüro
Beside port office
10-t-Forklift, auch Bootsvermietung und Tauchen / Schnuppertauchen
10-t-mobile crane; also boat rental and diving center (also test diving)

M 622 085 068 + 644 128 952
info@nauticacolonia.com
www.nauticacolonia.com
Mon-Fri: 9-13 +15-18,
ab/*from* 15/03: Sa 10-13 h

Shark Nautic, Toni Vadell
M 666 865 395
sharknautic@hotmail.es

YACHTAUSRÜSTER
MARINE SUPPLIERS

→ Siehe oben / *see above*

Portbook & Island Guide 105

Mallorca

Ruhepol: Keine 10 sm vor Mallorcas Küste liegt mit Cabrera ein Törnziel, das kaum jemand auslässt.

Haven of peace: less than 10nmi off Mallorca's coast, Cabrera is a destination which few boats fail to visit.

Ein Besuch im Archipel und Nationalpark vor der Südspitze Mallorcas ist beliebt und angesagt. Für Natur pur, einen Sternenhimmel zum Niederknien – und dunkle Geschichte...

A visit to the archipelago and national park at the southern end of Mallorca is a must. Enjoy unadulterated nature, a marvelous starry sky – and a sinister historic past...

Cabrera

39° 21,5' N 002° 55,3' E

Mysterious Cabrera

- Ruhe und Sterne genießen
- Hafenbucht mit 50 Bojen
- Online reservieren + zahlen
- Proviant besser mitbringen

- Enjoy peace among sparkling stars
- Harbour bay with 50 mooring buoys
- Book and pay in advance online
- Better bring along your own provisions

Mallorca

Isla Horarada – Punta Anciola

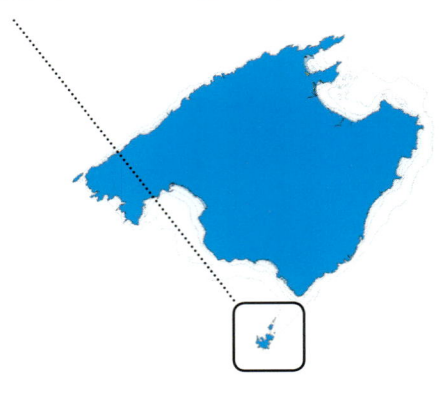

🇩🇪 Zu Cabrera zählen 19 Inseln und Inselchen. Die größte Fläche besitzt Cabrera selbst, gefolgt von der Isla de Conejera. Cabrera ist seit März 1991 maritimer Nationalpark. Seit Herbst 2012 werden für eine Übernachtung mit dem Boot Gebühren erhoben.

🇬🇧 *Cabrera archipelago includes 19 islets and islands; Cabrera Island itself has the largest surface, followed by Isla de Conejera. Since 1991 Cabrera has been a maritime nature reserve. Since autumn 2012, to reserve a mooring buoy is subject to fees.*

① Isla Horadada - 39° 12,4' N 002° 58,7' E → page 117
Viele, die Cabrera anlaufen, werden diesen Leuchtturm passieren.
Many vessels with destination Cabrera will pass this lighthouse.

② Blaue Grotte / Blue Cave - 39° 09,7' N 002° 56,8' E → page 118
Ausflugsboote fahren die Grotte regelmäßig an und einige auch hinein.
Excursion boats run regularly to the Blue Cave and some even into it.

③ Puerto de Cabrera - 39° 09,3' N 002° 55,6' E → page 118
Die Hafenbucht der Hauptinsel. Hier liegen die Übernachtungs-Bojen.
The natural harbour of the main island. The place to stay overnight.

④ Es Caló des Forn → page 118
Ein gemauerter Kalkofen gab den Namen. Bucht mit Bojen für Tagesnutzung.
A brick limekiln lent the name. Small inlet with buoys to use during the day.

⑤ Cala es Burri - 39° 08,7' N 002° 57,8' E → page 118
Die größte Bucht auf der Ostseite Cabreras mit 15 runden Festmachebojen.
The largest bay on the east side of Cabrera with 15 mooring buoys.

⑥ Castillo de Cabrera → page 118
Staubig und ein wenig anstrengend ist der Aufstieg, aber der Ausblick perfekt.
The path is dusty and to a climb up a little tiring, but the views are perfect.

⑦ Hauptpier / Main pier → page 120
Für die meisten Crews die bevorzugte Stelle für einen Landgang auf Cabrera.
For most crews the preferred location for their first landfall on Cabrera.

⑧ La Cantina → page 120
Die einzige Lokal ist bei der Hauptpier, neben dem Nationalpark-Büro.
The only pub is located at the main pier and next to the National Park office.

⑨ Pier für Dingis & Ausflugsschiffe / Pier for dinghies & excursion boats
Aber selten stark belegt. / *Rarely occupied by boats.*

⑩ Strände / Beaches → page 121
Klein, aber fein: Die Alternative zum Schnorcheln rund um das eigene Boot.
The alternative: If you do not like to snorkel around your boat all the time …

⑪ Museum und Denkmal / Museum and memorial → page 121
Stilvolle Ausstellung zur wechselhaften Geschichte der Insel. Kleiner Eintritt.
Elegant exhibition about the changeful history of the island. Small fee.

⑫ Punta Anciola - 39° 07,7' N 002° 55,1' E → page 121
Der Klassiker unter den Wanderungen führt zum Leuchtturm im Südwesten.
The classical hike leads to the red-and-white lighthouse in the southwest.

⑬ Mehr Wanderungen / More hikes → page 121
Es scheint, als könnten mehr Wege ohne Führung erwandert werden.
Today more hikes seem to be possible without a guide. So much to discover…

Portbook & Island Guide

Cabrera

1 Isla Horadada
2 Blaue Grotte / Blue Cave
6 Castell de Cabrera
3 Puerto de Cabrera
5 Cala es Burri
CABRERA
12 Punta Anciola

Mallorca

- Eine Bucht mit 50 Bojen…
- … für vier Bootsgrößen
- Anlanden an zwei Stellen

Bay with 50 buoys…
… for four different boat sizes
Landing on two different spots

Puerto de Cabrera

🇩🇪 Fakt ist: Im Naturhafen Puerto de Cabrera an einer der 50 Bojen zu hängen, ist der perfekte Kontrast zur Inselmetropole Palma de Mallorca – nicht einmal 30 sm liegen dazwischen. Die Zeiten kostenloser Bojenplätze inmitten geschützter Natur sind Geschichte. Im Reservierungsvorgang muss bezahlt werden, je nach Jahreszeit und Bootslängen unterschiedlich viel. **Achtung:** Wer keine Reservierung vorweisen kann, wird bei Kontrollen am Abend aufgefordert, die Hafenbucht zu verlassen – selbst wenn noch Bojen frei sind. Ankern ist an keiner Stelle des Nationalparks erlaubt. Fischen ist verboten und es dürfen keine Tiere an Land gebracht werden.

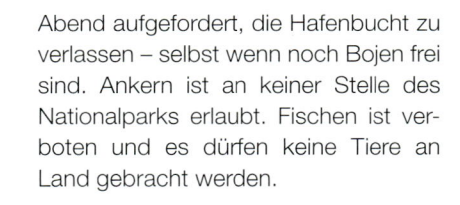

🇬🇧 *It is a fact that stopping at one of the mooring buoys in Puerto de Cabrera natural harbour is a jarring contrast to island's capital Palma de Mallorca, though it is only less than 30nmi away. Those good times when mooring buoys within Puerto de Cabrera were free are history. Fees are charged for each booked mooring buoy, depending on boat length and time of the year. **Caution:** those who cannot prove their reservation during controls in the evening will be requested to leave the harbour bay immediately – even though individual buoys may still remain vacant. Anchoring is not permitted in any bay inside Cabrera*

Hauptpier / *Main pier*

Cabrera

National Park. Fishing is prohibited and pets may not be brought ashore.

ANSTEUERUNG
APPROACHING

Die Gewässer rund um die Einfahrt in den Naturhafen Puerto de Cabrera mit dem Bojenfeld sind durchgängig sehr tief. Das wichtigste Einfahrtfeuer steht auf dem Cabo de Llebeig (Fl(4)W 14,5s) westlich der Einfahrt in 74m Höhe, Nenntragweite 7 sm. / *Coastal waters surrounding the entrance to Puerto de Cabrera natural harbour with its buoy field are all very deep. The main entrance lights are situated on Cabo de Llebeig (Fl(4)W 14,5s) to the west of the entrance, at 74m altitude, regular range 7nmi.*

BOJENFELD / BUOY FIELD

[A] Bojen für Yachten / *Mooring Buoys for yachts,* < 12 m

[B] Bojen für Yachten / *Mooring Buoys for yachts,* 12-15 m

[C] Bojen für Yachten / *Mooring Buoys for yachts,* 15-20 m

[D] Bojen für Yachten / *Mooring Buoys for yachts,* 20-35 m

€ Boje reservieren und bezahlen

Die Festmachebojen auf Cabrera sind seit Herbst 2012 kostenpflichtig. Hier die Bojen-Gebühren pro Nacht für die Zeit vom 1.5. -30.9. eines Jahres. In der Wintersaison zwischen dem 1. 10. und 30.4. wird der halbe Betrag kassiert.
bis 12 m Länge (weiße Bojen): 15 EUR
bis 15 m Länge (gelbe Bojen): 24 EUR
bis 20m Länge (orangene Bojen): 42 EUR
über 20 m Länge (rote Bojen): 129 EUR

Anfang 2016 wurden diese Tarife bei der Reservierung abzüglich von 21%

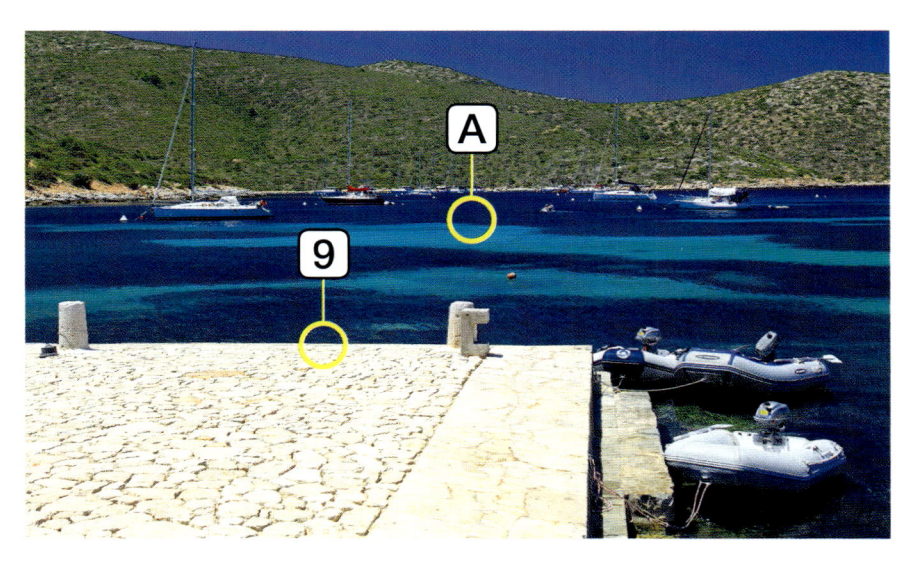

Mallorca

Blaue Grotte / Blue cave

MwSt. ausgegeben. Die Tarife sind identisch für Charter- und Privatyachten. Bei der Anmeldung muss man sich in einem der ersten Schritte dennoch entsprechend eingruppieren.

Zuletzt konnten maximal diese Anzahl von Tagen gebucht werden:
- Juli + August: max. 1 Nacht
- Juni + Sept.: max. 2 Nächte
- Okt.-Juni: bis zu 7 Nächte

Ein schneller Einstieg in den Reservierungsvorgang für eine Festmacheboje gelingt über die Webseite www.balearsnatura.com. Auf der Startseite lässt sich die Sprache auf Deutsch umstellen. Es werden verschiedene Naturparks zur Auswahl gestellt, darunter links der Nationalpark Cabrera. Anklicken.

Auf der folgenden Seite „Information" anklicken. Der nächste wichtige Menüpunkt ist nun „Anker-, Tauch- und Schifffahrtserlaubnisse". Anklicken.

Ab jetzt wird es Englisch, man wählt zwischen „Anchoring reservation" (Reservierung einer Übernachtungsboje), „Cancelation ancoring" (Stornierung einer Übernachtungsboje), „Reserve diving" (Tauchgenehmigung) und „Permit for navigation" (Jahreserlaubnis zur Nutzung der Tagesbojen). Für die Jahreserlaubnis wird keine Gebühr fällig.

Wir klicken auf „Anchoring reservation" und kommen direkt in die englische Sprachauswahl. Die Reservierung beginnt hier mit der Auswahl „Privat" oder „Charter" und Angabe der Bootslänge. Danach wählt man die Tage aus, die man bleiben möchte. Bojen werden nicht mehr fest vergeben, man wählt bei der Ankunft eine aus der gebuchten Kategorie. Alle Tage, die weiter als 20 Tage voraus liegen, erscheinen grau und können nicht reserviert werden.

Danach öffnet sich eine Seite, in die man die persönlichen Daten und die des Schiffes einträgt. Am Ende gelangt zum Bezahlvorgang (mit Visa- oder Mastercard). Wer vor 17 Uhr des gebuchten Tages storniert, kann 50% der Gebühren zurück erhalten. Hat man gleich für mehrere Tage reserviert, dann soll nur eine anteilige Stornierung möglich sein.

€ *How to reserve and pay a mooring buoy*

Mooring buoys on Cabrera have been subject to charge since autumn 2012. Here are mooring fees per night for the summer season (1.05.-30.09.). In the winter season (1.10.-30.04.), charges are half-price.

Boat length up to 12m (white buoys): 15 EUR

Kontrolle / Checking the papers

Cabrera

Einfahrt mit Kastell / Entrance with ancient fortress

up to 15m (yellow buoys): 24 EUR
up to 20m (orange buoys): 42 EUR
over 20m (red buoys): 129 EUR
Beginning of 2016 these rates were issued during the reservation process minus 21% VAT.

The fees are identical for charter and privately owned yachts, although vessels must still be classified when booking.

The following maximum no. of nights can be booked:
- July & August: 1 night max.
- June & September: 2 nights max.
- Oct.-June: up to 7 nights are possible.

Reservations for mooring buoys may be done via the web site (www.reservasparquesnacionales.es). On the Home page, click on „Archipiélago de Cabrera". On the following page click on „Fondeo" („Buceo") below is for diving permits, 5 EUR/day, the third item „Navegación" is for annual navigation permit, necessary if one wants to use the mooring bouys for use during the day.

On the following page, click on „Pulsar en este enlace" („press this link") for the Balearic Island Government page to open. Now the reservation process itself begins, language can be changed to English. Select the „private" or „charter" use of vessel and input vessel length. Afterwards select the dates you would like to stay. Bouys are no longer given individually, sailors choose their category upon arrival. Dates more than 20 days in advance are highlighted grey and cannot be booked.

Afterwards a page opens for input of personal data and boat data. Payment is due at the end of the booking process. Visa / Mastercard accepted. If a booked date is cancelled until 5. p.m. on that day 50% of the fees can be refunded. If one has reserved for several days, only a partial cancellation may be possible.

ANSCHAUEN / WHAT TO SEE

1 **Isla Horadada**
... mit dem schwarz-weiß gesteiften Leuchtturm Fl(2)12s markiert die Nordspitze des Cabrera-Archipels. Es gibt hier, wie auf dem Bild andeutungsweise zu erkennen, eine Anlegestelle und einen Weg nach oben für das Wartungspersonal.

Isla Horarada with this black & white belted lighthouse, Fl(2)12s, marks the northern tip of the Cabrera archipelago. As might be vaguely discerned on the image, there is a landing stage and a path further up for technical inspectors.

Fl(2)12s

Isla Horadada

Mallorca

Es Caló des Forn

Cala es Burri

Kastell / Fortress

2 Blaue Grotte / *Blue Cave*
Das schönste Farbenspiel erlebt man ab dem Mittag, wenn die Sonne hinein scheinen kann. Man kann die Grotte durchschwimmen und auch mit einem kleinen Boot hinein fahren. Das dürfen nicht nur die Ausflugsboote …

Colours are most vibrant in the afternoon with the sun shining in. Sail into the cave with a small craft, this is not limited to excursion boats. Or cross the bays interior by swimming …

3 Puerto de Cabrera
Der Name sagt alles: Wenn eine Bucht in den Rang eines Hafens befördert wird, dann weil sie ebenso sicher ist, wenn es ungemütlich wird. Die Bucht ist 0,7 sm tief und mit 50 Bojen für Yachten bis 35 m Länge belegt. Eigner größerer Schiffe haben keine Möglichkeit, Cabrera zu besuchen. Einfahrtsfeuer stehen auf dem Cabo Llebeig, Fl(4),14,5 s, und auf der Punta de sa Creveta, FlR4s.

As the name implies: if a bay is classified as a harbour, then it is because it is equally safe should the weather become unsettled. The bay is 0.7nmi deep and counts 50 buoys for yachts up to 35m in length. Owners of larger vessels do not have the opportunity to visit Cabrera. The entrance is marked by lighthouses on Cabo Llebeig, Fl(4)14.5s, and on Punta de sa Creveta, FlR4s.

4 Es Caló des Forn
In der kleinen, westlichen Ausbuchtung von Puerto de Cabrera findet man 8 runde Bojen für den Aufenthalt nur am Tage. 10 weitere unterhalb des Kastells nahe der Hauptpier. Die Zeit der Nutzung läuft von eine Stunde nach Sonnenaufgang bis eine Stunde vor Sonnenuntergang. Anmeldung: M 630 982 363 / *In the western part of Puerto de Cabrera there are 8 round buoys laid out. They are designated for day time use only, starting from one hour after sunrise to one hour before sunset. 10 more of these round bouys can be found below the castle close to the main pier. Contact: M 630 982 363*

5 Cala es Burri
Die größte Bucht auf der Ostseite Cabreras. Hier liegen 15 runde Festmachebojen aus für den Aufenthalt nur am Tage. Die Zeit der Nutzung läuft von eine Stunde nach Sonnenaufgang bis eine Stunde vor Sonnenuntergang. Anlanden ist hier nicht erlaubt.

The largest bay on the east side of Cabrera. Here one will find 15 round buoys designated for day time use only, starting from one hour after sunrise to one hour before sunset. Landing is not permitted here.

6 Castillo de Cabrera
Der Aufstieg zum Kastell ist ein Muss. Kurz bevor man die Festung über einen staubigen Pfad erreicht hat, passiert man einen kleinen, ummauerten Friedhof. Um ganz nach oben zu gelangen, muss man eine schmale Wendeltreppe hinauf. Dann genießt man den Rundumblick über Bucht und Einfahrt. Die umkämpfte Festung wurde allein im 16. Jhd. zehnmal zerstört und wieder aufgebaut.

Cabrera

Freude am Segeln

SUN CHARTER

Willkommen bei Sun Charter, der grössten deutschen Charterflotte im Mittelmeer

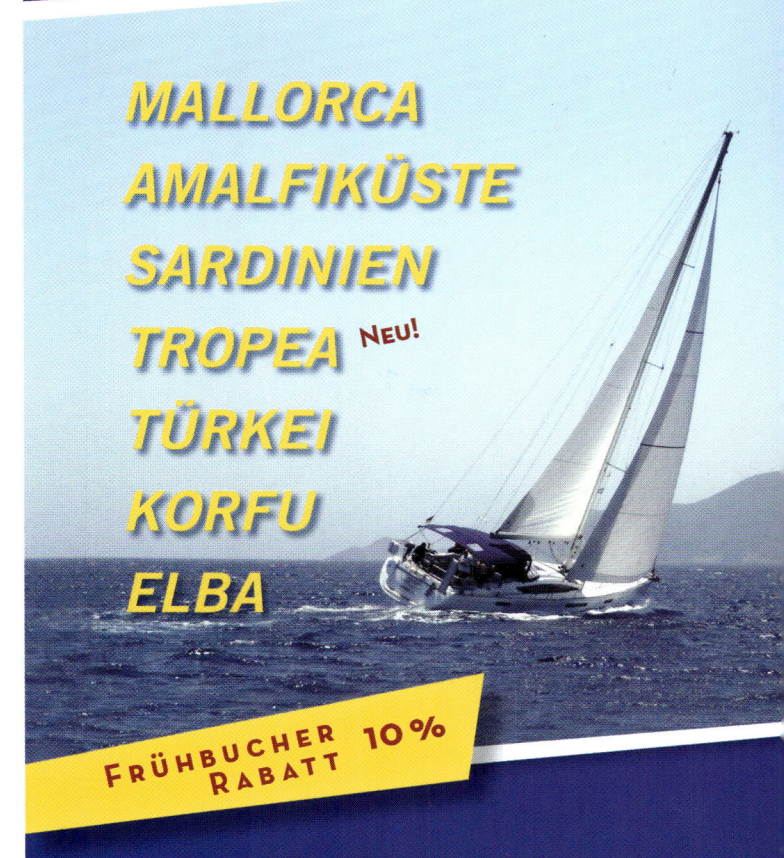

MALLORCA
AMALFIKÜSTE
SARDINIEN
TROPEA Neu!
TÜRKEI
KORFU
ELBA

Frühbucher Rabatt 10%

Ihre persönliche Buchungshotline:

+49 8171 / 29905

sail@suncharter.de

Unser kompetenter Kundenservice berät Sie gerne über unsere Buchungshotline oder per E-mail zu ihrer Buchung, den Yachten und Revieren.

Sie haben die Wahl:
aus 100 Sun Charter Yachten von 33 bis 57 ft an 8 Sun Charter Stützpunkten.

www.suncharter.de | sail@suncharter.de

Mallorca

Punta Anciola

Fl(3) 15s

The ascent to the fortress is a must. Before reaching its basement, you will pass a small, walled cemetery. To reach the very top, you have to go up a narrow spiral staircase. Then you can enjoy the panoramic view of the bay and its entrance channel. This fortification testifies many struggles, having been destroyed and rebuilt ten times in the 16th century alone.

7 Hauptpier / *Main pier*

Hier legen die Fischer an (und verkaufen manchmal einen Teil des Fangs direkt), hier liegen die Schlauchboote der Nationalpark-Mitarbeiter. Manchmal auch Arbeitsboote. Auch zum Anlanden mit dem Dingi ist es der richtige Platz – und wenn es nur für einen Drink in der Cantina ist …

The place where fishermen tie their boats (and sometimes sell directly parts of the daily catch) and where the National Park staff have their RIBs. Sometimes workboats moor here also. For landing with the dinghy, it is the right place – even if it is just for a drink at the cantina …

8 La Cantina

An der Hauptpier unterhalb des Kastells und neben dem Nationalpark-Büro liegt die einzige Gaststätte. Hier gibt es Getränke und Snacks und sogar ein Mittagsgericht. Neben der Terrasse eine alte Kanone. Öffnungszeiten: 09-22 Uhr

On the main pier below the fortress and next to the National Park office the only pub is located. You will get drinks and snacks and even a lunch. Next to the terrace there is an old cannon. Opening hours: 09-22 h

9 Pier für Dingis und Ausflugsschiffe / *Pier for dinghies and excursion boats*

Die von Colònia de Sant Jordi kommenden Ausflugsschiffe legen nur hier kurz an, um Tagesgäste zu bringen oder abzuholen. Zum Anlanden mit dem Dingi bleibt dennoch ausreichend Platz. Direkt hinter der Pier gibt es sanitäre Einrichtungen. Wenige Meter in Richtung Kastell liegen die Unterkünfte, die man seit 2014 buchen kann. Zur Verfügung stehen zwölf Zweibettzimmer.

Excursion boats coming from Colonia de Sant Jordi dock here only briefly to bring or pick up day visitors. Even then enough space remains for landing with a dinghy. Directly behind the pier there are sanitary facilities. From here a few meters towards the fortress one will find the accommodation that since 2014 can be booked. Twelve twin rooms are available.

July-Sept.: 60 EUR, April, May, Oct. + Nov.: 50 EUR; Dec-March: closed
www.cvcabrera.es/albergue-de-cabrera
www.cvcabrera.es/reservas-albergue

10 Strände / *Beaches*

Zum Bojenfeld hin abgetrennt. Hier tummeln sich tagsüber vor allem Besucher, die mit Ausflugsbooten von Colònia de Sant Jordi kommen. Aber auch Bootsfahrern ist der Zutritt nicht verwehrt …

Separated from the mooring buoy field, these beaches are full of day trippers coming over from Colònia de Sant Jordi by excursion boat. But sailors are also welcome …

11 Museum

Funde aus dem Meer erzählen vom regen Handel früherer Jahre. Neben dem Museum gibt es eine Gedenkstelle für die vielen tausend französischen Kriegsgefangenen, die hier ihr Leben ließen.

Archaeological finds from the sea testify a flourishing trade in former times. Next to the museum there is a memorial for those many thousands of French prisoners of war who died here.

Open: 11.30-14 + 16-18 h, 2 EUR

12 Punta Anciola

Ein rot-weißer Leuchtturm, Fl(3)15s, markiert die Südwestspitze Cabreras. Die Wanderung von Puerto de Cabrera ausgehend dauert zirka eine Stunde, ein Weg. Es sind einige Höhenmeter zu bewältigen. Getränke nicht vergessen. Wer am Leuchtturm angekommen rastet, bekommt alsbald Besuch von Eidechsen. Und die sind sehr neugierig und gar nicht scheu …

A red-and-white lighthouse, Fl(3)15s, marks Cabrera's southern tip. A hike starting from Puerto de Cabrera takes about an hour, one way. There is some altitude to tackle. Do not forget to put a water bottle into the backpack. Hikers resting beside the lighthouse building will soon be joined by many lizards. They are definitely not shy but curious.

13 Mehr Wanderungen / *More hikes*

Der Weg zur Punta Anciola muss nicht die einzige Wanderung auf Cabrera bleiben. Seit Touristen auf Cabrera übernachten können, können offenbar mehr Wege frei begangen werden. So könnte man ohne Führer zum Aussichtspunkt La Miranda östlich der Bucht und weiter auf einem Höhenweg entlang der Südküste zum Puerto de Cabrera zurückkehren und auch auf der Westseite der Hafenbucht einen Weg entlangwandern.

Geführte thematische Wanderungen, vorrangig zu Flora und Fauna werden vom Nationalpark-Büro angeboten. Sie starten abends gegen 17.45 Uhr von dort (neben der Cantina) und dauern bis zirka 20.30 Uhr. Preis: 4 EUR, ermäßigt 2 EUR.

Since there are accomodations to be rented since 2014 some more hikes seem to be possible without a guide. So one can walk to the viewpoint La Miranda east of the bay and return to Puerto de Cabrera on a trail along the south coast. Another path leads along the west side of the harbour bay.

Guided Walks, primarily to explore flora and fauna, are offered by the National Park Office. They usually start in the evening around 17.45 h from the office (next to the Cantina) and last until 20.30 h. Price: EUR 4, reduced 2 EUR.

La Cantina

Museum

Mallorca

Calas Fantásticas

Calas: Mit diesem Wort bezeichnet man Buchten in einer Kliffküste. Oft lockt hier sandiger Ankergrund, das Meer leuchtet in Türkistönen. Ein Traum. Mallorcas Osten ist mit diesen Calas überreich gesegnet.

Cala: a narrow cut in the sheer cliff coast, a sandy anchorage and bright turquoise sea – that is what sailors dream of. Mallorca's east coast lies waiting to be explored.

Der Osten Mallorcas / The East of Mallorca

Cala Barcas

- Ankerbuchten im Meilentakt
- Sieben Häfen und Marinas
- Bootfahren einfach genießen

- *Beautiful calas every mile*
- *Seven harbours and marinas*
- *Just enjoy boating and relax*

Mallorca

Cala Marmols – Portocolom

🇩🇪 Cala Figuera, Mallorcas kleinster Yachthafen, ist der erste Meilenstein an der Ostküste. Glücklich, wer hier unterkommt. Unter all den Buchten zählt die Cala Mondragó zu den beliebtesten. Große Hafenbuchten haben Portopetro und Portocolom.

🇬🇧 *Cala Figuera, the smallest of Mallorca's marinas, is the first milestone. You really need some luck to find a vacant berth here. Nearby Cala Mondragó is a highly recommended anchorage. And don't miss the natural ports at Portopetro & Portocolom.*

1 Cala Marmols - 39° 17,2' N 003° 05,6' E → page 126
Von hohen Felsen flankiert. Aber klein und schon mit wenigen Booten belegt.
Small, but flanked by high cliffs. Fills up with only a few pleasure boats.

2 Cala s'Almunia & Cala de sa Comuna (Calo d'es Moro) - 39° 18,8' N 003° 07,5' E → page 126
Eine Felsnase trennt die beiden Buchten. Vor allem sa Comuna fasziniert.
A rocky outcrop separates the two bays. Especially sa Comuna fascinates.

3 Cala Llombards - 39° 19,4' N 003° 08,8' E → page 127
Beliebte Badebucht mit Strandbar. Dahinter eine touristische Ansiedlung.
Popular bay with a beach. Behind a tourist settlement.

4 Cala Santanyi - 39° 19,5' N 003° 09,0' E → page 127
Tagesankerbucht, im Sommer sehr belebt durch Badetourismus.
Day anchorage. During summer very popular beach.

5 Cala Figuera - 39° 19,6' N 003° 10,5' E → page 128
Mallorcas kleinster Sportboothafen. Fünf Liegeplätze für Gäste.
As small as it gets. Five berths for guests. A must see place.

6 Cala Mondragó / Cala d'es Burgit - 39° 20,8' N 003° 11,8' E → page 132
Naturgeschützt, aber von Land wie vom Meer stark frequentiert.
Nature reserve, but highly frequented from sea and shore alike.

7 Portopetro - 39° 21,3' N 003° 13,1' E → page 134
Kleine Marina, großes Bojenfeld. Viele Restaurants am Hafen.
Small marina, large buoy field. Plenty of restaurants along the harbour.

8 Cala d'Or - 39° 22,1' N 003° 14,2' E → page 138
Die größte Marina der Ostküste; Ortschaft lebt nur im Sommer.
Largest marina on the east coast; the village is only alive in summer.

9 Cala Esmeralda, Ferrera, Serrena - 39° 22,4' N 003° 14,6' E → page 142
Dreierbucht mit starker Bebauung, aber guter Schutz bei Nordwind.
Triple bay with many flats and hotels; good at northerly winds.

10 Cala Mitjana - 39° 23,2' N 003° 15,0' E → page 142
Schöne Umgebung, auch weil von privat gepflegt; keine Versorgung.
Beautiful surroundings maintained by private owners; no supply.

11 Cala Arsenau - 39° 23,6' N 003° 15,2' E → page 143
Platz für nur wenige Yachten; sieht von oben schöner aus, als sie ist.
Bay for only few yachts; more impressive from above than in reality.

12 Cala Marsal - 39° 24,6' N 003° 15,9' E → page 143
Hat vergleichsweise viel Platz für Yachten. An Land alles vorhanden.
Spacious anchorage and sandy bottom. On land everything available.

13 Portocolom - 39° 24,8' N 003° 16,1' E → page 144
Hafenbucht, die alles hat: Stegplätze, Bojenfeld, Restaurants am Wasser.
Natural harbour that has it all: berths, buoy field, waterfront restaurants.

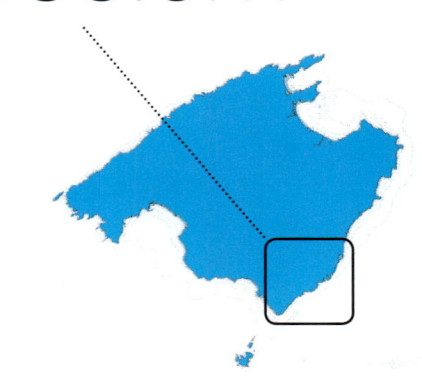

Der Osten Mallorcas I / The East of Mallorca I

MALLORCA

- 13 Portocolom
- 11 Cala Arsenau
- 12 Cala Marsal
- 9 Cala Esmeralda, Ferrera, Serrena
- 10 Cala Mitjana
- Cala d'Or
- 8
- 7 Portopetro
- 6 Cala Mondragó / Cala d'es Burgit
- 5 Cala Figuera
- 4 Cala Santanyi
- 3 Cala Llombards
- 2 Cala s'Almunia / Cala de sa Comuna
- 1 Cala Marmols

SANTANYI

Portbook & Island Guide 125

Mallorca

Cala Figuera

🇩🇪 Welch ein Kontrast zum nahen Cala d'Or! Nicht einige hundert, nein, gerade fünf (!) Liegeplätze für Yachten gibt es in Cala Figuera (übersetzt: Feigenbucht) an einer kurzen Mole. Und das seit vielen Jahren unverändert. So läuft man bis heute Cala Figuera an, weil es hier so anders ist: Die schmale Hafenbucht mit ihren zahlreichen traditionellen Fischerbooten und auch einer modernen Fangflotte hat etwas ganz Besonderes.

Man hat Cala Figuera nicht gesehen, ohne den alten Hafenteil einmal zu Fuß zu umrunden. Dabei wird man feststellen, welch entspannte Atmosphäre noch immer über diesem alten Fischerdorf liegt.

🇬🇧 *A complete contrast to nearby Cala d'Or! Not hundreds of berths but a mere 5 (!) wait for yachts in Cala Figuera (Fig Bay) on a short pier. There have been no changes for many years, and that is precisely the reason for going in; it's different. The narrow harbour is a gem with its traditional fishing boats as well as a modern fishing fleet. Walking once around the entire old port is a must for any visitor to Cala Figuera. Here you will realize this special relaxed atmosphere in this old fishing village.*

ANSTEUERUNG
APPROACHING

Keine Untiefen zu beachten. Diese Landmarken markieren die Einfahrt:
Auf der Nordseite: der alte Wachturm „Torre d'en Beu", daneben eine Radarstation auf einem sechseckigen, schwarzweiß längsgestreiften Leuchtfeuer (FlW 5s). Auf der Südseite: die im Bauhausstil errichtete, moderne Wohnanlage Cap Blau.
Einlaufend an Backbord, kurz vor den Liegeplätzen, liegen ein paar kleine Bojen aus, die man übersehen könnte, wenn sie nicht belegt sind. Sie sind privat und sollten nicht benutzt werden. Ankern ist hier nicht erlaubt, schon wegen der zahlreich ein- und auslaufenden, auch größeren Fischerboote.
Bei den Liegeplätzen guter Schutz, starker auflandiger Wind trägt jedoch Schwell herein. Dann erlebt man schon vor der Steilküste konfusen Seegang durch reflektierende Wellen.

Achtung: Die Fischerboote fahren beim Ein- und Auslaufen schnell und werfen Wellen auf. Abstand zur Pier ist deshalb wichtig.

There are no shallow areas. Observe the following landmarks when entering: On the north side the old watchtower Torre d'en Beu, next to it a radar station on a hexagonal lighthouse with black and white stripes. On the south side the modern housing estate Cap Blau.

Upon entering some small buoys can be seen on the port side, situated right before the short pier – they are easily overlooked when unoccupied. These are for private use only, so please keep off. Anchoring is not permitted either because of the busy fairway (including larger fishing boats).

The berths are sheltered, but strong inshore winds create swell. In that case in front of the cliffline cross seas build up due to wave reflection.

Caution: *Fishing boats leave and enter with speed. This causes waves at the berths, so keep a bit more distance.*

FESTMACHEN
FIND A BERTH

A Es sind wirklich nur die wenigen Liegeplätze im vorderen Teil der kurzen Pier. Die Bojen im schmalen Seitenarm neben den Liegeplätzen sind privat und sollten als solche respektiert werden.
Auf der Außenseite der Mole („Moll Transit") Anlegen mit Bug oder Heck an Muringleinen; ca. 5-3 m Wassertiefe. Holzplattform unterhalb der Mole zum leichteren Übersteigen. 220+380 V+Wasser vorhanden.

Only these few berths are available for visitors. Buoys in the small branch off the berths are private and must be respected as such. Berthing at the outer part of the pier („Moll Transit") with mooring lines, lying bow or stern to. Depth approx. 5-3m. Wooden platform below the pier for convenient access. 220+380V and water supply available.

Reservierung notwendig, mindestens drei Tage im Voraus über www.portsib.es. Bezahlung per Kreditkarte. Stornierung oder Umbuchung über die Webseite und das Kundentelefon: 902 024 444 + 971 628 089

Reservation recommended at least 3 days in advance at www.portsib.es. Payment by credit card. For cancelation or changes please go to the web-

Cala Figuera

- Mallorcas „Fjordhafen" – ein Unikum
- Große Fischfangflotte – viele Restaurants
- Wenige Liegeplätze – aber preiswert

- *A Mallorcan fjord port – unique*
- *Large fishing fleet – many restaurants*
- *Few berths – but inexpensive*

Fl(3)R 10s

page or call customers helpline:
902 024 444 + 971 628 089

Office:
Im Obergeschoss der Fischauktionshalle, nur wenige Meter von den Liegeplätzen entfernt / *In upper storey of fish market hall at only a few metres' distance from the berths*
T 971 645 242
port.calafiguera@portsib.es
🕑 8-15 h (winter), 8-20 h (summer)
€ EUR/m2: 0,60 (01/06-30/09); 0,18 (01/10-31/05). Water: 5,50 EUR; Electr.: 5,50 EUR. Alle Preise / *All prices plus 21% MwSt. /VAT*

Sanitäreinrichtungen unter dem Hafenbüro. / *Sanitary facilities below harbour office.*
Abpumpstation für Bootstanks am Kopf der Mole / *Extraction unit for holding tanks at the pier's head*

TANKEN / *FUEL*

Die Station hier bedient nur die Fischer. Nächste Bootstankstelle in Cala d'Or.
This filling station is for fishing boats only. Next one in Cala d'Or.

RESTAURANTS & BARS

1 Am Hafen / *Above the harbour:*

Bon Bar, Café gleich oberhalb der Mole mit schöner Aussichtsterrasse
Situated next to the pier, with a nice terrace overlooking the harbour.
Mistral, T 971 645 118
www.mistral-restaurante.com
Cala, T 971 645 018
hostalcala@hotmail.com
La Marina, T 971 645 270
L'Arcada, T 971 645 032
Bar Restaurant Pizzeria
Es Port, T 971 165 140
Restaurant Pizzeria

2 **Petit Iglesia**,
T 971 645 009
C./ de la Marina; franz. Küche / *French*

Portbook & Island Guide 129

Mallorca

3 **Pura Vida**
Aussichtsrestaurant auf der Steilküste / *Restaurant with Cabrera view*
Ab Spätherbst geschlossen; Wiedereröffnung meist kurz vor Ostern / *Closed at end of autumn – reopens just before Easter*

Täglich/daily 10-23 h, T 971 165 571
info@pura-vida-mallorca.com
www.pura-vida-mallorca.com

EINKAUFEN / *SHOPPING*

Gleich oberhalb der Mole ein kleiner Supermarkt. Spar-Markt und Bio-Markt im höher gelegenen Teil der Ortschaft.

Small supermarket located directly above the pier. Spar supermarket and whole food shop can be found in the higher part of town.
C./ San Pere and C./ d'Iglesia

DANCING / DISCOS

La Gota, Musicbar, C./Pintor Bernareggi

AUSFLÜGE / *EXCURSIONS*

Spaziergang um den inneren Hafenteil, der von alten Bootshäusern umgeben ist. Weiter zum Wach- und Leuchtturm auf der Nordseite der Hafeneinfahrt. Der Weg führt im Nordzipfel der Bucht auf die Hochebene und dort nach rechts Richtung Meer.

Take a walk around the inner harbour, surrounded by old boat houses. Continue to the watchtower and lighthouse north of the harbour entrance. The route leads to the bay's northern corner and upstairs, later turns right towards the sea.

Spaziergang zum Südteil der Hafeneinfahrt mit Steilküste und Blick auf Wach- und Leuchtturm. / *Or hike to the southern harbour entrance with steep cliffs, overlooking the watchtower and lighthouse.*

Santanyi

4,5 km entfernt. Bus Linie 503. Von dort u.a. Verbindung nach Palma.
4.5km away. Bus no. 503, from there connections to Palma etc.
Fahrpläne/*Timetables*:
www.tib.org/portal/de/web/ctm/autobus/seccio/500

Anlässe können die Märkte sein (immer Mittwoch und Samstag, 9-13 h) oder aber einfach ein Streifzug durch Geschäfte und Galerien.

Your goal might be a visit to the market (always on Wed and Sat, 9-13h) or simply take a stroll around the shops and galleries.

39° 19,6' N 003° 10,6' E

Cala Figuera

Sehenswürdigkeiten in Santanyi:
- Die Kirche mit einer großen Orgel des bekannten mallorquinischen Orgelbauers Jordí Bosch. Sie befindet sich in einem Seitenschiff der Kirche.
- Das Rathaus mit Glockenturm. Auf dem Platz davor finden Märkte statt.

Sightseeing in Santanyi:
- *The church boasts a huge organ made by famous Mallorcan organ builder Jordi Bosch, located in the side aisle.*
- *The town hall with belfry. The markets are held on the square in front.*

MIETWAGEN / CAR RENTAL
Vima Rent a car
C/. La Marina, 25, T 971 645 353
www.vimarentacar.com

FAHRRÄDER / BIKES
„bike total", C./Bernareggi 26
Richtung / towards Santanyí
T 971 645 271, M 650 422 233
www.bike-total.com

TAUCHEN / DIVING
Cabrera Divers, T 971 645 300
Neben dem Hafenbüro
Close to the harbour office
www.cabrera-divers.com

FIW 5s

Cala Mondragó / Cala d'es Burgit

ANKERPLÄTZE
ANCHORAGE AREAS

A Cala Mondragó
39° 20,8' N 003° 11,8' E

🇩🇪 Eine der bekanntesten Buchten der Ostküste. Naturgeschützt, aber dennoch stark frequentiert, von Land, wie vom Meer. Liegt mittig zwischen Cala Figuera und Portopetro. Der westliche der beiden Strände wird S'Amarador genannt.
Ankern vor einer abgetrennten Badezone für beide Strände auf 5-7 m. Grund: fast reiner Sand. Café und Restaurant an beiden Stränden. Duschen und Toiletten vorhanden. Es besteht eine Busverbindung nach Portopetro und Cala d'Or.

🇬🇧 *One of the best known bays on the east coast. Though a nature reserve, Cala Mondragó is nevertheless much frequented. Situated almost in the middle between Cala Figuera and Portopetro. Depth in front of separated bathing area for both beaches 5-7m. Bottom: basically all sand, only some spots of weed. Bar and restaurant on both beaches. Toilets and showers available. Bus connection to Portopetro und Cala d'Or.*

B Cala d'es Burgit
Eine kleine Einbuchtung unmittelbar östlich mit Platz für maximal drei Yachten. Grund: ebenfalls Sand. Tiefe 5-8 m. Schnorcheln und Fische gucken am besten an den Felswänden. / *A small neighbouring bay with space for three yachts only. Bottom: sand, depth 5-8m. Good snorkeling along the cliff walls.*

Cala Mondrago – Cala d'es Burgit

Cala d'es Burgit

**BUY YOUR NEW BOAT
FOR THE PRICE OF A PREOWNED**

SAVE 40% OFF - DOWNPAYMENT: 35% ONLY
66 MONTHS CHARTER MANAGEMENT PROGRAM - ZERO OPERATING EXPENSES
RECIPROCAL OWNER USE WORLDWIDE - 42 CHARTER BASES, OVER 800 BOATS

+33 (0) 4 94 62 31 67 - +33 (0) 6 71 69 66 17 - yachtsales@dreamyachtcharter.com

DREAM YACHT CHARTER

www.DreamYachtCharter.com

AMERICA | ASIA | CUBA | CARIBBEAN | ENGLAND | INDIAN OCEAN | PACIFIC | FRANCE | CORSICA | CROATIA | GREECE | TURKEY | BALEARICS

Mallorca
Mallorca

Fl(2)R 7s

Dinghies

Náutica Amengual
T 971 654 353, M 686 099 755
nauticaamengual@hotmail.com

YACHTAUSRÜSTER
CHANDLERIES

D Mas Nautica
T 971 643 578

RESTAURANTS & BARS

Vom Dingi-Anleger sind es nur wenige Schritte zu den zahlreichen Restaurants. Eine Auswahl: / *The numerous restaurants are only few steps away from the dinghy pier. A selection:*

1 Ca'n Martina
Nicht der perfekte Hafenblick, aber guter Service. / *Not the perfect harbour view, but good service.*
T 971 657 517 + 971 657 218

2 Beim Yachthafen ... mehrere Restaurants, zum Teil mit schönem Blick auf die Bucht.
Some restaurants close to the marina, partly with a beautiful view on the bay.

Blend, T 971 092 118,
www.blendmallorca.com, Bar & Snacks, WiFi kostenlos für Gäste/ *free for guests*

Es Bergant, T 971 648 400
La Caracola, T 971 657 013
Antichi Sapori, T 971 658 002
www.antichisaporiportopetro.com

3 Porto Petro, T 971 657 704
Nautic, T 643 565
Restaurant Maritimo,
T 971 658 050
Schnitzelhaus, T 971 659 182,
www.suremar.com

4 Restaurant Rafael y Flora
T 971 657 809
La Aventura, T 971 657 167

Portopetro

Fl(2+1)G 12s

39° 21,3' N 003° 13,1' E

EINKAUFEN / SHOPPING

Zwei kleine Supermärkte, einer davon direkt vom Hafen. Dort auch ein Bankautomat. / *Two small supermarkets; one in front of the port, where there is also an ATM.*

AUSFLÜGE / EXCURSIONS

Spaziergang entlang der Hafenbucht und vorbei am Hotel „Blau Porto Petro" zum Leuchtfeuer auf der Südhuk an der Einfahrt.
A walk along the bay, passing hotel "Blau Porto Petro" towards the lighthouse on the southern head of the bay entrance.

D **Mas Nautica**, Verleih von Fahrrädern, Seekajaks, Stand-Up-Padel boards / *rents bikes, sea kayaks, Stand-Up-Padel boards.* T 971 643 578

E **Petro Divers**, M 660 75 91 91 Tauchschule / *Diving school.* www.petro-divers.eu

MIETWAGEN / CAR RENTAL

Neben dem kleinen Supermarkt an der Hafenstraße / *Next to the small supermarket on the harbour street.*

Busverbindungen
Bus Connections

Entlang der Ostküste und nach Palma, Verbindungen und Fahrpläne unter:
Along the east coast and to Palma, connections and timetables on:
www.tib.org/portal/de/web/ctm/autobus/seccio/500

Die Linie 501 stellt eine Verbindung nach Palma her. / *Bus no. 501 connects the bay with Palma.*

Portbook & Island Guide 137

Cala d'Or

Mallorca

🇩🇪 Als der Bauboom Mallorca erfasste, bekam nahezu jede Bucht mit Sandstrand ihre Hotels, Apartmentanlagen und Villen. Hier in der Cala Llonga wurde ein Yachthafen errichtet und mehrfach erweitert. Seinen Namen erhielt er von der Nachbarbucht, Marina Cala d'Or. Sie ist mit über 500 Liegeplätzen der zentrale Bootsparkplatz an Mallorcas Ostküste. Gastplätze sind im Sommer dennoch rar. Besucher sollten sich anmelden.

Vom Wartekai bei der Tankstelle an der Außenmole blickt man auf den alten Teil von Cala d'Or: eine Reihe Fischerhäuser mit kleinen Bootschuppen – bemerkenswert in dieser touristisch geprägten Umgebung. Die Ortschaft Cala d'Or ist jedoch nur in den Sommermonaten und zu Ferienzeiten belebt, dann aber sehr.

🇬🇧 *When the construction boom hit Mallorca, almost every bay with a sandy beach was covered with hotels, apartment buildings and villas. Here in Cala Llonga they started the construction of a marina which later was enlarged several times. It was named Cala d'Or, according to the adjoining bay. With around 500 berths Cala d'Or is today the central marina on the east coast. Visitor's berths are rare during high season, it's recommended to make a reservation.*

From the the filling station one looks at the old part of Cala d'Or: A row of fishermen's houses with small boat sheds – remarkable in a touristic center like this. Cala d'Or is lively only in the summer months and during holiday periods, but then it's a place to enjoy.

ANSTEUERUNG
APPROACHING

Ein schwarz-weiß längst gestreiftes Einfahrtsfeuer, **Fl (1+2) 20s**, auf der Südseite der Bucht beim restaurierten Kastell Forti. Befeuerte Tonnenpaare markieren ein Fahrwasser bis hinein in die Marina. Dort Wassertiefen zwischen 4 und 2,5 m.

Black-and-white striped entrance light at southern shore of the bay near restored Forti castle. Green and red buoys mark the channel directly in front of the marina. Here depths 4 to 2.5m.

FESTMACHEN
FIND A BERTH

A Marina de Cala d'Or

Gastplätze befinden sich im hinteren Teil der Marina an Backbord und nehmen am sommerlichen Leben im Hafen teil. Bei der Tankstelle an der Einfahrt gibt es einen Wartekai.

Guests' berths are situated in the back of the marina at port side, where they share in the marina's summer bustle. At the filling station located at the marinas entrance there is also a waiting pier.

€ 12,50 m – 62 EUR (Jun-Sept),
47 EUR (April, May + Oct.),
31,40 EUR (Jan.-March + Nov., Dec.)

Cala d'Or

- Motoryachten prägen das Bild
- Sommer-Trubel – Winter-Stille
- Restaurants und Bars in Fülle

- *Motor yachts dominate the scene*
- *Busy in summer – quiet in winter*
- *Many restaurants and bars*

39° 22,1' N 003° 14,3' E

inkl. Wasser, Strom, plus 21% MwSt. *Water, electricity included, plus 21% VAT.* / Für Yachten, deren Besatzung tagsüber nur für 2-3 Stunden anlegen will, zum Einkaufen, Essen gehen oder Wasser tanken, gibt es Kurzzeit-Tarife: 10 oder 20 EUR, je nach Größe. Details auf Anfrage. *For yachts docking during the day only for 2-3 hours (for shopping, eating or fill up water) there are short-term rates: 10 or 20 EUR, depending on the size. Details on request.*

UKW/VHF 09 (24 h)
info@marinacalador.es
www.marinacalador.es
T 971 657 070
Office, Mon-Fri 9-13 h, 15-19 h; Sat, Sun+hol.9-13 h

Duschen und Toiletten: in der Nähe des Marinabüros in neuen Gebäuden und am Ende des Hafenbeckens beim Werftgelände (hinter dem Yachtclub Cala d'Or), 24 Stunden geöffnet / *Toilet and shower facilities: located near the marina office inside new buildings, at the end of the port basin next to the yard (behind Yacht Club Cala d'Or); open 24 h*

WiFi Kostenlos im Marinabüro und in der näheren Umgebung. Es gibt für Dauerlieger und Gäste eine Wi-Fi Lounge angrenzend an das Marina-Büro. *Free of charge in the marina's office and close surroundings. For permanent berth holders and guests there is a Wi-Fi lounge adjacent to the Marina office.*

Mallorca

ANKERPLÄTZE
ANCHORAGE AREAS

B **Cala Llonga**
Kurz vor der Einfahrt zur Marina vor einem kleinen Strand mit abgeteilter Schwimmzone. Wassertiefe um 5 m, Ankergrund Sand und Seegras. Schwell passierender Yachten.
Just before the entrance to the marina in front of a small beach with swimming zone. Depth around 5 m, bottom sand and weed. Swell of passing yachts.

C **Cala d'Or**
Vor einer abgeteilten Schwimmzone. Wassertiefe um 5 m, Ankergrund Sand und Seegras. / *Anchorage in front of a beach with seperated swimming zone. Water depth around 5 m, bottom sand and weed.*

D **Cala Gran**
Beim Anlaufen der Marina die erste Bucht an Steuerbord. Ankern vor dem abgeteilten Schwimmbereich. Hier guter Schutz gegen auflandige Winde. An Land Bars und Restaurants. Grund: Sand mit Seegras, Tiefe 4-6 m.
When entering the marina this is the first bay on starboard side. Anchorage in front of a marked bathing area. Well protected against inshore winds. Bars and restaurants ashore. Bottom: sand with weed, depth 4-6m.

TANKEN / *FUEL*

D + B; Mit Bedienung / *With service*
April + May: Mon-Sat 10-14 h, Sun + hol. closed
June: Mon-Sat 10-14 h + 16-19 h, Sun + hol. 10-14 h
July + August: Mon-Sat 10-14 h + 16-20 h, Sun + hol. 10-14 h
Sept.: Mon-Sat 10-14 h + 16-19 h, Sun + hol. 10-14 h
Oct.: Mon-Sat 10-14 h + 16-19 h, Sun + hol. closed
Außerhalb der Zeiten Selbstbedienung
Outside of opening hours self service
Nov.-March: Selbstbedienung mit Kartenzahlung / *self-service and payment by credit card*

TECHNISCHER SERVICE
TECHNICAL SERVICES

1 **Werftgelände der Marina**
Shipyard Travellift: 65 + 45 t
Mon-Fri: 8-13 h + 14-17 h
Motor-Service: Volvo Penta, Cat, Mercruiser; Anstriche, Osmose-Behandlung
Painting, Osmosis treatments

Fahrwasser vor der Marina / *Marked channel in the marina entrance*

Cala d'Or

YACHTAUSRÜSTER / *CHANDLERIES*

2 **Nautica Guimar**
T 971 846 010, M 678 469 291
info@nauticaguimar.com
In der Marina / *inside marina premises*

6 **Nautica Martin,** T 971 657 157
nautica@nauticamartin.com
Im Ort, nahe Kreisverkehr Richtung Calonge / *In Cala d'Or, near the roundabout towards Calonge*

RESTAURANTS & BARS

3 Auf der Nordseite der Marina:
At the marinas northern part:
Restaurant Proas, T 971 643 380
Mallorquinische Küche zu fairen Preisen; höher gelegen mit schönem Blick auf den Hafen. / *Mallorcan cuisine at fair prices; situated on the upper level with a fine harbour view.*
restauranteproas@hotmail.com
Peking Duck, T 971 643 441
China-Restaurant / *Chinese restaurant*
Port Petit, T 971 643 039
gehobenes Niveau / *exalted level*
www.portpetit.com
La Vida
T 971 659 573, M 638 071 997
www.lavida-calador.com
Sa Ancora, T 971643492
Treffpunkt vieler Eigner / *favourite place of many yacht owners*
La Scala
Italienische Küche, erhöhte Terrasse / *Italian cuisine, elevated terrace*
T 971 643 325, M 679 662 781
www.lascalarestaurante.com
19-23 h, Mon closed

Auf der Südseite der Marina:
Located at the marinas southern part:

4 **Yachtclub Cala d'Or**
Zutritt für Gäste: ab 15 EUR/Tag (Nebensaison). Angebot des Clubhauses: Bar, Bistro, Restaurant, Pool, Tischtennis, Wi-Fi, Computerraum, Bücherei, Sauna etc. / *Entrance fee for guests min. 15 EUR /day (low season). The club building houses: bar, bistro, restaurant, pool, ping-pong, Wi-Fi, computer room, library, sauna etc.*
T 971 648 203, www.yccalador.com

2 **Gadus,** T 971 659 134
Restaurant, Bar, Bistro
Tue-Sun 12-15 +18-24 h

5 **Botavara,** T 971 658 035
Porto Cari, T 971 657 947

EINKAUFEN / *SHOPPING*

Großes Angebot an Läden für internationale Mode etc. im Zentrum. Ein kleiner Supermarkt gegenüber vom Hafenbüro. Größere Supermärkte in Cala d'Or, fußläufig erreichbar. / *Large range of shops for international fashion etc in the town centre. Small supermarket in front of the harbour office. Several large supermarkets can be reached on foot.*

6 Einer der größten befindet sich beim Kreisverkehr am Ortsrand Richtung Calonge, „Eroski". / *One of the biggest is situated on the outskirts roundabout in S'Horta direction.*

NIGHTLIFE

Eine überreiche Auswahl an Discos & bars im Ort Cala d'Or / *A rich selection of bars and clubs in Cala d'Or*

SERVICE

MIETWAGEN / *CAR RENTAL*
Die meisten Autovermieter haben ihren Sitz an der vierspurigen Allee am Ortsrand in Richtung Calonge. Mit Europcar ein größerer Vermieter im Zentrum des Ortes, Avenida Es Ravells.
Most car rentals are located at the four-lane avenue on the edge of town towards S'Horta. Larger Europcar branch resides in the town's centre at Avenida Es Ravells. T 902 105 055

Busverbindungen / *Bus Connections*
Entlang der Ostküste und nach Palma, Verbindungen und Fahrpläne unter
Along the east coast and to Palma, timetables and connections on:
www.tib.org/portal/de/web/ctm/autobus/seccio/500

ACTIVITIES

Das Zentrum von Cala d'Or hat ein sehr breites Angebot an Geschäften und Restaurants auf kleinem Raum.
Wide variety of shops and restaurants to settle the small centre of Cala d'Or.

Besuch der Festung Forti (17. Jhd.)auf der Südseite der Einfahrt zur Hafenbucht. Sie ist die einzige historische Sehenswürdigkeit von Cala d'Or (Eintritt frei). / *A visit to the fortress Forti (17th century) on the south side of the bay's entrance. It's the only historical monument in Cala d'Or (free entrance).*

Sommer-Jazz-Festival
24.05.2016 - 31.05.2016
www.jazz-rolf.de => Termine

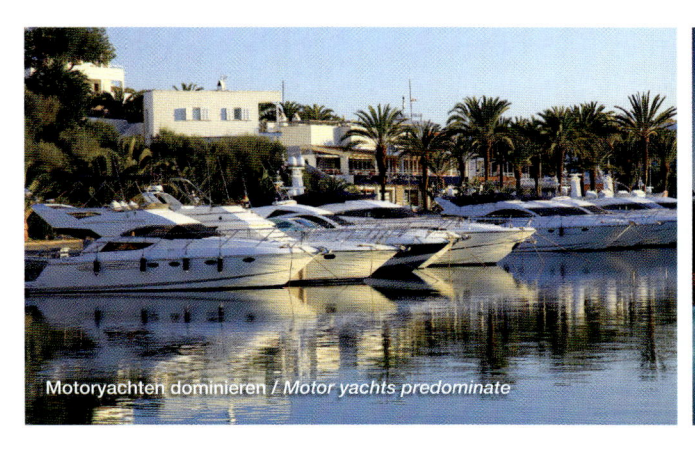

Motoryachten dominieren / *Motor yachts predominate*

Yachtclub Cala d'Or

Mallorca

Cala Esmeralda – Cala Marsal

ANKERPLÄTZE
ANCHORAGE AREAS

A   Cala Esmeralda, Cala Serena, Cala Ferrera
39° 22,5' N 003° 14,6' E

🇩🇪 Dreifingerbucht gleich nördlich von Cala d'Or. Hier liegt man nördlichen Winden gut geschützt. Umgebung viele Hotel- und Apartment-Anlagen mit zahlreichen Gaststätten und Geschäften. Große Wassertiefen im Zufahrtsbereich der Bucht, 16-10 m. An der Nordseite der Einfahrt eine kleine Insel (El Illot), die landseitig passiert werden kann, Durchfahrtstiefe 17 m. Ankerplätze vor abgetrennten Badezonen auf 7-4 m. Grund überwiegend Seegras mit Sandflecken.
ACHTUNG: Etwas außerhalb der Küstenlinie liegt vor der Cala Esmeralda eine unbezeichnete Untiefe, die mit 4,4–3,5 m in Seekarten eingetragen ist, Bajos de Cala Ferrera. Ebenfalls zirka 4 m hat eine weitere Untiefe vor der Steilküste zwischen Marina Cala d'Or und diesen Buchten.

🇬🇧 *Bay with three small beaches fringed by hotels and apartment buildings. Many restaurants and shops can be found here. Good protection against northerly winds. Drop achor in front of the marked bathing areas. Bottom: mostly weed with some sandy spots, depth 7-4m. Isle El Illot at the north side of the entrance can be passed on both sides, depths up to 17 m.*
CAUTION: *In front of Cala Esmeralda there is a shoal called Bajos de Cala Ferrera with only 4.5-3.5m water depth. There is another shoal almost in the middle between Marina Cal d'Or and these bays with again around 4m water.*

B   Cala Mitjana
39° 23,2' N 003° 15,0' E

Eine kleine und dabei sehr geschützte Bucht, gut eine 1 sm nordöstlich von Cala d'Or. Sie ist umgeben von einem parkähnlichen Anwesen. An der Steuerbordseite der Einfahrt steht ein weißer Signalmast. Untiefen sind nicht zu beachten. Ankern im Nordzipfel der Bucht auf 8-4 m, Grund viel Sand, wenig Seegras. Im Zipfel der Bucht ein kleiner Sandstrand, davor ein abgesperrter Bereich. Ist die Bucht stark belegt, können Landleinen zum Ostufer nötig sein.
A small, very sheltered cove, 1nmi northeast of Cala d'Or, surrounded by a park-like property. On the starboard side of the entrance white signal mast. No shoals. Drop anchor in the northern tip of the bay, where bottom mostly sand with little weed. Depths 8-4m. There is a small sandy beach with a marked swimming zone. Depending on

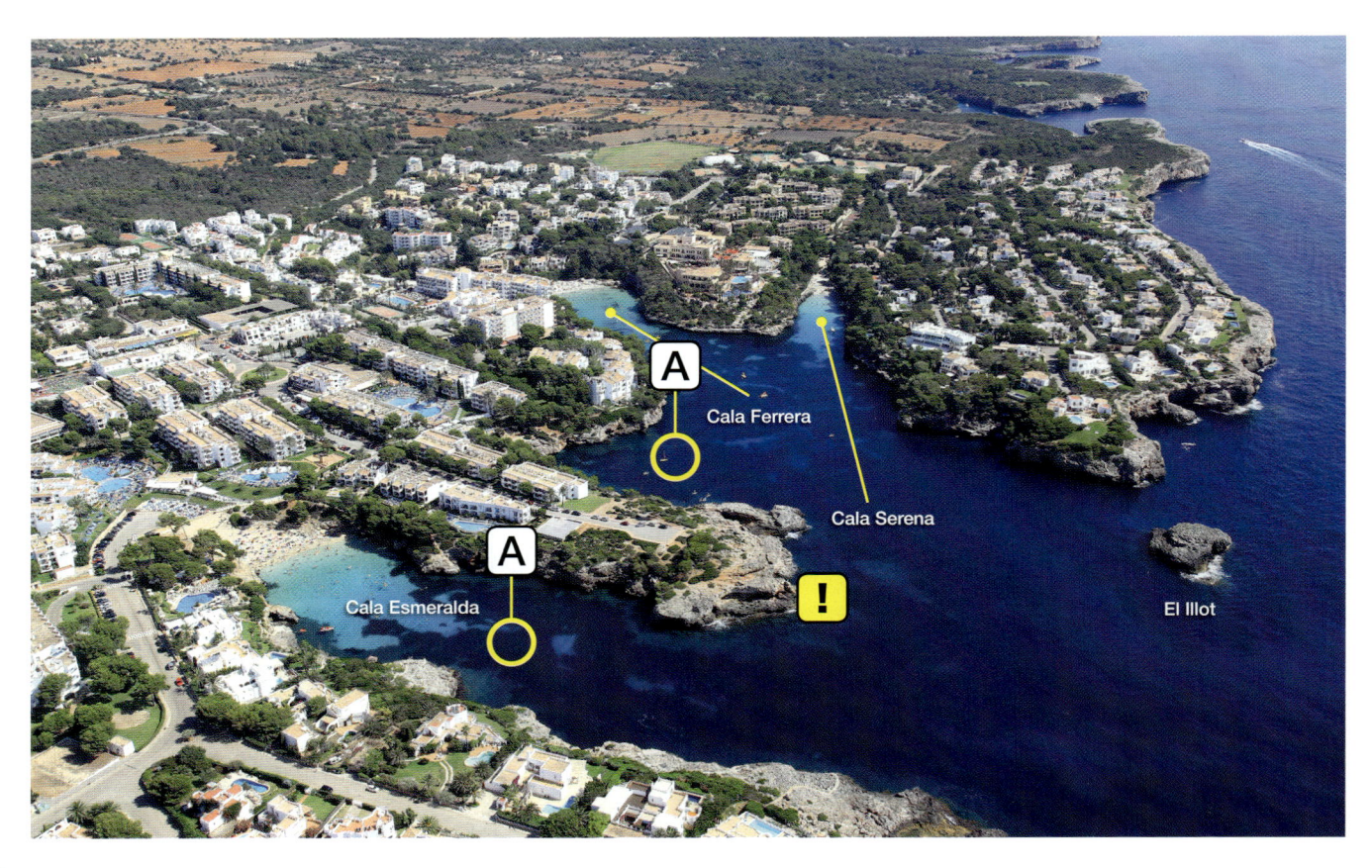

Cala Esmeralda – Cala Marsal

how far the bay is occupied, a mooring may be necessary to the eastern shore.

C Cala Arsenau
39° 23,6' N 003° 15,2' E

Diese Bucht liegt nur 0,5 sm nördlich der Cala Mitjana. Bucht und Einfahrt sind frei von Untiefen. Ankern über Sand und Seegras, Wassertiefen 6-4 m, direkt vor der Badezone nur noch 2,50 m. Störend sind die ein- und auslaufenden Ausflugsboote. Es gibt eine Strandkneipe (Chiringuito), sonst keine Versorgung.

This bay is located only 0.5nmi north of Cala Mitjana. Bay and entrance are free of shoals. Drop anchor over mostly sandy bottom, water depths 6-4m, directly in front of the bathing area only 2.50m. Disturbing are the incoming and outgoing tour boats. There is a beach bar (Chiringuito), otherwise no supply.

D Cala Marsal
39° 24,6' N 003° 15,9' E

Die Strandbucht von Portocolom, südlich der Einfahrt zum Naturhafen. Bei nördlichen und auflandigen Winden unruhig.

Auf der Südseite Hotels und Appartement-Anlagen, aber viel Ankerraum und fast reiner Sandgrund. Wassertiefen 6-4 m vor einer Badezone. Ansteuerung frei von Untiefen. Bars, Restaurants und Geschäfte auf der Südseite der Bucht und Richtung Portocolom. Dazu: Bankautomaten und Autovermieter.

Mehrmals am Tag kommt mit hoher Geschwindigkeit ein Ausflugsboot, um an der Südseite der Bucht Passagiere aufzunehmen oder abzusetzen.

The main beach of Portocolom, south of the entrance to the natural harbour. Less protection when northerly or onshore winds occur.

Plenty of space to drop anchor over almost pure sandy bottom. Water depths 6-4m in front of a swimming zone. No shoals of concern. Some hotels and apartment buildings on the south side and behind the beach, more direction Portocolom. Car rentals and ATM can be found also in the vicinity.

Excursion boats enter several times per day to board or land passengers at the south side of the bay.

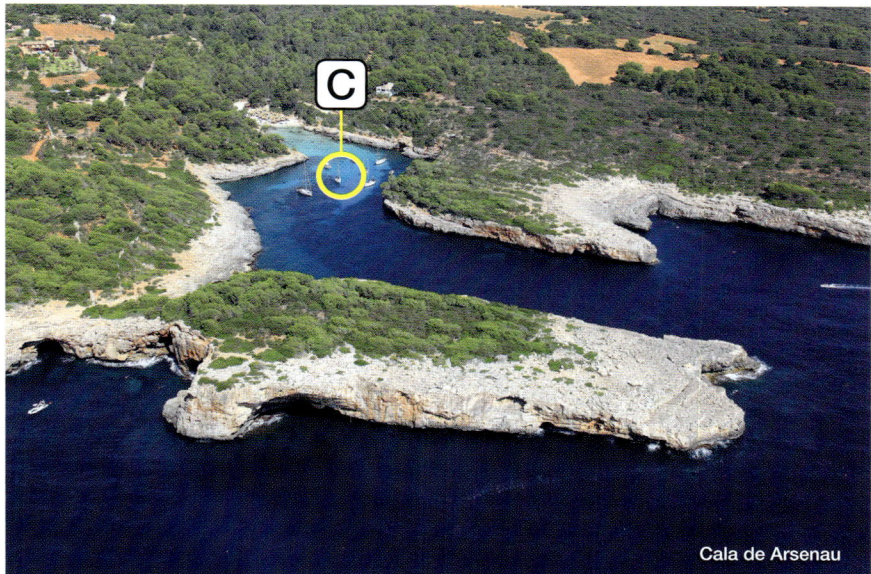

Cala Mitjana

Cala de Arsenau

Portocolom

Cala Marsal

Mallorca

Portocolom

🇩🇪 Es ist das Unprätentiöse, das in Portocolom den Gast gefangen nimmt. Denn die Ortschaft, ehemals Handelshafen der 10 km im Hinterland gelegenen Gemeinde Felanitx, hat dem Tourismus seit Jahren nur bedingt Tribut gezollt und in großen Teilen ihren Charakter bewahrt.

So gibt es bis heute keine große Marina, sondern nur die modernisierte Steganlage eines Yachtclubs und ein großes Bojenfeld. Typisch für Portocoloms Hafenbucht sind die farbenfrohen Bootshäuser im südwestlichen Teil der Bucht und die Llauts, wie die traditionellen Fischerboote heißen, rund um den alten Ortskern. Immer präsent ist der hohe, schwarz-weiß gestreifte Leuchtturm am Eingang zur Hafenbucht. 1965 wurde er das zweite Mal aufgestockt, um weitere 10 m.

Ankern ist in der Hafenbucht nur noch vor dem kleinen Strand S'Arenal in der Einfahrt unweit des Leuchtturms und über Sandflecken erlaubt. Es wurde an dieser Stelle kontrolliert, dass Yachten nicht für Tage bleiben.

🇬🇧 *The visitor will be captured by Portcolom's unpretentiousness. The former trading port to Felanitx, 6mi inland, it is hardly affected by tourism (only close to Cala Marsal) and has maintained its character. One will only find a small marina run by a local yacht club. So berths for vistors can be rare in summer but fortunately there is large buoy field.*

Typical for Portocolom are the colourful boat sheds found in the southwestern part of the bay and the numerous traditional fishing boats, so-called llauts, to be found first of all around the old centre. The black and white, striped lighthouse stands imposingly at the harbour's entrance and has been enlarged twice, the last time in 1965, adding another 10m in height.

Anchoring is only permitted in front of the small beach S'Arenal at the bay entrance close to the lighthouse and above sandy spots. Authorities have checked from time to time that yachts do not stay here on anchor for longer than 24 hours.

ANSTEUERUNG
APPROACHING

Befeuerte, grüne und rote Tonnen markieren in der Bucht ein Fahrwasser. Es führt durch ein großes Bojenfeld bis zu verschiedenen Liegeplätzen im nördlichen Teil der Bucht (Steganlagen des Club Náutico Portocolom und von portsIB), siehe Karte auf der folgenden Seite.

Lighted red and green buoys mark a channel into the bay; that leads along large buoy fields up to the berths on the north side (piers of Club Nàutic Portocolom and of portsIB), see chart on the following pages.

FESTMACHEN
FIND A BERTH

A **Ports Islas Baleares, portsIB**
Schwimmstege. Anlegen mit Bug oder Heck an Muringleinen. Wassertiefe in der äußeren Hälfte der beiden langen Stege 2,50 m und mehr. Rund um den kurzen Steg nicht mehr als 2 m. *Floating pontoons. Use mooring lines, bow or stern to. Depth around the outer part of the two long pontoons 2.50 m and more. Around the short one is not more than 2 m.*

Reservierung notwendig, mindestens drei Tage im Voraus über www.portsib.es. Bezahlung per Kreditkarte. Stornierung oder Umbuchung über die Webseite. / *Reservation required at least 3 days in advance at www.portsib.es. Payment by credit card. For cancelation or changes please visit the website.*

Office
Nahe der Moll Comercial, wo sich auch die Tankstelle befindet. / *Near Moll Comercial, where filling station is located as well.* T 971 824683
port.portocolom@portsib.es
8-15 h (winter), 8-20 h (summer), daily

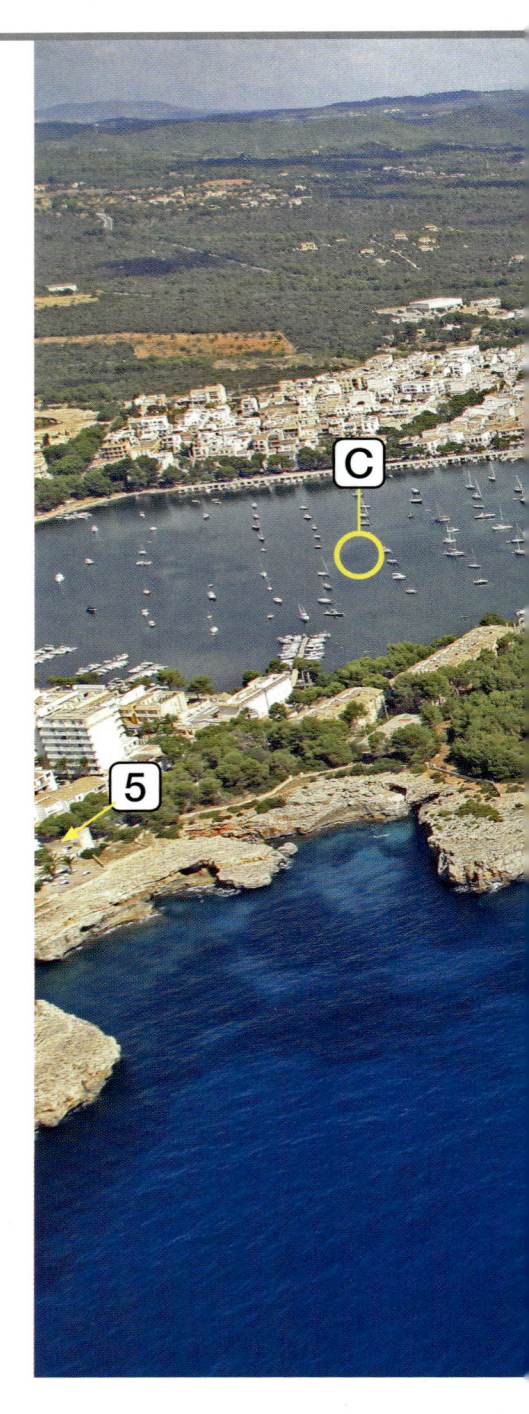

€ Steg/Pier: 0,60 EUR/m2 (01/06-30/09); 0,18 (01/10-31/05), Boje / *Buoy:* 0,18 EUR/m²; Water: 5,50 EUR; Electr.: 5,50 EUR. Alle Preise / *All prices plus 21%* MwSt. / *VAT*

Einfache Duschen und Toiletten im Gebäude des Hafenbüros. / *Simple sanitary facilities in harbour office building.*

B Auf der Außenseite der Handelsmole „Moll Comercial" (mit Tankstelle), wenn frei. Häufiger wird für das Anlegen hier nicht kassiert. Im Sommer

Portocolom

39° 24,6' N   003° 16,3' E

Fl(2)10s

- Hafenbucht mit großem Bojenfeld
- Viele Steganlagen für Gastyachten
- Zahlreiche Restaurants am Wasser

- *Harbour bay with large buoy field*
- *Many berths for yachts in transit*
- *Numerous restaurants on waterfront*

hier viel Betrieb durch Ausflugsschiffe. Kein Strom. Für Wasser nehmen wird meist 5 EUR kassiert.
On the outside of the commercial pier (with filling station), when unoccupied. Probably free of charge. Intensively frequented by excursion boats in summer. No electricty. Filling up water is usually charged with 5 EUR.

C Bojenfeld im Südwesten der Bucht (Zona II). Für Boote bis 1,30 m Tiefgang und 7 m Länge. Die Bojen sind zum überwiegenden Teil an Dauernutzer vergeben.
Buoy field in the southern part of the bay (Zona I). For boats with draught up to 1.30 m and max. 7m length. Nearly all buoys are given to long term users. Boje/ *Buoy:* 0,18 EUR/m²/day

Club Nàutic Portcolom
Liegeplätze Gastyachten / *Visitor berths:*

D Auf der Außenseite der Außenmole / *outer side of the breakwater*

E Moll Sis Cents (Schwimmstege / *floating pontoon* (15/04 – 15/10)

36 Plätze bis 15 m Länge, ca. 3 m Wassertiefe / *36 berths, max 15 on length, around 3m depth*

F Bojenfelder / *Buoy fields:*
Auf beiden Seiten des betonnten Fahrwassers; die Bojen sind mit Buchstaben für eine maximale Bootslänge markiert. A: bis 12 m, B: bis 15 m, C bis 20 m
On both sides of buoyed channel; mooring buoys carry letters indicating maximum boat length. A: up to 12 m, B: up to 15 m, C up to 20 m

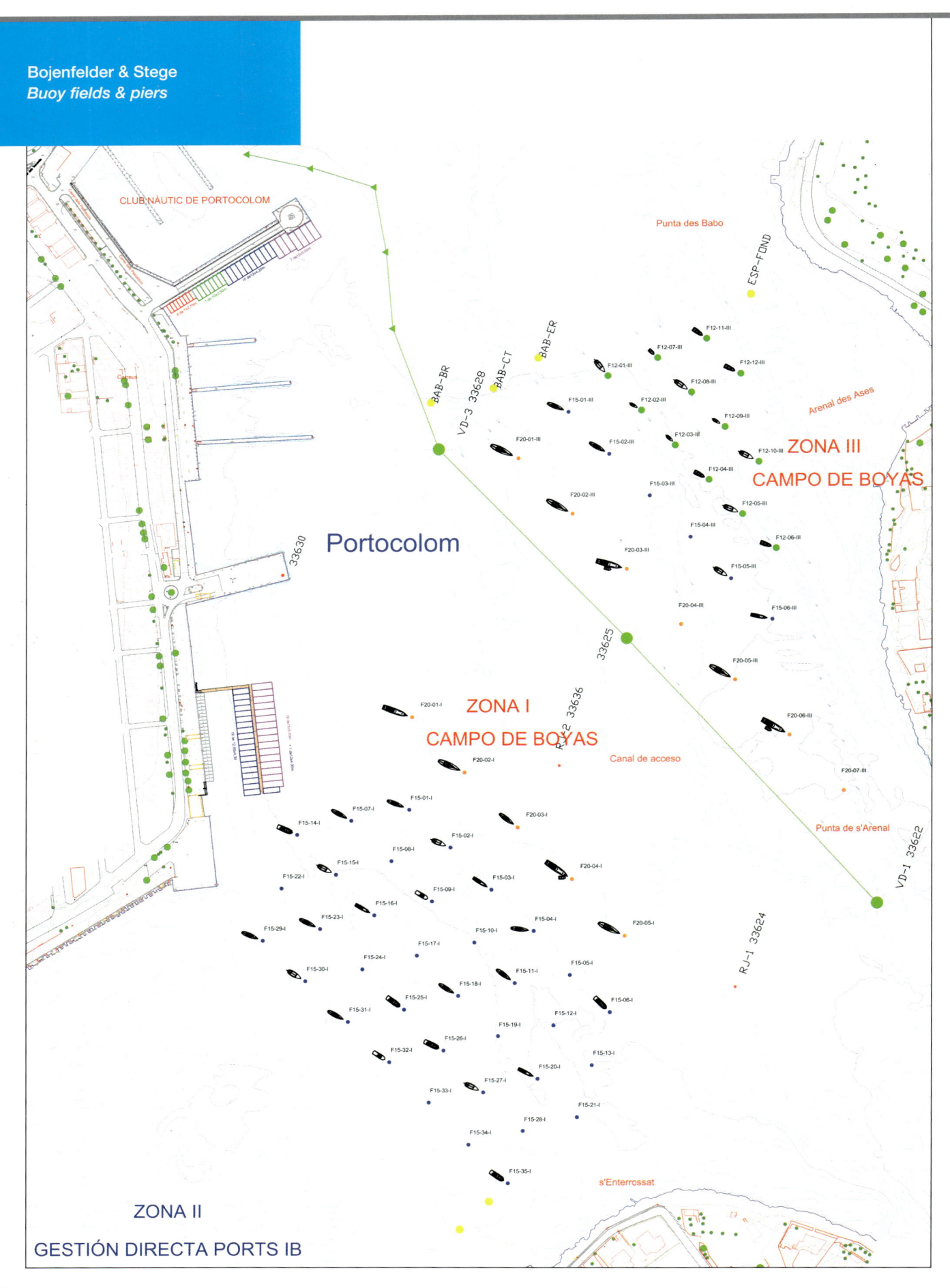

Mallorca

Bojenfelder & Stege
Buoy fields & piers

Portocolom

ZONA III CAMPO DE BOYAS

ZONA I CAMPO DE BOYAS

ZONA II — GESTIÓN DIRECTA PORTS IB

Portocolom

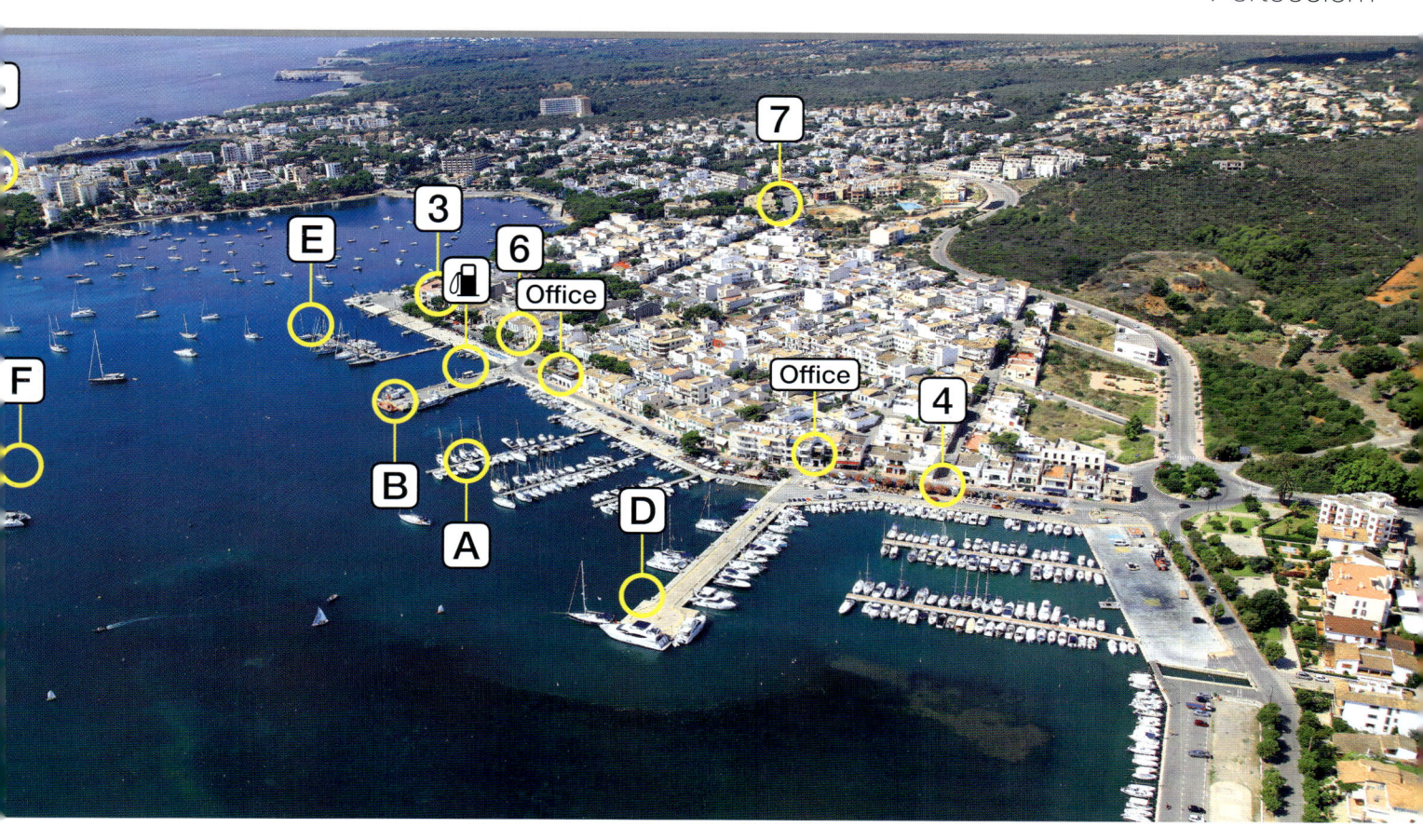

Achtung: Das Bojenfeld Zona III östlich des Fahrwassers liegt entsprechend der Konzession nur in dieser Zeit aus: 15/04–15/10; das Bojenfeld Zona I ist ganzjährig installiert.
Caution: The buoys field Zona III east of the bouyed channel is in place in accordance with the concession only at this time: 15/04–15/10; The buoys field Zona I west of the bouyed channel is in place all year round.

Office 📱 UKW/VHF-Kanal 9
T 971 824 658 (Club), M 604 117 605 (Marineros)
Sprachen/*Language*: Deutsch / English
administracio@cnportocolom.com
www.cnportocolom.com

🕒 01/06-30/09: 8-15 + 15.30-19.30 h (Mon-Fri), 9-14 h (Sat) | 01/10-31/05: 9-13.30 + 15.30-19 h (Mon-Fri)

€ Auf der Außenseite der Clubanlage
Outer jetty: 12-13 m: 70 EUR (June-Sept), 56 EUR (Oct.-May)
Sommersteg Moll Sis Cents / *floating pontoon*, 13-14 m: 70 EUR (July+Aug.), 60 EUR (June+Sept.)

Bojen-Kategorien / *Buoys categories*
A: bis 12 m, EUR 24 / 19 (1/10-31/05)
B: bis 15 m, EUR 35 / 28 (1/10-31/05)
C: bis 20 m, EUR 56 / 45 (1/10-31/05)
Wasser, Strom und MwSt. inkl. / *Water, electr., VAT incl.*

inklusive Mehrwertsteuer und Hafengebühr G-5, Benutzung der sanitären Anlagen unterhalb des Büros des Yachtclubs und Wasserbunkern. / *Including VAT and harbour tax G-5, use of toilet and shower facilities underneath the yacht club's office, water refill.*

ANKERPLÄTZE
ANCHORAGE AREAS

[G] Vor dem kleinen Sandstrand Playa s'Arenal mit Badezone bei der Einfahrt in die Hafenbucht. Grund: Sand und Seegras, Tiefe ca. 4 m. Strandbars (u. a. „Blue Bar") für Snacks und Drinks.
In front of small sandy beach Playa s'Arenal with bathing area at the entrance to the port bay. Bottom: sand with sea weed, depth around 4m. Beach bars (e.g. Blue Bar) serving snacks and drinks.

TANKEN / *FUEL*

D + B, Moll Comercial, T 971 824 201
esport@benzineradesport.com
www.benzineradesport.com
Mon-Sat: 8-14 h, Sun: 9-12 h, Jan-Dec

TECHNISCHER SERVICE
TECHNICAL SERVICES

Power Boats Service S.L.
(Volvo Penta etc.)
T 971824266, M 639 386 318
www.mallorca-boats-service.com

Náutica Gomilla, T 971 824 034
www.nauticagomila.com

Porto Colom Yachting S.L
Oliver Wallpott
T+F 971 879 459 + 971 826 078

YACHTAUSRÜSTER
CHANDLERIES

Ferreteria Artigues
Carrer de Marina, 14, T 971 825 521
www.ferreteriaartigues.com
Ferreteria in der / *at*
C./ Cristofor Colom, 73

Portbook & Island Guide

Mallorca

Cala Murada – Cala Rajada

🇩🇪 Der Buchten-Marathon geht weiter. Cala Rajada mit dem Cabo de Pera ist Mallorcas östlicher Punkt. Von hier sind es nur 20 sm bis Menorca.

🇬🇧 *Further north we see again some of Mallorca's finest bays. Cala Rajada is the easternmost town of the island. From here, the distance to Menorca is a mere 20nmi.*

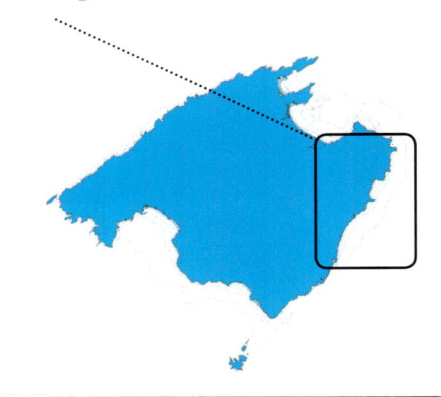

1 **Cala Domingos - 39° 27,4' N 003° 16,8' E** → page 152
An Land große Hotels und Apartment-Anlagen; bester Ankergrund.
Large hotels and apartment facilities ashore; bottom pure sand.

2 **Cala Antena – 39° 28,0' N 003° 17,0' E** → page 152
Schöne Atmosphäre zwischen hohen Kliffs. Auf der Südseite ein hohes Hotel.
Nice atmosphere between high cliffs. On the south side an elevated hotel.

3 **Cala Virgili, Pilota, Magraner - 39° 29,0' N 003° 17,6' E** → page 152
Pure Natur umgibt diese Buchten. Freeclimber in der Cala Magraner.
Bays surrounded by pure nature. Watch free-climbers in Cala Magraner.

4 **Cala Barcas - 39° 29,9'N 003° 18,1'E** → page 155
Die vielleicht beliebteste Bucht im Nordteil der Ostküste, entsprechend voll.
Perhaps the most popular bay in this area, and frequented accordingly.

5 **Cala Estany, Mandia & Angulia - 39° 31,0' N 003° 19,1' E** → page 155
Nur die Cala Estany war zuletzt als Ankerplatz nutzbar. Viel Landtourimus.
Only Cala Estany can be used as anchorage. Many touristic resorts.

6 **Porto Cristo - 39° 32,2' N 003° 20,5' E** → page 156
Für eine Überfahrt von und nach Menorca die Alternative zu Cala Rajada.
Can be a good alternative to Cala Rajada for a passage to and from Menorca.

7 **Cala Petita - 39° 32,8' N 003° 21,4' E** → page 160
So groß kann klein sein: Mit Glück findet man hier seine Privatbucht auf Zeit …
So small, it's great: With luck you will find your private bay for a while …

8 **Cala Morlanda - 39° 33,3' N 003° 22,3' E** → page 160
Feiner Sandboden, ruhige Umgebung. Nur ab und an stört ein Ausflugsschiff.
Bottom pure sand, tranquil surroundings. Only excursion boats can disturb.

9 **Ensenada de la Moreyra - 39° 34,4' N 003° 22,8' E** → page 161
Ein offener Ankerplatz, aber von betörender Wasserfarbe. Schutz bei Mistral.
Breathtaking ocean colour makes a stop worthwhile. Protection during Mistral.

10 **Cala Bona - 39° 36,9' N 003° 23,7' E** → page 162
Die Bucht ist ein Hafen, einer der kleinen auf Mallorca. Geringe Wassertiefe.
One of Mallorca's small harbours. Rather shallow water depth.

11 **Cala Canyamel - 39° 39,3' N 003° 26,6' E** → page 164
Ein sehr offener Platz, aber bei ruhigem Wetter ideal für die Höhle von Artá.
Perfectly suited for a visit to Artá cave in calm weather.

12 **Font de Sa Cala - 39° 39,3' N 003° 26,6' E** → page 165
Trotz Bebauung stimmungsvolle Bucht. Kleinboote können unterwegs sein.
An evocative bay. Many small boats may cruise here.

13 **Cala Rajada - 39° 42,5' N 003° 27,8' E** → page 166
Der Ort ist im Sommer lebhaft, sehr schöne Promenade am Meer.
Very lively town in summer, beautiful seaside boardwalk.

Der Osten Mallorcas II / The East of Mallorca II

- 1 Cala Domingos
- 2 Cala Antena
- 3 Cala Virgili, Pilota & Magraner
- 4 Cala Barcas
- 5 Cala Estany, Mandia & Angulia
- 6 (Porto Cristo)
- 7 Cala Petita
- 8 Cala Morlanda
- 9 Ensenada de la Moreyra
- 10 Cala Bona
- 11 Cala Canyamel
- 12 Font de Sa Cala
- 13 Cala Rajada

Portbook & Island Guide

Mallorca

Cala Domingos – Cala Mandia

ANKERPLÄTZE
ANCHORAGE AREAS

A Cala Domingos
39° 27,4' N 003° 16,8' E

🇩🇪 Bucht mit zwei stark frequentierten Sandstränden. Nutzbar bei ablandigen Winden oder insgesamt ruhigen Bedingungen. Ankern auf 5-3 m. Reiner Sandgrund. Dingi-Passagen neben abgetrennten Badezonen. Umgebung Hotels, Apartments, Strandbars, Restaurants, Geschäfte. Zwei Kabellängen südlich liegt die Cala Murada. Ankergrund hier eine Mischung aus Sand, Seegras und Fels.

🇬🇧 *Bay with two highly frequented sandy beaches. Good with offshore winds or in calm conditions. Drop anchor on 5-3m depth. Pure sandy bottom. Dinghy passages next separated bathing areas. Ashore hotels, apartments, beach bars, restaurants, shops. Two cable lengths south lies Cala Murada. Bottom here sand, weed and rocks.*

B Cala Antena
39° 28,0' N 003° 17,0' E

Schöne Atmosphäre zwischen hohen Kliffs. Auf der Südseite ein hohes Hotel. Bei der Einfahrt näher zur Nordseite halten. Ankern auf 6-4 m über fast reinem Sandgrund. Im Scheitel ein kleiner Strand, Versorgung in der Siedlung auf der Steilküste. Auch die unmittelbar nördlich anschließende Einbuchtung ist als Ankerplatz nicht zu verachten. 0,5 sm nördlich liegt Cala Bota. Sie ist nur für kleine Boote geeignet. **Achtung:** Knapp überspülte Felsen auf der Südseite! / *Nice atmosphere between high cliffs. On the south side an elevated hotel. At the bays entrance keep closer to the north side. Anchor at 6-4m over almost pure sandy bottom. Supply in the tourist resort on the cliff coast. Also the directly adjoining bay can be used as an anchorage. 0.5nmi north there is Cala Bota. This bay is only suitable for small boats.* **Caution:** *rocks on the south side of the bay's entrance!*

C Cala Virgili, Pilota & Magraner
39° 29,0' N 003° 17,6' E

Drei Buchten in unbebauter Umgebung. Bei auflandigen Winden kein, bei Nord- und Südwind wenig Schutz. Die Strände werden auch von Land besucht, die Kliffs im nördlichen Arm, Cala Magraner, sind das Ziel von Freeclimbern. Der Meeresboden in den Einfahrten ist frei von Untiefen. Cala Virgili: In der Einfahrt noch Seegras, später überwiegend Sandgrund, geankert wird auf etwa 5-4 m Tiefe. Auf der Nordseite dieser Bucht gibt es die Cova de ses Dones (Höhle der Frauen), in die man hineinschwimmen kann. Cala Pilota und Cala Magraner: ebenfalls Ankern auf 5-4 m über Sand.

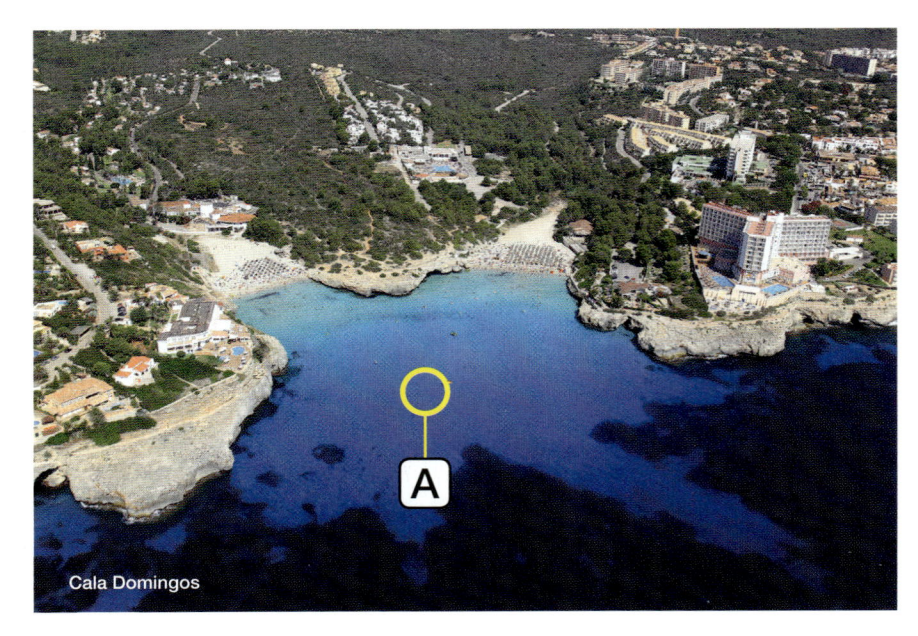

Cala Domingos – Cala Mandia

0,5 sm nördlich giot es eine weitere Dreifingerbucht, deren Einschnitte aber weniger ausgeprägt sind. Überwiegend sandige Ankergründe, keine Untiefen.

Three bays in undeveloped surroundings. No protection with onshore winds and little when northerly and southerly winds occur. The beaches are also visited by regular tourists, the steep cliffs in Cala Magraner, are frequently used by free climbers. No shoals to take care of. Cala Virgili: further out weed, later sandy bottom. Drop anchor at about 5-4m depth. Cala Pilota and Cala Magraner: also at 5-4m above sand. 0.5nmi north again three, but smaller bays can be found lying close together. Mostly sandy bottom, no shallows.

Mallorca

154 Portbook & Island Guide

Cala Domingos – Cala Mandia

D Cala Barcas
39° 29,9'N   003° 18,1'E

Diese wunderschöne Bucht mit ihrem türkisfarbigen Wasser ist auf der Nordseite von Kliffs mit einem bekannten Felsbogen flankiert. Einige Besucher springen von hier gerne ins Meer. Immer wieder kommen Ausflugsboote mit Urlaubern aus den nahen Hotelanlagen und Küstenorten. Die Schiffe legen auf der Südseite der Bucht an.

Der Meeresboden in der Einfahrt ist frei von Untiefen, der Ankergrund reiner Sand. Man ankert auf 5-3 m Wassertiefe. Die Bucht ist gegenüber dem Meer recht offen. Keine Versorgungsmöglichkeiten. Die Strände werden auch von Land aus stark frequentiert. Unmittelbar nördlich finden wir die Cala Falcó, mit ebenfalls schönem Sandgrund.

This beautiful bay with its turquoise waters is flanked on the north side by cliffs with a well known arch. Visitors jump down here. Frequently excursion boats dock on the south side of the bay carrying tourists from nearby resorts and coastal towns. The bottom is free of shoals and pure sand. Boats go on anchor at 5-3m depth. The bay is not well protected to the sea. No supply ashore. The beaches are frequented also by regular tourists.

E Cala Estany, Cala Mandia, Cala Angulia
39° 31,0' N   003° 19,1' E

Drei Buchten dicht nebeneinander, 1,5 sm südwestlich von Porto Cristo. Nur die Südseite der Cala Estany ist frei von Bebauung, sonst zahlreiche Hotels, Appartements und Ferienhäuser. Nur die südliche Cala Estany war zuletzt als Ankerplatz nutzbar, es gab keine abgetrennte Badezone. Vor den beiden anderen Buchten waren die gelben Tonnen soweit Richtung Meer ausgelegt, dass sich Ankern nicht mehr anbot.

Die Zufahrten zu den Buchten sind frei von Untiefen. In der Cala Estany ankern auf 6-3 m über reinem Sandgrund. Bei östlichen Winden unruhig. Restaurants, Bars und Geschäfte auf der Nordseite der Bucht. Busse verkehren zum nahen Porto Cristo.

Three bays in between 0.5nmi, 1.5nmi southwest of Porto Cristo. Only the southern side of Cala Estany is free of buildings, the rest is covered with numerous hotels, apartments and summer residencials. At last only the southernmost Cala Estany could be used as an anchorage, without a separated bathing area. At Cala Anguila and Cala Mandia the yellow bouys were laid out extremly far out. Approaches to the bays are free of shoals. In Cala Estany anchor at 6-3m depth over pure sandy bottom. Unsettled with easterly winds. Restaurants, bars and shops on the north side of the bay. Buses to nearby Porto Cristo.

Mallorca

Porto Cristo

🇩🇪 Porto Cristo hat alles, was man sich von einem Hafenort wünschen kann: Fjordartig umschließen Felswände beschützend die Liegeplätze, man findet einen schönen Sandstrand, Crews können zwischen zahlreichen Restaurants wählen. Und sollte die Technik mal streiken, dann gibt es hier gute Service-Betriebe, einen großen Yachtausrüster und einen Werftbetrieb mit Bootstankstelle.

Porto Cristo ist auch ein wichtiger Hafen Richtung Norden, will man die recht offenen Liegeplätze in Cala Rajada vermeiden. Und es ist der Heimathafen von Rafael Nadal, Tennisstar aus dem nahen Manacor.

🇬🇧 *Porto Cristo has it all: Fjord-like cliffs give shelter to the berths, there is a nice beach, crews can choose between several restaurants. In case of a technical breakdown you will find here experienced service companies, a large chandlery and a shipyard that also runs the boat filling station.*

Porto Cristo is also the last important harbour for all heading north and like to avoid the unsheltered berths of Cala Rajada. And it's the homeport of tennis champion Rafael Nadal, born in the nearest town, Manacor.

ANSTEUERUNG
APPROACHING

Die Einfahrt ist problemlos, überall ausreichend Wassertiefen. Aber Fischer, Ausflugsschiffe und schnelle Tauchboote sind zu beachten.

An easy approach with sufficient water depths everywhere. But pay attention to fishing, excursion and fast going diving boats.

FESTMACHEN
FIND A BERTH

A **Club Nàutic Porto Cristo**
Einlaufend an Backbord Schwimmstege mit Muringleinen. Gäste liegen an der Innenseite des ersten Stegs am darauf folgenden Steg. Auf der Innenseite des Wellenbrechers werden für die Sommermonate acht Festmachemöglichkeiten und Versorgungsterminals für Yachten bis 20 m Länge installiert. Gute sanitäre Anlagen.

Floating pontoons with mooring lines on portside when entering. Guests dock at the inside of the first pontoon and the following. Inside the breakwater, eight berths with mooring lines and supply terminals are provided during summer months for yachts up to 20m long. Good sanitary facilities.

€ 11-12 m
85,03 EUR (June-Sept), 76,53 EUR (March-May+Oct), 59,52 EUR (Nov-Feb) *incl. water, electr., Wi-Fi, pool, showers* plus 21% VAT
Ebenfalls eingeschlossen: die Benutzung des Schwimmbads (Juni.-Sept,)
Also included: the use of swimming pool (June-Sept.)
Keine Monatstarife im Sommer, aber Winterangebote (01/10-31/05) / *no monthly fees in summer, but special offers for the winter period* (12,50: 350 EUR/month)
T 971 821 253 📱 UKW/VHF 09
direccion@cnportocristo.com
www.cnportocristo.com
🕐 21/03-30/09: Mon-Fri: 9-13+16-19, Sa 9-13 h; 01/10-20/03: Mon-Fri: 9-16, Sa 9-14 h

B **PortsIB**
Einlaufend an Steuerbord: Anlegen mit Bug oder Heck an Muringleinen. 25 Plätze sind online buchbar, davon 15 bis 15 m Länge. Achtung: Es gibt einen Mauervorsprung bei den weiter innen liegenden Plätzen. Beim Anlegen mit dem Heck hier auf ausreichend Abstand achten.
Reservierung notwendig, mindestens drei Tage im Voraus über www.portsib.es. Bezahlung per Kreditkarte. Stornierung oder Umbuchung über die Webseite.

Entering on starboard: Berthing, bow or stern to, with available mooring lines. 25 berths are available for booking online, of which 15 are up to 15 m length. Caution: There is a ledge at the more inward berths. When you dock here stern to keep distance.
Reservation required at least 3 days in advance at www.portsib.es. Payment by credit card. For cancelation or changes please visit the website.
Office: T 971 820 419
Bei den Liegeplätzen.
Close to the berths.
port.portocristo@portsib.es

Porto Cristo

- Bekannt für seine Höhlen
- Inmitten toller Buchten
- Schönes Hafenambiente

- *Famous for its caves*
- *Surrounded by many bays*
- *Nice harbour ambience*

Fl(3)R 10s
4,0
6,0
8,0
39° 32,2' N 003° 20,5' E
Fl 5s

ANKERPLÄTZE
ANCHORAGE AREAS

[C] Einlaufend an Steuerbord für max. 6 Boote auf 5-3 m. Sandgrund mit Seegras. Verschiedene Plätze zum Anlanden mit dem Dingi. Etwas unruhig durch passierende Schiffe, aber kostenlos.

Entering on starboard, for max 6 boats only at 5-3m depth. Sandy bottom and weed. Several dinghy landing options. Slight swell from passing vessels, but free of charge.

TANKEN / *FUEL*

T 971 820 653
01/06-31/09: 9-19 h (Mon-Fri),
10-14 h (Sat, Sun + hol.)
01/10-31/05: 9-17 h (Mon, Wed, Fri),
10-14 h (Sat), Sun + hol.: closed

TECHNISCHER SERVICE
TECHNICAL SERVICES

Yacht Concept Mallorca
Peter Kuklok – Boots-Technik, Lackierungen etc. / *Engineering, paintwork et cetera*. C./ Vela 22, Porto Cristo
T 971 820 976, M 619 658 312
www.yachtconceptmallorca.com

Marina Marbella Balear
Betreibt die Tankstelle und das Werftgelände; dort 60-t-Travellift & 12-t-Kran
Runs the filling station for boats and the shipyard with 60t travellift & 12t boatcrane. T 971 820 653,
www.marinamarbella.net

🕐 **Office**
16/03-14/10: 9-19 h
15/10-15/03: 9-18 h

Mallorca

Jaume Vermell, C./ Port, 126
Großer Yachtausrüster und Bootshändler am Kreisverkehr Richtung Manacor
Big chandlery and boat dealer at the roundabout direction Manacor
T 971 822 022, M 649 406 094
www.vermell.com

Swi-Tec, Neveta Náutica S. L.
Schweizer Hersteller hochwertiger Yachtausrüstung; auch Einzelanfertigungen; Propeller-Reparatur mit Spezial-Maschine etc. An der Straße von Porto Cristo nach Manacor, km 9
Swiss manufacturer of quality yacht equipment; also custom-made devices; propeller repair with special machine etc. On the road from Porto Cristo to Manacor, km 9, T 971 822 426
SWI-TEC Produkte / *products*:
www.swi-tec.com, info@swi-tec.com
Propeller-Reparatur / *Repair*:
www.neveta-nautica.com
info@neveta-nautica.com

YACHTAUSRÜSTER / *CHANDLERIES*

Yacht Concept Mallorca,
→ s.o. / see above
Jaume Vermell
→ s.o. / see above
Swi-Tec, Neveta Náutica S. L.
→ s.o. / see above

WÄSCHEREI / *LAUNDRY*

Tintoreria / Lavanderia Miguel
C./Port, 40; gutes Preis-/Leistungsverhältnis / *good value for money*

RESTAURANTS & BARS

1 Im Gebäude des Club Nàutic Porto Cristo / *inside the building of Club Nàutic Porto Cristo*

2 **Restaurant Soma**
Beim Werftgelände – Interessante Speisekarte und nicht überteuert; man sitzt erhöht, z. T. mit Blick auf den inneren Hafenteil / *Close to shipyard premises – Interesting menu and not overpriced; i. a. terrace overlooking the inner part of the marina.*
T 971 820 450, soma2013@outlook.es

3 **Es Revet**
Kult-Kneipe für den „Sundowner" an der Straßenbrücke hinter dem letzten Hafenteil. Einfache Bestuhlung.
Hip pub for sundowner, at the road bridge behind the inner part of the port. Simple seating.

4 Am inneren Teil des Hafens mit erhöhter Terrasse: / *in the inner part of the harbour, with elevated terrace:*
Siroco, T 971 822 444

Sa Pedra, T 971 820 932
Ein Bild zeigt Tennis-Star Rafael Nadal in jüngeren Jahren, gebürtig aus Manacor, als Gast / *A photograph shows young Rafael Nadal, the tennis star from Manacor, as a guest.*
www.restaurantsapedra.com

Quince
T 971 821 830, info@quince15.es

Trattoria d'il Porto
T 971 820 198
latrattoriadilporto@gmail.com

5 **Hotel THB Felipe**
4 Sterne, Terrasse, zivile Preise
4 stars, terrace, decent prices
T 971 820 750
www.thbhotels.com

EINKAUFEN / *SHOPPING*

2 Neben dem Eingang zum Restaurant „Soma" Mini-Supermarkt „Varadero", auch für Brot und Brötchen.
Next to the entrance of restaurant „Soma" mini-supermarket „Varadero", even for bread and rolls.

6 Kleine Supermärkte (Spar etc.) am Marktplatz und in den angrenzenden Straßen; Wochenmarkt immer Sonntagsvormittag.
A couple of small supermarkets are situated on the market square and in the adjacent streets; weekly market on Sundays.

7 Größere Supermärkte Richtung Manacor und Cala Millor am Ortsrand / *Larger supermarkets direction Manacor and Cala Millor, on the outskirts of town.*

AUSFLÜGE / *EXCURSIONS*

Cuevas del Harms & Cuevas del Drach
Die „Drachenhöhlen" liegen in unmittelbarer Nähe des Hafens. Ein Besuch der Drachenhöhle ist interessant, aber nicht spektakulär. Die Cuevas del Harms befinden sich an der Straße von Porto Cristo nach Manacor.

The caves of Harms and Drach are close to the port. A visit is interesting but nothing spectacular. The Cuevas del Hams are located on the road from Porto Cristo to Manacor.
www.cuevasdeldrach.com
www.cuevas-hams.com

🚌 Bus-Verbindungen vom Marktplatz, Fahrplan: / *Bus connections via market place, timetable:* www.tib.org/portal/de/web/ctm/autobus/seccio/500

Cuevas del Drach

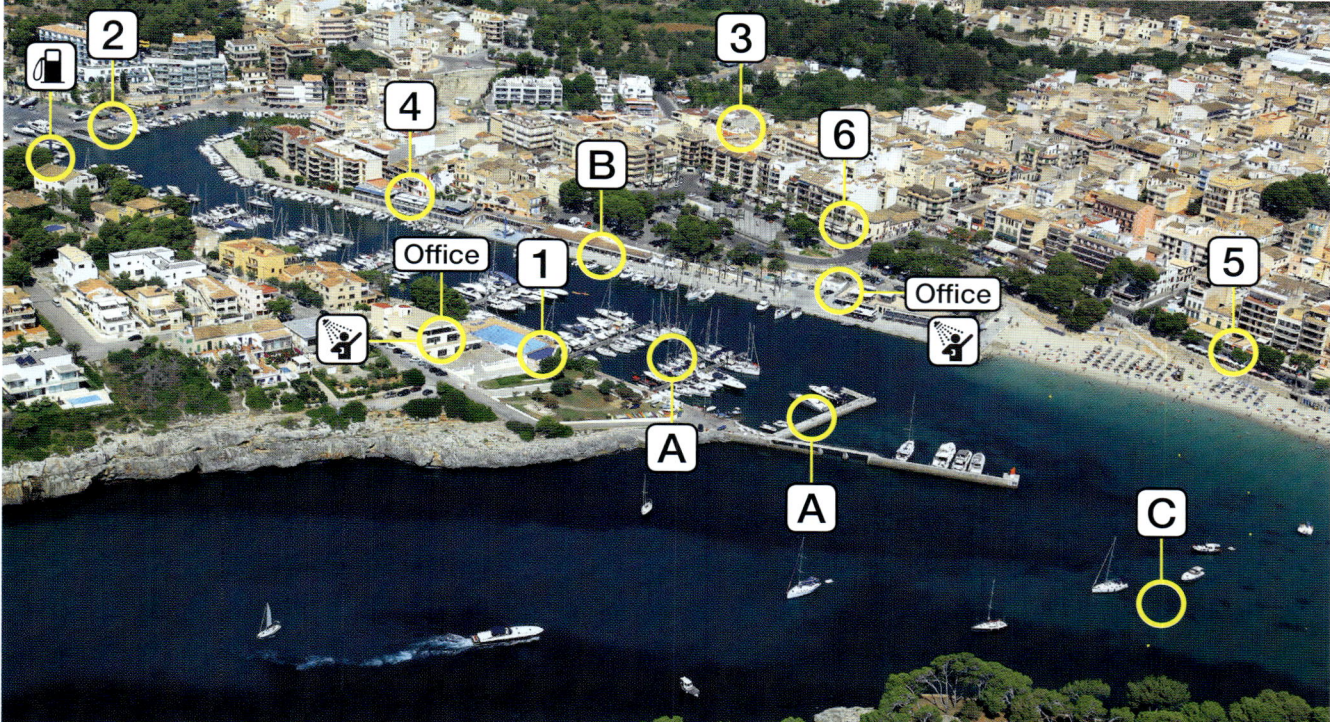

Porto Cristo

Werftgelände, Tankstelle und Liegeplätze
Boat yard, petrol station and berths on both sides

Portbook & Island Guide 159

Cala Petita – Ens. de la Moreya

Mallorca

ANKERPLÄTZE
ANCHORAGE AREAS

A Cala Petita
39° 32,8' N 003° 21,4' E

Ein Stück stille Natur. 1 sm nördöstlich von Porto Cristo. Wie der Name sagt, klein und schmal, so dass man sie auf der Seekarte leicht übersieht. Ankern erst im letzten Zipfel über Sandgrund. Wassertiefen hier 4-3 m. Evtl. ist eine Landleine nötig. Keine Untiefen in der Ansteuerung.

Just quiet nature at 1nmi NE of Porto Cristo. As the name indicates, this bay is small and narrow, easy to miss on the chart. Anchoring above sandy bottom. Deths here 4-3m. Depending on the conditions a mooring line ashore might be neccesary. No shoals in the approach.

B Cala Morlanda
39° 33,3' N 003° 22,3' E

Eine gern übersehene Bucht. Feiner Sandboden, ruhige Umgebung. Nur ab und an stört ein Ausflugsschiff. Keine Untiefen, Wassertiefen zum Ankern 8-5

Cala Petita – Ensenada de la Moreya

m. Für Schutz gegen nördliche Winde besser die Ensenada de la Moraya aufsuchen, gut 1 sm nördlich. Geschäfte, Restaurants etc. zirka 1 km nördlich Richtung S'Illot.

An underrated bay. Bottom pure sand, tranquil surroundings. Only excursion boats can disturb. No shallows, water depths for anchoring 8-5m. For protection against northerly winds better visit Ensenada de la Moraya, only 1nmi north. Shops, restaurants etc. about 0,5mi north towards S'illot.

C Ensenada de la Moreya
39° 34,4' N 003° 22,8' E

Ein offener Ankerplatz südlich der Landzunge von Punta de Amer mit einer kleinen Festungsanlage. Aber guter Schutz bei Nordwind Mistral. Betörende Wasserfarben. Ankern auf 6-3 m Wasser, Grund überwiegend Sand. Keine Untiefen zu beachten. Mit Sa Coma, dem südlichen Teil von Cala Millor, gibt es an Land eines der großen Urlaubszentren Mallorcas, so dass man sich hiermit allem nötigen versorgen könnte.

An open anchorage south of the headland of Punta de Amer with a small fortress. But good protection if northwind Mistral occurs. Breathtaking sea colour makes a stop worthwhile. Drop anchor on 6-3m depth, mostly sandy bottom. No shoals to take care of. With Sa Coma, the southern part of Cala Millor, you will find ashore one of the big touristic centres of Mallorca. Therefore nearly everything is available here.

Cala Petita

Cala Morlanda

Ensenada de la Moreya

Mallorca

Cala Bona

🇩🇪 Der Ortsteil Cala Bona liegt am nördlichen Rand des touristischen Zentrum Cala Millor. Hier gibt es diesen kleinen Hafen für lokale Fischerboote und einige wenige Yachten mit bis zu 1,80 m Tiefgang.

🇬🇧 *The district Cala Bona is located on the northern outskirts of the tourist resort Cala Millor. There is this small harbor for local fishing boats and a few yachts of up to 1.80m depth.*

ANSTEUERUNG
APPROACHING

Keine Untiefen in der Ansteuerung. Die Molen sind befeuert, Fl(2)G 10s und Fl(2)R 10s. Das rote Feuer steht weiter außen und ist von daher evtl. früher zu sehen vor der hellen Beleuchtung der den Hafen umgebenden Ortschaft. Wassertiefe In der Hafeneinfahrt 3m.

No shallows in the approach. The heads of the breakwaters are lighted, Fl (2) G 10s and Fl (2) R 10s. The red light is further out and is therefore possibe to recognize in front of the bright lights of the surrounding buildings. In front of the breakwaters heads around 3m depth.

FESTMACHEN
FIND A BERTH

A In der Mitte des Hafenbeckens befindet sich die durch ein Schild gekennzeichnete „Moll Transit" für Gastyachten. Hier auf der Außenseite ein halbes Dutzend Liegeplätze mit Muringleinen. Wasser und Strom. Empfohlener max. Tiefgang: 1,80m. Reservierung notwendig, mindestens drei Tage im Voraus über www.portsib.es. Bezahlung per Kreditkarte. Stornierung oder Umbuchung über die Webseite.

In the middle of the harbour basin the visitor's pier is indicated by a sign „Moll Transit". On the outside half a dozen berths with mooring lines. Water and electricity available. Recommended max. draft: 1.80m.

Reservation required at least 3 days in advance at www.portsib.es. Payment by credit card. For cancelation or changes please visit the website.

Office:
T 971 586 256
port.calabona@portsib.es
Bei den Liegeplätzen.
Close to the berths.

🕐 08-18 h (01/10-31/05), 08-21 h, Mo-Fri, 08-15.30 h, Sat, Sun + hol. 08-15.30 h (01/06-30/09)

€ Steg/*Pier*: 0,60 EUR/m2 (01/06-30/09); 0,18 (01/10-31/05), Water: 5,50 EUR; electr.: 5,50 EUR. Alle Preise / *All prices* plus 21% MwSt. /VAT
Duschen und Toiletten im Gebäude des Hafenbüros. / *Sanitation inside the harbour office building.*

TANKEN / *FUEL*

Die Tankstelle neben den Gastliegeplätzen (Repsol) soll 2016 wieder in Betrieb gehen. Wassertiefe hier angeblich nur 1,70 m. Es gab dort 2015 auch eine funktionierende Absauganlage für Rückhaltetanks.

The gas station next to the guest berths (Repsol) is to go into operation in 2016. Water depth here supposedly only 1.70m. 2015 there was a operating extraction system for holding tanks.

TECHNISCHER SERVICE
TECHNICAL SERVICES

Ca'n Pep Thomàs
10 Min. zu Fuß Richtung Cala Millor.
10min. walk towards Cala Millor.
Paseo Maritimo,26, T 971 585 875

RESTAURANTS & BARS

1 Im Hafen Bar / Restaurant Thalassa, Rund um den Hafen ein halbes Dutzend Restaurants und Bars. / *Inside the port Bar / Restaurant Thalassa, around the harbour in addition half a dozen restaurants and bars.*

ANKERPLÄTZE
ANCHORAGE AREAS

B Im Nordwesten der Bahia de Arta zwischen Port Vey und dem Minihafen Costa del los Pinos (Wassertiefe zirka 1 m) lässt sich auf zirka 4-3 m Tiefe ankern. Sandgrund mit Seegras und Felsen. An Land ein Hotel, Mini-Markt, Bankautomat, Gaststätte.

The northwestern part of Bahia de Arta between Port Vey and the Mini Port Costa del los Pinos (water depth about 1 m) can be a sheltered place even with strong northerly winds. Anchor at 4-3m, bottom sand with weed and rocks. Ashore a hotel, convenience store, ATM, restaurant.

Cala Bona

Fl(2)R 10s

39° 36,9' N 003° 23,7' E

Costa de los Pinos

Portbook & Island Guide 163

Mallorca

Cuevas de Artà

Cabo Vermey

Cala Canyamel – Font de Sa Cala

ANKERPLÄTZE
ANCHORAGE AREAS

A Cala Canyamel
Cuevas de Artà
39° 39,3' N 003° 26,6' E

An der Cala de Canyamel liegt im vorspringenden Cabo Vermey eine der bekannten Tropfsteinhöhlen der Insel, Cuevas de Artà. Bei ruhigem Wetter und wenn man eine Ankerwache an Bord lassen kann, ist dieser Platz ein guter Ausgangspunkt zur Besichtigung der Höhle. Warme Kleidung mitnehmen. Man ankert im Nordwesten der Bucht auf 7-5 m reinem Sandgrund vor einem abgetrennten Schwimmbereich. Anlanden am Strand oder an einer Betonpier. Hinter einer Brücke über einen Süßwasserzufluss führt eine Treppe hoch zur Straße, die zur Höhle

Cala de Canyamel

Cala Canyamel – Font de Sa Cala

Font de sa Cala

führt. In der touristischen Ortschaft Canyamel gibt es Supermärkte Bars und Restaurants. Das wahrscheinlichste beste befindet sich in der Nähe der Brücke. Hier im Beach Hotel Cap Vermell kann man Blick auf das Boot vor Anker erlesen speisen.

Im Hinterland gibt es ein bekanntes Restaurant im Torre de Canyamel, ein alter Wehrbau. Spezialität: Spanferkel.

🇬🇧 *At Cala de Canyamel with the promontory Cabo Vermey one will find one of the famous caves of the island, Cuevas de Artà. In calm weather and with watchkeeping this achorage is a good starting point for a visit. Bring warm clothes. Drop anchor in the northwestern part of the bay in front of a separate swimming area. Depths 7-5m, pure sandy bottom. Landing on the beach or at a concrete pier. Behind a bridge over a freshwater inlet a staircase leads up to the road that terminates in front of the caves entrance. In the tourist resort of Canyamel you do provisioning. There are also bars and restaurants. One of these is located close to the mentioned bridge. The terrace of Beach Hotel Cap Vermell offers the perfect view over the anchorage. 3mi away there is a well known restaurant inside Torre de Canyamel, an old fortification. Speciality: suckling pig.*
www.cuevasdearta.com
€ 14 EUR, red. 7 EUR, < 7 J./y. free
🕙 10-18-h (April-Oct., daily)
10-17 h (Nov.-March. Daily)
www.capvermellbeachhotel.com,
T 971 841 157
www.torredecanyamel.com,
Tel. 971 841 310, reservas@restauranteporxadadesatorre.com

B Font de Sa Cala
39° 39,3' N 003° 26,6' E

Auf halber Distanz zwischen Cala Canyamel und Cala Rajada. Rund um die Bucht Einzelhäuser, Hotels und Appartementanlagen. Betrieb durch Ausflugsboote, Surfer, Strandkatamarane und Tretboote. Überspülte Felsen liegen vor der Nordseite der Bucht. In der Mitte der Einfahrt 10 m Wassertiefe, danach gleichmäßig abnehmend. Ankern auf reinem Sandgrund über 5-4 m Wasser vor einer abgetrennten Badezone. Hinter dem Sandstrand und an der Straße Richtung Cala Ratjada verschiedene Supermärkte, Bars und Restaurants.

Half distance between Cala Rajada and Canyamel. Around the bay private villas, hotels and apartment buildings. Excursion boats, surfers, beach catamarans and pedal boats are using the bay frequently. Submerged rocks on the north side of the bay. In the approach you will find depths around 10m decreasing steadily.
Anchors on pure sandy bottom about 5-4m of water in front of a swimming area. Behind the sandy beach and on the road to Cala Ratjada various supermarkets, bars and restaurants.

Mallorca

39° 42,5' N 003° 27,8' E

Fl G 5s

FlR 3s

TANKEN / *FUEL*

D+B, Mon-Sun 9-13 + 14-19h, (15/04-31/10),
Mon-Fri 9-13 + 16-19 h (01/11-14/04)

TECHNISCHER SERVICE
TECHNICAL SERVICES

Motonautica, T 971 563 188
Volvo Penta + div.
C./Monturiol, 20, Cala Rajada

RESTAURANTS & BARS

Die Reihe der Cafés und Restaurants rund um den Hafen ist fest geschlossen. / *An uninterrupted row of bars and restaurants lines the harbour.*

1 Restaurant Es Mollet
Italienisch / *Italian*; T 971 565 005
Es Llaut, T 971 563 561
Meeresfrüchte; etwas teuer, viel Einheimische / *Seafood: a bit expensive, many locals.*
Escorat, T 971 818 699
Spezialitäten Caldereta und Lagusten
Specialities: caldereta and lobsters
2 Auf der Westseite
on the west side:
Sa Fonda 74, Musikbar
T 971 818 222, www.safonda74.es
Portofino Sea Side, T 971 818 722
Fischrestaurant, Steakhouse; edel
Fish restaurant & steakhouse; elegant
www.portofino-calaratjada.com
Noah's, T 971 818 125
Sehr gutes Frühstück, leckere Snacks und Drinks. Blick auf den Hafen.
Good breakfast, tasty snacks and drinks. Overlooking the harbour.
Reservierungen auch über
Reservations: www.cafenoahs.com
3 Weitere Dutzend Lokale entlang der Promenade Richtung Playa de Son Moll. / *Many more establishments exist along the promenade towards Playa de Son Moll; notably:*
Café 3, T 971 565356
Einer der ersten Cocktail-Bars am Paseo Marítimo. Lifebands treten auf.
Among the first cocktail bars at Paseo Marítimo. Live band performances.
www.cafe3mallorca.com
Restaurant del Mar
April-June 11.30-15.00 + 18.30-24 h
July-Oct. 18.30-24h, Wed closed
T 971 565 836, M 689 263 067
www.mallorca-delmar.com

Cala Rajada

DANCING / DISCOS

Hier ist nachts einiges los: Zum Tanzen ins Physical, Chocolate, Keops etc.
Busy Nightlife: For dancing: Physical, Chocolate, Keops etc.

EINKAUFEN / SHOPPING

Im Ort Geschäfte (fast) aller Art und Güte, dazu verschiedene Supermärkte, kleinere auch in Hafennähe. / *Shops of almost every kind and quality in town, and several supermarkets as well, smaller ones also in harbour vicinity.*

FESTE / EVENTS

Immer Anfang Oktober wird ein Wochenende lang rund um den Hafen

Cala Gat

Cabo Pera

Portbook & Island Guide 169

Made by Gustavo: „Fischerpaar kommt in einem schwarzen Boot aus Antwerpen und wartet auf den Regenbogen in Cala Rajada"

die „Mostra de la Llampuga" gefeiert. Es ist die Zeit der Goldmakrele, die nur im Herbst vor Mallorca gefangen wird.
Each year in the first weekend of October people from Cala Rajada celebrate around the harbour the „Mostra de la Llampuga". It's because this kind of fish is only caught during autumn.

AUSFLÜGE / *EXCURSIONS*

4 Zwei großformatige Kachelbilder des im Nordosten Mallorcas lebenden und arbeitenden Künstlers Gustavo senden einen farbenfrohen Gruß an die Seefahrer, denn sie prangen auf der Innenseite der Außenmole. Es lohnt sich, sie aus der Nähe zu betrachten. Das jüngste wurde im Frühjahr 2015 eingeweiht. Es besteht aus 1700 Kacheln, die in Handarbeit hergestellt wurden und zusammen eine Fläche von 16x4 m ergeben.
Two large-format tile paintings by the well know artist Gustavo who lives and works in the northeast of Mallorca send a colourful salute to the sailors from the inner part of the breakwater. It is worthwhile to consider them at close range. The latest image was inaugurated in spring 2015. It's composed of 1,700 tiles that were handmade, forming an area of 16x4m.
www.artgustavo.com

5 Palau March / Sa Torre Cega
Das auffällige Gebäude mit einem Turm liegt auf einem Hügel östlich des Hafens inmitten einer weiten Parkanlage und gehört der Bankiersfamilie March. Ein Fußweg dorthin führt vom Hafen am Meer entlang. Im Park und in der Villa gibt es seit vielen Jahren eine Skulpturensammlung, die auch der Öffentlichkeit zugänglich ist. Besuche im Rahmen von Führungen.
Guided tour around the garden and inside of the March villa; this is situated on top of the hill overlooking the harbour and belongs to the banker family March. From the port one can take a footpath eastwards along the sea. There is a sculpture collection of several well-known artists in the park and inside the villa which is open to public.

Reservation, tourist office:
C./ de l'Aguila, 50
T 971 819 467, M 689 027 353
www.fundacionbmarch.es
🕐 01/05-30/11: Wed, Thu, Fri 10.30–12 h, Sat+Sun 11–18 h | 01/02-30/04: Wed+Sat 11–12.30 h, Fri 11 h
€ 4,50 EUR, red. 3,80 EUR, < 12 Jahre / *years* free

6 Cabo Pera
Der Leuchtturm hier ist leider nur von außen zu bestaunen, wie fast alle Leuchttürme der Balearen. Vorbei am Palau March und der Cala Gat führt der Weg am Meer entlang und anschließend leicht bergan. Man kann nun „querfeldein" weiter gehen (kürzer) oder hält den Kontakt zum Meer.
Mallorca's easternmost lighthouse can unfortunately be admired from outside only, like most lighthouses. Take a walk passing Palau March and Cala Gat along the sea, later hike slightly uphill. Then either go cross-country (which is shorter) or follow the coastline.

7 Talaia de Son Jaumell
Es geht zu Berge, genau 272 m hoch zum alten Wachturm Torre d'es Telegraf und zur Talaia de Son Jaumell. Vom Nordrand von Cala Rajada führt der Weg entlang der Traumbucht Cala Guya und zur Nachbarbucht Cala Molto. Von dort führt ein breiter Weg zur Cala Mesquida und dabei immer leicht bergan. Dauer: für Hin- und Rückweg vom Hafen ausgehend vier Stunden.
This hike leads uphill for exactly 272m and takes you to the old watchtower Torre d'es Telegraf and Talaia de Son Jaumell. The way starts at the marvelous bays of Cala Guya and Cala Molto towards Cala Mesquida. With clear skies Menorca can be seen on the horizon. Duration: return trip from harbour approx. 4 h.

8 Capdepera
Ortschaft mit Festung zirka 5 km vom Hafen entfernt. Sehenswert. Schöner Ausblick. Kleines Heimatmuseum.
Village with fortress in some 5km distance from the harbour. Worth a visit. Nice views. Small museum about local history. www.castellcapdepera.com

Die Insel und das Meer von oben
Island and coastline from above

Around Mallorca

Deutsch & Englisch
English & German
39,90 EUR

Martin Muth

BONA NOVA BOOKS

Das perfekte Geschenk! Die Trauminsel von oben – Großformatiger Bildband mit 180 Seiten

The perfect present! Isla bonita from the air – photo book in large format with 180 pages

Bona Nova Books

www.bonanova-books.com

Mallorca

- Große Kaps und weite Buchten
- Ankerplätze vor Bergkulisse
- Cabo Formentor runden!

- *Big headlands and wide bays*
- *Mountainous anchorage areas*
- *Rounding Cabo Formentor!*

Große Buchten prägen den Norden Mallorcas: Bahia de Pollença und Bahia de Alcúdia. In beiden finden wir moderne Yachthäfen und im Sommer regelmäßig thermische Winde.

Two large bays shape Mallorca's north coasts: Bahia de Pollença and Bahia de Alcúdia. Both shelter modern marinas and in summer sailors benefit from quite a regular sea breeze.

Der Norden Mallorcas / The North of Mallorca

Up North

Cabo Farrutx & Bay of Alcúdia

Mallorca

Cala Guya – Isla Alcanada

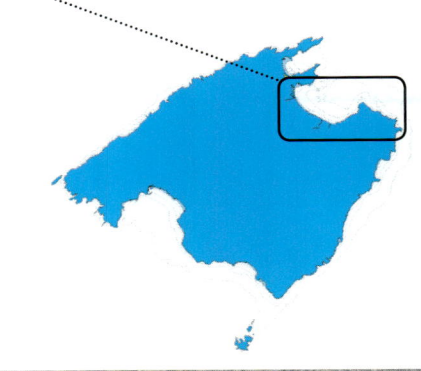

🇩🇪 Menorca ist jetzt nur noch 20 sm entfernt. Doch kann Mallorcas Nordosten mehr sein als ein Sprungbrett zur Nachbarinsel. An Ankergründen herrscht kein Mangel, nur sind die meisten zum Meer hin offen.

🇬🇧 *From here the distance to Menorca is only 20nmi. But Mallorca's northeastern part is far more than a link to the neighbouring island. There is no lack of anchorages, although these are mostly open to the sea.*

1 Cala Guya, Cala Molto - 39° 43,6' N 003° 27,5' E → page 176
Doppelbucht mit Dünen. Ihre Sandstrände haben Cala Rajada groß gemacht.
Without their beaches Cala Rajada would still be a fishing village.

2 Cala Mesquida - 39° 44,9' N 003° 26,2' E → page 176
Bucht für ruhige Bedingungen. Dahinter touristische Ortschaft und Dünen.
A bay perfect for calm conditions. In the backdrop Mallorca's highest dunes.

3 Cala Torta / Cala Mitjana - 39° 45,3' N 003° 25,1' E → page 176
Zwei naturbelassene Buchten in Nachbarschaft. Aber reger Badebetrieb.
Two bays in unspoiled nature. But Cala Torta can be crowded ...

4 Cala Matsoch - 39° 45,7' N 003° 24,6' E → page 178
Wird markiert durch das vorgelagerte Inselchen Farayo d'Aubarca.
Marked by the islet Farayo d'Albarca and an ancient watchtower.

5 Cala Port Salada - 39° 46,1' N 003° 22,9' E → page 178
Rückzugsgebiet ... Selbst im Hochsommer nur wenig Betrieb am Strand.
Boaters refugium ... Even in high season no overcrowded beaches.

6 Cala es Caló - 39° 46,4' N 003° 19,9' E → page 179
Einstige Fischerbucht mit Mole, Teil der Reserva Marina de Levante.
A bay that belonged to fishermen. Part of Reserva Marina de Levante.

7 Cala Mata - 39° 45,6' N 003° 19,4' E → page 179
Ankerplatz nordöstlich der Ortschaft Betlem; Grund Sand; Tiefe um 5 m
Anchorage north-east of the village of Betlem; Bottom sand; Depths appr. 5 m

8 Colònia de Sant Pere - 39° 44,3' N 003° 16,3' E → page 180
Club-Marina vor den Bergen von Artá; zahlreiche Restaurants am Meer.
Marina in front of Artá mountains; numerous waterfront restaurants.

9 Son Serra de Marina - 39° 44,5' N 003° 13,3' E → page 182
Ein Fluttor kann den kleinen Club-Hafen abriegeln, wenn es Not tut.
A tidal gate can lock Son Serra marina, if necessary. Depths around 1.2m

10 Punta Llarga - 39° 44,9' N 003° 12,6' E → page 182
Schönwetter-Ankerplatz nw-lich von Son Serrra. Zum Meer hin offen.
Fair-weather anchorage northwest of Son Serra. Open to the sea.

11 C'an Picafort - 39° 46,1' N 003° 09,6' E → page 183
Club-Marina mit weniger als 1,80 m Wasser. Schwierige Einfahrt.
Marina run by a yacht club. Less than 1.8m water depth in the approach.

12 Port d'Alcúdia / Alcúdiamar - 39° 50,0' N 003° 08,1' E → page 184
Im Norden der Platz für große Motoryachten; vielfältiges Angebot. Ankerfeld.
In the north part of Mallorca the designated marina for large motor yachts.

13 Isla Alcanada - 39° 50,0' N 003° 09,9' E → page 190
Ankerplatz westlich der Insel. Grund: Sand, Fels, Seegras. 2-m-Flachstellen!
Anchorage area west of the small island. Shallow spots with only 2m!

Der Norden Mallorcas I / The North of Mallorca I

- 4 Cala Matsoch
- 5 Cala Port Salada
- 6 Cala es Caló
- 7 Cala Mata
- 3 Cala Torta / Cala Mitjana
- 2 Cala Mesquida
- 1 Cala Guya, Cala Molto
- 8 Colònia de Sant Pere
- 9 Son Serra de Marina
- 10 Punta Llarga
- 11 C'an Picafort
- 12 Port d'Alcúdia
- 13 Isla Alcanada

MALLORCA

Portbook & Island Guide 175

Cala Guya – Cala Mata

ANKERPLÄTZE
ANCHORAGE AREAS

A Cala Guya, Cala Molto
39° 43,6' N 003° 27,5' E

Vor allem die außerordentliche Schönheit der Cala Guya nördlich von Cala Rajada hat die Entwicklung des Ortes beflügelt. Bei ruhigen Bedingungen traumhaftes Ankern auf ca. 4 m über Sandgrund vor einem dünengesäumten Strand. Hinter einer schmalen Halbinsel liegt die kleinere Cala Molto. Weil Sandstrand fast völlig fehlt, geht es hier wesentlich ruhiger zu. Etwas Felsgrund auf der Nordseite.

The exceptional beauty of Cala Guya north of Cala Rajada has driven the town's rapid development. In calm conditions, anchoring is simply marvelous at 4m depth on sandy bottom in front of a long beach surrounded with dunes. Behind a narrow peninsula you will find the smaller Cala Molto with only very small sandy beaches. Therefore it is more quiet here. Some rocky patches on the north side.

B Cala Mesquida
39° 44,9' N 003° 26,2' E

Tagesankerbucht für ruhige Bedingungen vor einem schönen Sandstrand mit den höchsten Dünen Mallorcas und einer Feriensiedlung. Gleichmäßig abfallender Sandgrund. Keine abgetrennte Badezone. Distanz zum Hafen Cala Rajada: 4 sm.

Daytime anchorage area in calm weather with a beautiful sand beach as backdrop, surrounded by the highest dunes of Mallorca and holiday homes. Evenly sloping sandy bottom. No separated bathing area. Distance: 4nmi to Cala Rajada.

C Cala Torta / Cala Mitjana
39° 45,3' N 003° 25,1' E

Ankern vor diesen zwei benachbarten, naturbelassenen Buchten über reinem Sandgrund. Wassertiefen um 5 m. Keine gefährlichen Untiefen. Vor allem die östliche Cala Torta wird von Land aus stark frequentiert, eine Straße endet hier. Der Strand ist bewacht und es gibt eine Bar mit Imbiss. 1,5 km oberhalb der Bucht liegt „Agroturismo Sa Duaia", ein Gebäude aus dem 15. Jahrhundert. Das Restaurant dort hat vom späten Frühjahr bis in den Oktober hinein geöffnet. Von der Terrasse ein schöner Blick aufs Meer.

Drop anchor in front of the two adjacent natural beaches with sandy bottom. Water depths around 5m. No dangerous shoals. Especially the beach of eastern Cala Torta is heavily frequented, a road terminates here. Lifeguards on duty and there is a beach bar with refreshments. 1mi along the road one will find „Agroturismo Sa Duaia", a building from the 15th century. The restaurant there is open from late spring until well into October. From the terrace a beautiful sea view.

M 658 958 890, www.saduaia.com

Cala Guya – Cala Mata

B Cala Mesquida

C Cala Torta

Cala Mitjana

Mallorca

D Cala Matsoch
39° 45,7' N 003° 24,6' E

Kleine Bucht mit Platz für ein, zwei Boote. Wassertiefen unter 5 m. Ankergrund Sand, Seegras und Fels. Wird markiert durch das vorgelagerte Inselchen Farayo de Aubarca vor dem Cabo Morro de Aubarca mit einem Wachturm.
Achtung: Es gibt eine unbezeichnete Untiefe unmittelbar nordöstlich der Bucht mit nur etwas mehr als 2 m Wassertiefe.

Small bay with room for one or two boats. Water depths less than 5 m. Bottom sand, weed and rock. Is marked by Farayo de Aubarca islet 0,4nmi away from Cabo de Morro Aubarca with a Medieval watchtower.
Caution: *there is an unmarked shoal in the northeastern approach of the bay with only slightly more than 2m of water.*

E Cala Port Salada
39° 46,1' N 003° 22,9' E

Ankern vor allem vor dem westlichen der beiden Strände auf zirka 5 m Tiefe. Fast reiner Sandgrund, Grund sanft abfallend. Pure Natur, nur Wanderer kommen an diesen Platz. An Land ein nicht öffentliches Gebäude.

Anchorage at around 5m depth, gently sloping, in particular at the western beach. Almost purely sand with little weed, unadulterated nature, only hikers come to this place. Ashore a non-public building.

Cala Guya – Cala Mata

Cala Port Salada

F Cala es Caló
39° 46,4' N 003° 19,9' E
Ankerplatz südlich einer alten Mole. Sie trägt schon lange kein Feuer mehr. Im inneren Teil gibt es unmarkierte Untiefen, vorsichtig navigieren. Südlich der Mole ankert man auf 4-3 m. Das Seegras wächst zum Teil dicht und hoch und an einigen Stellen liegen größere Steine sowie ältere Muringgeschirre der Fischer. Die Bucht gehört zur Reserva Marina de Llevant, Anker und Kette dürfen Seegras nicht berühren. Es wird fallweise kontrolliert. Versorgungsmöglichkeiten in der kleinen Ortschaft Betlem, gut 2 km Weg entlang der Küste.
Anchorage south of an old breakwater, unlit since many years. In the inner part there are unmarked shoals, so navigate with caution. Drop anchor at 4-3m. The weed grows partly dense and high, and in some places there are larger stones and chains formerly laid out by fishermen. The bay is part of Reserva Marina de Llevant, anchor and chain may not touch weed. It is occasionally checked. Supplies only in the small village of Betlem, over 2mi along the coast.

G Cala Mata
39° 45,6' N 003° 19,4' E
Ankerplatz nordöstlich der Ortschaft Betlem; Grund Sand; Tiefe um 5 m. In der nahen Ortschaft Betlem Restaurant und Mini-Markt.
Anchorage north-east of the village of Betlem; Bottom sand; Depths approx. 5m. In the nearby village of Betlem restaurant and minimarket.

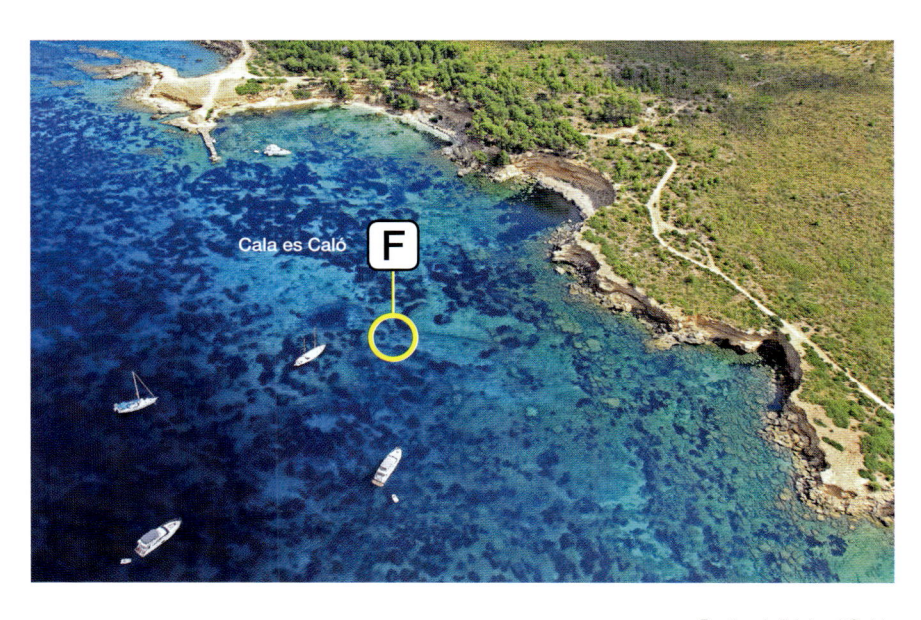

Cala es Caló

Mallorca

Colònia de Sant Pere

🇩🇪 Wenn die tiefere Nachmittags- oder Abendsonne den steilen Westflanken der Berge von Artá ihr tiefes Rotbraun entlockt, dann möchte man auch als Bootsfahrer dieser Szenerie möglichst nahe sein. Das geht seit Anfang des neuen Jahrtausends durch die Marina des Club Nàutic in Colònia de Sant Pere.

🇬🇧 *When the sunset colours the steep mountains of Arta with a dark reddish brown, yachtsmen wanting to view this spectacle from nearby can enjoy it at the marina of Club Nàutic in Colònia de Sant Pere.*

ANSTEUERUNG
APPROACHING

Nachts ist das rote Molenfeuer relevant. Keine Untiefen. Wassertiefe in der Einfahrt 4-3 m, ebenfalls innerhalb der Marina. **Vorsicht** bei starkem auflandigen Wind mit Seegang: Die Wellen laufen dann quer zum Einsteuerungskurs! *At night the red light at the head of the outer breakwater is important. No shallow areas. Depth of 4-3m at the entrance and inside the marina.* **Caution:** *with strong onshore winds waves can run across the steered course in front of the marinas entrance.*

FESTMACHEN
FIND A BERTH

[A] 308 Liegeplätze für Yachten bis 18 m. Wartepier bei der Tankstelle. Gepflegte und moderne Duschen und Toiletten im Clubgebäude beim Bistro „Sa Cantina".
308 berths for yachts up to 18m. Waiting pier at petrol station. Modern, well maintained showers and toilets in club building next to bistro "Sa Cantina".

T+F 971 589 118,
oficinacncsp@gmail.com

📱 UKW/VHF 09
Reservierung / *Reservations on ...*
www.cncoloniasp.com
🕐 daily: 08–21 h (01/06 - 30/09);
08–17 h (01/10 - 31/05)
Symbol EUR
€ 12 x 4 m; 45,78 EUR (01/06-30/09);
19,23 EUR (01/10-31/05)
Wasser, Elektr., Duschen inkl., plus 21% MwSt. / *Water, electr., showers incl., plus 21% IVA*

TANKEN / *FUEL*

D+B, daily: 07–20.30 h (01/06 - 30/09); 07–19.00 h (01/10 - 31/05)

TECHNISCHER SERVICE
TECHNICAL SERVICES

35-t-Travellift Club Nàutic
Günstige Tarife / *Fair rates*
Techniker / *Technician,*
Juan/Manuel, M 629 308 715
Sancho, M 687 076 232
Motonautica (Cala Rajada)
T 971 563 188

RESTAURANTS & BARS

Zahlreiche Restaurants, primär am Meer: / *Numerous Restaurants, particularly on the sea boulevard:*

Es Mollet, T 971 589107
Del Náutico, T 971 589 009
Club-Restaurant
Es Playa, T 971 589 017
bekannt für Paella und Meeresfrüchte
known for great paellas and seafood

Cala Estret, nördöstlich von / *northeasterly of* Colònia de Sant Pere

7,0

Colònia de Sant Pere

39° 44,3' N 003° 16,3' E

Fl(4)R 12s

- Clubhafen auf Marina-Niveau
- Vor den Bergen von Artá
- Viele Restaurants am Meer
- *Marina built by a yacht club*
- *With Arta mountains in the backdrop*
- *Many restaurants on the seafront*

Blau Mari, T 971 58 94 07
Küche mit Anspruch / *ambitious cuisine*
www.restauranteblaumari.es
Es Vivers
Italienisch angehaucht; *Italian cuisine*
T 971 589 478, M 659 799 507
www.esvivers.com

EINKAUFEN / SHOPPING

[1] Supermarkt vor der Zufahrt zur Marina im Souterrain eines Gebäudes. / *Supermarket at the entrance of the marina in the basement of a building.* 🕒 Mon-Sat: 08-13.30 + 16.30-19.30 h; Sun + hol.: 08-13.30 h

SERVICE

Autovermietung / *Rent a Car*
C&H, C./Vivers / C./ de Ca'n Matxo
T 971 589 135, M 908 407 033

Wäscherei / *Launderette*
C./ de Ca'n Metxo, M 609 375 902
Apotheke / *Pharmacy*
C./ de Ca'n Metxo

AUSFLÜGE / EXCURSIONS

Wanderung am Meer und zu Berge: Vom Ortsausgang ca. 2 km am Meer entlang zur Cala Camps, zu erkennen an ihrer flachen Steilküste mit Bootshäusern. Einige hundert Meter weiter, noch vor der Ortschaft Betlem, den zweiten Weg nach rechts nehmen, weg von der Küste. Bald ist die Straße beim Ortseingang von Betlem erreicht.
Hier beginnt der ausgeschilderte Wanderweg GR 222 zur Ermita Betlem, die auf zirka 250 m liegt. Von dort könnte man u. a. weiter wandern zu den Aussichtspunkten Puig de sa Creu und Talaja Freda, 560 m, und weiter. Zeit bis zur Ermita und zurück: 3-4 h

Hike along the sea and to the mountains. From the village continue ca. 2km along the sea to Cala Camps, recognisable by its shallow cliffs with boat houses. A few hundred metres onwards, before arriving at Betlem village, take the 2nd road to the right leading away from the coast. Soon you will arrive at Betlem where the marked walkway GR 222 to Ermita Betlem begins, up to altitude 250m. From there you might continue to scenic points Puig de Sa Creu and Talaja Freda at 560m, and proceed further on to the north coast. Duration to and from the Ermita: 3-4 h

In Betlem schön Gaststätte mit Blick aufs Meer: / *Nice restaurant in Betlem, overlooking the sea:*

Casablanca
Paseo Artá, T 971 589 404
info@brunocasablanca.com

Mallorca

Punta Llarga

Son Serra – Ca'n Picafort

ANKERPLÄTZE
ANCHORAGE AREAS

**Son Serra de Marina /
Club Náutico Serranova**
39° 44,5' N 003° 13,3' E

🇩🇪 Ein Fluttor kann den kleinen Club-Hafen abriegeln, wenn es Not tut. Ohnehin könnte man hier nur einfahren bei ruhigen Bedingungen. Wassertiefe im schmalen Hafenbecken 1,20 m. Es ist mit Booten der Clubmitglieder belegt. Im Clubhaus gibt es ein kleines Restaurant.

🇬🇧 *A tidal gate can lock Son Serra marina, if necessary. Anyway, you could only enter in calm conditions. Water depth in the narrow harbour basin 1.2m. It is occupied with boats of club members. In the clubhouse there is a small restaurant.*

A Am östlichen Ende der Ortschaft ein Spot für Kiter und Surfer und beliebte Restaurants und Bars. Weiter östlich schöne Ankerplätze für ruhige Bedingungen über gleichmäßig abfallendem Sandgrund vor Stränden, Tiefe um 5 m. / *At the eastern end of the village you find a hot spot for kiters and surfers and popular restaurants and bars. Further east beautiful anchorages for calm conditions. Anchor on gently sloping sandy bottom in front of beaches, depth to 5m.*

B **Punta Llarga**
39° 44,9' N 003° 12,6' E
NW-lich davon Schönwetter-Ankerplatz. Nur 1 sm weiter nw-lich liegt die phönizische Grabstätte Son Real auf der Punte Fenicis (7.-4. Jhd. v. Chr.). Sie ist die größte bisher aufgefundene und freigelegte Nekropole auf den

Son Serra de Marina

Son Serra de Marina – Ca'n Picafort

C'an Picafort

Fl(2)G 7s
Fl(2)R 7s
VQ(3)W 5s
39° 46,1' N 003° 09,6' E

Balearen. Das Küstengebiet Son Real ist nach einem Landgut benannt, das besichtigt werden kann.

Fair-weather anchorage northwest of Punta Llarga. Only 1nmi northwest the Phoenician burial Son Reel shows up on the Punta Fenicis (7-4. century BC.). It is the largest so far discovered and exposed necropolis in the Balearic Islands. The coastal area Son Real is named after a rural estate, which can be visited. www.balearsnatura.com

C'an Picafort
39° 46,1' N 003° 09,6' E

In die Jahre gekommene Marina mit weniger als 1,80 m Wasser im Einfahrtsbereich und auch danach. Achtung: Einfahrt neben einem Riff, markiert durch ein Kardinalzeichen, VQ(3)W 5s. Innerhalb der Mole markieren kleine grüne und rote Tonnen das Fahrwasser. Selbst bei ablandigem Wind kann es vor dem Molenkopf durch Schwell zu deutlich ausgeprägten Wellen kommen. **Achtung:** In solchen Fällen waren Leinen quer über die Einfahrt gespannt, um Yachten zu sichern. Dann kann man nur provisorisch festmachen. Vorher informieren! Es gibt einen 30-t-Travellift. Der touristische Teil von C'an Picafort beginnt nw-lich der Marina. Rund um den neu gestalteten Yachtclub (mit Clubhaus und Restaurant) verschiedene weitere Restaurants und eine ganz besondere Bar, „Bahia" – ein Stück altes Spanien.

Marina run by a yacht club, not in a good shape. Less than 1.8m water in the approach. Caution: Port entrance next to a reef, highlighted by a cardinal sign, VQ (3) W 5s. Within the breakwater small green and red bouys mark the entrance. Even with offshore winds significantly pronounced waves may occur at the breakwaters head. **Note:** *In such cases ropes can be stretched across the entrance to secure yachts. Ask in advance! A 30-t-travellift is operating on the hard.*

The touristic part of C'an Picafort starts northwest of the marina. Around the redesigned Yacht Club (with clubhouse and restaurant) several other restaurants can be found and a special Bar, „Bahia" – Spain like it was decades ago.

Club Nàutic de C'an Picafort
T 971 850 185, 971 728 322
Marineros 608 057 533
www.cncanpicafort.com
UKW/VHF 09
🕐 Mon-Fri 09.30–13.30 + 15.50–18 h, Sat 9.30–13.30 h

Mallorca

PUERTO DE ALCÚDIA
PORT OF ALCÚDIA

Legend:

- Zona portuaria / Port area
- Zona ajardinada / Gardens
- Edificios / Buildings
- Casco urbano / Urban area
- Viales / Roads
- Límite zona servicio del puerto / Limits of the port service area
- Accesos / Access
- Faro / Lighthouse
- Baliza / Landing beacon
- Sirena / Siren
- Grupo 2 destellos rojos / Group of 2 red flashes
- Destellos aislados rojos / Isolated red flashes
- Destellos aislados verdes / Isolated green flashes
- Grupo 2 destellos verdes / Group of 2 green flashes
- Grupo (2+1) destellos rojos / Group of (2+1) red flashes
- Grupo 4 destellos amarillos / Group of 4 yellow flashes
- Marca especial ciega / Special daymark
- Grupo 3 destellos verdes / Group of 3 green flashes
- Grupo 3 destellos rojos / Group of 3 red flashes
- Grupo 4 destellos verdes / Group of 4 green flashes
- Destellos aislados amarillos / Isolated yellow flashes

Map labels: MUELLE TRÁFICO LOCAL, DÁRSENA PESQUERA, MUELLE VIEJO, A.P.B., MUELLE PESQUERO, Cofradía pescadores, ALCUDIAMAR, NUEVO MUELLE, Muelles de, DESCARGA GASES LICUADOS

Street names: MAR, CANET, MARE DE DÉU DEL CARME, GOMERA, CIUDADELA, TABARCA, ISLAS BALEARES, SAN PEDRO

Buoy numbers: 33140, 33160, 33134, 33150, 33133, 33132, 33128, 33126, 33130, 33122

Port d'Alcúdia

Hafenplan / Harbour map – Port d'Alcúdia

Portbook & Island Guide 185

Mallorca

Port d'Alcúdia

🇩🇪 Die Stadt am Meer ist ein Zentrum des Pauschal-Tourismus mit ungezählten Hotels, einem großen Einkaufs- und Vergnügungsangebot, Souvenirgeschäften und Discotheken, Restaurants und Bars. Dieses Gebiet erstreckt sich vom Hafen aus über einige Kilometer südwestlich hinter dem langen Sandstrand Playa de Muro.
Die Marina Alcúdiamar ist im Norden Mallorcas bedeutend, in keiner anderen liegen so viele große Motoryachten. Guter Landschutz bei Mistral (Starkwind aus nördlichen Richtungen).

🇬🇧 *Port d'Alcúdia is a centre for package tourism with plenty of hotels, large shopping and entertainment facilities such as souvenir shops, discos, bars and restaurants. This area extends from the harbour a few miles southwest behind long Playa de Muro beach.*
Marina Alcudiamar is important in the north of Mallorca; no other marina shelters so many large power boats. Well protected against Mistral (strong north wind).

- Motoryacht-Marina des Nordens
- Zahlreiche Service-Betriebe
- Geschütztes Ankerfeld

- *Many large power boats*
- *Plenty of service companies*
- *Well protected anchorage*

ANSTEUERUNG
APPROACHING

Zwei Schornsteine markieren den Hafen von weitem. Sie stehen hinter dem Handelshafen, der auf dem Weg zur Marina passiert werden muss. Vor allem Fähren und Schnellfähren sind hier zu beachten. Zwischen Fährhafen und Marina bzw. dem Ankerplatz vor der Außenmole gehen die Wassertiefen auf unter 3 m zurück. Es gibt Fahrwassertonnen, die beim Einlaufen in die Marina beachtet werden sollten.
Two chimneys mark the harbour from far away. They are located behind the commercial port, which has to be passed on the way to the marina. Between the comercial port and the marina or the anchorage area in front of the breakwater water depths fall below 4m, in parts even receding to under 3m. There is a buoyed channel when entering the marina.

FESTMACHEN
FIND A BERTH

A Wartekai der Marina Alcudiamar einlaufend an Backbord an der Tankstellenpier. Anmeldung im Sommer wichtig. Auch über die Webseite möglich.
Waiting pier of marina Alcudiamar on portside when entering, at the filling station. Reservations required in summer, possible also on the marinas website.
T 971 546 000/04
alcudiamar@alcudiamar.es
www.alcudiamar.es
€ 12 m x 4 m
50,05 EUR (01/07-31/08), 39,33 EUR (01/09-30/06), plus Gebühren G-5 und T-0 und 21% MwSt. / *plus harbour fees G-5 and T-0 and 21% VAT*
Preisliste siehe / *Pricelist see*
www.alcudiamar.es/Tarifas_Alquiler_Amarres.pdf
Die Marina bietet für Dauerliegeplätze

Port d'Alcúdia

für Yachten unter 10 m und generell für die Wintermonate signifikante Abschläge. / *For permanent berths for yachts under 10m and generally for the winter months the Marina offers significant discounts.*

📱 UKW/VHF 09
🕐 01/04-30/06: Mon-Fri 08-19 h, Sat 09-13 h, Sun closed
01/07-31/08: Mon-Fri 08-19 h, Sat 09-13 h, Sun 9-13 h
01/09-30/09: Mon-Fri 08-19 h, Sat 09-13 h, Sun closed
01/10-31/03: Mon-Fri 08-16 h, Sat 10-13 h, Sun closed

Wartekai von Alcudiamar einlaufend an Backbord an der Südseite der Tankstellenpier. Anmeldung im Sommer wichtig. *Waiting pier of marina Alcudiamar on portside when entering, at the south side of the filling station. Reservations required in summer.*

€ 12 m x 4 m
50,05 EUR (01/07-31/08), 39,33 EUR (01/09-30/06) Plus Hafengebühren und 21% MwSt. / *plus harbour fees and 21% VAT*, T 971 546 000/04
📱 UKW/VHF 09

alcudiamar@alcudiamar.es
www.alcudiamar.es/Tarifas_Alquiler_Amarres.pdf
🕐 Mon-Fri: 8.30-13.30 h + 16.30-19.30 h; Sun 10.13 h

B Liegepätze an der Nordmole des Fährhafens. Verwaltet durch Mallorca Yates, Büro im Fährgebäude Estación marítima de Alcudia.

Berths in front of the ferry terminal. Managed by Mallorca Yates, office inside the ferry terminal.
T 971 825 135, M 619 248 070

Mallorca

ANKERPLÄTZE
ANCHORAGE AREAS

C Ankerplatz südwestlich der Außenmole. Kostenlos und im frischen Wind mit Blick über den östlichen Teil der Bucht von Alcúdia bis Colònia de Sant Pere. Wassertiefen 4-2,50 m. Sehr gut haltender Grund aus Sand und Ton, wenig Seegras.

Well protected anchorage southwest of the breakwater, free of charge, overlooking the eastern part of the bay from Alcúdia to Colònia de Sant Pere. Depths 4-2.5m; bottom sand and clay with patches of weed.

D Anlanden vor dem Restaurant „Aqua". / *Dinghies may land in front of Lounge Bar „Aqua".*

TANKEN / FUEL

D+B, 24 h; Nach Anmeldung im Marinabüro; auch Wassertankstelle und Absauganlage für Rückhaltetanks
After applying at the marina office; service station also for water and extraction system for holding tanks

TECHNISCHER SERVICE
TECHNICAL SERVICES

E Werft der Marina / *Shipyard* Alcudiamar; 150-t-Travellift
In der Marina / *On marina premises:*
Multimar Alcudia
T 971 897 167, M 620 870 193
www.multimar-alcudia.com
Nautica Mahón Yacht Service
T 971 546 750, M 670 234 732
www.nauticamahon.com
Parker Yacht Services
M 685 130 634
www.parkeryachtservices.com
Nautico Matxet, M 687 788 215

F Bennasar
Yachtwerft außerhalb der Marina
Shipyard outside the marina
T 971 546 700, M 649 989 950
cnavals.bennasar@gmail.com

YACHTAUSRÜSTER
CHANDLERIES

In der Marina / *On marina premises:*
Multimar Alcudia, T 971 897 167
www.multimar-alcudia.com
Motonautica Alcúdia, T 971 546 130
www.motonautica-alcudia.com

RESTAURANTS & BARS

Riesige Auswahl an Gaststätten, direkt bei der landseitigen Marina-Zufahrt, hier vor allem rechter Hand. Weitere Restaurants (Auswahl): *There is a large choice of restaurants situated directly at the exit of the marina, mainly on the right side. Other restaurants (selection):*

1 Restaurante Aqua
T 971 544 626
In der Marina. Wunderschöne Terrasse neben der Ankerbucht. Breitgefächerte Speisekarte. Dazu Chill-out-Bereich mit Cocktailbar und eine Frühstückskarte. *Inside the marina. Fantastic terrace overlooking the bay. Chill-out area with cocktails, also breakfast.*
June-Aug.: daily, 12-24 h
April, May, Sept., Oct.: 12-16 + 19-24 h

Piero Rossi, T 971 548 611
guter Mittagstisch / *tasty lunch*
täglich / *daily*, 11-16 h + 19-23 h

Sa Taverna des Ports, T 971 897 939
Mit Blick auf die Bootsstege, großer Außengrill / *Close to the jetties, large outdoor barbecue*
www.alcudiarestaurants.com

Stadttor / City gate in Alcúdia

Port d'Alcúdia

[2] El Jardin, T 971 892 391
Eines der Top-Restaurants Mallorcas: Seit 2011 glänzt das Restaurant El Jardin mit einem Michelinstern. Neben dem Restaurant das Jardín-Bistro mit Außenplätzen und preiswerter Karte. / *One of Mallorca's premier restaurants: El Jardin, boasting a Michelin star since 2011. Next to the restaurant, Jardin Bistro offers outside seating and a less expensive menu.*
C./ Diana / C./Triton s/n
Restaurant: (Fri, Sat + Sun) 13.30-15.30 h, 20-23 h.
Bistro: Mon-Sun: mittags / *at noon*, Fri + Sat: auch abends / *also in the evening*
www.restaurantejardin.com

[3] Gran China, Chinesisches Restaurant / *Chinese cuisine*
östlich der Hafenzufahrt am Strand, mit Terrasse im 1. Stock und Blick über die bucht; gut und preiswert
East of the harbour entrance behind the beach, terrace on the 1st floor overlooking the bay. Good value for money
T 971 549 624

[4] Bodega des Port
Mallorquinische Küche, Tapas / *Local food & tapas*
T 971 549 633
info@bodegadesport.com
www.bodegadesport.com

[5] In der Altstadt von Alcúdia, ca. 2 km entfernt / *In the old town of Alcúdia, ca. 2 km off:*

Satyricón
In einem ehemaligen Kino. Mittags preiswerte Salatbar. Zum Abendessen reservieren.
In a former cinema. Inexpensive salad bar during lunchtime. Reservations recommended in the evening.
Plaça Constitució, 4; 11-23 h
T 971 544 997, M 616 126 959
www.alcudiarestaurants.com

Sa Portassa, T 971 548 819
Span. Restaurant, Tapas
C./Sant Vicenç, 7

EINKAUFEN / *SHOPPING*

Im Hafen eine kleiner Supermarkt und ein Geschäft für die schönen Dinge des Lebens, Son Fè Tiendas.
Große Auswahl an Geschäften und Supermärkten nach Verlassen der Marina linker Hand.
Small supermarket inside the harbour and a shop for something special, Son Fè Tiendas.
Large choice of shops and supermarkets outside the marina. If you leave turn left.

SERVICES

Rent-a-car / Bikes / Taxi / Cabs
… alles zu finden nach Verlassen der Marina linker Hand / *… all located after leaving the marina to the left.*

🚌 http://www.tib.org/portal/web/ctm/autobus/seccio/300
Linie 351 fährt nach Palma; nach Alcúdia verschiedene Linien
Bus 351 takes you to Palma; several bus routes to Alcúdia

AUSFLÜGE / *EXCURSIONS*

Altstadt Alcúdia entdecken (ca. 1,5 km)
Die Stadt ist eine römische Gründung aus dem Jahr 123 v. Chr., genannt Pollentia (lat. Macht/Herrschaft). Neugründung durch Mauren zu Beginn des 8. Jhd. als „Al Kudia". Stadtmauer mit Pfarrkirche Sant Jaume, den Uhrenturm am Rathaus, die römischen Ausgrabungen und die das Amphitheater. Alles auf dieser Karte:

The city was founded by Romans in 123 B.C. and called Pollentia (lat. power/dominion). In the 8th century A.D. under Arab rule it was renamed Al Kudia. The city wall with the church of Sant Jaime, the town halls belfry, Roman excavations and the amphitheatre are all on this map:

www.alcudiamallorca.com/fdb/f52bdc96e371248b.pdf

Trofeo Almirante Conde de Barcelona
Ende August findet in der Bucht von Alcúdia diese traditionsreichen Regatta mit klassischen Segelyachten statt.
End of August Alcúdia bay celebrates this traditional regatta with sailing yacht classics.
www.fundacionhispania.org

Rathaus / *Town hall* in Alcúdia

Fiesta de Sant Pere
Immer Ende Juni feiert man den Heiligen Sant Pere, den Beschützer der Fischer. Eines der schönsten Feste des Jahres in Port d'Alcúdia. Jeden Tag verschiedene Aktivitäten: Konzerte, Wettbewerbe, Kinderspiele, Sportereignisse … Am letzten Tag: Prozession über Land und Meer mit der Figur des Heiligen. Großes Feuerwerk vor der Marina zum Abschluss.

One of the most beautiful festivals of the year in Alcúdia's harbour: celebrating harbour patron Sant Pere, protector of the fishermen. There are different activities every day: concerts, competitions, children's games, sports events … On the last day, a procession takes place on land and by boat, parading the figure of the saint. A huge firework in front of the marina closes the festivities.

Mallorca

Isla Alcanada – Cala Pinar

ANKERPLÄTZE
ANCHORAGE AREAS

A Isla Alcanada
39° 50,0' N 003° 09,9' E

Der Ankerplatz bei der Leuchtturminsel (Fl 5s) liegt ca. 2 sm östlich von Port d'Alcúdia. Yachten ankern überwiegend auf der Westseite innerhalb der Fünf-Meter-Tiefenlinie auf Sand mit Seegras. Achtung: häufig sind Taucher unterwegs und es gibt Stellen mit nur 2 m Wassertiefe. Bei hohem Sonnenstand lassen sie sich an der bräunlichen Wasserfarbe erkennen. Im Nordwesten der kleinen Insel kann man an einer Betonpier anlanden. Auf der Seite der Halbinsel Victoria gibt es zwei Strandrestaurants.

The anchorage near the islet with its white lighthouse (Fl 5s) is about 2nmi east of Port d'Alcudia. Yachts drop anchor mostly on the west side within the 5m depth contour above sandy bottom with weed. Watch out for divers and spots with only 2m of water. When the sun is high these spots can be identified by brown colour. On the northwestern tip of Alcanada there is a concrete pier for dinghies. Ashore, on Victoria Peninsula, two beach restaurants can be visited.

B Cala de Coll Baix
39° 51,9' N 003° 11,4' E

Eine Bucht mit rundpolierten Steinen am Strand und ganz ohne Sand. Dennoch sehr beliebt, bei Bootfahrern und Landtouristen. Auf der Nordostseite der Halbinsel Victoria, fast 5 sm von Port d'Alcúdia entfernt. Von hohen Felswänden umgeben. Ankergrund Sand und Seegras, Tiefe nur in Strandnähe unter 10 m. Umgebung: pure Natur.

A bay with pebble beach. Surrounded by unadulterated nature. To be found on the northeast side of the Victoria peninsula, almost 5nmi away from Port d'Alcúdia. Surrounded by cliffs. Bottom: sand and weed. Depths only close to the beach less than 10m.

C Cala Pinar
39° 53,2' N 003° 11,1' E

0,5 sm südwestlich des Leuchtfeuers Cabo Pinar liegt diese Bucht mit zwei Stränden. Sie sind zum Meer hin separiert, weil sich an Land militärisches Sperrgebiet befindet. Vor der Absperrung lässt auch 8-4 m Wassertiefe ankern, der Grund besteht aus Seegras mit sandigen Flecken. Im Hintergrund ein dichter Pinienwald, der Kap und Bucht seinen Namen lieh.

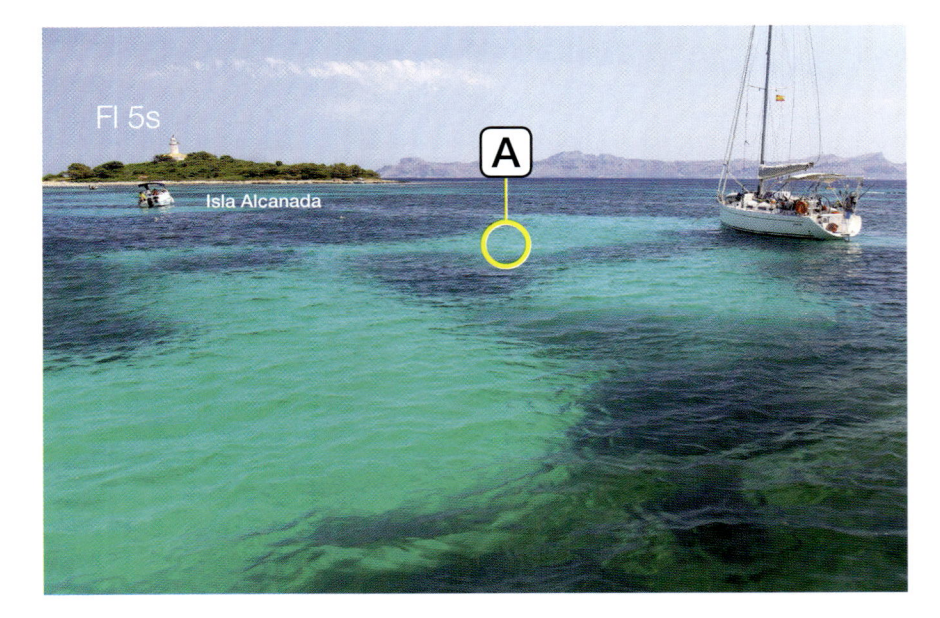

0.5nmi southwest of lighthouse Cabo Pinar one will find this bay with two beaches. They are separated towards the sea, because the tip of this peninsula is one of the few remaining restricted military areas of Mallorca. The anchorage in front of the bay has water depths of 8-4 m, the bottom consists of weed with sandy spots. In the background a dense pine forest.

Isla Alcanada – Cala Pinar

B
Cala del Coll Baix

Fl (3) 13s
Cabo Pinar
C
Cala Pinar

Mallorca

Coll Baix – Cala Tuent

🇩🇪 Rund um das Cabo Formentor, Mallorcas nördlichster Punkt, finden wir beeindruckende Plätze mit Gebirgspanorama. Und dazu mit der Bucht von Pollensa eine Wasserfläche, die zum leichten Segeln einlädt.

🇬🇧 Around Cabo Formentor, Mallorca's most northerly point, we find impressive places with mountain panorama. And as with the Bay of Pollensa, a perfect spot for easy sailing.

1 Cala de Coll Baix - 39° 51,8' N 003° 11,3' E → page 190
Bucht mit Kiesstrand. Eingerahmt von Bergen. Drum herum nur Natur.
Bay with pebble beach, surrounded by hills. 100% nature all around.

2 Cala Pinar - 39° 53,2' N 003° 11,1' E → page 190
An Land militärisches Sperrgebiet. Im Hintergrund ein dichter Pinienwald.
Ashore one of the few remaining military areas of Mallorca. Framed by pines.

3 Marina de Bonaire - 39° 52,1' N 003° 08,5' E → page 194
Durch Sturm zerstört, stark wieder aufgebaut. Schön ruhig und nahe Alcúdia.
Destroyed by a storm and extensively rebuilt. A quiet place close to Alcúdia.

4 Port de Pollenca - 39° 54,0' N 003° 05,2' E → page 198
Verschiedene Anlegemöglichkeiten, dazu ein Ankerplatz vor Bergen.
Several berth options. Also a large anchorage in front of a mountain range.

5 Punta Avenzada - 39° 54,2' N 003° 06,2' E → page 200
Schöner Ankerplatz westlich einer markanten Landzunge. Einst Bojenfeld.
Fine anchorage west of a headland with lighthouse. Former bouy field.

6 Cala Formentor - 39° 55,4' N 003° 08,2' E → page 204
Gebührenpflichtiges Bojenfeld vor dem Hotel Formentor und Bergen.
Buoy field subject to charge in front of Hotel Formentor and mountains.

7 Cala Murta / Cala en Gossalba - 39° 56,2' N 003° 11,2' E → page 204
Schmale Ankerbuchten. Die Cala Murta ist atmosphärisch schöner.
Small-sized anchorages. Cala Murta has the more cosy atmosphere.

8 Cala Figuera - 39° 57,7' N 003° 11,2' E → page 204
Idyllisch zwischen hohen Bergen. Die schönsten Ankerplätze liegen innen.
Idyllic spot between high mountains. The best spots lie further inwards.

9 Cala Boquer - 39° 56,2' N 003° 06,3' E → page 206
Eingerahmt von steilen Höhenzügen. Das Tal führt nach Port de Pollensa.
Framed by two steep ridges. The valley leads to Port de Pollensa.

10 Cala San Vincente - 39° 55,8' N 003° 04,1' E → page 206
Kleiner Urlaubsort bietet Vollversorgung. Fast überall reiner Sandgrund.
Small tourist village offers full supply services. Mostly with sandy bottom.

11 Cala Castell - 39° 56,3' N 003° 02,3' E → page 206
Benannt nach der Ruine Castillo del Rey, die 2 km entfernt liegt.
Named after the ruin Castillo del Rey, which is 2 km away.

12 Cala de sa Calobra - 39° 51,6' N 002° 47,8' E → page 207
Einzigartiger Platz vor dem Durchbruch des Torrent de Pareis.
Unique location in front of the gorge Torrent des Pareis, depth 10m.

13 Cala Tuent - 39° 50,8' N 002° 46,2' E → page 207
Ankern mit Blick auf Mallorca höchsten Berg, den Puig Major, 1445 m.
Anchorage with a view of Mallorca's highest mountain Puig Major, 1445m.

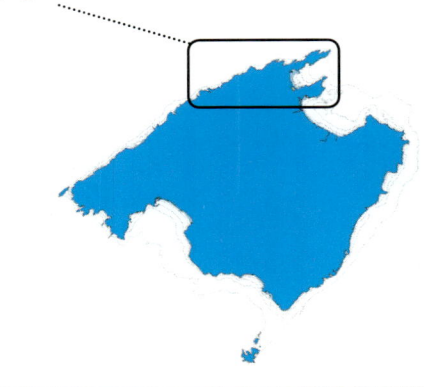

Der Norden Mallorcas II / The North of Mallorca II

Mallorca

Mallorca

Port de Pollença

- Hafenort vor Bergkulisse
- Großes Angebot an Gastplätzen
- Viel Ankerraum – Bojenfeld geplant
- *Port with mountain backdrop*
- *Wide choice of guest berths*
- *Large anchorage – plans for buoy field*

🇩🇪 Gelegen im Nordwestzipfel der gleichnamigen Bucht. Beliebt wegen des umfassenden Angebots an Land und der landschaftlichen Schönheit. An törnstrategisch wichtiger Stelle, für alle Yachtcrews, die Cabo Formentor runden.

🇬🇧 *Situated at the northwest tip of the bay of the same name. Popular because you find a lively touristic town. Beautiful surrounding landscape. For yacht crews planning to round Cabo Formentor this harbour is situated in a perfect position.*

ANSTEUERUNG
APPROACHING

Rund um den Hafen und im Innenteil geringe Wassertiefen, aber keine sonstigen Untiefen. Die Befeuerung des Hafens ist vor den Lichtern des Ortes schwierig und erst spät zu erkennen. Sehr oft ab Mittag einsetzende Thermik. Bei starken auflandigen Winden etwas Seegang vor der Hafeneinfahrt.

Around the harbour and inside not very deep, but otherwise no shallow areas. The entrance lights are hardly visible due to the town's backlight. Frequently summer breeze starting at noon. With strong onshore breeze some waves occur in front of the harbour entrance.

FESTMACHEN
FIND A BERTH

A **Reial Club Nàutic de Pollença (RCNPP)**
75 Gastplätze für Yachten bis 25 m, vor allem an der Außenseite der Nordmole. Wassertiefen bei der Einfahrt und an den Liegeplätzen 2,7 m.
75 guest berths for yachts up to 25m, mainly outside of the north pier. Depth 2.5m at the entrance and near berths.

€ 12-15 m
82,44 EUR (June-Sept),
47,11 EUR (Oct-May).
Wasser und Strom inkl., plus 21% MwSt. + Hafengebühren G-5 und T-0.
Water and electricity included, plus 21% VAT and harbour fees G-5 and T-0.

Duschen/WC im Clubhaus und auf der Außenmole
Bathrooms in the clubhouse and on the breakwater.

Office, T 971 864 635 + 864 636
UKW/VHF 09
oficina@rcnpp.net, www.rcnpp.net

B **PortsIB**
44 Gastplätze bis 15 m Länge. Anlegen mit Bug oder Heck an Muringleinen. Reservierung notwendig, mindestens drei Tage im Voraus über www.portsib.es. Bezahlung per Kreditkarte. Stornierung oder Umbuchung über die Webseite.

Port de Pollença

FI(2)G 6s

FI(2)G 6s

39° 54,1' N 003° 05,4' E

44 berths up to 15m length on a daily basis. Moor bow or stern to. Reservation recommended at least 3 days in advance at www.portsib.es. Payment by credit card. For cancelation or changes please use the web site.
Office, T+F 971 866 867
port.pollensa@portsib.es
€ EUR/m2: 0,60 (01/06-30/09); 0,18 (01/10-31/05). Water: 5,50 EUR; Electr.:5,50 EUR. Alle Preise / *All prices* plus 21% MwSt. /*VAT*

🕐 8-18 h (winter), 8-20 h (summer)
Sanitäreinrichtungen im Gebäude des Hafenbüros und 100 m entfernt
Sanitary facilities within the building of the harbour office and in 100m distance.

Das Hauptbüro von PortsIB befindet sich neben dem Club Nàutic
Ports IB main office next to Club Nàutic

🕐 8-14 + 17-18 h

C **Portocolom Nautic**
Schwimmsteg für Yachten bis 15 m Länge auf der Südseite der Werft Astilleros Cabanellas. Es sind Muringleinen ausgelegt. Wasser und Strom vorhanden. Ein Sanitärcontainer. Wassertiefen 2,5-2 m.
Floating pontoon for yachts up to 15m south of shipyard Astilleros Cabanellas. Laid out moorings. Water and electricity available. Toilets and showers. Water depths from 2.5-2 m.

Portbook & Island Guide 199

Mallorca

Oc (2) 8s

Punta Avenzada und die Ankerplätze vor Port de Pollença / and the anchorage areas in front of Port de Pollença

T 971 867 786, 971 200 571
M 619 248 070
UKW/VHF 09
www.mallorcayates.com
info@mallorcayates.com

ANKERPLÄTZE
ANCHORAGE AREAS

D Nördlich der Nordmole und östlich auf 2,5 bis 3,5 m Wasser über Sand und Seegras. / *Depth ranges from 2.5m to 3.5m at the north pier and eastwards, sandy bottom with weed.*

E Punta Avenzada
39° 54,2' N 003° 06,2' E
Schöner Ankerplatz westlich einer markanten Landzunge mit Leuchtfeuer, Oc(2)W 8s. 2006-2013 war hier ein Bojenfeld. Ankern über Sand mit Seegras, Tiefen 3,5-2,5 m.
Fine anchorage west of a headland with lighthouse, Oc(2)W 8s. Former bouy field. Drop anchor on depths of 3.5-2.5m. Bottom weed and sand.

TANKEN / FUEL

Am Kopf der Moll Pescadors
At the end of Moll Pescadores
D+B; UKW/VHF 09
15/05-15/10: Mon-Fri 8-20 h,
Sat+Sun: 8-13 + 15-20 h
15/10-15/05: Mon-Fri 8-13 + 15-19 h,
Sat+Sun: 8-12 h

TECHNISCHER SERVICE
TECHNICAL SERVICES

Astilleros Cabanellas
Alt eingesessener Werftbetrieb /
long-established shipyard
T 971 865 444
info@astilleroscabanellas.es
www.astilleroscabanellas.es

Reial Club Nàutic de Pollença (RCNPP)
50-t-Travellift, Absaugeinrichtung für Rückhaltetanks / *50 t Travel-lift, disposal pump for black and grey water tanks*

Náutica El Cano
Seit über 50 Jahren tätig. Bootslagerung, Bootsverkauf, neu und gebraucht. Alle Arbeiten rund ums Schiff, Motorenservice.
Exsisting for over 50 years. Boat storage, boat sales, new and used. All kind of craft, engine service.
C./ El Cano, 10; T 971 866 351
info@nauticano.e.telefonica.net

Nautinort, T 971 868 115
Bootshändler (Zar + Jeanneau), Vermietung, Winterlager, Bootservice. Am Ortsausgang Richtung Pollensa.
Boat dealer (Zar + Jeanneau), renting, winter storage, boat service. At the edge of town, towards Pollensa

YACHTAUSRÜSTER
CHANDLERIES

Ferreteria Puerto
Gut sortiertes Geschäft; hier gibt es u. a. Adapter für die Wasseranschlüsse an den portsIB-Liegeplätzen / *Well-stocked specialist store; among oth-*

Port de Pollença

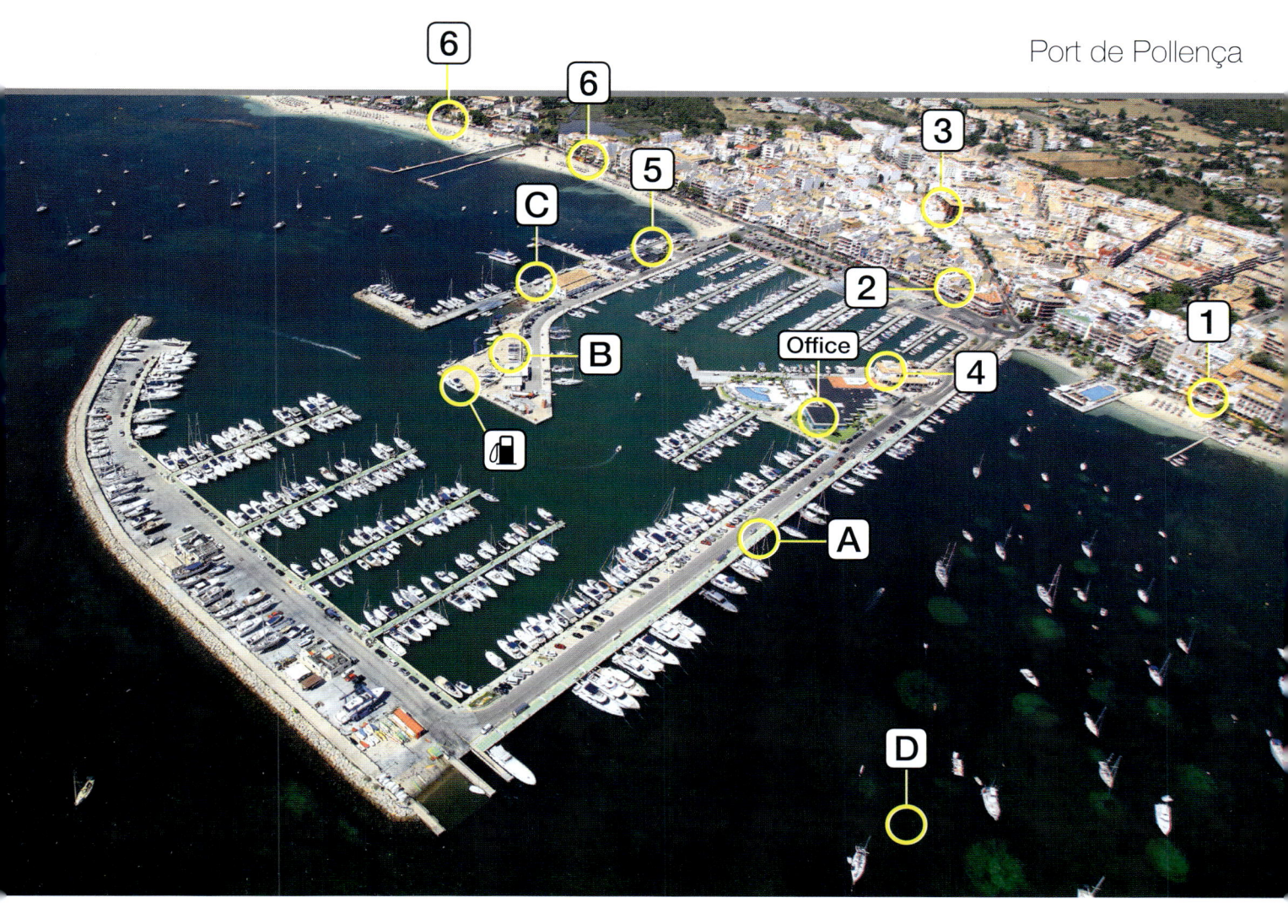

ers, water connectors for the berths at portsIB available here.
Carrer de la Verge del Carme, 41
T 971 86 53 15
www.ferreteriapuertopollensa.com

Náutica El Cano, T 971 867 173
Sehr große Bandbreite an Yacht- und Bootszubehör, Elektronik, Farben, Tauwerk etc. / *Great variety of boat accessories, electrical und electronical parts, paints, ropes etc.*
C./ El Cano, 10
info@nauticaelcano.com

La Nàutica d'eu Moll
C./ Virgen del Carmen, 86
T 971 867 880

RESTAURANTS & BARS

Unüberschaubare Vielfalt
unlimited variety

[1] Nach einem kleinen Fußweg an der Bucht entlang / *Walk on a small path along the bay to reach:*
Can Pescador, T 971 867 850
Traditionelle Küche in die Gegenwart übertragen. Normales Preisniveau.
Traditional cuisine with a modern twist. Average prices.
Passeig de Vora Mar, 1
www.canpescador.es

[2] **C'an Ferra**
Traditionsreiches Restaurant.
Traditional & typical restaurant.
Calle San Pedro, 3, T 971 867 006
www.canferra.com info@canferra.com

[3] **Celler La Parra**
Am Ortsausgang Richtung Pollensa. Der Clou ist schon die Eingangstür, man schreitet durch ein altes Weinfass. Hier wird mallorquinische Küche gepflegt. Gekocht wird mit Holz. Plätze drinnen (stimmungsvoll) und draußen. / *At the edge of town in*

Portbook & Island Guide 201

Mallorca

Formentor Peninsula

Pollensa direction. First highlight is the entrance door – visitors pass through an old wine barrel. Enjoy real Mallorcan cuisine, cooked over a wood fire. Seated within (great atmosphere) or outside. C./ Joan XXIII, 89
T 971 865 041, www.cellerlaparra.com
daily 13–15+19.15–23 h,
(winter 22.30 h)

4 Yachtclub RCNPP
T 971 865 622

La Llonja, T 971 868 430
In unmittelbarer Nähe des Yachtclubs, einige Tische in der Abendsonne; Terrasse im 1. Stock mit Blick über Bucht.
Right next to the yacht club, with a few tables warmed by evening sun; terrace on 1st floor overlooking the bay.
info@restaurantlallonja.com
www.restaurantlallonja.com

5 Stay
T 971 864 013 + 971 868 020
stay@stayrestaurant.com
www.stayrestaurant.com

6 Entlang der Uferstraße Richtung Süden weitere Gaststätten, u.a.
Along the coast towards south, there are more restaurants …

El Bistró, T 971 865 346
Segler-Treff: Gehört zur deutschen Segelschule Sail&Surf
The place to be: attached to the German sailing school Sail&Surf
info@sailsurf.de, www.sailsurf.de

Tolo's, T 971 864 046
Nur 50 m weiter. Großer Speisesaal und Terrasse zur Straße und zum Meer. Immer gut besucht.
Just 50m further. Large dining room and terrace on the street with sea view. Always well attended.
restaurante-tolos@hotmail.com

La Ruta del Tapeo
Jeden Donnerstag zwischen 20 und 24 Uhr bieten ein gutes Dutzend Bars ein Glas Wein oder Bier zusammen mit einem Imbiss-Häppchen (genannt Tapa) für 2 EUR an.
Every Thursday from 20-24 h a dozen bars offer a glass of wine or beer along with appetizers (called tapas) for 2 EUR.

DANCING / DISCOS

Buddha Bar, C./Corb Mari
(neben / next to Sail&Surf)

EINKAUFEN / SHOPPING

Eine reiche Auswahl an Supermärkten, z. B. 2x Eroski / *A varied choice of supermarkets - 2 Eroski supermarkets and other, smaller ones*

SERVICES

WÄSCHEREI / LAUNDRY
LaVaFur, Moll Pescadors,
Neben der Bootstankstelle
Close to the petrol station
Self Service, T 902 155 155
Summer: 8-20 h, Winter: 8-19 h

Port de Pollença

AUSFLÜGE / EXCURSIONS

Verschiedene Möglichkeiten:
- Wanderung zur Cala Sant Vicenç
- Wanderung in das Tal von Bóquer
- Besuch von Pollença: dort zum Markt im Zentrum am Sonntag; Kalvarienberg, römische Brücke
- zum Kloster Santa Maria oberhalb von Pollença (Aussichtpunkt, einfache Gerichte und Getränke)
- zum Cabo Formentor. Möglicher Abstecher zum Wachturm Torre Cabo Formentor: Blick auf die Cala Formentor und bis zur Westküste. Weitere Abstecher zur Cala Figuera, Cala Formentor und zur Cala Murta.

Various possibilities:
- *Hike to Cala Sant Vicenc*
- *Hike to the valley of Boquer*
- *A visit to Pollença: Sunday market in the centre, Calvary hill, Roman bridge*
- *to convent Santa Maria above Pollença (basic restaurant & bar, view point)*
- *to Cabo Formentor*
Possible side trip to the watchtower Torre Cabo Formentor: with a view over Cala Formentor and to the west coast. Other side trips to Cala Figueras, Cala Formentor and Cala Murta.

ZWEIRÄDER / BIKES

Pro Cycle Hire (sportlich / *sportive*)
C./ Corb Mari, 6
(neben / *next to* Sail&Surf)
T 971 866 857, info@procyclehire.com

Rent March, Räder aller Art, Mopeds.
Bikes & motor bikes; C./ Juan XXIII, 89
(Richtung / *direction* Pollensa)
T 971 864 784, www.rentmarch.com

MIETWAGEN / CAR HIRE

Hiper Rent a Car
Calle Juan XXIII, T 971 866768
www.hiperrentacar.com

Europcar, C/ Juan XXIII, 95-97
T 902 105 055, www.europcar.es

Formentor Rent a car
Passeig Saralegui, 106 (neben / *next to* Sail&Surf Pollença), T 971 865 492
www.rentacarformentor.com

Cabo Formentor

Mallorca

Cala Formentor – Cala Tuent

ANSTEUERUNG
APPROACHING

A Cala Formentor
39° 55,4' N   003° 08,2' E

🇩🇪 Gebührenpflichtiges Bojenfeld vor dem Hotel Formentor. 2,5 sm nordöstlich von Port de Pollença. Schöne Umgebung, vor Bergen. Am Ufer Sandstrand mit Bäumen. Für Festmachen an den Bojen zuletzt hohe Gebühren, selbst für kurzes Anlegen. Strandrestaurant. Dort Anlanden mit dem Beiboot. Anmeldung: UKW-Kanal 71.

🇬🇧 *Buoy field subject to charge in front of Hotel Formentor. 2.5nmi northeast of Port de Pollença. Mountains in the backdrop. Sandy beach lined with trees. Taking a buoy is rather expensive, even for a short time. Beach restaurant. One may land here by dinghy. Reservation possible via VHF 09.*

€ EUR (2015)

< 8 m	14,50	rot/red (23)
< 15 m	29,00	grün/green (28)
< 25 m	42,50	gelb/yellow (17)
< 35 m	112,00	weiß/white (7)
> 40 m	210,00	Kegeltonnen (4)
Einw./*Resid.* Pollensa, free, blau/blue		

B Cala Murta
39° 56,2' N   003° 11,2' E

Heimeliger Ankerplatz vor Bergen. Besonders schön möglichst weit innen. Ankergrund Seegras mit Sandflecken und Felsen. Kiesstrand. Von der Straße zum Cabo Formentor ist die Bucht zu Fuß zu erreichen. Versorgung: keine.

Small-sized anchorage. Best spots close to the small pebble beach. Bottom mostly weed with sandy spots, occasional rocks. From the road to Cabo Formentor this Cala can be reached by foot. No supplies.

C Cala en Gossalba
39° 56,4' N   003° 11,4' E

Ankern auf 6-8 m Wassertiefe, möglichst im Scheitel der Bucht. Lange größere Wassertiefen als in der Cala Murta. *Anchorage at 6-8m depths, best closely to the bays crest. When you enter you will find more water depths than in the Cala Murta.*

D Cala Figuera
39° 57,7' N   003° 11,2' E

Idyllisch zwischen hohen Bergen. Die schönsten Ankerplätze liegen innen bei

Cala Murta

Cala en Gossalba

Cala Formentor – Cala Tuent

Cala Formentor

Cala Figuera

Mallorca

einem Felsen. Wassertiefen dort noch knapp unter 10 m. Fast reiner Sandgrund. Vielleicht kriecht ein Oktopus am Anker vorbei ... Zahlreiche Besucher des Kiesstrands kommen von der Straße, die zum Cabo Formentor führt. Keine Versorgung.

Idyllic spot between high mountains. The best spots lie further inwards. Water depths there are still just under 10m. Almost pure sandy bottom. Eventually an octopus is crawling around the anchor ... Many visitors at the pebble beach step down from the road above that leads to Cabo Formentor. No supplies.

E Cala Boquer
39° 56,2' N 003° 06,3' E

Eingerahmt von steilen Höhenzügen. Das Tal dahinter führt nach Port de Pollensa, 1,5 Stunden zu Fuss. Auch hier muss man für Wassertiefen unter 10m recht weit in den Scheitel der Bucht fahren. An Land pure Natur.

Framed by two steep ridges. The valley behind leads to Port de Pollensa, around 1,5 hours on foot. Again, you have to navigate quite close to the inner part of the bay for water depths less than 10m. No supplies.

F Cala San Vincente
39° 55,8' N 003° 04,1' E

Ein kleiner Urlaubsort garantiert hier für die meiste Zeit des Jahres Vollversorgung. Fast überall reiner Sandgrund bei Wassertiefen um rund 5 m.

Small tourist village offers almost everything from spring to autumn. The anchorage has mostly sandy bottom, water depths are around 5m.

G Cala Castell
39° 56,3' N 003° 02,3' E

Benannt nach der Ruine Castillo del Rey (492 m), die Luftlinie 2 km entfernt liegt. Erst im letzten Teil der Bucht gehen die Wassertiefen auf unter 10 m zurück. Ankergrund Seegras mit sandigen Flecken. An Land pure Natur. Es führt ein Weg weg von der Bucht und zum Castell. Man befindet sich dort auf Privatbesitz, es ist möglich, dass man zurückgeschickt wird. Das Castillo del Rey war neben dem Kastell von Alaró einer der letzten Verteidigungsstellun-

Cala Formentor – Cala Tuent

gen der Mauren bei der Rückeroberung Mallorcas durch den christlichen König Jaime I de Aragón 1229 und wurde bis 1231 gehalten.

*Named after the ruin Castillo del Rey (492m), which is 1.5mi away as the crow flies. Only in the inner part of the bay depths drop below 10m. The bottom is weed with sandy spots. Ashore pure nature. There is a path leading away from the bay and up with a branch-off to the Castell. **Caution:** You are walking here on private property, it is possible that you will be refused entry. Next to the castle of Alaró Castillo del Rey was one of the last defensive fortifications of the Moors during the reconquest of Mallorca by the Christian king Jaime I de Aragón in 1229 and was defended until 1231.*

H Cala de sa Calobra
39° 51,6' N 002° 47,8' E

Einzigartiger Platz vor dem Durchbruch des Torrent de Pareis auf ca. 10 m Wassertiefe. Im Sommer sind Anker- und Schwimmbereich wahrscheinlich separiert. Anlegestelle für Ausflugschiffe in einem Seitenarm der Bucht. Dort Restaurants und ein kleiner Laden.

Unique location in front of the gorge Torrent des Pareis, water depth 10m. In summer anchorage and swimming area are probably separated. Restaurants and small shop can be found in a branch of the bay where the excursion boats dock.

I Cala Tuent
39° 50,8' N 002° 46,2' E

Keine 5 sm entfernt von Port de Sóller und 1,5 sm von Sa Calobra. Ankern mit Blick auf Mallorca höchsten Berg, den Puig Major, 1445 m. Grund Sand und Seegras, 10-4 m Tiefe. Auf der Südseite das Restaurant „Es Vergeret", große Terrasse.

Less than 5nmi distance to Port de Sóller and 1.5nmi from Sa Calobra. Anchorage with a view of Mallorca's highest mountain Puig Major, altitude 1445m. Bottom sand and weed, depth 10-4m. On southern side lies restaurant „Es Vergeret", with extensive terrace.

T 971 517 105, M 669 715 990
esvergeret@hotmail.com
www.esvergeret.com

Cala de sa Calobra / Torrent de Pareis

Cala de sa Calobra / Torrent de Pareis

Cala Tuent

Menorca

Ein Sommer-Idyll: Auf einem Törn rund Menorca gehört Ciutadella im Westen zum Pflichtprogramm. Die Hafenstadt bezaubert mit einem wunderschönen Mix aus zentrumsnahen Liegeplätzen und gepflegter Altstadt.

A summer paradise: On a trip around Menorca, Ciutadella is a highlight. The former capital enchants visitors with a wonderful mix of charming and convenient berths located on the doorstep to the well-preserved old town.

Menorca

- Umrundung in nur 80 sm
- Starke britische Einflüsse
- Häufig Nordwind Mistral

- *Circumnavigation in just 80nmi*
- *Noticeable British influences*
- *Frequent north wind Mistral*

Menorca

Ciutadella – Cala Escorxada

🇩🇪 Durch die Lage zu Mallorca wird Ciutadella häufig zuerst angesteuert. Wer im Sommer kommt, erlebt eine Hafenstadt, die vor Charme nur so sprüht. Entlang Menorcas Südwesten entdeckt man einige der schönsten Buchten der Balearen.

🇬🇧 *Yachts coming from Mallorca frequently visit Ciutadella first. Sailors arriving in summer will experience a charming harbour town. Along the southwest coast of Menorca one can discover some of the most beautiful bays in the Balearic Islands.*

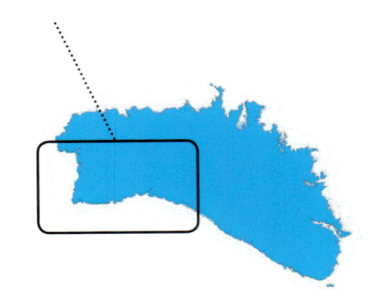

1 **Ciutadella - 39° 59,7' N 003° 49,4' E** → page 212
Im Sommer tolle Atmosphäre rund um den alten Hafen und die Altstadt.
During summer a great atmosphere around the old harbour and the old town.

2 **Cala Degollador - 39° 59,6' N 003° 49,5' E** → page 216
Beliebte hafennahe Bucht, die viele Yachten aufnahmen kann.
Popular bay close to Ciutadellas port, that can shelter many yachts.

3 **Cala Santandria - 39° 58,7' N 003° 49,7' E** → page 217
Viele Gaststätten, Supermarkt in der Nähe. Wassertiefe 7-3 m.
Many restaurants, nearby supermarket. Anchorage at 7-3m.

4 **Leuchtturm / *Lighthouse* d'Artutx: Fl(3)10s** → page 218

5 **Cala 'n Bosch - 39° 55,3' N 003° 50,3 E** → page 218
Zwei Ankerbuchten östlich des Sportboothafens, eine mit Schutz bei Mistral.
Two bays east of marina, one with good protection against northerly Mistral.

6 **Cala de Son Saura - 39° 55,3' N 003° 53,5 E** → page 220
Großer Ankerplatz mit Schutz gegen Wind aus Südost. Flache Umgebung.
Large bay with protection against wind from southeast. Level surroundings.

7 **Cala Talaier - 39° 55,4' N 003° 54,2 E** → page 220
Östlich der Cala Son Saura. Lebhafte türkise Wasserfarben.
Less than 0.5 nm east of Cala Son Saura. Lively turquoise water colours.

8 **Cala Turqueta - 39° 55,7' N 003° 54,9 E** → page 220
Ankern über 6-4 m vor Badezone & belebten Strand. Überwiegend Seegras.
Anchorage at 6 - 4m in front of busy beach. Bottom: predominantly weed.

9 **Cala Macarella - 39° 56,0' N 003° 56,3' E** → page 221
Für viele die schönste Bucht Menorcas – entsprechend stark besucht ...
For many, the most beautiful bay of Menorca - well attended in summer ...

10 **Cala Galdana - 39° 56,0' N 003° 57,3' E** → page 222
Touristisches Zentrum an der Südküste. Reizvoll trotz starker Bebauung.
Popular tourist centre. Attractive despite strong development.

11 **Cala Mitjana - 39° 55,9' N 003° 58,3' E** → page 222
Auf der ersten Blick sehr attraktiv – Yachten müssen weit draußen ankern.
On a first glance quite attractive – but yachts have to anchor quite far outside.

12 **Cala Trebeluja - 39° 55,7' N 003° 59,3' E** → page 222
Vielleicht die bessere Wahl, weil hier keine Badezone zu beachten ist ...
Perhaps the better choice as there is no swimming area laid out ...

13 **Cala Escorxada - 39° 55,4' N 004° 00,2' E** → page 223
Auch hier keine Badezone. Sollte man besucht haben.
Another must-see bay. No swimming zone.

Der Südwesten Menorcas / The South-West of Menorca

- 1 CIUTADELLA
- 2 Cala Degollador
- 3 Cala Santandria
- 4 Cabo d'Artutx
- 5 Cala 'n Bosch, Cala Xoriguer
- 6 Cala de Son Saura
- 7 Cala Talaier
- 8 Cala Turqueta
- 9 Cala Macarella
- 10 Cala Galdana
- 11 Cala Mitjana
- 12 Cala Trebaluguer
- 13 Cala Escorxada

MENORCA

Portbook & Island Guide 211

Ciutadella

🇩🇪 Keine andere Hafenstadt auf den Balearen hat diese perfekte Kombination von kleinen Yachthäfen und unmittelbar anschließender Altstadt wie Ciutadella, am westlichen Ende Menorcas. Dieser Vorteil kommt vor allem im Hochsommer zum Tragen. Wenn die Liegeplätze gefüllt sind und die Bars und Gaststätten entlang der Kaimauer nicht minder. Wer hier flaniert, hat nur wenige Meter oder Stufen zu steigen und steht auf dem großzügigen Platz vor einer Altstadt, die im Vergleich zu anderen einzigartig gepflegt erscheint. Darin zahlreiche Geschäfte und Restaurants.

Ciutadella hat seit 2013 mehr Liegeplätze für Yachten zu bieten als einst. Das ist die Konsequenz einer schweren Rissaga im Jahr 2006, bei der ein Schaden in Millionenhöhe entstanden war. Eine Rissaga bezeichnet im Spanischen einen Meteo-Tsunami und der von 2006 war nicht der erste und nicht der schwerste, der diesen Hafen heimsuchte. Dabei verschwindet innerhalb kurzer Zeit mehr als ein Meter Wasserhöhe aus dem Hafen, um ebenfalls binnen weniger Minuten mit einer mehr oder weniger starken Flutwelle zurückzukehren. Boote, die trocken gefallen sind, werden dann unter Stege gepresst, kollidieren und verkeilen sich mit anderen. Weil es in den Jahren davor schon schlimmere Rissages gab, entschlossen sich die Regierenden 2006 zum Handeln. Für Fähren und Handelsschiffe wurde der Port Comercial Son Blanc gleich vor dem Hafen neu gebaut und ist seit März 2011 in Betrieb.

In Ciutadella hat man m. E. die Wahl zwischen den Liegeplätzen des Vereins Club Nàutic und den von Ports Islas Baleares verwalteten. PortsIB, so die Kurzform, kann jedoch nur Skipper oder Eigner bedienen, deren Yacht nicht mehr als 12x4 m misst. Man liegt hier preiswerter, muss sich allerdings mit einfacheren Sanitäreinrichtungen zufrieden geben.

🇬🇧 *No other harbour town on the Balearic Islands offers this ideal combination of small marinas adjacent to a historic old town like Ciutadella, situated at the western end of Menorca. This is clearly seen in July and August when berths are filled up and bars and restaurants along the quay are bursting. When strolling along the marina, you just need to ascend a few steps to arrive at a wide plaza in front of the old town which, compared with others, is exceedingly wellgroomed. Numerous shops and restaurants can be found here.*

Since 2013, Ciutadella has significantly increased its number of yacht berths. This was due to a severe rissaga in

Einfahrt nach Ciutadella: Leuchtturm auf der Punta de Sa Farola und Torre de San Nicolás gegenüber.

Port entrance of Ciutadella: between Punta de sa Farola with its lighthouse and Torre de San Nicolás.

39° 59,7' N 003° 49,4' E

FlW 6s

Ciutadella

2006 which caused damages ranging into the millions. The Spanish term rissaga denotes a meteo sunami, and the 2006 event was neither the first nor the most severe one to afflict this harbour. Within a short time, water levels within the harbour sink by more than a metre, only to return within minutes in a more or less vehement flood wave. Consequently, boats having fallen dry become squeezed beneath piers, collide or become wedged together with others.

As worse rissages had occurred in the past, authorities decided in 2006 to take action. The Port Comercial Son Blanc was newly built directly in front of the harbour to serve ferries and commercial ships, and has been operational since March 2011.

In Ciutadella you can choose berths from Club Nàutic and others operated by Ports Islas Baleares. PortsIB, so the short form, however, can serve only skippers or owners with yachts no bigger than 12x4m. It is cheaper here, but you have to settle for more simple sanitation facilities.

ANSTEUERUNG
APPROACHING

Zeitweise ein- oder auslaufende Fähren im Handelshafen unmittelbar südlich der schmalen Einfahrt zu den Yachthäfen.

Der Leuchtturm auf der Punta de sa Farola auf der Nordseite der Hafeneinfahrt ist vor starken Lichtquellen erst aus circa 3 sm Entfernung auszumachen. Die Südseite der Einfahrt nach Ciutadella wird vom Torre de San Nicolás markiert (nachts angestrahlt). Wassertiefe in der Mitte des Hafens über 5 m.

Das Ampel-System an der Hafeneinfahrt, das viele Jahre den Zugang zum Hafen regelte, damit sich Schiffe und Sportboote nicht in die Quere kamen, hat sich mit der Inbetriebnahme des neuen Handelshafens überholt und ist abgeschaltet.

Be aware of entering or departing ferries at the commercial port just south of the narrow entrance to the marinas. The lighthouse on Punta de sa Farola on northern side of harbour entrance is visible only at some 3nmi distance, due to strong light sources in its background. The south side of the entrance into Ciutadella is marked by Torre de San Nicolás, illuminated at night. Water depth in harbour: mid-basin more than 5m.

The traffic light system at the harbour entrance, which for years regulated access to the harbour to prevent commercial and recreational ships from getting into each others way, has been switched off after the opening of the new commercial port.

FESTMACHEN
FIND A BERTH

A PortsIB

Seit Sommer 2013 gibt es Schwimmstege für Yachten bis 12 m Länge und 4 m Breite. Sie befinden sich auf der Nordseite der schmalen Hafenbucht, wo vorher die Fähren anlegten. Anlegen an Fingerstegen, keine Muringleinen.

Offiziell gibt es nur neun mögliche Gastliegeplätze, die via Internet über

Blick aus dem Inneren des schmalen Hafens Richtung Einfahrt.
View from the inner part of Ciutadellas port to the west.

- Der perfekte Sommerhafen
- Mehr Liegeplätze für Gäste
- Sehr gepflegte Altstadt

- *The perfect harbour in summer*
- *More berths for visitors*
- *Well-groomed Old Town*

Menorca

www.portsib.es gebucht werden können. Reservierung notwendig, mindestens drei Tage im Voraus über www.portsib.es. Bezahlung per Kreditkarte. Stornierung oder Umbuchung über die Webseite und das Service-Telefon 902 024 444.

Aber: Wenn dauerhaft vergebene Liegeplätze frei sind, weil der Eigner auf Törn ist, werden diese ebenfalls vermietet. Jedoch nicht über die portsIB-Webseite, sondern nur über das Büro vor Ort. Und das hört auf UKW-Kanal 14, telefonische Anfragen sind zwecklos. Die Preise sind identisch mit denen im Web.

Since summer of 2013 there are floating pontoons for yachts up to 12m length and 4m width. They are situated at the northern side of the narrow harbour bay, where ferries used to dock. Landing at finger piers, no mooring lines. Reservation obligatory at least 3 days in advance at www.portsib.es. Payment by credit card. For cancelation or changes please use the web site or the service line 902 024 444.

Officially there are only nine visitor berths, which can be booked via the Internet through www.portsib.es. However as all-year berth holders leave their berths for summer cruises, these are rented separately and only on VHF channel 14, telephone inquiries are useless. Worth a try! The prices are identical to those on the Web.

Office, T 971 484 455
(im altem Fährterminal / *in former ferry terminal*) port.ciutadella@portsib.es

€ EUR/m²: 0,60 (01/06-30/09); 0,18 (01/10-31/05)
Water: 5,50 EUR; Electr.: 5,50 EUR
Alle Preise plus 21% MwSt.
All prices plus 21% VAT

🕐 8-15 h (winter), 8-20 h (summer)

🚿 Toiletten und Duschen unterhalb des PortsIB-Büros bei der Werft Astilleros Llompart. / *Toilets and showers below the PortsIB-office close to shipyard Astilleros Llompart.*

B Club Nàutic, Moll de la Trona
170 m lange Pier an der Südseite der schmalen Hafenbucht, Wassertiefe an der Kaje 3,50 m. Tankstelle (Diesel, Benzin) sowie Strom und Wasser. Man legt jetzt mit Bug oder Heck zur Pier an, es gibt Muringleinen. Die Liegeplätze in der gegenüberliegenden Cala Busquetes und vor der Altstadt gehören ebenfalls zum Club, die Plätze sind aber fast komplett an Dauerlieger vergeben.

170m-long pier at southern side of the narrow harbour bay. Water depth at quay 3.50m. Refuelling station (diesel, petrol/gasoline) and electricity & water. Land bow or stern to pier, with mooring lines available. In Cala Busquetes vis-à-vis and further inside the bay more pontoons belong to the Club. These berths are mostly belonging to all-year-round contract holders.

T 971 383 918, 📱 UKW/VHF 09
Öffnungszeiten / *Opening hours*:
July/Aug.: Mon-Fri. 9-14 + 16-20 h;
Sa+Sun: 9-13 h
Sept.-June: 9-14 + 16-20 h;
Sa+Sun: closed
Reservierung über / *Reservation on*: www.cnciutadella.com (English!)

€ 12m - 15/07-31/08: 113 EUR, 15/06-14/07: 106 EUR, 01/09-31/05: 57 EUR - Während des San-Juan-Festes (20/06-25/06) Höchstsaisonpreise / *During San-Juan-Fiesta (20/06-25/06) highest price level*
Preise für Katamarane auf Anfrage / *Multihull rates on request*
Duschen, Wasser, Strom, WiFi, und MwSt. eingeschlossen / *Including showers, water, electricity, WiFi and VAT*

TANKEN / *FUEL*

Club Nàutic, Moll de la Trona
T 971 481 373
🕐 July-Aug: 9.15-13.15 h + 15-19 h (Mon-Sun)

Nun mit Muringleinen: die Liegeplätze des Club Nàutic
Moore bow or stern to: visitor's berths of Club Nàutic

Ciutadella

Innenteil des Hafens: links PortsIB, rechts Liegeplätze des Club.
Inner part of the harbour: to the left the berths of PortsIB, to the right berths of the Club.

June-Sept.: 9.15-13.15 h + 15-18 h (Mon-Sat), Sun closed
May+Oct.: 9.30-13.15 h + 15-18 h (Mon-Fri), Sat+Sun closed
Nov.-April: Mon, Wedn., Thursd. Auf Anfrage / *On request*

TECHNISCHER SERVICE
TECHNICAL SERVICES

Schiffswerft beim alten Fährterminal.
Shipyard close to former ferry terminal.

Astilleros Llompart, 12,5-t-crane
astillerosllompart@gmail.com
M 650 957 454 + 619 413 748
🕒 8-13 + 15.30-19 h

YACHTAUSRÜSTER
CHANDLERIES

Centre Nautic, T 971 382 616
C/ Bisuters 23, Ciudadela
centrenautic@centrenautic.com
www.centrenautic.com

EINKAUFEN / *SHOPPING*

Kleiner Supermarkt oberhalb der Liegeplätze von portsIB. Geschäfte aller Art im weiteren Bereich der Altstadt. Große Supermärkte an den Ausfallstraßen und in den Gewerbegebieten.

Small supermarket above berths of portsIB. All kinds of shops in extended Old Town area. Larger supermarkets at arterial roads and at business parks.

Südlich der Hafeneinfahrt: / South of the ports entrance: Torre de San Nicolás

Menorca

RESTAURANTS & BARS

Restaurant Club Nàutic
im Obergeschoss. Blick auf den Hafen.
in upper floor. Harbour view.
T 971 38 63 75

Oberhalb des Hafens zig Restaurants in der Altstadt. *Many restaurants in Old Town above the harbour.*

Cas Consòl, T 971 484 654
mit Sonnenuntergang- und Hafenblick / *with sunset & harbour view*
Plaça des Born, 17
www.casconsol.com

Am Hafen ein Restaurant neben dem anderen. Erwähnenswert: / *Restaurants galore in the harbour. Recommended:* **Café Balear** ... ist ein Restaurant im hinteren Teil der Bucht. Bekannt für frischen Fisch. Man fängt selbst. Die wenigen Tische sind immer belegt. Warten ist angesagt, Reservieren nur in Ausnahmefällen möglich. / *...is a restaurant in the back part of the bay. Famous for fresh fish caught by the company. Only few tables which are always occupied. Prepare for a wait, reservations done only in exceptional cases.*
T 971 380 005, www.cafe-balear.com

BARS & LATE NIGHT

Angesagte Chill Out Bars und Diskotheken findet man in den inneren Teil des Hafens. Vor 23 Uhr muss man sich nicht dorthin begeben. / *The chill out and dance clubs are located together in the inner part of the harbour area. Nothing starts to happen until 11 pm.*

AUSFLÜGE / EXCURSIONS

Ein Besuch der Altstadt ist Pflicht. Über die alte Fischertreppe ist sie von der Brücke aus verbunden mit dem Hafen. Einmal im Jahr lebt der ganze Ort im Ausnahmezustand. Ciutadella ist ausgebucht, wenn am 23. und 24. Juni in der Altstadt das Reiterfest San Juan gefeiert wird. Nur wenige Kilometer außerhalb der Stadt, an der Hauptstraße Richtung Mahón, kann man eine der bekanntesten und besterhaltensten frühgeschichtlichen Bauten der Insel besichtigen, Naveta des Tudons, eine Grabanlage aus dem 14. Jahrhundert v. Chr. / *One simply must visit the Old Town. It is connected to the harbour by the old fishermen's stairway. Once every year the entire town becomes a playground and Ciutadella is fully booked, when San Juan gymkhana is celebrated in the Old Town on June 23rd and 24th. Just a few kilometers outside the city, on the main road towards Mahón, you can visit one of the most famous and best-preserved prehistoric buildings on the island, Naveta des Tudons, a grave from the 14th century BC.*

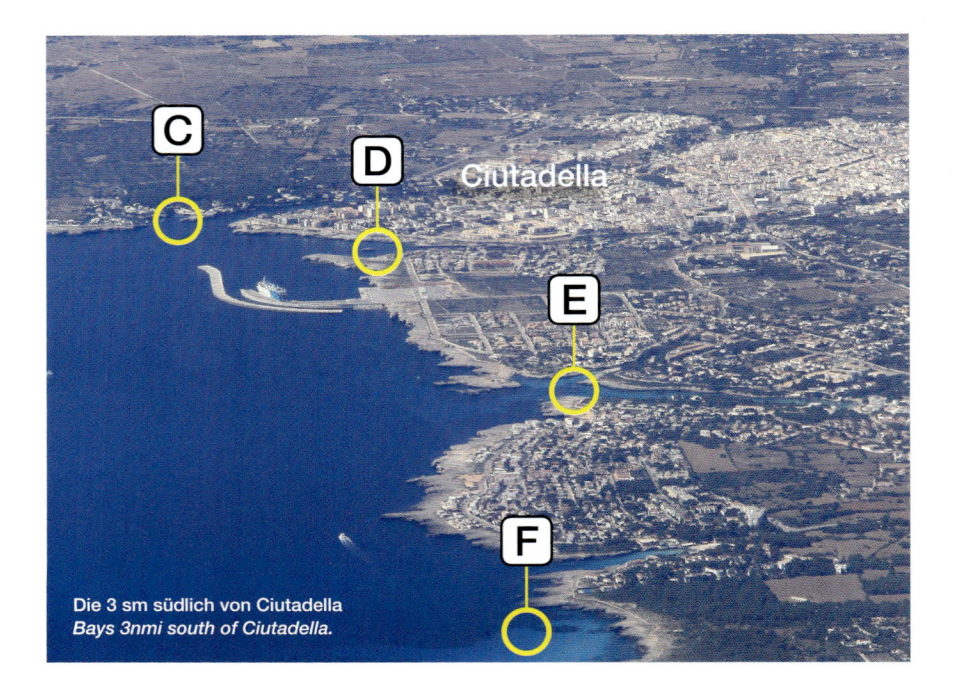

Die 3 sm südlich von Ciutadella
Bays 3nmi south of Ciutadella.

Cala d'es Frares – Cala Santandria

ANKERPLÄTZE
ANCHORAGE AREAS

C Cala d'es Frares
39° 59,7' N 003° 49,4' E

🇩🇪 Beim Einfahrtsfeuer auf der Nordseite des Hafens, Punta de sa Farola. Abgesperrte Badebereiche. Wenig Ankerraum. Je nach Belegung Ankern mit Landleine. Schwell durch vorbeifahrende Yachten. Tiefe: 8-6 m, Grund Seegras mit Fels und Sandflecken. Etwas weiterer Weg in die Stadt. Einige Crews benutzen das Beiboot.

🇬🇧 *At entry lights on northern side of the harbour, Punta de sa Farola. Separated swimming areas. Little anchorage space, if crowded a mooring ashore is needed. Swell caused by passing yachts. Depth: 8-6m, bottom weed with rock and sandy patches. Slightly further distance into the city. Some crews use the dinghy.*

D Cala Degollador
39° 59,6' N 003° 49,5' E

Ankerbucht zwischen der Einfahrt zum Hafen von Ciutadella und dem Port Comercial Son Blanc. Im schmalen Innenteil vor einer Badezone mit Landleine ankern. Tiefe zirka 4 m. Ankergrund: Sand mit Seegras. Weiter außen freies Ankern, zirka 7 m Tiefe. Restaurants und Supermärkte in fußläufiger Entfernung. Unruhig bei Mistral.

Lies adjacent to the south of Ciutadella harbour bay. While anchoring in narrow inner section, bring a mooring line

Cala d'es Frares – Cala Santandria

Cala Degollador

Fl(4)R 11s

ashore. Further out there is no need for it. Depth: 7-4m, bottom sand with some weed. Restaurants and supermarkets within walking distance. Unsettled conditions with Mistral.

E Cala Santandria
39° 58,7' N 003° 49,7' E
2 sm südlich von Ciutadella. Rundum mit Ferienhäusern bebaut. Ankern nur im vorderen Teil der Bucht auf 7-3 m Tiefe, der Grund ist Sand mit Seegras. Kein ausreichender Schutz bei Mistral. Gelbe Bojen trennen die Strandbucht und die lange, schmale Einbuchtung ab. In der tiefen, nach Osten reichenden Bucht, liegen Boote an dauerhaft vergebenen Plätzen. Viele Gaststätten an Land, Supermarkt in der Nähe.

2nm south of Ciutadella. Anchorage in the outer part of the bay at 7-3m, mostly sandy bottom with spots of weed. **Caution:** *no sufficient protection when Mistral is blowing. Yellow buoys separate the anchorage from the beach cove and the long, narrow inlet that stretches to the east. This part of the bay is designated to permanent berth holders. Many restaurants ashore. Supermarket within walking distance.*

F Cala Blanca
Wenn die Wetterlage ruhig ist, dann könnte die offene, namenlose Bucht südlich der Cala Blanca 1 sm entfernt eine Alternative sein. Der Ankergrund hier ist reiner Sand, man ankert auf ca. 5 m Wasser. Die Cala Blanca selbst eignet sich nicht.

South of Cala Blanca, 1nmi away, could be an option. The bottom here is pure sand, the depths are around 5m. Cala Blanca does not offer sufficient space for yachts.

Cala Santandria: Der Teil im Bild rechts ist Dauerliegern vorbehalten.
The part shown right cannot be used by visiting boats.

Menorca

Cala'n Bosch

🇩🇪 Ins Land hinein gebauter Sportboothafen, der im Sommer regelmäßig Gastyachten aufnimmt. Reservierungen werden empfohlen.

🇬🇧 *Inland built marina for yachts up to 18m which regularly receives boats for the summer months. It is recommended to make a reservation.*

ANSTEUERUNG
APPROACHING

Eine Brücke über den Einfahrtskanal limitiert die maximale Höhe auf 6,80 m. Einfahrtstiefe max. 1,20 m. Einfahrtsfeuer: Fl(2)R 7s und Fl(2)G 7s
A bridge over the entrance channel limits the maximum height to 6.80m. Entrance depth max. 1.20m. Entrance lights: Fl(2)R 7s und Fl(2)G 7s

FESTMACHEN
FIND A BERTH

[A] Liegeplätze für Yachten bis 18 m Länge. Man macht fest an Schwimmstegen mit Fingerstegen.
Berths for boats up to 18m in length. Yachts dock at floating pontoons with finger piers.

TANKEN / *FUEL*

(D+B), July+August 8-21 h, June+Sept. 9-13 + 16-19.30 h (Mon-Sat), 9-13 h (Sun); T 971 387 171; M 617 312 597; www.puertocalanbosch.com

EINKAUFEN / *SHOPPING*

Supermärkte, Autovermieter, Ärzte, Apotheke, Tauchschulen, Geldautomaten etc.
Supermarkets, car rental, doctors, pharmacies, diving schools, ATMs, etc.

RESTAURANTS & BARS

Rund um das Hafenbecken Restaurants in Hülle und Fülle
Around the harbour plenty of restaurants

Cala'n Bosch & Cala Xoriguer

Cala'n Bosch

Cala'n Bosch

39° 55,4' N   003° 50,1 E

ANKERPLÄTZE
ANCHORAGE AREAS

B Cala'n Bosch
Bucht östlich der Einfahrt zum gleichnamigen Sportboothafen. Ankern über Sand vor einer Badezone, 6-4 m Tiefe. Keine Untiefen. *Bay east of the entrance to the correspondent marina. Anchorage with sandy bottom in front of a swimming area, 6-4 m depth.*

C Cala Xoriguer
Schutz bei Mistral bietet erst die östlich anschließende Cala Xoriguer durch eine Landzunge. Hier weiträumig abgetrennte Badezone! Man ankert auf zirka 5 m über Seegras. An Land Supermarkt, Restaurants, Autovermieter.
Achtung: Vor der Cala Xoriguer befindet sich die Flachstelle Bajo d'Artuch mit zirka 1,60 m Wasser, die nicht in allen Seekarten verzeichnet ist. Bei hohem Sonnenstand ist sie an einer grünlichen Verfärbung des Wassers zu erkennen.
When northerly wind Mistral blows protection will not be found here but in Cala Xoriguer, the next bay eastwards behind a headland. Widely separated swimming area! One drops anchor at about 5m depth above weed. Ashore supermarket, restaurants, car rental.
Caution: *In front of Cala Xoriguer the flat spot Bajo d'Artuch with about 1.60m of water is marked, but only in some charts. When sun is high it can be recognised by a greenish spot in the sea.*

AUSFLÜGE / EXCURSIONS

D 1 km südwestlich (Luftlinie) steht der Leuchtturm Far Cabo d'Artrutx, Fl(3)W 10s, und markiert die Südwestspitze Menorca. Wer Lust auf einen kurzen Spaziergang verspürt, kann sich hier vor dem Rückweg stärken.
Less than 1mi southwest (beeline) is the lighthouse Faro de Cabo d'Artrutx, Fl(3)W 10s, and marks the south-western tip of Menorca. A short walk can be split by having a refreshment at the turning point.

Bar & Snack-Restaurant
„Far Cap d'Artutx",
T 871 552 286, M 654 397 300
Tue-Sun from 11.30 h, Mon closed

Menorca

Cala Son Saura – Cala Macarella

ANKERPLÄTZE
ANCHORAGE AREAS

A Cala Son Saura
39° 55,3' N 003° 53,5 E

🇩🇪 Platz für drei Dutzend Yachten in flacher Umgebung. Ankern auf ca. 5 m über Sandgrund vor Badezonen. In Teilen guter Schutz gegen Südostwind. Streifen aus Fels und Seegras durchzieht die Mitte der Bucht. Zirka 1 km entfernt ein Restaurant, das im Sommer täglich von 12-19 Uhr öffnet. T 618 640 389

🇬🇧 *Level surroundings, space for roughly three dozen boats. Anchorage at ca 5m above sandy ground in front of swimming areas. In parts good protection against SE-winds. Strip of rock and weed crosses the bay's middle. Approximately 1mi away a restaurant which opens daily from 12-19 h during summer. T 618 640 389*

B Cala Talaier
39° 55,4' N 003° 54,2 E

Weniger als 0,5 sm östlich der Cala Son Saura, Umgebung steigt nach Osten hin langsam an. Lebhafte türkise Wasserfarben, am schönsten kurz vor der abgetrennten Schwimmzone. Versorgung: siehe Cala Son Saura

Less than 0.5nmi east of Cala Son Saura, surroundings rise slowly to the east. Lively turquoise waters are most beautiful just in front of the separated swimming area. Supply: see Cala Son Saura

C Cala Turqueta
39° 55,7' N 003° 54,9 E

Mit Kiefern bewachsene Kliffs. Ankern über 6-4 m vor einer Badezone und einem belebten Strand. Mehr Seegras als Sand. Dingi-Passage zum Strand an der Ostseite. Snackbar in

Cala Son Saura – Cala Macarella

Cala Macarella

1 km Entfernung beim Strandparkplatz. *Cliffs overgrown with pines. Anchorage at 6-4m in front of a swimming area and a busy beach. Bottom: more weed than sand. Dinghy-passage to the beach on the east side of the bay. Snack-bar within 1mi distance at a car park.*

D Cala Macarella
39° 56,0' N 003° 56,3' E

Vom Landschaftseindruck her Menorcas Top-Bucht – und z. T. entsprechend voll. Die hohe, helle Klifküste suggeriert Geborgenheit. Tatsächlich guter Schutz bei Nord- und Westwinden. Vor Badezonen und schönen Sandstränden ankern über Sand mit wenig Seegras und 6-4 m. Strandbar.

In terms of landscape, this is Menorca's No. 1 bay – and therefore full of people and boats at times. The steep, light cliff coast is cosy and offers good protection against winds from north and west. Anchorage in front of swimming areas and beautiful sandy beaches above sandy ground and little weed at 6-4m. Beach bar.

Cala Turqueta

Cala Trebaluja

Cala Galdana – Cala Escorxada

ANKERPLÄTZE
ANCHORAGE AREAS

A Cala Santa Galdana
39° 56,0' N 003° 57,3' E

🇩🇪 Weiträumige Bucht, aber trotzdem nur Platz für zirka ein Dutzend Yachten, denn die Badezone ist großzügig ausgetonnt. Etwas Schutz gegen östliche Winde. Auf der Nordseite mündet der Barranc d'Algendar ein, der einzige ganzjährig wasserführende Fluss der Insel. Abgesehen von der Hotelbebauung landschaftlich reizvoll. Ankern auf 5-4 m und Sand. An Land Vollversorgung.

🇬🇧 *Spacious bay but can only serve around a dozen of yachts, because the swimming area occupies a large part of the bay. Some shelter against easterly winds. On the north side the estuary of Barranc d'Algendar flows in, as the only year-round water-bearing river of the island. Beautiful landscape with the exception of the hotel buildings. Anchorage at 5-4m and above sandy bottom. Ashore supermarkets, bars, restaurants etc.*

B Cala Mitjana
39° 55,9' N 003° 58,3' E

Eines der schönsten Naturschwimmbäder Menorcas – für Landtouristen. Yachten müssen recht weit draußen ankern. Keine Versorgung.

One of the most beautiful natural swimming pools of Menorca – for regular tourists. Yachts have to drop anchor pretty far away. No supply ashore.

C Cala Trebeluja
39° 55,7' N 003° 59,3' E

Weil Landtouristen recht weit wandern müssen, ist diese Bucht nicht überlaufen. Positiv für Skipper und Crews: Es gibt hier keine abgetrennte Badezone. Ein Flusslauf mündet hinter dem Strand, die Dünen sind abgesperrt. Schönes Schnorcheln bei den Felsen an der Ostseite, hier legt von Fall zu Fall ein Ausflugsboot an. Auch liegen hier zwei Bojen für Behördenboote. Keine Versorgung.

Because regular tourists have to walk quite far this bay is not overcrowded. A small river behind the beach forms

Cala Galdana – Cala Escorxada

Cala Galdana

Cala Mitjana

Cala Escorxada

a sweet water lake, the dunes are restricted area. And ideal for Skipper and crew: There is no swimming zone. Fine snorkeling around the rocks on the east side, excursion boats dock here sometimes. Also to be found are two buoys for authority boats. No supply ashore.

D **Cala Escorxada**
39° 55,4' N 004° 00,2' E

Ein flach auslaufender, reiner Sandgrund, ohne dass eine Zone für Schwimmer ausgelegt wäre. Dazu überschaubarer Andrang an Land, denn die Bucht ist maximal weit entfernt, um sie landseitig schnell erreichen zu können. Keine Versorgung.

Relatively flat, pure sandy bottom without any area designated to swimmers. The beach is not visited by crowds because of time-comsuming access by foot. No supply ashore.

Portbook & Island Guide 223

Menorca

Playa Binigaus – Cala Presili

🇩🇪 Im Land der aufgehenden Sonne: Wo die Balearen zuerst das Licht des neuen Tages erblicken, schlägt das Herz Menorcas. Die Hauptstadt Mahón liegt an einem der größten Naturhäfen. Ein begehrter Vorzug, davon zeugen Befestigungsanlagen.

🇬🇧 *Land of the Rising Sun: Where the new day's light touches the Balearic Islands first, we find the island's capital Mahón, situated at one of the largest natural harbours worldwide. Huge fortifications show how desirable this was in the past.*

1 Playa de Binigaus – Son Bou - 39° 54,0' N 004° 04,0' E → page 226
Die Strandzone im Süden Menorcas. Ein 3 sm langer Ankerplatz …
The beach area in the south of Menorca. Anchorage at more than 3nm …

2 Cala Porté - 39° 51,7' N 004° 08,6' E → page 226
40 m hohe Kliffs schaffen eine beeindruckende Atmosphäre. Große touristische Siedlung an Land. / *Cliffs reach 40 m height and create an impressive atmosphere. Large tourist resort ashore.*

3 Cala Covas - 39° 51,6' N 004° 8,6' E → page 227
Beliebte Bucht, hohe Kliffs vermitteln ein Gefühl der Geborgenheit. Keine Versorgung. / *Popular Bay, high cliffs give a feeling of security. Ashore no bar or restaurant. Bring your own provisions.*

4 Cala Canatuells - 39° 50,9' N 004° 10,1' E → page 227
Eine schmale, aber stimmungsvolle Bucht, in der kleine Boote dominieren.
A narrow, but evocative bay, dominated by small pleasure boats.

5 Cala Binibeca - 39° 48,7' N 004° 14,6' E → page 229
Beliebte Ankerbucht. Yachtclub vermietet zudem frei Bojen. Untiefe in der Ansteuerung. / *Popular anchorage. Yacht Club also rents vacant buoys. Lighted shoal only 0,5nmi away.*

6 Punta Prima / Isla del Aire - 39° 48,7' N 004° 17,3' E → page 229
Beliebter Ankerstopp an der Südostspitze Menorcas: beim Leuchtturm oder vor einem Strand / *Popular achorages on the southeastern tip of Menorca: at the lighthouse or in front of a beach*
Kennung Leuchtturm / *Lighthouse characteristic:* FlW 5s

7 Puerto de Mahón - 39° 52,0' N 004° 18,7' E → page 230
Einer der größten Naturhäfen der Welt. Beherbergt mehrere Marinas. Sehenswerte Altstadt. Starke britische Einflüsse. / *Among the world's largest natural harbours. Shelters several marinas. The old town is definitely worth a visit. Strong british influence.*

8 Cala Mesquida - 39° 58,8' N 004° 17,6' E → page 240
Die erste attraktive Bucht nördlich von Mahón. Es sind zahlreiche Untiefen zu beachten. / *The first attractive bay north of Mahón. Take care of various unmarked shoals.*

9 Es Grau / Isla Colom - 39° 57,2' N 004° 16,8' E → page 240
Ankerplatz vor einem kleinen Ort. Es gibt hier Bojen, die vermietet werden. Direkt nördlich ein sehr beliebtes Bojenfeld westlich der Isla Colom.
Anchorage in front of a small fisherman's village. There are also buoys for rent. Directly to the north a popular buoy field west of Isla Colom.

10 Cala Algaret & Presili - 39° 59,5' N 004° 15,8' E → page 240
Beliebte Buchten vor Stränden südlich des Leuchtturms beim Cabo Favaritx.
Popular bays with beaches south of the lighthouse on Cabo Favaritx.

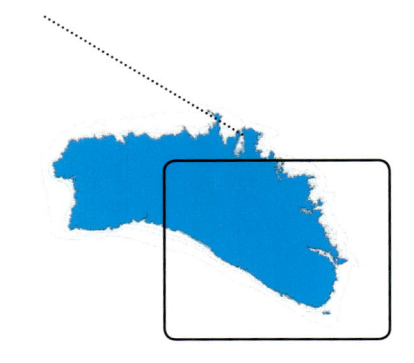

Der Osten Menorcas / The East of Menorca

- Playa Binigaus
- San Tomàs
- Son Bou
- **1**
- Cala Porté **2**
- **3** Cala Covas
- **4** Cala Canatuells
- MENORCA
- **7** MAHON
- Es Grau
- Isla Colom **9**
- **10** Cala Algaret & Cala Presili
- **8** Cala Mesquida
- Cala Binibeca **5**
- Punta Prima
- **6** Isla del Aire

Portbook & Island Guide   225

Menorca

Cala Binibeca

Cala Binibeca – Punta Prima / Isla del Aire

Isla del Aire

Cala Binibeca – Isla del Aire

ANKERPLÄTZE
ANCHORAGE AREAS

A **Cala Binibeca**
39° 48,7' N 004° 14,6' E

🇩🇪 Beliebte Ankerbucht mit Sandstrand und Blick auf die Isla del Aire, dahinter Feriensiedlungen. Ankergrund weiter außen um 10 m. Der lokale Yachtclub vermietet freie Bojen an Gäste, ca. 15 EUR. Supermarkt und Gaststätten ca. 300 m östlich in der Siedlung. Bar gleich beim Anleger.
Achtung: Befeuerte Untiefe Bajo Es Caragol (Q(6)W+LFl 15s) 0,5 sm südöstlich.

🇬🇧 *Popular anchorage with sandy beach and vista towards Isla del Aire, holiday resort ashore. Further out depth approx.. 10m. Local yacht club lets vacant buoys to guests, ca. 15 EUR. Supermarkets and restaurants some 300m east of the apartment blocks. Bar right next to pier.*
Attention: *Lighted shoal Bajo Es Caragol (Q(6)W+LFl 15s) 0.5 nmi southeast.*

B **Punta Prima / Isla del Aire**
39° 48,7' N 004° 17,3' E

An der Südostspitze zwischen Punta Mabres und Punta Prima ankern bei ruhigen Bedingungen über wunderschön türkisem Blau vor einer abgetrennten Badezone. Tiefe 7-5 m. An Land im Sommer Vollversorgung einer touristischen Siedlung, inkl. Apotheke. 0,5 sm südlich, im Nordwesten der Isla del Aire mit ihrem schwarz-weiß geringelten Leuchtturm (Fl 5s), könnte der Anker ebenfalls fallen, auf ca. 4 m Wassertiefe und felsigem Grund mit Seegras. Zum Anlanden gibt es einen Steg, ein Weg führt von dort zum Leuchtturm auf der Südseite.

On the southeastern tip of Menorca between Punta Mabres and Punta Prima one can find this wonderful anchorage over turquoise blue water in front of a separated swimming area. Depth 7-5m. Behind the beach during summer full supply of a tourist settlement, incl. pharmacy. 0.5nmi south, in the northwest of Isla del Aire, with its black and white striped lighthouse (Fl 5s), you may also drop anchor at about 4m depth of water. Rocky bottom covered with weed. There is a dinghy pier and from there a path leads to the lighthouse on the south side.

Menorca

Mahón

🇩🇪 Die Hauptstadt Menorcas markiert den östlichsten Punkt der Balearen und Spaniens. Ist Hafen für Fähren und Kreuzfahrtschiffe und von den Marinas hier haben Yachtcrews die kürzeste Distanz von und nach Sardinien. Mahóns Naturhafen ist einer der größten weltweit und so wurde dieser Platz über Jahrhunderte zum Spielball verschiedener Hegemonialmächte. Darunter das britische Empire. Festungsanlagen sind bis heute überall sichtbar – und Gin wird noch immer gebraut.

🇬🇧 *Menorca's capital marks the easternmost location of the Balearic Islands and Spain. Inside it's huge natural bay Mahón provides shelter for ferries and cruise ships and last but not least for pleasure boats. Starting from here they have the shortest distance possible to Sardegna, a widely often used passage in the western Mediterranean. Mahón's huge natural bay has for centuries attracted various hegemonic powers. Among these was the British Empire whose fortifications to this day remain visible everywhere – and gin is still being distilled here.*

ANSTEUERUNG
APPROACHING

Die 75 m hohe, stark befestigte Halbinsel La Mola markiert die Nordseite der Einfahrt in die große Hafenbucht. Zwischen ihr und der Isla del Lazareto zweigt gleich zu Beginn die Zufahrt zum einzigen erlaubten Ankerplatz ab, zur Cala Taulera.
Große Fahrwassertonnen zeigen an, dass Berufsschifffahrt hier regelmäßig vertreten ist. Die in der Länge 3 sm messende Bucht ist durchgängig befeuert. Im Hauptfahrwasser passiert man die Isla del Lazareto, Krankenhaus-Standort aus kriegerischen Zeiten. Auf der folgenden Isla Cuarantena, heute auch Isla Plana genannt, mussten Schiffsbesatzungen in Quarantäne gehen.
An der Nordseite der Hafenbucht gibt es nun die ersten Liegeplätze in der Cala Llonga und voraus westlich der Isla del Rey. Alle weiteren Anlegestellen folgen.
Anlegestellen, die hier in der Folge nicht explizit benannt sind, befinden sich in der Zuständigkeit der Hafenbehörde Autoridad Portuaria, die ausschließlich ganzjährige Liegeplatzverträge vergibt. Für die regelmäßig verkehrenden Fährschiffe wurde 2015 eine neue Estación Maritima an der Nordseite Bucht in der Nähe des Kraftwerks gebaut. Auf der Südseite, vor der Altstadt, machen jetzt ausschließlich Kreuzfahrtschiffe fest.

75m-high, heavily fortified La Mola peninsula marks the northern side of the harbour bay entry passage. Right at the beginning, between the peninsula and Isla del Lazaretto the access to the only permitted anchorage site branches off, leading to Cala Taulera.
Large lighted buoys at the entrance indicate that large vessels regularly pass here. The bay is continuously lighted throughout its 3nmi. In the main channel, vessels pass Isla del Lazaretto, which housed a military hospital in war times. On subsequent Isla Cuarantena ship crews were obliged to stay during quarantine.
Afterwards the first berths appear at the north side of the harbour bay in Cala Llonga and further ahead west of Isla del Rey. All other mooring sites are situated further inward.
Mooring sites, which are not explicitly

Mahón / Maó

- Sehr große Hafenbucht
- Marinas & ein Ankerplatz
- Bedeutende Altstadt

- *Huge harbour bay*
- *Marinas & one anchoring site*
- *Significant Old town*

39° 52,0' N 004° 18,7' E

named here subsequently, are the responsibility of the Port Authority (Autoridad Portuaria) that awards only year-round mooring contracts.

For regularly scheduled ferries a new Estación Maritima was built in 2015, located on the north side of the inner bay close the power plant. On the south side, in front of the old town, cruise ships have their exclusive berths.

FESTMACHEN
FIND A BERTH

Diese Liegemöglichkeiten für Yachten gibt es in Mahón:
Skippers find several marinas in Mahón:

Marina Menorca
Vermietet Liegeplätze an verschiedenen Stellen innerhalb der Hafenbucht.
Berths at various locations.
T 971 365 889, UKW/VHF 09
info@marinamenorca.com
www.marinamenorca.com
Für einige der Liegeplätze kann es notwendig sein, auf den Service des Watertaxi zurückzugreifen. / *For some berths it may be necessary to call the services of the Water Taxi Menorca.*
May–Oct. Mon–Sat: 9.30–21.30 h
www.watertaximenorca.com
watertaximenorca@gmail.com
T +34 616 428 891

[A] Schwimmstege im inneren Teil der Hafenbucht beim Kraftwerk. 230 Plätze mit Muringleinen für Boote von 5-25 m Länge. Die sanitären Einrichtungen sind gepflegt, jedoch am unteren Limit für die Zahl der Liegeplätze. Gäste erhalten pro Tag maximal drei Stunden ein Elektrorad umsonst, was für einen Besuch der höher gelegenen Altstadt oder anderer Stadtteile nicht zu unterschätzen ist.
Floating pontoons in the inner part of the harbour bay, opposite to the power plant. Moorings laid out for 230 boats between 5-25m in length.
Sanitary facilities are well maintained, but rather few considering the number of berths. Guests are granted use of an electric bicycle for max. 3 hours a day, which proves quite useful for visiting the Old Town or other town quarters situated higher above.

Menorca

Marina Port Mahón

12 m: 88,23 EUR (July/Aug.),
55,38 EUR (Sept.-Juni);
incl. water, electr., taxes

B **Islas Flotantes**
Zwei verankerte Pontons in zentraler Lage mit Liegeplätzen an Muringleinen und Versorgung mit Wasser und Strom. In der Nähe der Dingi-Pier auf der Südseite der Hafenbucht gibt es neue Sanitäreinrichtungen. / *Two fixed pontoons in central location with moorings as well as water and electric supply. Close to the dinghy pier on the south side of the harbour bay there are new sanitary facilities.*
12 m: 63,25 EUR (July/Aug.),
38,33 EUR (Sept.-Juni);
incl. water, electr., taxes

C Schwimmstege in der Cala Llonga auf der Nordseite der Hafenbucht. Versorgung mit Wasser und Strom. / *Floating pontoons in Cala Llonga on the northern side of harbour bay. Water and electric supply.*

12 m: 76,61 EUR (July/Aug.),
47,57 EUR (Sept.-Juni);
incl. water, electr., taxes

D Schwimmponton vor der Cala Llonga und westlich der Isla del Rey. Keine Versorgung mit Wasser und Strom. Dafür am günstigsten. / *Swimming pontoon in front of Cala Llonga and west of Isla del Rey. No water or electric supply, but cheapest fees.*
12 m: 42,12 EUR (July/Aug.),
27,60 EUR (Sept.-Juni);
incl. water, electr., taxes

E **Marina Port Mahón**
165 Liegeplätze an fünf Stegen mit Muringleinen, Strom und Wasser. Anlegehilfen rund um die Uhr und drahtloses Internet. Lage vor dem Club Náutico und der touristischen Wasserfront mit zahlreichen Bars & Restaurants. Gehobenes Preisniveau.
165 moorings on 5 pontoons all served with mooring lines, electricity, water. Marineros 24 h and free Wi-Fi. Situated in front of Club Náutico and touristy water front with many bars & restaurants. Elevated prices.
2,46 EUR/m² (July/Aug.), 0,5 EUR m² (Sept.-Juni); plus water (1,80 EUR/m³), electr.(0,197 EUR kWh), 21 % IVA, G-5, T-0, harbour taxes
T 971 366 787, UKW/VHF 09
info@marinamahon.es, WiFi
www.marinamahon.es

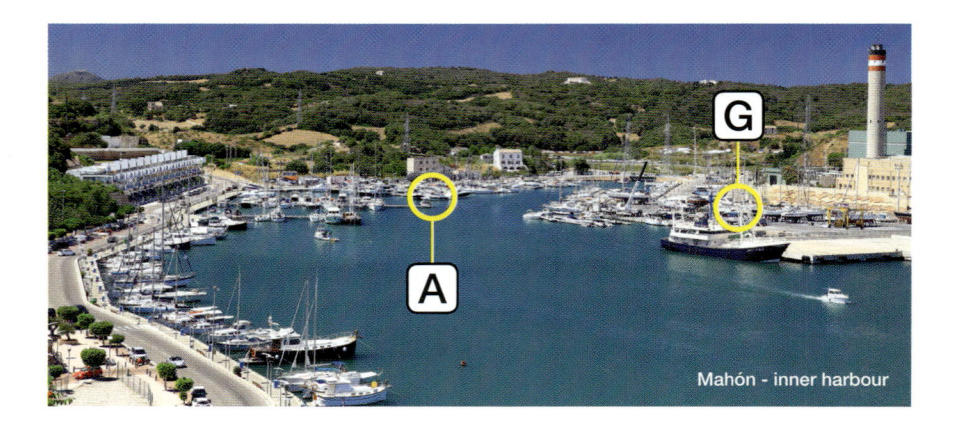

Mahón - inner harbour

Mahón / Maó

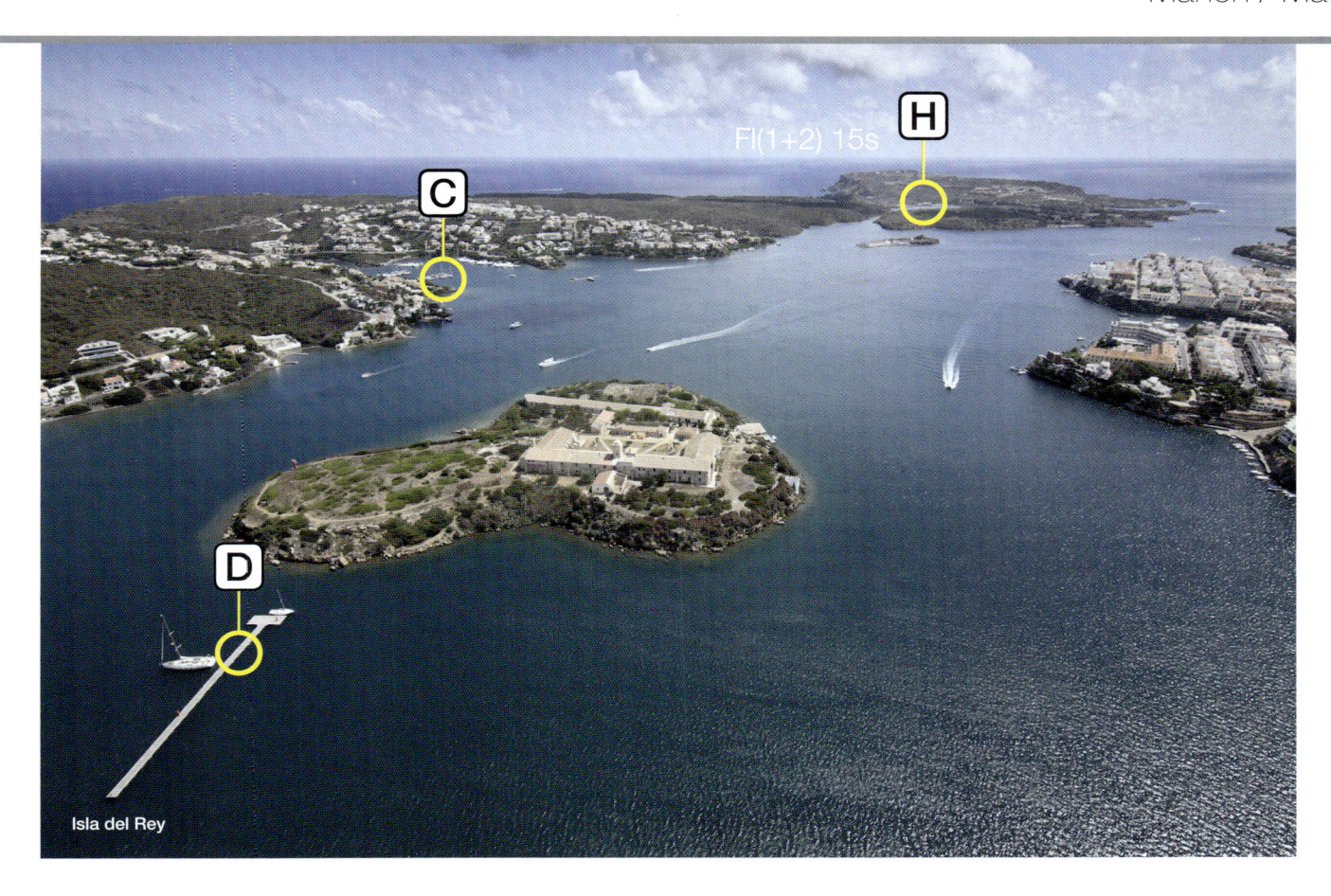

F **49 Liegeplätze westlich anschließend an Marina Port Mahón.** Bis 2015 in Regie des Club Marítimo de Mahón.
49 berths west of Marina Port Mahón. Until 2015 managed by the Club Marítimo de Mahón.

Preisbeispiel:
www.clubmaritimomahon.com/puerto/
T 971 354 116 + 971 365 022
M 620 801 859, UKW/VHF 09
oficina@clubmaritimomahon.com
www.clubmaritimomahon.com
Mon-Sat 8-20 h, Sun 8-14 h

G **Trockenplätze beim Kraftwerk.** Zwei Firmen bieten hier ihren Service an:
Hardstanding area at the power plant. Two companies offer their service here:

Pedro's Boat Centre
T 971 366 968
oficina@pedrosboat.com
www.pedrosboat.com
50-t-Travellift
€ Bis / until 12 m: 0,12 EUR/m²/Tag; over 12m: 0,18 EUR/m²/day

Nautic Center, T 971 354 499
www.nauticcenter.net

€ Die Preise variieren je nach Dauer des Aufenthalts auf dem Gelände, weil die Hafenbehörden für Yachten höhere Gebühren erhebt, je länger ein Boot bleibt. Angebot erfragen. Hier die Preise für den Travellift (entweder Heben oder Senken). Die Preise enthalten keine zusätzlichen Dienstleistungen, Gebühren der Hafenbehörden oder Steuern.
The prices vary depending on the total stay on the yard as port authorities apply higher fees for a boat that stays longer. Prices for single operation (lift out or launching). These prices do not include any additional services, port authorities fees and taxes.
Bis zu / *up to* 8m: 48 EUR
Bis zu / *up to* 11m: 93 EUR
Bis zu / *up to* 15m: 191 EUR

Menorca

Sant Francesc

TANKEN / *FUEL*

Stark frequentierte Bootstankstelle Im Scheitel der Cala Figuera in nächster Nähe der Marina Port de Mahón. Im Sommer warten oft viele Motorboote auf Treibstoff. Zeit einplanen oder früh morgens zum Tanken fahren. Eine der Zapfsäulen liefert 250 l pro Minute. Mengen ab 2000 Liter sollten dennoch 24 Stunden vorher angemeldet werden. Betreiber der Tankstelle ist der Club Marítimo Mahón.

Busy filling station at the peak of Cala Figuera close to Marina Port de Mahón. In summer, many motor vessels often wait for fuel. Allow for extra time, or go for refuelling early in the morning. One of their pumps delivers 250 l per minute. Quantities exceeding 2000 litres should still be notified 24 hours in advance. This refuelling station is operated by Club Marítimo Mahón.

T 971 354 116 + 971 365 022
M 620 801 859, UKW/VHF 09
oficina@clubmaritimomahon.com
www.clubmaritimomahon.com
June: Mon-Fri 8-14+16-19 h
July+Aug.: Mon-Sun 8-20 h
Sept.: Mon-Fri 8-14+16-19 h
Sat+Sun 8-14 h
Oct.-Dec.: Mon-Sat 9-14 h, Sun closed
Jan-May: Mon-Sat 8-14 h, Sun closed

TECHNISCHER SERVICE / *TECHNICAL SERVICES*

Pedro's Boat Service
Büro Werkstatt / *office and workshop*:
Anden de Poniente, 75 (Nähe Kreuzfahrt-Terminal / *close to cruise ships terminals*)
T 971 366 968, M 699 527 123
taller@pedrosboatcentre.com

Nautica Reynes
T 971 365 952, Bajoli, 42
(Industriegebiet Richtung Flughafen)
(industrial zone towards airport)
info@nauticareynes.com

Nautic Center Menorca
T 971 363 273 + 971 369 592
+ 971 354 499
www.nauticcenter.net

YACHTAUSRÜSTER / *CHANDLERIES*

→ Siehe / *see* „TECHNISCHER SERVICE / *TECHNICAL SERVICES*"

EINKAUFEN / *SHOPPING*

Supermercado Es Port
Lieferung frei Haus/Boot; *Delivery Service*
Moll de Levant, 332, T 971 368 956

Größere Supermärkte (Lidl, Mercadona, Eroski etc.) in den höher gelegenen Stadtteilen und im Industriegebiet an der Straße, die zum Flughafen führt. Alle liefern zum Boot.
Larger supermarkets (Lidl, Mercadona, Eroski etc.) can be found in higher-up town quarters and in the industrial zone alongside the road leading to the airport. All deliver to the boat.

RESTAURANTS & BARS

An der Uferstraße zwischen Bootstankstelle und dem Kreuzfahrthafen ein sehr großes Angebot. Eine Auswahl:
Very large variety on offer on quay between the dedicated filling station for yachts and the new cruise terminal. A small choice:

Jagaro, T 971 362 390
Das auch bei Einheimischen beliebte Restaurant liegt gleich neben der Bootstankstelle. Höheres Preisniveau.
Locals like this restaurant located right next to the boat service station. Higher price level.
www.jagaromenorca.com

Restaurante Pierro, T 971 354 360
Gutes Preis-Leistungsverhältnis, gerade beim Mittagstisch. / *Good value for*

Mahón / Maó

Venice house: 2015 renoviert / renovated

money, also for daily lunch.
www.restaurantepierro.com

Restaurante Pizzeria Roma
T 971 35 37 77
Immer gut besuchtes Restaurant in der Nähe des Club Maritimo.
Always lively restaurant with an Italian touch close to Club Maritimo.
www.restaurantepizzeriaroma.com

Can Vermut, T 971 361 726
Tapas-Bar an der Hafenpromenade. Drinks, Musik, gute Stimmung, freundliche Bedienung. / *On the harbour promenade. Drinks, music, good atmosphere, friendly service.*
www.canvermut.com

NAUTISCHE EVENTS/ NAUTICAL EVENTS

Menorca Maxi
www.menorcamaxi.com
Stelldichein der Wally-Superyachten; Ende Mai / *Tryst of Wally-superyachts; end of May*

Copa del Rei Panerai
www.velaclasicamenorca.com
Eine Station im weltweiten Klassiker-Regatta-Zirkus, Ende August
An event in the worldwide classic regatta circuit at the end of August

AUSFLÜGE / EXCURSIONS

Altstadt
Von der Marina Menorca aus am Ende der Hafenbucht kommt man schnell dorthin. Die Straße Costa de Dr. Guardia führt von der Uferstraße aus sanft ansteigend hinauf in Richtung des ehemaligen Franziskanerklosters Sant Francesc, heute Museo de Menorca. Die schönsten Teile der Altstadt entdeckt man in der Folge, wenn man sich zunächst nicht zu weit von der Hafenbucht entfernt.

Historic centre
Quick access from Marina Menorca at the end of harbour bay. Take Costa de Dr. Guardia street from the quay, gently

Canal de Sant Jordi

Talayot Trepucó

Menorca

ascending towards former Franciscan monastery Sant Francesc, today Museo de Menorca. Discover the prettiest sites of the old town while not leaving the harbour bay too far behind.

La Mola
Zum Schutz des Hafens wurde zwischen 1848 und 1875 die imposante Festung Isabel II. auf der Halbinsel La Mola errichtet. Sie diente damals der Abwehr einer drohenden, neuerlichen Besetzung der Insel durch die Briten, die Menorca als Stützpunkt im Krieg gegen die Franzosen benutzen wollten, als Frankreich und England um die Seeherrschaft im Mittelmeerraum rangen. Details, auch für eine Besichtigung, unter:

Castle "Fortaleza de Isabel II" was constructed from 1850 to 1875 on the northern side of the harbour entrance at the cliffs of La Mola, when France and England fought for naval supremacy in the Mediterranean. Details, also concerning a tour, on:

www.fortalesalamola.com
🕐 June-Sept.: 10-20 h, May: 10-18 h, Oct-April.: 10-14 h (Oct.-May: Mon closed)
€ 8 EUR, red. 4 EUR, under 6 y.: free
T 971 364 040; M 686 659 400
info@fortalesalamola.com

Talayot Trepucó
Die Talayot-Kultur war eine prähistorische Kultur zwischen dem 13. und 2. Jahrhundert v. Chr., auch auf den Balearen, gekennzeichnet durch Bauten in Großstein-Bauweise, den Talayots. Etwa zwei Kilometer von Mahón Richtung Ortschaft Sant Lluís entfernt liegt der Talayot Trepucó. Er zählt zu den größten Menorcas und besteht aus einem großen, festungsähnlichen Hügel aus Steinen, und der Taula – eine senkrecht stehende Steinplatte mit einer liegenden Steinplatte obenauf. Über alle frühzeitlichen Siedlungen Menorcas informiert:

The Talayot civilization was a prehistoric civilization flourishing from the 13th to 2nd century B.C. on Menorca and Mallorca, leaving megalith structures called Talayots. Some 1.5mi from Mahón towards Sant Lluís village there is Talayot Trepucó. It numbers among the largest in Menorca and consists of one large, fortress-like hill made of stone, and its Taula – a vertical stone slab with a horizontal slab resting upon it. These websites cover more or less all prehistoric settlements on the island of Menorca:
www.menorcatalayotica.info + www.talayots.es

Es Castell
Es Castell ist die nicht nur die östlichste Ortschaft Menorcas sondern auch des spanischen Staates. Hier lassen sich sehr gut die Spuren der englischen Herrschaft im 18. Jahrhunderts verfolgen. Die Ortsgründung hängt zusammen mit dem Bau des Castell de Sant Felip an der auf der bis dahin verwundbaren Südseite der Hafeneinfahrt.

Es Castell is not merely the easternmost municipality of Menorca, but of entire Spain as well. The marks left by English rule in the 18th century are very easily found here. The town was founded in connection with building Castell de Sant Felip at the southern side of the harbour entrance, which until then was quite vulnerable to attacks.

ANKERPLÄTZE
ANCHORAGE AREAS

[H] Cala Taulera
Der einzige zugelassene Ankerplatz in der Hafenbucht liegt östlich der Isla Lazareto, bei der Einfahrt zur Hafenbucht an Steuerbord. Laut Auskunft der Hafenbehörde Autoridad Portuaria darf dieser Ankerplatz nur für maximal drei Tage und bei schlechtem Wetter benutzt werden. Wann dies der Fall ist und wie diese Regelung umgesetzt wird, liegt in der Zuständigkeit der Hafenpolizei, die zuletzt entsprechende Handzettel an die Ankerlieger verteilte. Wassertiefen neben einem vorbeiführenden, betonnten Fahrwasser: 5-3 m. Der Ankergrund: gut haltend, tonig-schlammig, zum Teil viel Seegras. Es gibt einen kleinen Strand im Ostzipfel. Von hier führt ein kurzer Fußweg zur Festung Fortaleza de Isabel II auf der Halbinsel La Mola. Nach Nordwesten hin hat die Cala eine weitere Verbindung zum großen Teil des Naturhafens durch den kurzen, befeuerten und 3 m tiefen Canal de Sant Jordi.

The only permitted anchorage inside Mahon's harbour bay lies east of Isla Lazareto, when entering the big harbour bay change course to starboard. According to information from the Port Authority Autoridad Portuaria this anchorage may only be used for a maximum of three days and in bad weather. How this rule is applied is the responsibility of the Harbour Police, who distribute updated information to the captains.
Water depths next to bouyed fairway: 5-3m. Bottom: clay & mud, in parts much weed. There is a small beach at the eastern tip. From here it's only a short walk to the fortress Fortaleza de Isabel II on the peninsula of La Mola. Towards northwest this Cala has another connection to the larger part of the natural harbour, the short, lighted and 3m deep Canal de Sant Jordi.

Festung / *Fortress* La Mola

Mahón / Maó

Fähren habe ihre Liegeplätze im inneren Teil der Hafenbucht.
Ferries have to use the whole harbour bay to reach their berths ...

Canal de Sant Jordi

Cala Taulera

Cala Mesquida – Cala Algaret

ANKERPLÄTZE
ANCHORAGE AREAS

A Cala Mesquida
39° 58,8' N 004° 17,6' E

🇩🇪 Die erste attraktive Bucht nördlich von Mahón. Es gibt einen kleinen Ort an der Südseite und einen Sandstrand, der von Land aus gut frequentiert wird. Bei der Ansteuerung Vorsicht walten lassen, denn auf beiden Seiten der Bucht liegen Felsen und überspülte Untiefen. Die vorgelagerten Illots d'es Mesquida kann man landseitig passieren bei Wassertiefen von knapp unter 10 m. Man ankert über Sandboden mit Seegras und ein paar Felsen und 7-5 m Wasser vor einer markierten Badezone. Im Ort gibt es einen Mini-Supermarkt. Auf der Steilküste im Süden liegt das Restaurant Cap Roig mit Terrasse zur Bucht. T. 971 188 383, www.restaurantcaproig.com

🇬🇧 *The first attractive bay north of Mahón. There is a small village on the south side and a sandy beach, which is well visited. On approaching the bay take care of rocks on both sides. Illots d'es Mesquida can be passed on their westside. The water depths are just below 10m. One drops anchor on sandy bottom with some weed and rocks. Depths are 7-5m in front of a bouyed swimming area. In the village a mini-supermarket can be found and on the southside of the bay the restaurant Cap Roig with a large terrace.*
T. 971 188 383
www.restaurantcaproig.com

B Es Grau
39° 57,2' N 004° 16,8' E

Ankern vor dem Ort auf ca. 7 m und Sand mit Seegras. Es gibt hier abgetrennten Bojenfeld, das bewirtschaftet ist. Man kann, wenn verfügbar, für Boote bis 12 m Länge eine Boje reservieren, Mobil 696 890 854 (10-21.30 Uhr). Preis: Juni und September 1 EUR/m, July und August 2 EUR/m. Außerhalb dieser Zeiten sind keine Bojen ausgelegt.

Anchorage in front of the village with it's buoy field. Depths around 7m, bottom sand with weed. One can, if available, reserve a buoy for boats up to 12m length, M 696 890 854 (10-21.30 h). Price: June and September 1 EUR/m, July and August 2 EUR/m. Rest of the year no buoys are laid out.

C Isla Colom
39° 57,7' N 004° 16,3' E

Sehr beliebtes Bojenfeld westlich der Isla Colom. Bojen buchen unter www.balearslifeposidonia.eu. Kielyachten können zwischen dem Südteil der Isla Colom und Menorca im nicht passieren, Wassertiefen hier um 1 m. Die Ansteuerung aus Nord ist unproblematisch. Aber vor dem Ostkap der Isla Colom, Cabo Levant, liegt eine unbezeichnete Untiefe, die sich ca. 100 Meter weit ins Meer erstreckt. Vor den beiden Stränden in der Cala Tamarells-auf Menorca (Nationalpark S'Albufera des Grau) darf nicht geankert werden. Versorgung im Ort Es Grau.

Very popular buoy field west of Isla Colom. Buoys can be reserved at www.balearslifeposidonia.eu. Keel yachts can not pass between the south Part of Isla Colom and Menorca, depths only around 1m. Caution: shoals occur east of Isla Colom. Keep distance! Anchoring is strictly prohibited at the Menorca side in Cala Tamarells North and South (National Park S'Albufera des Grau). Supply in Es Grau.

D Cala Algaret & Presili
39° 59,5' N 004° 15,8' E

Beliebte Buchten vor Stränden südlich des Leuchtturms auf dem Cabo Favaritx, aber mit vielen Untiefen. Ankergrund überwiegend Sand, Wassertiefen zwischen 10 und 5 m. An Land keine Versorgung. Ein kleiner, sehr schöner Ankerplatz liegt unmittelbar südlich des Leuchtturms.

Popular bays with beaches south of the lighthouse on Cabo Favaritx, but with many shoals that have to be avoided. Bottom mostly sand, depths from 10 to 5 m. No facilities ashore. A small, very beautiful anchorage is just south of the lighthouse.

Cala Mesquida

Es Grau

Cala Mesquida – Cala Algaret

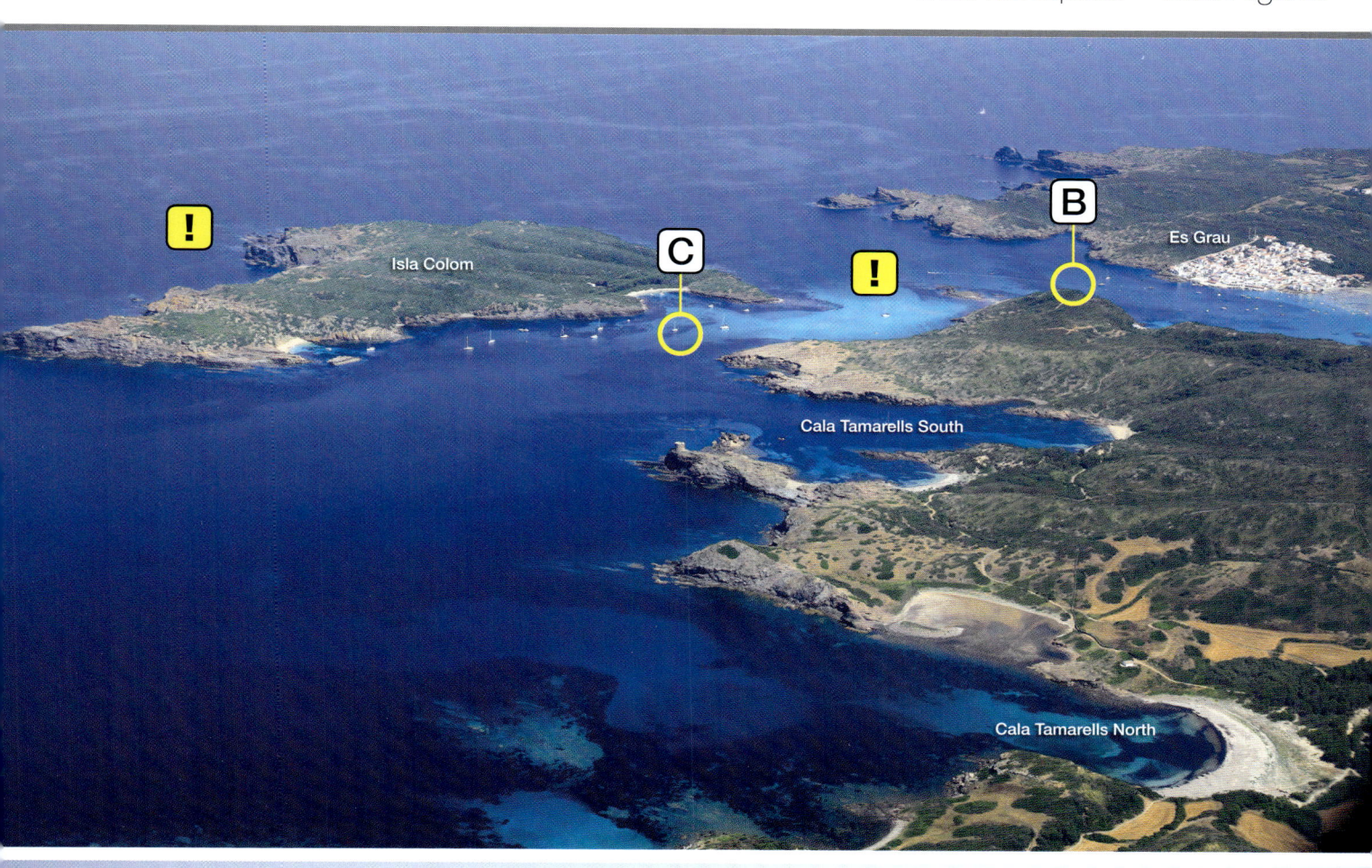

Isla Colom
Es Grau
Cala Tamarells South
Cala Tamarells North

Cala Algaret & Presili

Portbook & Island Guide

Menorca

Addaya – Cala Morell

🇩🇪 Der Norden ist die Mistralküste von Menorca. Der starke Nordwind vereitelt immer wieder Törnpläne, auch im Sommer. Auch auf die Seekarte ist hier besonders zu achten, fast jedem zweiten Kap sind Untiefen vorgelagert.

🇬🇧 *The north coast of Menorca is dominated by the Mistral, a strong northerly wind, that continues to interrupt sailing trips, even in summer. Care should also be taken because of shallow areas, particularly close to capes.*

① Addaya - 40° 01,4' N 004° 12,3' E → page 244
Die 1 sm lange Zufahrt zur kleinen Marina und dem Ankerplatz ist jetzt an ihrem Anfang befeuert. / *A bouyed channel leads over 1nmi to a small marina and an anchorage. The outer bouys are now lighted.*

② Cala Arenal de Castell - 40° 01,4' N 004° 10,9' E → page 248
Geschützte Bucht vor einer touristischen Anlage. **Achtung:** zwei überspülte Untiefen 0,5 sm nördlich. / *Sheltered bay except during north winds.* ***Caution:*** *two dangerous shoals 0,5nm north of the bay.*

③ Cala Olla - 40° 02,2' N 004° 09,8' E → page 248
Die perfekte Badebucht vor Sandstrand und Dünen.
A nearly perfect bay with sandy beach and dune backdrop.

④ Cala Fornells - 40° 04,0' N 004° 08,0' E → page 249
Fast rundum geschlossene, mehr als 2 sm tiefe Einbuchtung. Stark frequentiertes Bojenfeld. / *Almost entirely closed off bay, more than 2nmi deep. Highly frequented buoy field.*

⑤ Playa Cavalleria & Cala Ferragut - 40° 03,7' N 004° 04,4' E → page 252
Menorcas Nordkap liegt in Sichtweite. Ankerbucht in natürlicher Umgebung.
Mallorca North Cape is in sight. Anchorage in natural surroundings.

⑥ Cala Pregonda - 40° 03,5' N 004° 02,8' E → page 252
Bei Nordwind kein Platz zum Bleiben. Sonst sehr idyllisch. Gefährliche Untiefe!
With northerly winds no place to stay. Otherwise very idyllic. Dangerous shoal!

⑦ Cala Algaryens - 40° 03,4' N 003° 54,8' E → page 252
Stark frequentierte Ankerbucht, frei von Untiefen. Aber Vorsicht bei den Kaps.
In high season visited by dozen of boats and the beach is also crowded. When approaching round the capes with distance.

⑧ Cala Morell - 40° 03,4' N 003° 52,7' E → page 252
Bucht mit Feriensiedlung. Restaurant am Wasser. Alte Begräbnisstätten.
Interesting bay with a holiday resort. Waterfront restaurant. Old burial sites.

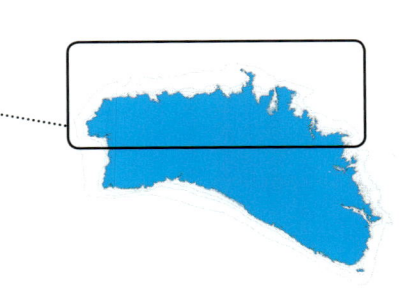

Der Norden Menorcas / The North of Menorca

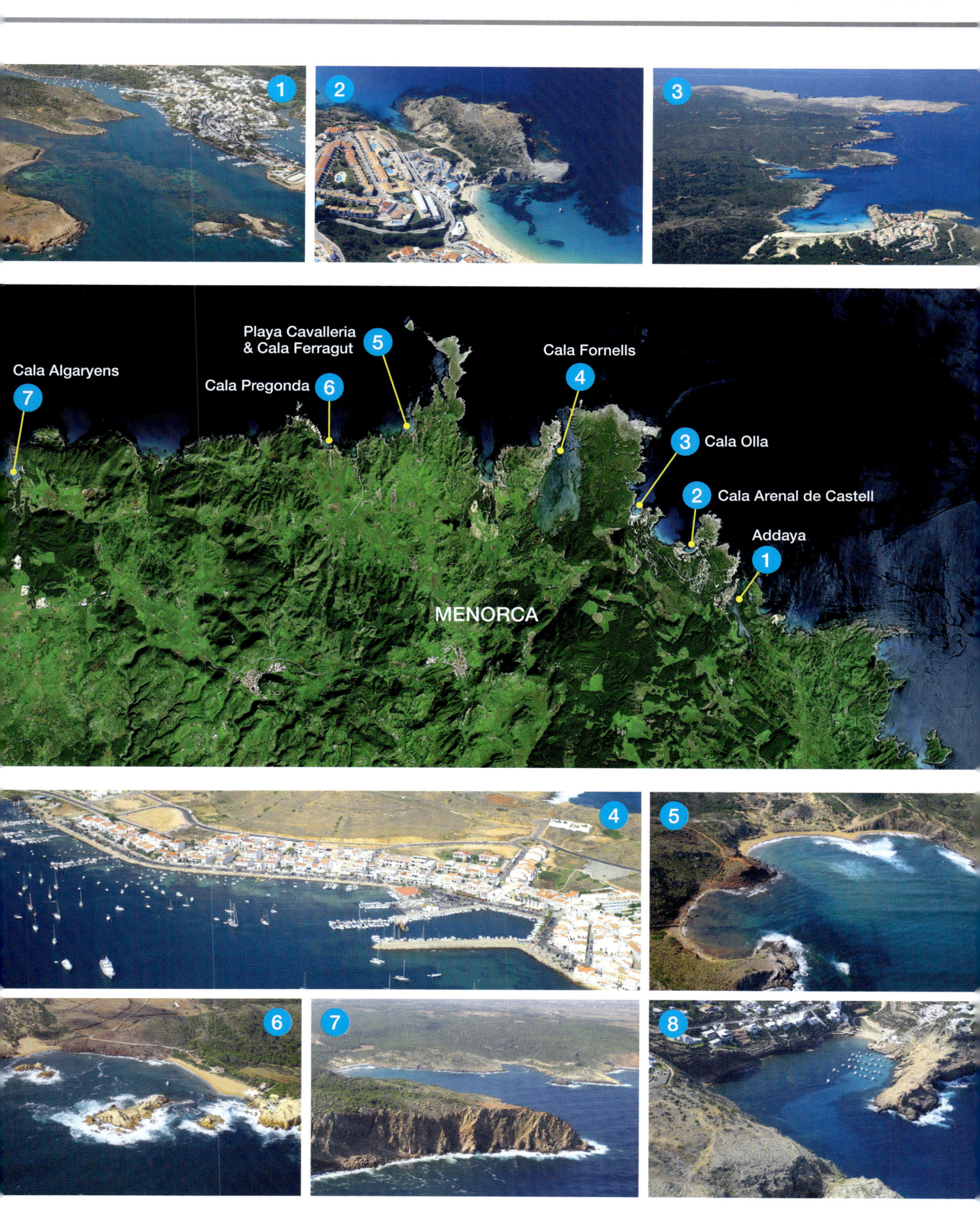

Cala Algaryens 7
Playa Cavalleria & Cala Ferragut 5
Cala Pregonda 6
Cala Fornells 4
Cala Olla 3
Cala Arenal de Castell 2
Addaya 1

MENORCA

Portbook & Island Guide 243

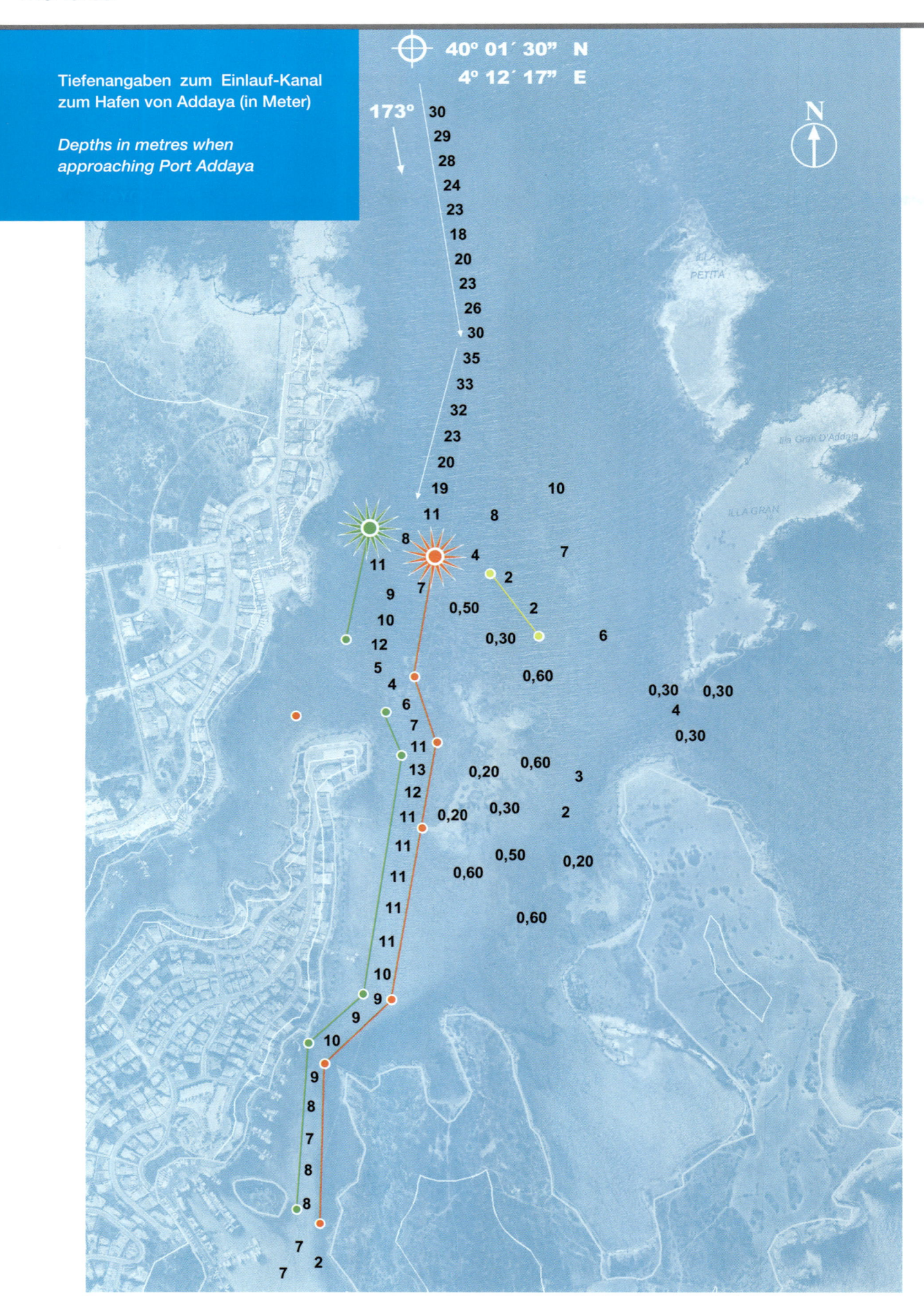

Menorca

Tiefenangaben zum Einlauf-Kanal zum Hafen von Addaya (in Meter)

Depths in metres when approaching Port Addaya

40° 01′ 30″ N
4° 12′ 17″ E

173°

30
29
28
24
23
18
20
23
26
30
35
33
32
23
20
19   10
11   8
    8   10
11   4   2
   7   0,50   7
 9   2
  10   0,30   6
 12
  5   0,60
   4
    6   0,30   0,30
     7   4
      11   0,30
       13   0,20 0,60
        12   3
         11 0,20 0,30 2
          11   0,50 0,20
           11 0,60
            11
             11
              10
               9
                9
                 10
                  9
                   8
                    7
                     8
                      8
                       10
                      7 2
                     7

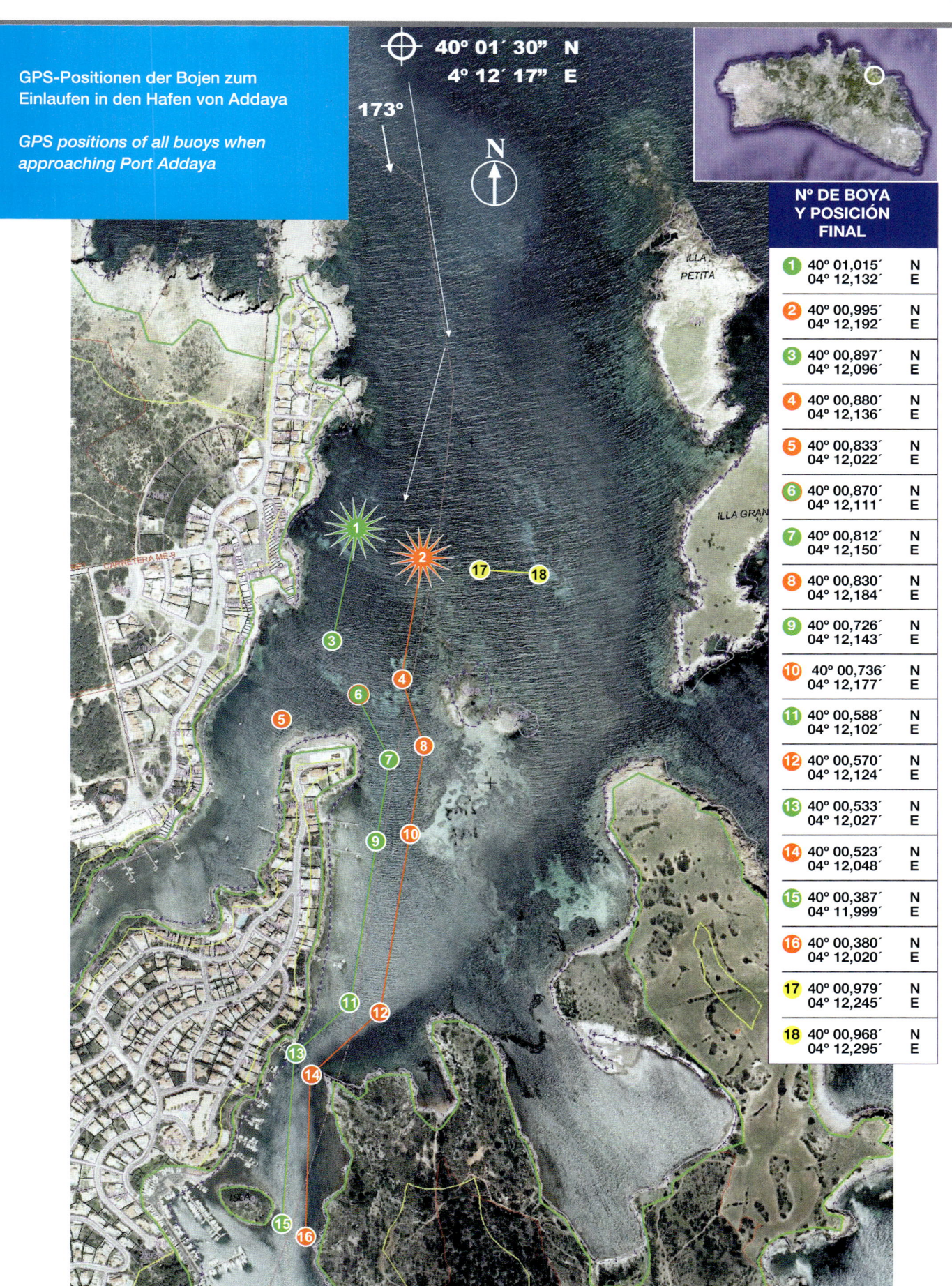

Addaya

GPS-Positionen der Bojen zum Einlaufen in den Hafen von Addaya

GPS positions of all buoys when approaching Port Addaya

40° 01′ 30″ N
4° 12′ 17″ E
173°

Nº DE BOYA Y POSICIÓN FINAL		
1	40° 01,015′	N
	04° 12,132′	E
2	40° 00,995′	N
	04° 12,192′	E
3	40° 00,897′	N
	04° 12,096′	E
4	40° 00,880′	N
	04° 12,136′	E
5	40° 00,833′	N
	04° 12,022′	E
6	40° 00,870′	N
	04° 12,111′	E
7	40° 00,812′	N
	04° 12,150′	E
8	40° 00,830′	N
	04° 12,184′	E
9	40° 00,726′	N
	04° 12,143′	E
10	40° 00,736′	N
	04° 12,177′	E
11	40° 00,588′	N
	04° 12,102′	E
12	40° 00,570′	N
	04° 12,124′	E
13	40° 00,533′	N
	04° 12,027′	E
14	40° 00,523′	N
	04° 12,048′	E
15	40° 00,387′	N
	04° 11,999′	E
16	40° 00,380′	N
	04° 12,020′	E
17	40° 00,979′	N
	04° 12,245′	E
18	40° 00,968′	N
	04° 12,295′	E

Portbook & Island Guide

Menorca

Addaya

- Schöne Bucht mit Marina
- Bojenfeld und Ankerplatz
- Schwierige Zufahrt bei Nacht

• Beautiful bay with marina
• Bouy field and anchorage
• Difficult access at nighttime

🇩🇪 Cala Addaya wirkt wie die Mündung eines Flusslaufs, der sich zwischen Felsen und grünen Kiefern ins Land hineinzieht. Schöne Landschaft umgibt auch die sehr geschützte kleine Marina Puerto Addaya am Rande einer touristischen Siedlung. Südlich davon gibt es ein Bojenfeld und einen Ankerplatz.

Cala Addaya gehört zum Nationalpark S'Albufera des Grau. Hier ist Ankern über Seegrasfeldern untersagt. Ankerverbote gibt es für das Flachwassergebiet südlich der Islas Carbo auf der Ostseite des Tonnenweges zur Marina und im hintersten Teil der Cala Addya.

🇬🇧 *Cala Addaya gives the impression of an estuary extending into the countryside between cliffs and green pines. Beautiful countryside surrounds the very protected small marina Puerto Addaya close to a tourist settlement. South of the marina one can find a buoy field and an anchorage.*

Cala Addaya is part of the National Park S'Albufera des Grau. Here it's prohibited to drop anchor where weed covers the bottom. Anchor bans exist for the shallow water area south of the Islas Carbo on the east side of the bouyed channel that leads to the marina and at the southernmost tip of Cala Addaya.

ANSTEUERUNG
APPROACHING

Detailpläne / *maps* > S./p. 244 / 245

Die Ansteuerung ist für ortsunkundige Skipper etwas heikel, denn es gibt Untiefen, Felsen und Flachstellen in der schmalen Passage nach Puerto de Addaya. Bei auflandigem Starkwind sollte man von einem Anlaufen absehen.

Von Osten kommend, passiert man zunächst die Flachstelle Llosa d'Emmig mit ausreichend Abstand und hält sich dann an der Westseite der Einbuchtung. Das ist auch bei Ansteuerung aus Nord empfehlenswert.

Nördlich der Punta de sa Torre, wo die kleinere Cala Molins nach Südwest abzweigt, gibt es ein befeuertes Tonnenpaar (FlG + FlR). Es markiert die Untiefen nordwestlich der Islas Carbo und bildet den Beginn des im folgenden unbefeuerten Fahrwassers zur Marina. Es ist schmal, aber tief, 9-6 m neben einer Flachstelle. Die Richtung des Fahrwassers wechselt bisweilen abrupt. Im Hafen 3-2 m, auf dem Anker- und Bojenplatz neben dem Hafen bis 5-3 m Wasser.

Piloting is rather difficult as there are shoals, rocks and shallows. Captains unfamiliar with local conditions should refrain from landing during strong onshore winds.

When arriving from the east, vessels pass shallow Llosa d'Emmig within distance and afterwards keep to the west shore of the bay. This side of the bay is also recommended to boats coming from north.

North of Punta de sa Torre, where the smaller Cala Molins branches to the southwest, there is a pair of lighted bouys (FLG + FLR). It marks the shallows northwest of Islas Carbo and forms the beginning of the hereafter unlighted channel to the marina. This part of the entrance is narrow but deep, at 9-6m next to a shoal. The direction of the channel sometimes changes abruptly. Harbour depth 3-2m, at anchorage and buoy field next to the harbour up to 5-3m water depth.

Marina Puerto Addaya

40° 01,5' N 004° 12,3' E

Addaya

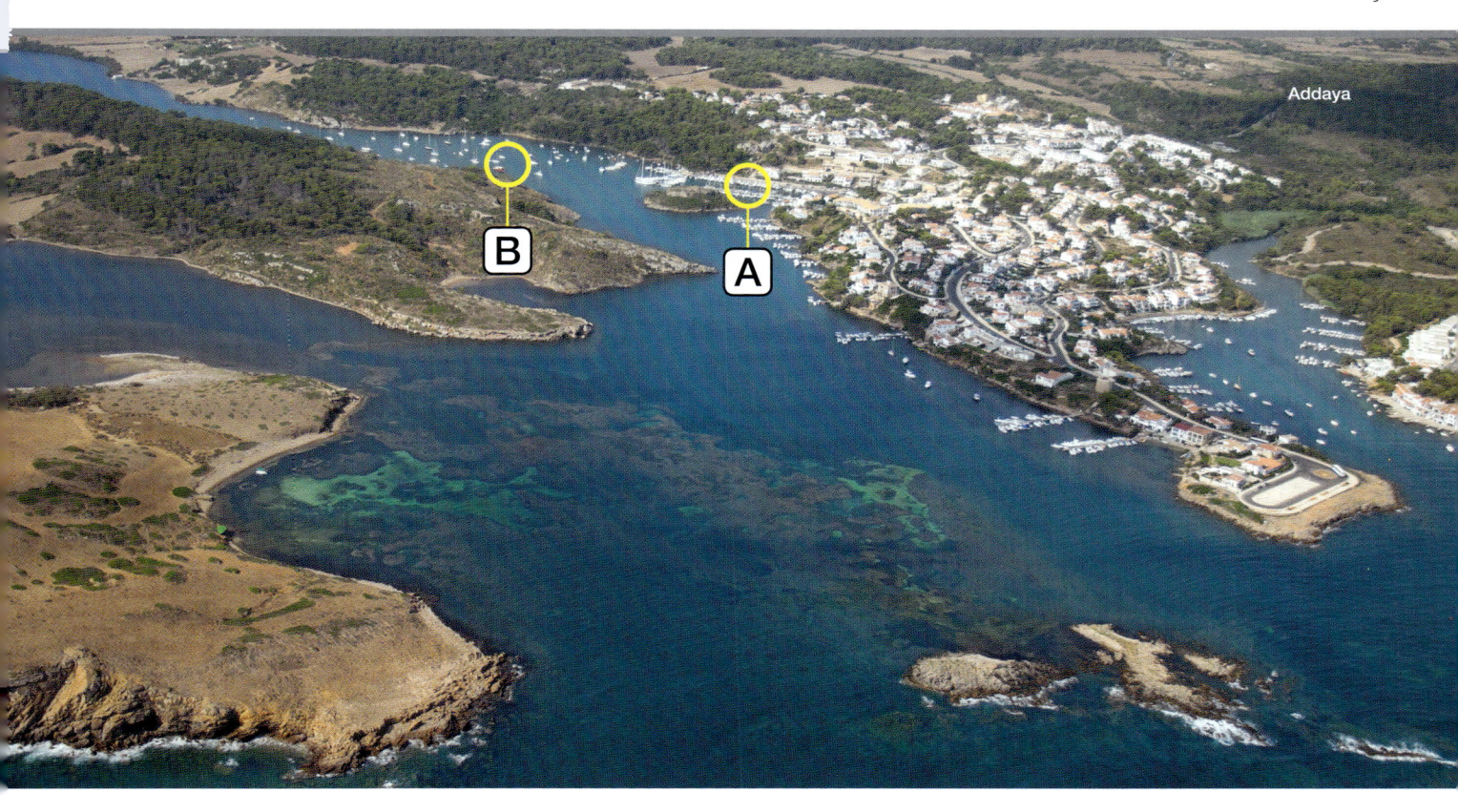

FESTMACHEN
FIND A BERTH

A Die Stege der kleinen Marina zeigen sich erst wenn das vorgelagerte Inselchen passiert ist. Wenige Gastplätze, Reservierung empfohlen. Wassertiefe 3-2 m.
The pontoons of the small marina become visible first when the islet Isla de la Monas lies at starboard. Few berths with mooring lines, reservation is recommended. Water depth 3-2m.

€ 12,50 m: 78,20 EUR (Aug.+July), 58,65 EUR (June+Sept.), 28,25 EUR (May+Oct.), 25,65 (Nov.-April); MwSt./VAT incl.
T + F 971 358 649 📱 UKW/VHF 09
puertoaddaya@puertoaddaya.com
www.puertoaddaya.com

TANKEN / *FUEL*

In Fornells, ca. 6 sm westlich
In Fornells, some 6nmi to the west

TECHNISCHER SERVICE
TECHNICAL SERVICES

25-t-Bootslift, bis 1,80 m Tiefgang
25t ship lift up to 1,80m draught

Dináutica Menorca
Auf dem Gelände der Marina. Alle Arbeiten rund uns Schiff.
On marina premises. Any kind of ship repair and maintenance work provided.
T 971351 478 + 971356270
M 699061 990 + 650653426
dinautica@terra.es

Astilleros Mardaya, T 971 379 196
In Alaior, 5 km südlich / *3mi to the south*
mardaya@mardaya.com

YACHTAUSRÜSTER
CHANDLERIES

Dináutica Menorca, T 971 358 185
Auf dem Gelände / *On the premises*

EINKAUFEN / *SHOPPING*

Restaurant/Bar „Sa Cantina" neben dem Marinabüro. Hier kann man sich morgens auch mit Brot und Brötchen versorgen. Der nächste kleine Supermarkt ist ca. 2 km entfernt.

Small restaurant/bar „Sa Cantina" beside the marina office also provides bread and rolls in the morning. The closest small supermarket is at some 1.5mi distance.

RESTAURANTS & BARS

Restaurant/Bar „Sa Cantina" auf dem Marina-Gelände. Weitere Restaurants in der Feriensiedlung neben dem Yachthafen. / *Restaurant/Bar „Sa Cantina" on marina premises. More restaurants in the resort next to yacht harbour.*

ANKERPLÄTZE
ANCHORAGE AREAS

B Die 20 Festmachenbojen vor der Marina gehören Mitgliedern einer Fahrtensegler-Vereinigung und dürfen von durchreisen Yachten nicht belegt werden. Es ist aber erlaubt, zwischen Marina und Bojenfeld für maximal 24 Stunden vor Anker zu gehen. Der letzte Zipfel der Bucht darf nicht benutzt werden, er gehört zu einem Naturpark. 5-2 m Tiefe, Schlickgrund mit viel Seegras.
The 20 mooring buoys in front of the marina belong to members of a local Cruising Association and are not available to passing by yachts. However, it is permitted to go on anchor between marina and buoy field for 24 hours. The last tip of the bay may not be used, it belongs to a natural reserve.
Depth 5-2m, mud bottom, covered frequently with weed.

Arenal de Castell – Cala Olla

ANKERPLÄTZE
ANCHORAGE AREAS

A **Cala Arenal de Castell**
40° 01,4' N 004° 10,9' E

🇩🇪 Geschützte Bucht vor einer touristischen Anlage, nur gegen Nordwind ist sie offen. Ankern auf ca. 5 m über Sand und Seegras vor einer Badezone. **Achtung:** zwei überspülte Untiefen 0,5 sm nördlich der Bucht! In Strandnähe Bars und Restaurants. In der Feriensiedlung gibt es vielfältige Versorgungsmöglichkeiten, sogar einen Arzt wird man finden.

🇬🇧 *Sheltered bay except during north winds in front of a tourist apartment estate. Anchorage at ca 5m over sandy bottom with weed patches in front of a swimming area. Depths around 5 m. **Caution:** two dangerous shoals 0,5nmi north of the bay. Bars, restaurants, supermarkets and doctors can be found close to the beach.*

B **Cala Olla**
40° 02,2' N 004° 09,8' E

Die perfekte Badebucht vor Sandstrand und Dünen. Ankern auf 6-4 m über Sand vor einem abgetrennten Schwimmbereich. Keine Untiefen im Bereich der Einfahrt. Bars, Restaurants und Supermarkt in der Nähe.

A nearly perfect bay with sandy beach and dune backdrop next to an apartment facility. Anchor at 6-4m over sandy bottom in front of a swimming area. No shallows to take care of while entering. Bars, restaurants and supermarket nearby.

Cala Fornells

- Große Bucht im Norden
- Bei Mistral sehr wichtig
- Ausgedehntes Bojenfeld

- *Large bay in the north*
- *Best shelter during mistral*
- *Extended buoy fields*

Cala Fornells

🇩🇪 Fornells ist ein hübscher kleiner Ort und im Sommer Zentrum des Wassersports, auch mit kleinen Booten. Wegen der zentralen Lage in der Mitte der Nordküste und einer großen, sehr geschützten Bucht, kommen hier regelmäßig viele Yachten zusammen.
Der kleine Hafen spielt mit seinem äußerst beschränkten Liegeplatzangebot für Gastyachten nur eine Nebenrolle. Aber das große Bojenfeld und die Ankerplätze haben eine magische Anziehungskraft, vor allem wenn der Nordwind Mistral auffrischt. Im Sommer sind eine Menge kleiner Jollen und Surfer in der Bucht unterwegs.

Die 2 sm tiefe Cala Fornells gehört zur Reserva Marina Menorca Nord mit Einschränkungen für Taucher und den Fischfang. Yachten können überall ankern, nur in der Kernzone (Integral oder „A" und hier der Südostteil der Bucht) ist zu beachten, dass Seegrasfelder dabei nicht berührt werden.

🇬🇧 *Fornells is a pretty little town and in summer a centre for sailing with dinghies and for windsurfing. Thanks to its central location in the middle of the north coast and due to its large, well-protected bay, many yachts gather here regularly.*

The small harbour with a limited number of berths designated to boats in transit plays a minor role. The large buoy field and numerous anchorage sites, magically attract boats, especially when northern Mistral winds start getting stronger. Many dinghies and surfers use the bay in summertime.
Cala Fornells stretches 2nmi from north to south and is part of Reserva Marina Menorca North with restrictions for diving and fishing. Yachts can anchor anywhere, except in the core zone (integral or "A" and here the southeastern part of the bay) weed fields have to be avoided.

ANSTEUERUNG
APPROACHING

Die große Bucht mit ihrer nur 200 m Passage an der engsten Stelle kann auch bei Mistral, dem hier immer wieder auftretenden starken Nordwind, angelaufen werden. Auf der flacheren Westseite der Einfahrt mit dem Cabo de sa Paret wird sie markiert durch einen Wachturm (nachts angestrahlt) und ein Leuchtfeuer (Fl 2s). Die Einfahrt ist in der Mitte über 10 m tief, in der Bucht wird es nur langsam flacher. Auf der Isla Sargantanes in der Cala Fornells steht ein Richtfeuer (bei 177,2° in Deckung, QR 1s + IsoR 4s).
The large bay with its 200m wide passage, can be entered at its narrowest point even with the Mistral, the strong northerly wind, which occurs here from time to time. The western side of the bays entrance with Cabo de sa Paret is more level and marked by a watchtower (illuminated at night) and a beacon

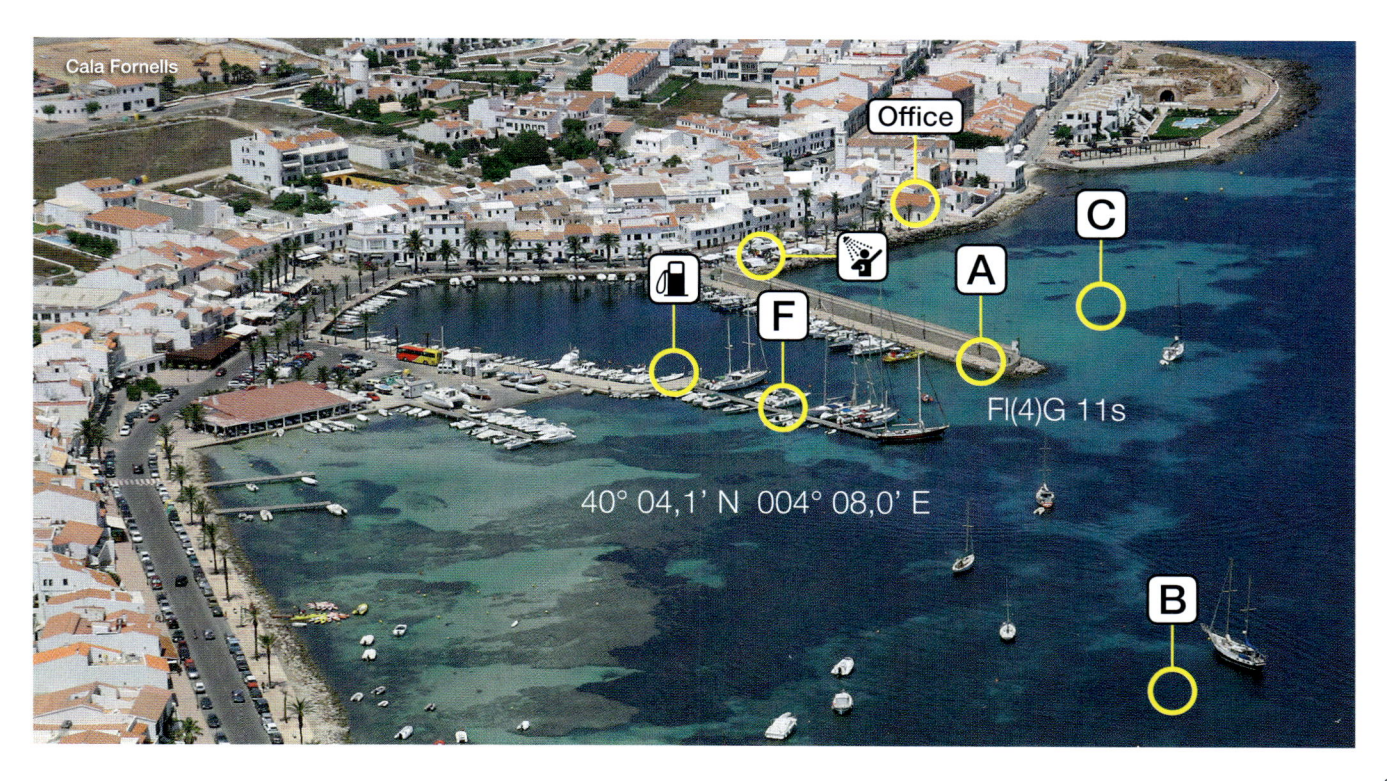

Cala Fornells

40° 04,1' N 004° 08,0' E

Fl(4)G 11s

Portbook & Island Guide

Menorca

Cala Fornells

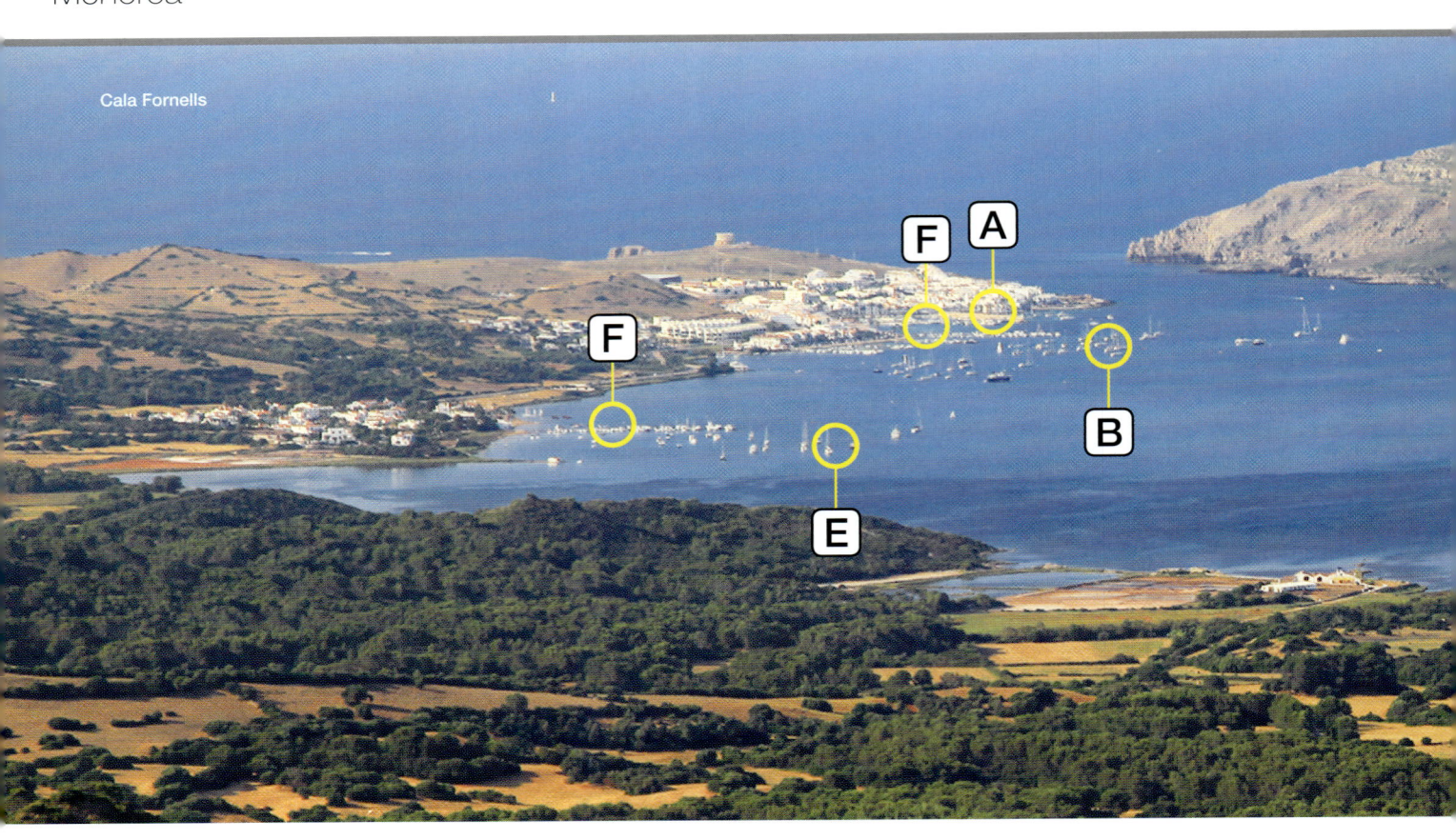

(Fl 2s). In its middle the entrance is more than 10m deep, becoming shallower very gradually within the bay. On Isla Sargantanes inside Cala Fornells there is a leading light (overlap at 177.2 degrees, QR 1s + IsoR 4s).

FESTMACHEN
FIND A BERTH

A Am Kopf der großen Außenmole sind die äußeren acht Plätze für durchreisende Yachten. Muringleinen liegen aus. Beim Festmachen ist Vorsicht angebracht, Segelyachten sollten besser mit dem Bug voraus anlegen, denn vor der Kaimauer befinden sich eine vorspringende Stufe und ein paar Felsen. Strom und Wasser vorhanden. Reservierung notwendig, mindestens drei Tag im Voraus über www.portsib.es. Bezahlung per Kreditkarte.

At the head of the large breakwater, the eight outermost berths are assigned to visiting yachts. Mooring lines available. Be careful when docking, sailing yachts should land bow to because of the jutting step and various rocks in front of the quay wall. Electricity and freshwater supply available.
Reservation recommended at least 3 days in advance at www.portsib.es. Payment by credit card.

Office
T 971 376 604 + M 639 404 816
port.fornells@portsib.es
€ EUR/m2: 0,60 (01/06-30/09); 0,18 (01/10-31/05) Water: 5,50 EUR; Electr.: 5,50 EUR. Alle Preise / *All prices plus 21% MwSt. /VAT*
🕗 8-15 h (winter), 8-21 h (summer)
🚿 Toiletten und Duschen am Fuß der Außenmole. / *Toilets and showers close to the breakwater.*

BOJENFELD / *BUOY FIELDS*

B Die meisten Festmachebojen liegen auf der Westseite der Bucht und südlich des Hafens aus. Weitere nördlich der der Isla Sargantanes. 2015 wurden für Yachten bis 14 m Länge 29,10 EUR kassiert, darüber und bis max. 16 m 48,50 EUR. Es gibt keinen Tarif für kurzzeitiges Festmachen. Reservierung notwendig über www.balearslifeposidonia.eu. Details S. 320

A large number of mooring buoys are installed on the western side of the bay and south of the harbour. More north of Isla Sargantanes. In 2015 fees for yachts up to 14m length amounted to EUR 29.10 and up to 16 m to EUR 48,50 EUR; no short-term mooring fee. Reservations required, on: www.balearslifeposidonia.eu. Details p. 320

TANKEN / *FUEL*

Gegenüber den Liegeplätzen von PortsIB. / *Opposite to the berths of PortsIB.*

YACHTAUSRÜSTER
CHANDLERIES

Vivelmar
An der Uferstraße / *On the quayside*
Paseo Marítimo, 34
Mon-Sun 10.30-15 + 18-21 h
T 971 158 490, M 605 885 336
Vivelmar.com

Astilleros Mardaya
siehe unten / *see below*

TECHNISCHER SERVICE
TECHNICAL SERVICES

Astilleros Mardaya
Am Hafen in 2. Reihe /
Close to the marina in 2nd row
C/ Rosari, 6, T 971 376 579
www.mardaya.com

Cala Fornells

RESTAURANTS & BARS

Entlang der Uferstraße und im Ort zahlreiche Restaurants. Oftmals auf Fisch und Schalentiere spezialisiert. Hinsichtlich der Qualität gehen die Meinungen vielfach auseinander: / *Many restaurants on the quayside and in the town. Often specialiced in fish and shellfish. In terms of quality opinions often vary.*

Es Pla, T 971 376 655
Beste Lage am Hafen / *Waterfront*
Es Cranc
Hafenähe, 2. Reihe / *close to the harbour*
C. Escoles 31, T 971 376 442

EINKAUFEN / *SHOPPING*

Im Sommer ein großes Angebot an Geschäften. Dazu auch Post, Bank und Apotheke etc. / *Large variety of shops, post office, bank, pharmacy etc.*

AUSFLÜGE / *EXCURSIONS*

Der alte Wachturm auf der Westhuk an der Einfahrt auf dem Cabo de sa Paret ist restauriert und zu besichtigen. Der Weg dorthin am Ufer entlang führt vorbei an der alten Verteidigungsanlagen El Castillo de San Antonio aus dem 17. Jahrhundert.
Fornells ist ein guter Ausgangspunkt, um das Kloster auf dem gut 350 m hohen Berg Toro zu besuchen, die höchste Erhebung Menorcas. Beste Aussicht. / *The historic watchtower at the bays entrance on Cabo de sa Paret is restored and worth a visit. Walking along the shore one will pass the restored fortification El Castillo de San Antonio built in the 17th century.*
Fornells is a good starting point to visit the monastery situated on mount Toro, at 350m altitude the highest point of Menorca. Fantastic views.

ANKERPLÄTZE / *ANCHORAGE AREAS*

C Vor der Außenmole. Ankergrund Sand und Seegras. Tiefen: 4-2 m / *In front of breakwater. Bottom: sand and sea weed. Depth: 4-2m*

D Nordöstlich der Isla Sargantanes Einbuchtungen mit abgetrennten Bereichen. Davor wird geankert. / *At eastern side of bay, north of Isla Sargantanes. Anchorage permitted exclusively above sandy bottom.*

E Vor allem südlich der Bojenfeldes auf der Westseite der Bucht bis zirka auf Höhe der Steganlage des Club Nàutic Fornells beim Ortsteil Ses Salines zirka 1 km südlich der Ortschaft Fornells. / *Especially south of the buoy field on the west side of the bay down to the pontoon of Club Nàutic Fornells in Ses Salines less than 1nmi south of the town of Fornells.*

F Club Nàutic Fornells

Steg in Fornells
35 Liegeplätze für Boote von 5–12 m, max. Tiefgang 4 m
Steg in Ses Salines
74 Liegeplätze für Boote von 4–12 m
An beiden Stegen gibt es nur in Ausnahmefällen Kurzzeitplätze.

Pier in Fornells
35 berths for boats 5–12m length, up to a depth of 4 m.
Pier in Ses Salines
74 berths for boats 4–12m length
At both locations, berths are only available by chance

T 971 376 328, info@cnfornells.com
www.cnfornells.com

Playa Cavalleria – Cala Morell

ANKERPLÄTZE
ANCHORAGE AREAS

A Playa Cavalleria, Cala Ferragut
40° 03,7' N 004° 04,4' E

🇩🇪 Liegeplatz Natur. Die Strände sind allerdings im Sommer von Land aus sehr gut besucht, dennoch gibt es keine Versorgungseinrichtungen an Land. Unproblematische Ansteuerung, ein Fels in der Mitte der Bucht formt zwei Strandabschnitte. Wassertiefen 8-4 m, Sandgrund.

Der Ankerplatz liegt keine 2 sm südlich von Menorcas Nordkap, dem Cabo de Cavalleria mit seinem Leuchtturm, Kennung Fl(2) 10s. Zwischen der vorgelagerten Isla Porros gibt es eine Passage mit 6 m Wassertiefe in der Mitte.

🇬🇧 *Pure nature. The beaches, however, are very well attended in the summer from the mainland, but there are no bars and restaurants. Straightforward approach, a rock in the middle of the bay formes two beaches. Dephts from 8-4 m, sandy bottom.*
This anchorage is less than 2nmi south of Menorca's North Cape, Cabo de Cavalleria with its lighthouse, character Fl (2) 10s. Between Isla Porros and Cabo de Cavalleria there is a passage with 6 m water depth in its middle.

B Cala Pregonda
40° 03,5' N 004° 02,8' E

Eingerahmt von Felsen. Die Umgebung wirkt, als sei sie vulkanischen Ursprungs. Achtung: nicht markierte, knapp überspülte Untiefe im Bereich der Ansteuerung, nur drei Kabellängen NNE. Ankern auf 6-4 m, Grund Sand. Restaurant vom Strand nach 2 km Richtung Osten.

Framed by rocks. The surroundings give the impression of having volcanic origins. Caution: not marked, just washed over shoal only three cable lengths NNE. Drop anchor at 6-4m above sandy bottom. Restaurant 1.5mi eastwards, starting from the beach. Otherwise no supply.

C Cala Algaryens
40° 03,4' N 003° 54,8' E

Schöne Bucht (im Bildhintergrund) mit Sandstrand. Im Sommer tagsüber stark frequentiert, auch landseitig. Ankern auf 6-3 m über Sandgrund. Keine Versorgung. Die Kaps zu beiden Seiten mit Abstand runden!

Beautiful bay (see background) with sandy beach. Many yachts visitors come here during the daytime in summer. Anchorage at 6-3m above sandy bottom. No supply service. Round the headlands with distance on both sides!

D Cala Morell
40° 03,4' N 003° 52,7' E

Keine 10 sm von Ciutadella entfernt. Nur etwas Schutz gegen nördliche Winde. Ankern vor einem Bojenfeld für kleine Boote. Ankergrund Sand mit Seegras und Fels. Untiefe Bajo Morell 0,7 sm westlich! Restaurants an der Bucht. Kein Mini-Markt! Im Scheitel der Bucht kann man Höhlen besichtigen, die in der Zeit zwischen 1200 v. Chr. und 600 n. Chr. in den Fels gehauen worden sind.

Less than 10nmi distance to Ciutadella. Anchorage in front of a buoy field for smaller boats. Bottom is sand with weed and rocks. Shoal Bajo Morell is 0.7nmi to the west! Some shelter against northern winds. Anchorage in front of a buoy field for small boats. Restaurants close to the pier, no supermarket. You can visit caves, carved into the rock between 1200 BC and 600 AC.

Playa Cavalleria / Cala Ferragut

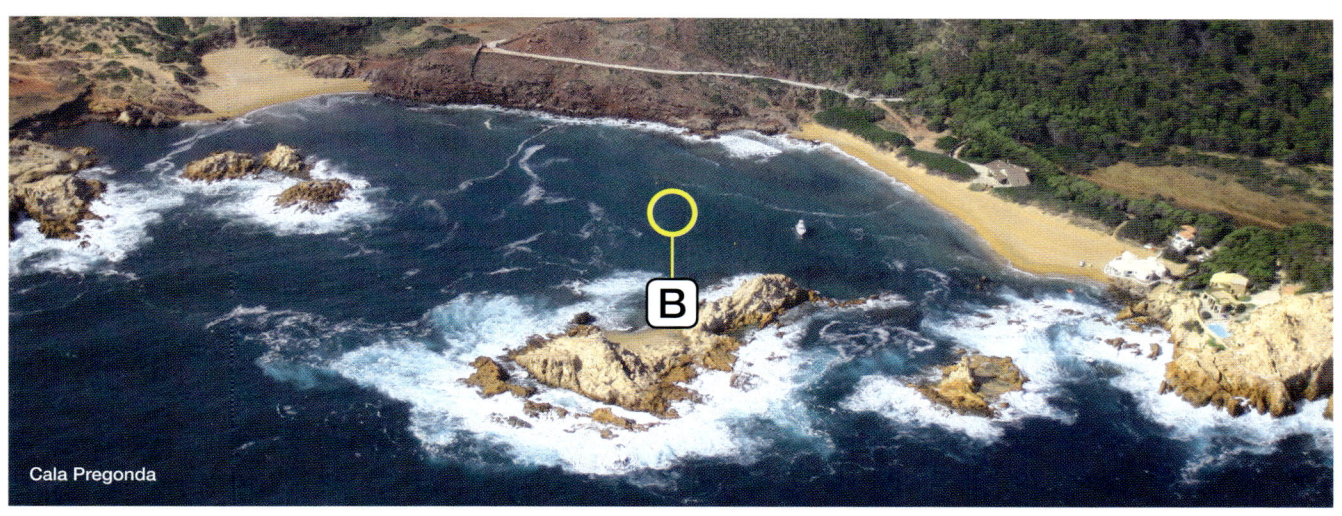

Playa Cavalleria – Cala Morell

Cala Pregonda

Cala Algaryens

Cala Morell

Portbook & Island Guide 253

Ibiza

Ibiza – Dalt Vila: Die Festungsanlage mit der Altstadt genießen UNESCO-Schutz.
The citadel complex with the old town enjoy UNESCO protection.

Hot spot Ibiza

Für einen Törn nach Ibiza gibt es viele gute Gründe: Die einen kommen wegen der Altstadt mit der Festungsanlage, für andere zählt vor allem das legendäre Nachtleben.

There are many good reasons to take a sailing trip to Ibiza: some want to visit the historical old town and its fortress, others come for the legendary nightlife of the island.

Ibiza – Port Sant Miguel

🇩🇪 Yachten aus Richtung Mallorca lernen üblicherweise zuerst diese Seite von Ibiza kennen. Mit der Hauptstadt und Santa Eularia liegen hier die beiden größten Orte. Ihre Marinas sind dem Andrang im Sommer kaum gewachsen.

🇬🇧 *Yachts coming from Mallorca will most likely explore the eastern part of Ibiza first, making a stop at the island's two biggest cities, the capital Ibiza and Santa Eularia. Their marinas can hardly manage the huge demand for berths in the summer.*

1 Ibiza - 38° 54,0' N 001° 26,7' E → page 258
Die Hauptstadt hat fünf Marinas, aber im Sommer trotzdem wenige Gastplätze.
Five marinas are located here, but have few berths to offer during summer.

2 Cala Talamanca - 38° 54,5' N 001° 27,9' E → page 268
Ankerbucht unmittelbar östlich des Hafengebiets von Ibiza und ähnlich groß.
Anchorage directly east of the port area of Ibiza and similar in size.

3 Cala Llonga - 38° 57,2' N 001° 31,9' E → page 268
Touristischer Ort mit Restaurants und Supermärkten. Ankern auf 8-5 m.
Touristy village. Many restaurants and supermarkets. Drop anchor at 8-5m.

4 Santa Eulalia - 38° 58,5' N 001° 32,7' E → page 270
Zweitgrößte Stadt Ibizas. Sportboothafen mit Ankerplatz vor der Einfahrt.
Second biggest town in Ibiza. Marina with anchorage close to the entrance.

5 Cala Nova / Cala Llena - 39° 00,6' N 001° 35,4' E → page 272
Zwei wenig bebaute Buchten, nur durch eine Huk getrennt. Sandstrände.
Two little unspoiled bays, separated by a small headland. Sea floor mainly sand.

6 Cala Boix - 39° 01,6' N 001° 36,4' E → page 272
Eine offene, aber recht beliebte Bucht unmittelbar bei Cabo Roig. Restaurant.
An open, but quite popular bay directly at Cabo Roig. Restaurant on the beach.

7 Isla Tagomago - 39° 02,1' N 001° 38,2' E → page 272
Privatinsel; große, private Bojen; Ankergrund Seegras; Strandbar öffentlich.
Private island; large, private buoys; bottom weed, beach bar open to the public.

8 Cala San Vicente - 39° 04,2' N 001° 35,8' E → page 273
Im Sommer ein lebhafter touristischer Ort. Es gibt fast alles, aber keinen Laden.
During summer a lively tourist spot. Offers almost everything, but no shop.

9 Cala Portinatx - 39° 07,0' N 001° 30,6' E → page 274
Ankern vor einer Badezone auf 9-4 m. Im Sommer ein touristisches Zentrum.
Anchorage in front of a bathing zone, depth 9-4m. Busy village during summer.

10 Ensenada Xarraca - 39° 06,1' N 001° 29,9' E → page 276
Der schönste Ankerplatz ist im südwestlichen Zipfel. Sommer-Restaurant.
The best place to anchor lies in the southwestern tip. Restaurant in summer.

11 Cala Blanca - 39° 06,3' N 001° 29,1' E → page 276
Weit innen ankern auf 8-3 m bei einem einzelnen Haus. Sandgrund.
Drop anchor in the inner part, close to a white building, depths 8-3m.

12 Cala Binirras - 39° 05,6' N 001° 26,8' E → page 277
Im Sommer öffnen ein halbes Dutzend Restaurants; Ankergrund meist Seegras.
In summer, half a dozen restaurants open here; bottom mainly weed.

13 Port Sant Miguel - 39° 05,3' N 001° 26,5' E → page 277
Schutz durch Insel, Ankergrund viel Sand. An Land im Sommer sehr touristisch.
Protected by an island, bottom mostly sand. During summer a busy village.

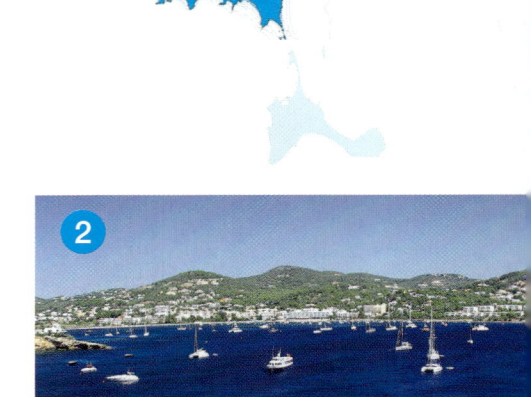

Der Osten Ibizas / The East of Ibiza

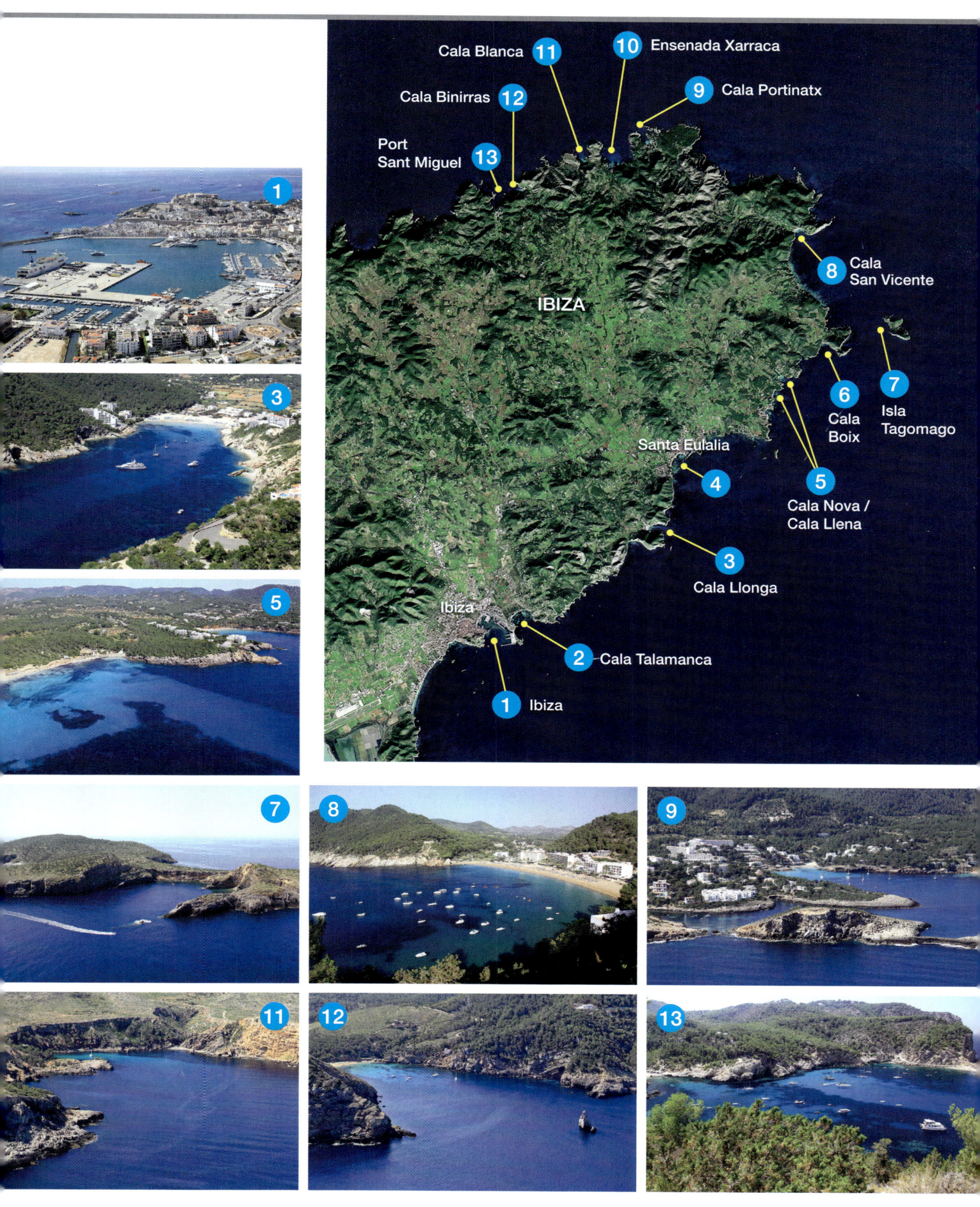

- Cala Blanca 11
- Ensenada Xarraca 10
- Cala Binirras 12
- 9 Cala Portinatx
- Port Sant Miguel 13
- 8 Cala San Vicente
- IBIZA
- 6 Cala Boix
- 7 Isla Tagomago
- Santa Eulalia
- 4
- 5 Cala Nova / Cala Llena
- 3 Cala Llonga
- Ibiza
- 2 Cala Talamanca
- 1 Ibiza

Ibiza

Ibiza Stadt / Ibiza Town

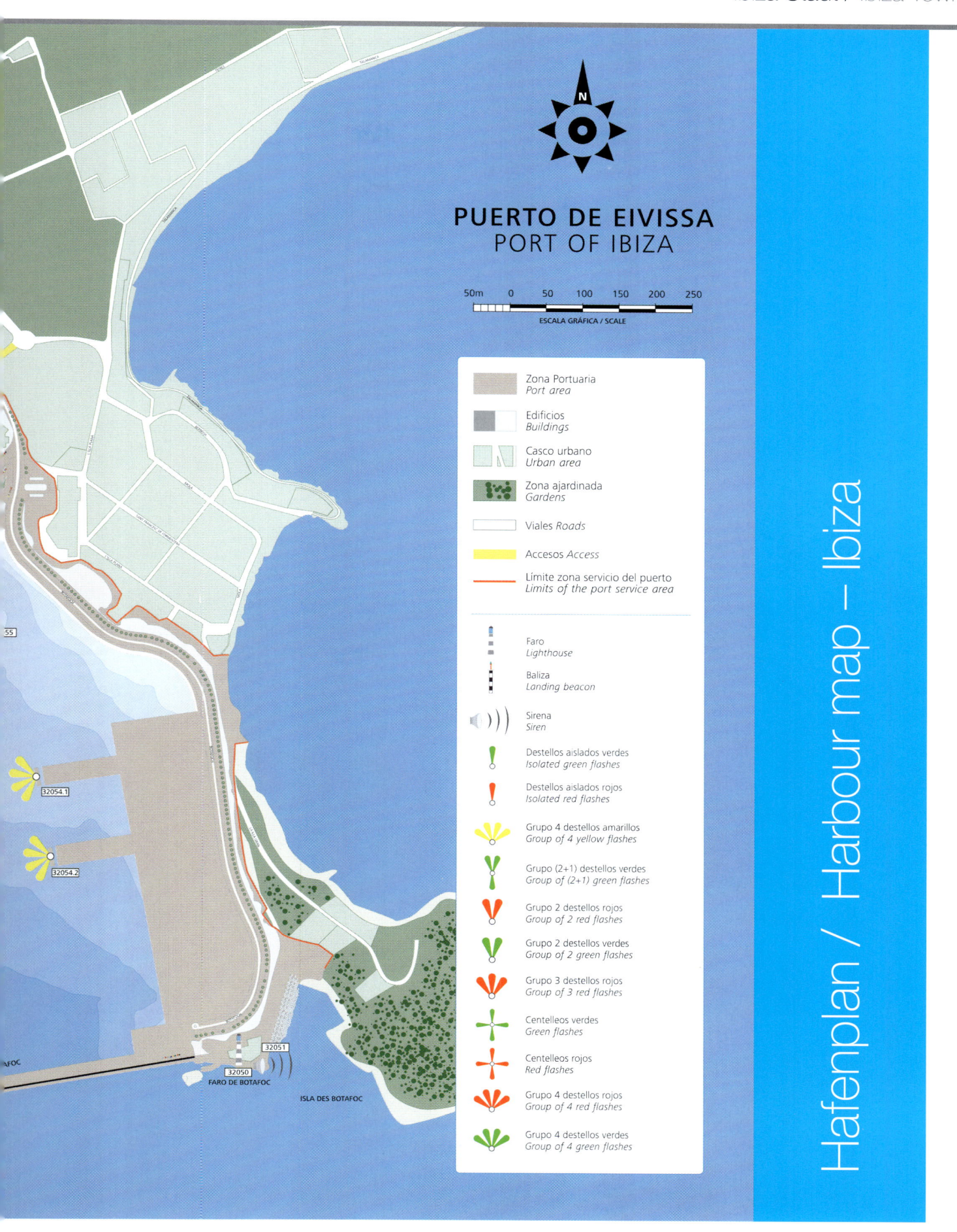

PUERTO DE EIVISSA
PORT OF IBIZA

ESCALA GRÁFICA / SCALE

	Zona Portuaria / Port area
	Edificios / Buildings
	Casco urbano / Urban area
	Zona ajardinada / Gardens
	Viales / Roads
	Accesos / Access
	Límite zona servicio del puerto / Limits of the port service area
	Faro / Lighthouse
	Baliza / Landing beacon
	Sirena / Siren
	Destellos aislados verdes / Isolated green flashes
	Destellos aislados rojos / Isolated red flashes
	Grupo 4 destellos amarillos / Group of 4 yellow flashes
	Grupo (2+1) destellos verdes / Group of (2+1) green flashes
	Grupo 2 destellos rojos / Group of 2 red flashes
	Grupo 2 destellos verdes / Group of 2 green flashes
	Grupo 3 destellos rojos / Group of 3 red flashes
	Centelleos verdes / Green flashes
	Centelleos rojos / Red flashes
	Grupo 4 destellos rojos / Group of 4 red flashes
	Grupo 4 destellos verdes / Group of 4 green flashes

32054.1
32054.2
32051
32050
FARO DE BOTAFOC
ISLA DES BOTAFOC

Hafenplan / Harbour map – Ibiza

Portbook & Island Guide

Ibiza

Mega-Port Ibiza

Isla Grossa

OcWR 7s

Fl(2)R 7s

260 Portbook & Island Guide

Ibiza Stadt / Ibiza Town

Ibizas Stadtmarinas haben Platz für Megayachten. Der Andrang im Sommer ist beträchtlich, die Partyszene und der Lifestyle der Insel-Hauptstadt ziehen magisch an.

Ibiza's port with its marinas is prepared for sheltering mega-sized yachts. The demand on berths is really high in summer, as the capital's night life and lifestyle attract people magically.

Formentera, Ostteil / eastern part

Fl(2)W 5s
Islotes los Dados

FlG 3s

38° 54,0' N   001° 26,7' E

Fl R 3s
Isla Negra del Este

Islotes Malvines

- Wenige Gastplätze im Sommer
- Große Festung mit Altstadt
- Zentrum des Nachtlebens

- *Few visitor berths in summer*
- *Important castle, historic old town*
- *World famous for its nightlife*

Portbook & Island Guide   261

Marinas in Ibiza

🇩🇪 Eivissa, wie die Hauptstadt im Katalanischen heißt und wie es auf jedem Straßenschild steht, ist der Platz für Megayachten auf der Insel. Die größten unter ihnen machen unterhalb der befestigten Altstadt Dalt Vila fest. Es gibt fünf Marinas in dem großen Hafenbecken, aus dem die größten Fähren verlegt wurden in einen neuen Hafen, der bei der Isla Grossa errichtet wurde. Dennoch kann ohne Reservierung die Suche nach einem Liegeplatz in den Sommermonaten schwer bis unmöglich werden. Und das, obwohl im nahen Formentera mit seinen bezaubernden Sandstränden und dem Farbenspiel des Meeres hunderte Yachten auch über Nacht bleiben. Vor Anker und in den zwei nicht weniger teuren Marinas. Wer keinen Platz in einer Marina findet, für den kann das Aufnehmen von Trinkwasser im Sommer problematisch werden.

🇬🇧 *Eivissa, as the capital is named in Catalan and as it is written on every street sign, is the place for mega yachts on the island. The biggest among them dock below the fortified Dalt Vila. There are five marinas in the large harbour bassin, which only shelter a few ferries. Most vessels use the new cruise port, constructed close to Isla Grossa. Nevertheless, without any reservation it can be difficult or impossible to find a vacant berth in the summer. Despite the fact that in nearby Formentera with its enchanting beaches and colourful sea, some hundreds of yachts stay overnight. Options are anchoring or staying in one of two equally pricey marinas. For those who cannot find a space in a marina, refilling freshwater may turn to be difficult during summer months.*

ANSTEUERUNG
APPROACHING

Die wichtigsten Einfahrtsfeuer, den Leuchtturm auf der Isla Botafoch und die Befeuerung vorgelagerter Inselzeichen zeigt das große Bild. Es sind jedoch nicht alle Inselchen im Seeraum vor Ibiza-Stadt befeuert, so dass Aufmerksamkeit gefordert ist. Die ist schon notwendig wegen der Schnellfähren und konventionellen Fähren vor allem zwischen Ibiza und Formentera, wo sie fast im Minuten-Takt verkehren. Hinzu kommen viele schnell fahrende Motoryachten. Kreuzfahrtschiffe laufen vor allem in den Morgen- und Abendstunden ein- und aus.

The large image shows the main entry lights, i.e. the Isla Botafoch lighthouse and the lights on small islands. Not all islets off Ibiza City have lights, which requires close attention by skippers. Attention is also required particularly because of speed ferries and regular ferries between Ibiza and Formentera, which operate very frequently. These are joined by numerous fast motor yachts. Cruise ships enter and leave mainly in the morning and evening hours.

Marina Botafoch

Ibiza Stadt / Ibiza Town

Marina Ibiza

FESTMACHEN
FIND A BERTH

A **Marina Botafoch**

Am Nordufer des Hafens von Ibiza und am nächsten zu den neuen Fährmolen innerhalb des Wellenbrechers gelegen. Wartekai bei der Tankstelle, neben dem Marinabüro. Kleine Pendelfähre zwischen Marina und Stadtzentrum.

428 Liegeplätze von 6-30 m; 60 Lokale in der Geschäftszone, Ausrüster, Immobilienfirmen, Yachtbroker, Modeläden, Bars, Restaurants etc.

At the north shore of Ibiza port and closest to the new ferry piers within the breakwater. Waiting quay situated at petrol station next to marina office. Small shuttle ferry connects marina and town centre.

428 berths from 6-30m; 60 bars and restaurants, shops, outfitters, real estate companies, yacht brokers, fashion, etc.

T 971 312 231   UKW/VHF 09
info@marinabotafoch.com
www.marinabotafoch.com

Anlegehilfe / *Mooring support*
🕘 09-22 h (summer), 09-18 h (winter)

🕘 Office
01/07-30/09: Mon-Fri: 9-14 + 16-20 h, Sat, Sun + hol.: 9-14 + 17-20 h (summer) 01/10-31/05: Mon-Fri: 9-14 + 16-19 h (winter)

€ 12,01x4,01 – 15x4,8 m
01/07-31/08: 202; 01/06-30/06 + 01/09-30/09: 90; 01/04-31/05+01/10-31/10: 45; 01/11-31/03: 27

Jeweils plus 21% MwSt., plus Wasser und Strom (gut 10 EUR/Tag) und Hafengebühren G5+T0

All prices plus 21% IVA, plus water and electr. (more than 10 EUR per day) and harbour taxes G5+T0

Duschen hier evtl. außerhalb der Öffnungszeit geschlossen. Beim Werftgelände evtl. länger geöffnet. / *Showers here may be closed outside working hours. At the shipyard possibly longer.*

B **Marina Ibiza**

Hier liegen große Motoryachten. Gute Shopping-Möglichkeiten auf dem Marinagelände. Verschiedene Restaurants und Lounge Bars. Concierge-Service. Gehobenes Entertainment im „Lio"-Nightclub. Mehr Angebote nahe des Marinazugangs.

Zwei Hafenbecken (Dársena norte und Dársena sur). Hier Liegeplätze von 18-55 m, im Nordbecken bis 40 m. Es gibt einen dritten Hafenbereich, Marina Seca, anschließend an den nördlichen

Portbook & Island Guide   263

Ibiza

Hafenteil. Hier liegen Boote von 5-8 m an Land und können mit einem Forklift bewegt werden. Man kooperiert mit der Werft Varadero Ibiza.

Large motor yachts berth here. Good shopping facilities on the marina premises. Various restaurants and lounge bars. Concierge service. First class entertainment at "Lio" night club. Further venues close to marina entrance.

There are two port basins (Dársena norte and Dársena sur). Berths here are sized 18-55m, in northern basin up to 40m. There is a third port section, Marina Seca, joined to the northern port section. Vessels sized 5-8m are beached here and may be moved by a forklift. Cooperation with shipyard Varadero Ibiza.

T 971 318 040, UKW/VHF 09
info@marinaibiza.com
www.marinaibiza.com

Office
Mon-Sun: 09-14.30 + 15.30-20.30 h
€ 10– 14,99 m Länge / length
01/07-31/08: 4/m²; 01/05-30/06 + 01/09-30/09: 2/m01/10-30/04: 0,67/m². Jeweils plus 21% MwSt., plus Wasser und Strom und Hafengebühren G5+T0. *All prices plus 21% IVA, plus water and electr. and harbour taxes G5+T0.* plus WiFi free

C Club Náutico
Üblicherweise sind alle Plätze belegt. Gastyachten werden im Sommer nur in Ausnahmefällen aufgenommen. Muringleinen sind vorhanden. Parallel zur betagten Steganlage wurde ein moderner Schwimmsteg ausgelegt, aber der enorme Schwell durch die schnell ein- und auslaufenden Formentera-Fähren ist geblieben. Auf ausreichend Abstand zum Steg achten. Wasser und Strom am Steg, Duschen und Toiletten im Clubhaus. / *Usually fully occupied, berths in summer, are only rarely offered to yachts in transit. Mooring lines available. A modern floating pontoon was installed in parallel to the old concrete pier, enormous swell caused by ferries to Formentera remains. So keep sufficient distance to the pontoon. Water and electricity available, toilets and showers are inside the clubhouse.* T 971 313 363
info@clubnauticoibiza.com
www.clubnauticoibiza.com

D Ibiza Magna
In der NW-Ecke des Hafenbeckens neben der Anlegestelle für die Schnellfähren nach Formentera und in nächster Nähe zur Altstadt. 85 Liegeplätze für Schiffe von 10-60 m und 12 m Breite an der Contramuelle de Poniente und an zwei Schwimmstegen. Keine Duschen und Toiletten. / *Situated at port basin's northwest corner, close to the speed ferry landings to Formentera and very close to the old town Dalt Vila. 85 berths for vessels sized 10-60m length and 12m beam at Contramuelle de Poniente and at two floating jetties. No showers or toilets.*

€ **12x4m** (48 m²) / Steg /jetty
107,84 EUR (July/August),
43,21 EUR (Sept-June)
30m (ca. 240 m², Contramuelle:
459,60 EUR (July/August),
229,80 EUR (Sept-June)
plus water, electr. G5, T-0 + 21% IVA
T 971 193 870 UKW/VHF 09
info@ibizamagna.com
www.ibizamagna.com

🕘 01/06-30/09: Mon-Sat: 9-20 h, Sun: 09-13 h, 01/04-31/05: Mon-Fri: 9-16 h, Sat+Sun: closed; 01/10-31/03: Mon-Fri: 09-15.30 h, Sat+Sun+hol.: closed

E Port Ibiza Town
Gegenüber von Ibiza Magna. Liegeplätze für Yachten von 60 m bis 140 m Länge und bis 7 m Tiefgang. Wasseranschluss, WLAN, Müllabfuhr, 24-Stunden-Sicherheitsdienst, Concierge-Service (Catering, Wäscherei, Pakete, Reservierungen, etc.). Die Lie-

Ibiza Stadt / Ibiza Town

geplätze werden vom Büro von Ibiza Magna verwaltet.
On the opposite side of Ibiza Magna. The marina can accommodate yachts of 60m to 140m in length and 7m draught. Water connection, WiFi, refuse collection, 24-hour security, concierge service (catering, laundry, packages, reservations, etc). Berths are managed by the office of Ibiza Magna.

T 971 193 870
UKW/VHF 09,
info@portibizatown.de
www.portibizatown.com
€ 01/07-31/08: 4/m²; June+Sept.: 3 €/m². Jeweils plus 21% MwSt., plus Hafengebühren G5+T0. *All prices plus 21% IVA, plus harbour taxes G5+T0*

TANKEN / *FUEL*

Marina Botafoch
Mon-Fri: 9-14 + 15-19 h, Sat, Sun + hol.: 9-14.30 h (summer)
Mon-Fri: 9-18 h,
Sat, Sun + hol.: 9-14 h (winter)

Marina Ibiza
Tankstelle direkt vor dem Marinabüro. Absaugung von Schwarz- und Grauwasser. / *Filling station situated directly in front of marina office. Extraction of black and grey water available.*

Marina Ibiza Magna
vom Tankwagen (für große Yachten, nach Anmeldung) / *from tank vehicles (for larger yachts, upon notification)*

TECHNISCHER SERVICE
TECHNICAL SERVICES

[K] Marina Botafoch
60-t-Travellift
Mon-Fri: 08:30-13 h + 15-18 h
Sat: 08:30-11 h

24-h-Notdienst / *emergency service*
(UKW/VHF 09, T 971 311 711)
Doppelter Normaltarif / *100 per cent additional charge*

Electrofrancisco
Marine Electrical Service, T 971 313 854
info@electrofrancisco.com

Siamarine
Antriebe und Generatoren / *marine engines, gearboxes and generators*
T 971 194 536, info@siamarine.com
www.siamarine.com

Tecnomar Ibiza
Motoren und Generatoren / *engines and generators*
(Mercury + Cummins), T 971 19 06 05
info@tecnomaribiza.com

[L] Varadero Ibiza
(Tanit Ibiza Port S.A.)
Travellift max. 160 t, bis 10 m Breite. Spezialisiert auf Großyachten, Refit, Anstriche und jedwede technische Dienstleistung. / *Travel lift services (max. 160t, up to 10m width). Specialises in large yachts, antifouling and painting facilities, refit & repair,* T 971 806 755
www.varaderoibiza.com
info@varaderoibiza.com

[M] ServiNautic
T 971 314 001 + 971 191 318
Werft und Motorenservice / *boat yard and engine service* (Volvo, Yanmar,

Ibiza

Varadero Ibiza

MerCruiser etc.)
🕐 Mon-Fri 08-13 + 15-18 h
Summer: auch /*also* Sat 10-12

Sun Supermercado Náutico
An der Straße Richtung Santa Eularia.
On the main road that leads to Santa Eularia. Av. de Sant Joan de Labrija
www.supermercadonautico.es
T 971 191 782

YACHTAUSRÜSTER / *CHANDLERIES*

N **Náutica Viamar**
Marina Botafoch, T 971 314958
Shop Carretera Sta. Eulalia, km 1.3,
T 971 191 782
www.viamar-ibiza.com

O **Nautico Ereso**
Kennt sich auch bei Seglerbedarf aus… / *Also well-versed in sailing equipment …*
www.nauticaereso.com
info@nauticaereso.com
T 971 199 605 / 971 314 122
Mon-Fri: 9-13+ 16-19 h, Sat: 9-13h

EINKAUFEN / *SHOPPING*

1 Spar-Supermarkt an der Cala Talamanca, von der Zufahrt zur Marina Botafoch keine 5 Min. zu Fuß
Spar supermarket at Cala Talamanca, in front of access to Marina Botafoch, less than 5 min. walk

2 Ein kleiner Supermarkt (7Mart Market) in der Nähe des Zugangs zur Marina Ibiza. / *Small supermarket (7Mart Market) near entrance to Marina Ibiza.*
Umfassende Angebote im Innenstadt-Gebiet von Ibiza und entlang der Ausfallstraßen.
Numerous offers in Ibiza town centre and along the trunk roads.

3 Kleine Supermärkte in den Straßen hinter dem Anleger der Formentera-Fähren. Ein größerer Supermarkt an der Straße Richtung Santa Eularia.
Small Supermarkets behind the shipping pier for the ferries that leave for Formentera. A bigger supermarket „Eroski" on the main road that leads to Santa Eularia, Av. de Sant Joan de Labrija.

RESTAURANTS & BARS

4 **Marina Botafoch**
Große Auswahl auf dem Marina-Gelände. / *Great variety on marina premises.*

5 **Marina Ibiza**
Auf dem Gelände, fast alle mit Blick auf die Altstadt-Festung Dalt Vila: *On the premises, places offering views of old town fortification Dalt Vila:*
Lío Restaurant Club Cabaret, Pacha-Gruppe; Dinner + live show
Calma Bistró, Frühstück bis Sonnenuntergang; *early in the day with breakfast until dawn*
Cappuccino Grand Café
Blue Marlin, von Frühstück bis Disco *offers range from breakfast to disco*

6 Vor der / *In front of* Marina Ibiza:
Nuba club
Ibiza Gran Casino + Jackpot Rest., Nightclub Downtown Ibiza

7 Große Auswahl in der Altstadt, u. a. *Large choice within old town, i. a.*

La Marina, T 971 578 774
nahe /*near* Estacion Maritima

Damit wurde Dalt Vila verteidigt … / This is how Dalt Vila was defended…

Ibiza Stadt / Ibiza Town

Die Altstadt Dalt Vila mit ihrer Kathedrale, UNESCO-Weltkulturerbe
Dalt Vila, citadel complex with the old town, UNESCO world heritage

Cala Talamanca

DANCING / DISCOS

Ibizas Nachtleben und die Clubszene sind einzigartig. Das gilt auch für die Preise. Eine Übersicht zu Ibizas Nachtleben und die Clubszene plus Partykalender gibt es unter:
www.ibiza-spotlight.de/nachtleben/club_infos_a.htm
Ibiza's night life and club scene are really one of a kind. This also applies to prices. For an overview of Ibiza's night life and club scene plus party schedule please see:
www.mydestination.com/ibiza/nightlife/22

Eine Auswahl großer Clubs auf Ibiza:
A selection of large clubs on Ibiza:

Amnesia – San Rafael
Booom! – next to Marina Ibiza
DC10 – next to the airport
Eden – San Antonio
Es Paradis – San Antonio
Pacha – Marina Ibiza
Privilege – next to San Rafael
Sankeys – Playa d'en Bossa
Space – Playa d'en Bossa
Ushuaïa – Playa d'en Bossa

AUSFLÜGE / EXCURSIONS

8 Durch die Gassen der Altstadt geht es hoch hinauf zur Kathedrale Nuestra Señora de las Nieves unmittelbar neben dem Kastell. Von hier aus hat man einen wunderbaren Ausblick über die Meerenge zwischen Formentera und Ibiza, über die Stadt, den Hafen und das grünbewaldete Hinterland. Dort oben am Platz der Kathedrale ist auch das Archäologische Museum der Insel beheimatet mit Funden aus dem Altertum, aus den Zeiten der Phönizier, Punier und Römer bis zum ausgehenden Mittelalter. 2015 geschlossen.

Through Old town alleyways ascend to Nuestra Señora de las Nieves cathedral, immediately next to the castle. Enjoy a fantastic sweeping vista of the straits between Formentera and Ibiza, including the town, harbour and forested back country. Right at Cathedral Square there is the island's archaeological museum, showing objects dating from antiquity, the age of the Phoenicians, Carthaginians and Romans up to the Late Middle Ages. 2015 closed.

9 Autovermietung / *Car rental*
Zahlreiche Vermieter in der Nähe des Club Náutico. PKW sind im Vergleich zu Mallorca mind. doppelt so teuer. Motorroller können eine Alternative sein.
Many rentals close to Club Náutico. Car rentals are at least twice the price of Mallorca. Scooters are an alternative.

Cala Talamanca – Cala Llonga

ANKERPLÄTZE
ANCHORAGE AREAS

A Cala Talamanca
38° 54,5' N 001° 27,9' E

Eine (auch wegen des Liegeplatzmangels in Ibiza-Stadt) vielgenutzte Ankerbucht unmittelbar östlich anschließend an das große Hafengebiet und ähnlich groß. Ankergrund überwiegend Seegras. Ankertiefen um 10 m. Der innere Teil ist vor allem im Nordosten sehr flach. Vier gelbe Leuchttonnen (FlY) markieren eine Speerzone im südwestlichen Teil der Bucht. Sehr oft Schwell durch auflandige, thermische Winde. Auch nordöstliche Winde wehen hinein. Strand-Restaurants und kleine Supermärkte auf beiden Seiten der Bucht.

Intensively frequented bay (also because of lack of berths in Ibiza Town) just east to the large port area and similar in size. Sea floor predominantly weed. Depths around 10m. The inner part is quite shallow especially in the northeast.

Four yellow lighted buoys (FlY) mark a restricted area in the southwestern part of the bay. Swell is caused by thermal onshore winds. Also northeasterly winds reach into the bay. Beach-restaurants and small supermarkets on both sides of the bay.

B Cala Llonga
38° 57,2' N 001° 31,9' E

Eine von hohen Felswänden eingerahmte Bucht, knapp 2 sm südlich von Santa Eulalia. Achtung: kein Schutz bei Mistral (starker Nord- bzw. Nordostwind). Eine gute Landmarke ist das über 220 m hohe Cabo Librell südlich der Bucht. Beide Seiten der Bucht sind mit Hotels bebaut. In der Einfahrt beträgt die Wassertiefe 16 m und nimmt danach gleichmäßig ab. Untiefen sind keine zu beachten, aber Schwimmer, Taucher und Ausflugsboote, die Richtung Santa Eulalia pendeln. Ankern auf 8-5 m über Sand vor einem großzügig abgetrennten Badebereich. Cala Llonga ist ein touristischer Ort mit

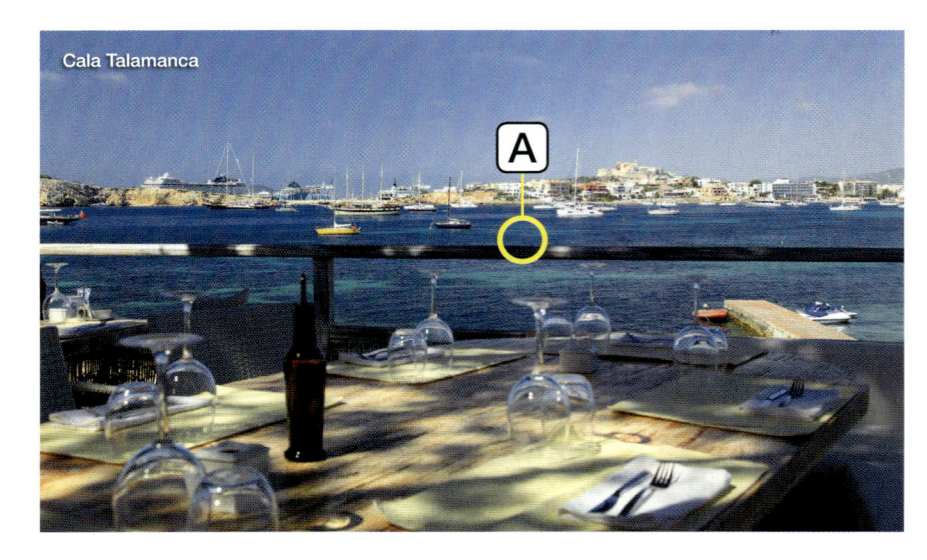

Cala Talamanca – Cala Llonga

Restaurants und Supermärkten, Ärzten, Apotheke, Autovermietungen, Bankautomaten etc.

A bay framed by high cliffs, nearly 2nmi south of Santa Eulalia. **Note:** *no protection during Mistral (strong north or north-east wind). The 220m high Cabo Librell south of the bay is a good landmark.*
Both sides of the bay are built with hotels. In the approach the water depth is 16m and then decreases steadily. No shallows have to be observed but swimmers, divers and excursion boats to and from Santa Eulalia. Drop anchor at 8-5m in front of a marked swimming area. Sandy bottom. Cala Llonga is a busy touristy village. Many restaurants and supermarkets, doctors, pharmacies, ATM, car rental et cetera.

Ibiza

Cala Nova – Cala San Vicente

ANKERPLÄTZE
ANCHORAGE AREAS

A Cala Nova / Cala Llenya
39° 00,6' N 001° 35,4' E

🇩🇪 Cala Nova ist eine wenig bebaute Bucht, nur durch eine Huk von der nördlicheren Cala Llenya getrennt. Sandiger Ankergrund bei zirka 5-3 m Wassertiefe. Es gibt mehrere Restaurants am Strand.
Cala Llenya wird flankiert von Hotels und Appartements. Auf der Nordseite liegen alte Bootshäuser der Fischer. In der Mitte der Einfahrt 10 m Wassertiefe, danach gleichmäßig abnehmend. Ankern vor dem weiträumig abgesperrten Badebereich auf 6-5 m über Sand. Eine Strandbar ist vorhanden.

🇬🇧 *Cala Nova is a little built-up bay, seperated from the northern Cala Llenya only by a small headland. Sandy sea floor, one can drop anchor at 5-3 water depth. There are several restaurants at the beach.*
Cala Llenya is flanked by hotels and apartments. On the north side old boathouses of local fishermen appear. In the approach 10m water depth, followed by a steady decrease. Anchorage at 6-5m above sand in front of a widely seperated swimming area. A beach bar is available.

B Cala Boix
39° 01,6' N 001° 36,4' E
Eine offene, aber recht beliebte Bucht bei Cabo Roig. Frei von Untiefen. Die Wassertiefen nehmen gleichmäßig ab. Yachten ankern auf ca. 5 m Wassertiefe über fast reinem Sandgrund. Die Bucht ist Schwell aus südlichen Richtungen schutzlos ausgesetzt. Guter Schutz jedoch bei nördlichen Winden. Gaststätte am Strand.

An open, but quite popular bay at Cabo Roig. Free of shoals. Water depths decrease steadily. Yachts drop anchor in about 5m depth with a sea floor of predominantly sandy. The bay is exposed to swell from the south. But well protected during northerly winds. Restaurant on the beach.

C Isla Tagomago
39° 02,1' N 001° 38,2' E
Privatinsel, die von einer Immobilienfirma zur Miete angeboten wird. Man kann an verschiedenen Stellen ankern, u. a. an der Westseite auf ca. 6 m Wassertiefe. Grund: überwiegend Seegras, Sand erst nahe der Steilküste. Man kann mit dem Beiboot zu einer kleinen Pier übersetzen und die Strandbar beim Anleger besuchen. Bis dahin ist die Insel öffentlich zugänglich. Es gibt einige große, private Bojen, die nicht belegt werden dürfen.

Achtung: Es überspülte Felsen (Losa Figueral) 1 sm nordwestlich von Tagomago. Die Kennzeichnung (Einzelgefahrenstelle) kann nach den Wintermonaten fehlen.

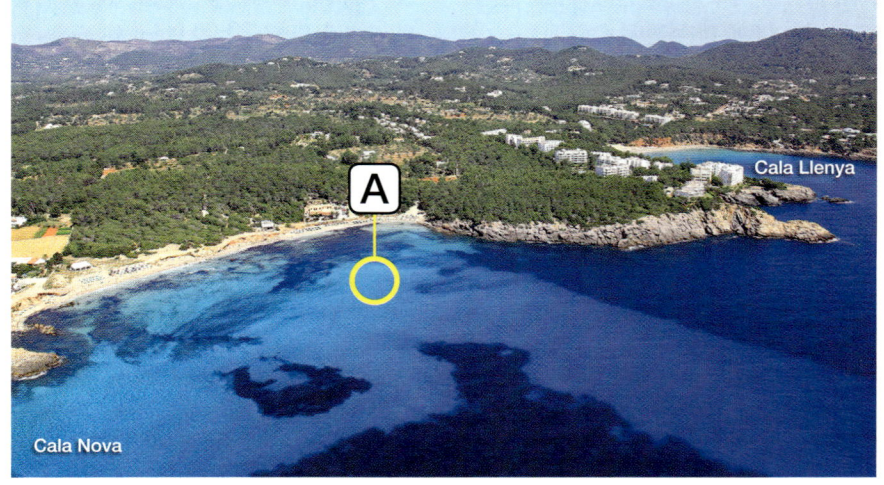

Cala Nova – Cala San Vicente

Isla Tagomago

Private island. Anchoring is possible at various spots, first of all the west side of Tagomago is visited frequently by yachts. Here one can anchor in about 6 m depth of water. Some big, private buoys may not be occupied. The sea floor consists mostly of weed. Sandy bottom can be found closer to the cliffs. One can land by dinghy to visit the beach bar. Further inland the island is not accessible to the public.
Caution: *1nmi to the northeast there are washed over rocks (Losa Figueral). Beacon topmark may be missing after the winter period!*

www.island-tagomago.com

D **Cala San Vicente**
39° 04,2' N 001° 35,8' E

Im Schutz der 174 m hohen Punta Grossa finden wir die weite, nach Südost offene Cala de San Vicente, eingerahmt von grünen Hügeln, die teilweise bebaut sind. Hinter dem 500 m langen Strand stehen viele Hotels.
Der Meeresgrund vor der Bucht ist tief, selbst nah an der Steilküste. Doch Vorsicht: Vor der Ostseite der Bucht können Fischernetze und -bojen ausliegen. Etwas mehr als ein Dutzend Yachten finden in der Bucht vor der abgesperrten Badezone Platz. Man ankert auf 10-7 m Wasser, der Grund besteht aus Sand und Seegras.
Hinter dem Strand einige Bars und Restaurants, aber kein Supermarkt.

Protected against wind from north and west we find Cala de San Vicente close to Punta Grossa towering 174m. Behind the beach numerous hotels appear. **Note:** *On the east side of the bay permanent fishing nets may be laid out marked with very small bouys and quick white lights. One drops anchor in front of a separated swimming zone. Depths are around 10-7m, the sea floor consists of sand, partly covered with weed. Behind the small beach you will find bars and restaurants, but no supermarket.*

Cala Boix

Cala San Vicente

Cala Portinatx

🇩🇪 Nur gegen Winde aus nördlichen Richtungen verspricht diese vielbesuchte Ankerbucht wenig Schutz, bei allen anderen Windrichtungen ist man hier sehr gut aufgehoben. So kommen hier an einem Sommerabend gerne 40 Yachten und mehr zusammen. Die Bucht ist auch groß genug, sie alle aufnehmen zu können. An Land finden die Crews im Sommer einen sehr belebten Ferienort mit einem umfassenden Angebot. Von daher: Leise ist es hier nachts in der Bucht nicht.

🇬🇧 *It is only during northerly winds that this much visited bay does not offer good protection, in all other conditions it is a safe and charming place. Consequently, some 40 yachts or more may congregate here on a beautiful summer evening. The bay is large enough to leave enough space for all. On shore, crews can enjoy a very popular resort town with comprehensive offerings in summer. So be aware: this is definitely no quiet bay by night.*

ANSTEUERUNG
APPROACHING

Keine Untiefen direkt vor dem Hafen. Aber auch keine Einfahrtsbefeuerung. 1 sm östlich steht jedoch der schwarzweiß geringelte Leuchtturm auf der Pta. Moscarter, FlW 5s. Die Wassertiefen gehen erst im inneren Teil der Bucht unter 10 m zurück.

No shallows immediately in front of harbour, but there are also no lights at the entrance. Luckily, 1nmi southeast there is a black-and-white striped lighthouse on Pta. Moscarter, FlW 5s. Water depths rise to less than 10m only within the bay itself.

ANKERPLÄTZE
ANCHORAGE AREAS

A Ankern vor einer abgeteilten Badezone auf 9-4 m. Nur weit innen Sandgrund, sonst viel Seegras.
Anchorage in front of separate bathing area over 9-4m. Sandy bottom only far within, lots of weed elsewhere.

B Es gibt Sandflecken zwischen Seegras auf 6-8 m Wassertiefe. Einer der schönsten Plätze, vor dem kleinen Hotelstrand mit kleiner Badezone unterhalb einer Steilküste. Hier Verleih von Seekayaks und Surfbrettern. Anlanden mit dem Beiboot möglich.
Sandy patches between seaweed at 6-8m water depth. This is one of the most beautiful spots to visit, right in front of a small beach of a hotel with bathing area below a steep cliff. Seagoing kayak and surfboard rental here. Use dinghy to land.

C Hier ankern mit Landleinen.
Use mooring lines to anchor here.

D Schmaler Seitenarm mit zunächst noch großen Wassertiefen. Am Ende Mini-Sandstrand mit Bars & Restaurants und Blick auf den Leuchtturm.
Narrow branch, initially providing deep water. Ends in a small sandy beach with bars & restaurants and a view of the lighthouse.

EINKAUFEN / *SHOPPING*

Drei kleine Supermärkte in direkter Nähe der Bucht. Bankautomaten vorhanden. Auch Arzt und Apotheke.
Three small supermarkets near the bay. ATMs available, and a doctor and pharmacy as well.

RESTAURANTS & BARS

1 Zahlreiche Restaurants, auch in Wassernähe. Eine Terrasse mit sehr schönem Blick auf die Bucht hat das Grop's Lounge (chinesische + thailändische Küche).
Many restaurants, some near the water. For a terrace with beautiful view of the bay go to Grop's Lounge (Chinese + Thai cuisine).

2 Restaurant Jardin del Mar
Dingi-Landeplatz am nahen Sandstrand / *with dinghy landing spot on nearby sandy beach*
T 971 337 659

AUSFLÜGE / *EXCURSIONS*

Neben Bus-Verbindungen, Fahrpläne unter www.ibizabus.com, gibt es gleich drei Vermieter von Autos und Zweirädern.

Bus connections – schedules see: www.ibizabus.com – are supplemented by three car and bike rental services.

Cala Portinatx

- Wichtige Bucht im Norden
- Kurze Distanz nach Mallorca
- Sehr touristische Umgebung

- *Important bay in the North*
- *Short distance to Mallorca*
- *Very touristy area*

39° 07,1' N   001° 30,6' E

Cala Portinatx

Cala Portinatx

Ibiza

Ens. Xarraca – Port Sant Miguel

ANKERPLÄTZE
ANCHORAGE AREAS

A Ensenada Xarraca
39° 06,1' N 001° 29,9' E

🇩🇪 Unmittelbar westlich an die Cala Portinatx schließt die Ensenada oder Cala Xarraca an. Sie ist 0,7 sm tief. Der vielleicht schönste Ankerplatz befindet sich im südwestlichen Zipfel, wo im Sommer auch ein Restaurant öffnet. Man ankert auf gut 5 m Wassertiefe und überwiegend sandigem Grund. Felsige Abschnitte und andere mit Seegras lassen sich gut vermeiden, der Andrang an Booten hält sich meist in Grenzen. Ob es daran liegt, dass die Uferstraße nach Cala Portinatx vorbeiführt?

🇬🇧 *Just west of Cala Portinatx, Ensenada or Cala Xarraca connects to the bay. The bay measures 0.7x0.7nmi. Perhaps the most beautiful anchorage is located in the southwest, in summer a restaurant opens here. Anchorage on 5m water depth with predominantly sandy sea floor. Rocky sections and others with weed can be well avoided. Not too many boats visit this place, possibly because of the passing coastal road to Cala Portinatx.*

B Cala Blanca
39° 06,3' N 001° 29,1' E

Viel Sandgrund im inneren Teil dieser wenig besuchten und unterschätzten Bucht. Dort am Südwestufer ein auffälliges, weißes Haus. Davor Ankern auf 8-2 m. Gegenüber im Südwesten ein Kiesstrand. Von dort Spaziergänge, auch in unwegsamem Gelände. Keine Angebote an Land.

Lots of sandy sea floor in the inner part of this unfrequented and underrated bay. In the southeastern part a single, white private building. Drop anchor here, depths around 8-2m. Opposite a pebble beach where one can land by dinghy. From there interesting hikes are possible, also through rough terrain.

Ens. Xarraca – Port Sant Miguel

Ensenada Xarraca

C Cala Binirras
39° 05,6' N 001° 26,8' E

Die lotrechte Felsspitze Islote Bernat markiert die Einfahrt zur Bucht. Deren Ankergrund besteht direkt vor einer abgetrennten Schwimmzone aus Sand mit Seegras, weiter außen überwiegt Seegras. Die äußeren Ankerplätze haben 13-10 m Wasser, erst vor der Badezone findet man mit 7-6 m moderate Tiefen vor.

Im Sommer öffnen ein halbes Dutzend Restaurants, die auch von Land aus stark frequentiert werden. Die Wassertiefen sind überall üppig, es gibt hier keine gefährlichen Untiefen.

The vertical crag Islote Bernat marks the entrance to the bay, one drops anchor in front of a separate swimming area. Sea floor in the inner part sand with weed, further out mainly weed. The anchorage area here has depth from 13-10m, in the inner part 7-6m. In summer, half a dozen restaurants open here, which are mainly frequented by beach visitors. The water depths are generous everywhere, no dangerous shoals to be avoided.

D Port Sant Miguel
39° 05,3' N 001° 26,5' E

Der westliche Teil dieser Ankerbucht ist gut geschützt durch eine bebaute Halbinsel. Gegen Nordwind besteht dennoch wenig Schutz. Die vorgelagerte Insel Isla Murada kann landseitig ohne Probleme passiert werden.

Man ankert vornehmlich auf der Westseite vor einer Steilküste auf 7-5 m zwischen zwei Bojenfeldern für kleine Boote und über Sandgrund mit wenigen Seegrasflecken.

Die Ortschaft hinter dem Strand bietet in den Sommermonaten fast alles: von Restaurants über Supermärkte und Autovermieter bis zu Geldautomaten.

The western part of this anchorage is well protected by an built-up peninsula. Nevertheless with northerly winds there is little protection. Small island Isla Murada to the northwest can be passed on all sides without problems.
One drops anchor on the west side in front of a cliff. Water depths are 7-5m between two buoy fields for small boats, the sea floor consists of sand with few spots of weed.
The village behind the beach offers in the summer months almost everything from restaurants, supermarkets and car rental companies to ATMs.

Ens. de Aubarca – Ens. del Canal

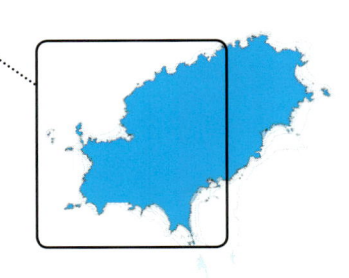

🇩🇪 Buchten und Beachclubs – vor allem zwischen Sant Antoni de Portmany und der Südspitze mit der Nachbarinsel Formentera ist die Insel voll damit. Sant Antoni ist der einzige Hafen an Ibizas Westseite, mit Marina und einem Bojenfeld.

🇬🇧 *Bays and beach clubs line the coastline between Sant Antoni de Portmany and the southern tip, continuing on to the neighbouring island of Formentera. Sant Antoni is the only port on Ibiza's west side, with a marina and a buoy field.*

1 Ensenada de Aubarca - 39° 03,9' N 001° 22,3' E → page 280
Ankern im Südwestteil auf 15-8 m. Sand und Seegras. Natur pur.
Anchorage in the southwestern part, 15-8 m. Sand & weed. Pure nature.

2 Islas Margaritas - 39° 03,1' N 001° 18,8' E → page 280
Auffällige Felsformation mit einem Loch zwischen Fels und Meer.
Striking rock formation with a hole between rock and sea.

3 Cala Salada - 39° 00,5' N 001° 17,5' E → page 280
Größere Wassertiefen zum Ankern. Grund überwiegend Seegras. Restaurant.
5-10m water depth on the anchorages. Bottom mostly weed. Restaurant.

4 Sant Antoni - 38° 58,6' N 001° 17,6' E → page 282
Einziger Yachthafen im Westen, aber wenige Gastliegeplätze. Ort touristisch.
The only marina on the west side of Ibiza. Few guest berths. Very busy place.

5 Port del Torrent - 38° 58,4' N 001° 15,9' E → page 286
Reiner Sandgrund. Tagsüber unruhig durch Motorboote.
Sandy bottom. Choppy during the day because of speed boats.

6 Cala Bassa - 38° 58,3' N 001° 14,8' E → page 286
Ankern auf ca. 10 m vor Badestrand mit Beachclub. Viel Seegras, Sandflecken.
Depth is mostly 10m, bottom weed with sandy patches. Beachclub ashore.

7 Cala Compte - 38° 58,1' N 001° 13,4' E → page 286
Sandgrund. Eine Barre schützt vor Seegang aus West. Strandrestaurants.
Sandy bottom. Underwater reef southwest of the bay. Beach restaurants.

8 Cala Tarida - 38° 56,3' N 001° 14,1' E → page 287
Nach Westen offene Bucht vor Feriensiedlungen. Feiner Sandgrund. Restaurants.
Not well protected to the west. Ashore vacation resorts. Restaurants.

9 Cala Badella - 38° 54,8' N 001° 13,0' E → page 287
Nordhuk läuft flach aus. Große Wassertiefen, Seegras. Ankern mit Landleine.
Lots of weed. It's recommended to use a land connection where neccesary.

10 Cala Horts - 38° 53,1' N 001° 13,0' E → page 288
Blick auf Isla Vedra. Ankern über Sand, 7-4 m. Restaurants am Strand.
Isla Vedra view. Anchorage with sand, depths 7-4m. Restaurants on the beach.

11 Cala de Port Roig - 38° 52,0' N 001° 18,0' E → page 288
Im Nordteil Sand, ca. 4 m Tiefe. Sonst Seegras und tiefer. Private Bojen.
In the north sandy bottom, about 4m depth. Otherwise weed, deeper. Private buoys.

12 Cala Jondal - 38° 51,9' N 001° 18,9' E → page 290
Bucht mit Beachclubs im Süden Ibizas. Viele Megayachten.
Bay with beach clubs in the south of Ibiza. Attracts also many super yachts.

13 Ensenada de la Canal - 38° 50,2' N 001° 23,6' E → page 291
Bucht mit Bojenfeld und Ankergrund und gleich mehreren Beachclubs.
A bay with buoy field, an anchorage and several beach clubs ashore.

Der Westen Ibizas / The West of Ibiza

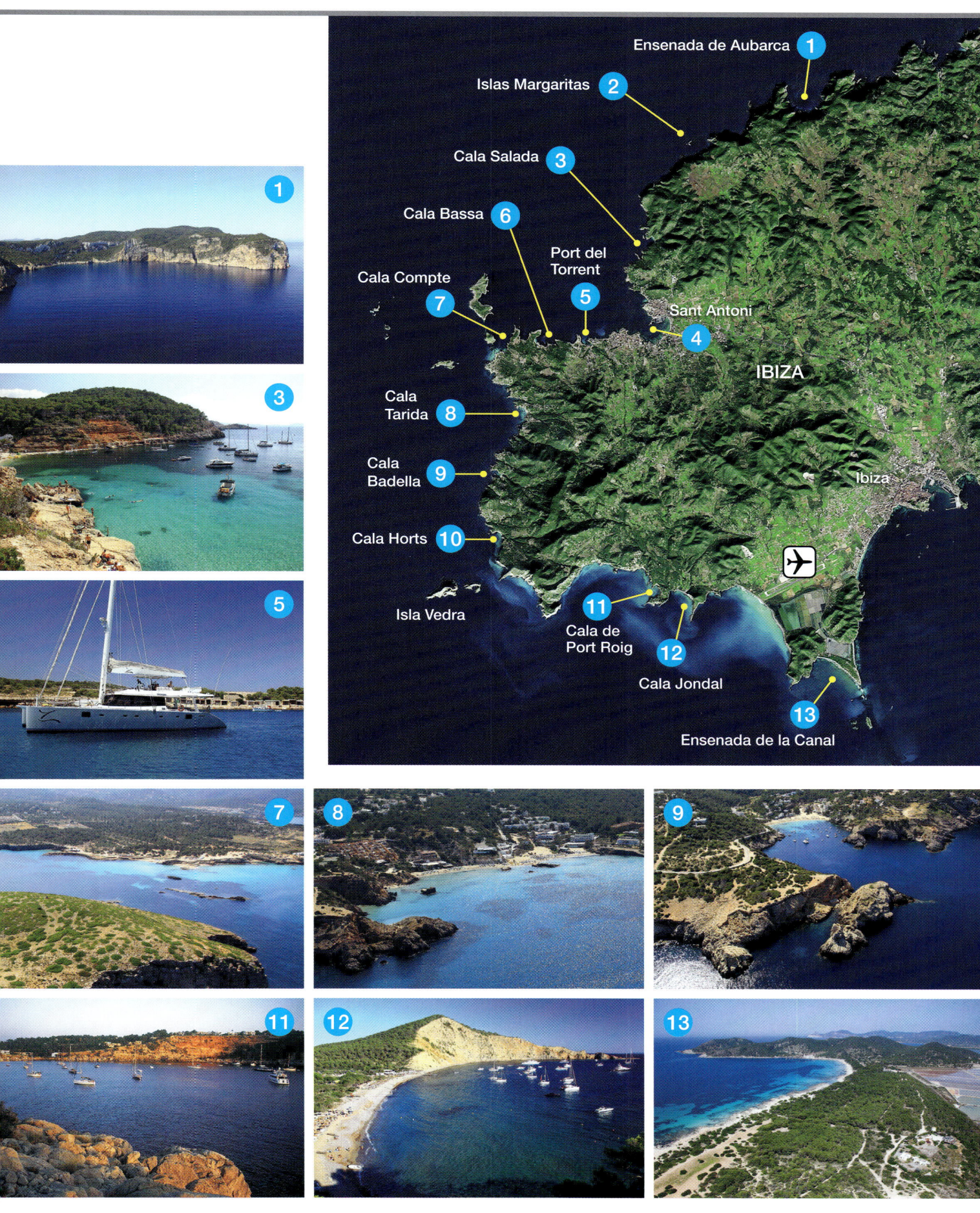

1. Ensenada de Aubarca
2. Islas Margaritas
3. Cala Salada
4. Sant Antoni
5. Port del Torrent
6. Cala Bassa
7. Cala Compte
8. Cala Tarida
9. Cala Badella
10. Cala Horts
11. Cala de Port Roig
12. Cala Jondal
13. Ensenada de la Canal

Isla Vedra

IBIZA

Ibiza

Ens. de Aubarca – Cala Salada

ANKERPLÄTZE
ANCHORAGE AREAS

A Ensenada de Aubarca
39° 03,9' N   001° 22,3' E

Eine tiefe Bucht, die beim Vorbeisegeln unspektakulär wirkt. Man muss schon bis ans Ende hineinfahren, um ihren Zauber zu entdecken und die spektakuläre hohe Steilküste. Ankern im Südwestteil auf 15-8 m. Sand und Seegras. Keinerlei Versorgung an Land. Natur pur, schnorcheln und mit dem Dingi zum Landausflug und zu einer kleinen Wanderung starten. Handy vergessen, das fällt leicht, denn die Mobilfunk-Abdeckung kann hier schwach sein …

A deep bay, which seems unspectacular when passing by boat. You have to explore right to the end of it to discover its magic and the impressive high cliffs. Drop anchor in the southwest part at 15-8m depth of water. The sea floor consists of sand and weed. Shore pure nature, close to the rocks good snorkeling. One can also launch the dinghy for an excursion and a short hike. Forgot your cellphone, that's easy here, as cellular coverage may be weak …

B Islas Margaritas
39° 03,1' N   001° 18,8' E

Auffällige Felsformation mit einem Loch zwischen Fels und Meer. Die Inseln vor Sant Antoni sind hier schon in Sichtweite. Viele Seevögel nisten hier. Sehr große Wassertiefen auf der Westseite, geringer auf der Ostseite. Ein beliebter Tauchspot. Mit einem Dingi kann man den Felsbogen durchfahren, ein tolles Erlebnis.

Striking rock formation with a hole between rock and sea. The islands off Sant Antoni are already in sight. Many seabirds nest here. Huge water depths on the west side, less on the east side. A popular diving spot. With a dinghy you can drive through the natural arch, a great experience.

C Cala Salada
39° 00,5' N   001° 17,5' E

3 sm nördlich von Sant Antoni. Rundum hohe Ufer, bewaldet. Bootsschuppen, die als Sommerdomizil genutzt werden. Zwei Strände, die stark frequentiert sind. Als Nachtankerplatz beliebt, wenn auch nach Westen offen. In der Ansteuerung überall große Wassertiefen. Ankern im nördlichen Teil auf 5-7 m, vor einem Bereich mit weniger als 3 m Wasser. Im Südteil auch über 10 m. Grund mehr Seegras als Sand. Restaurant am Strand.

Ensenada de Aubarca

Ens. de Aubarca – Cala Salada

Cabo Nono

Islas Margaritas

Cala Salada

3nmi north of Sant Antoni. High cliffs, well visited beaches. Boathouses, which are used as a summer residence. Two well frequented beaches. A popular bay for the night, even if it's unprotected to the west. When approaching large water depths throughout. Depths around 5-7m in the northern part, 10m and even more in the southern part. Bottom predominently weed. Restaurant ashore.

Ibiza

Sant Antoni

- Einziger Hafen im Westen
- Sehr touristische Stadt
- Wenige Gastliegeplätze

- *Only port in the west*
- *Very touristy town*
- *Few berths for visitors*

🇩🇪 Sant Antoni de Portmany ist ideal für alle Yachten, die vom spanischen Festland kommen oder dorthin wollen. Nur hier gibt es entlang der 30 sm messenden Nordwestseite Ibizas Yachtliegeplätze, auch für Gäste. Jedoch nicht in ausreichender Zahl.
Der Hafenort ist durch den zunehmenden Massentourismus gewuchert und hat wenig schöne Seiten. Aber man kann sich entsprechend gut versorgen, an Restaurants und Supermärkten herrscht kein Mangel. Zu allen Seiten gibt es schöne Ankerplätze.

🇬🇧 *Situated in the West of Ibiza, San Antonio de Portmany is perfect for all yachts coming to or from to the Spanish mainland. This is the only place along the 30nmi northwestern coast of Ibiza offering yacht berths, even for visitors. However: insufficient for the summer rush. The port town has mushroomed due to increasing package tourism and offers few lovely spots. But getting supplies is easy as there is no lack of restaurants and supermarkets. Beautiful anchorages on all sides.*

ANSTEUERUNG
APPROACHING

Die Bucht vor Sant Antoni ist frei von Untiefen. Vier Seemeilen westlich des Hafens liegt die auffällige Isla Conejera mit einem Leuchtturm auf der Nordspitze. Von Westen und Süden kommend ist man versucht, diese Insel südlich zu passieren. Die Wassertiefen in der Passage mit der kleineren Isla del Bosque gehen jedoch auf max. 4 m zurück, so dass man hier nur bei ruhigen Bedingungen durchfahren sollte.
Der Hafen wird auch von Fähren angelaufen, deren Liegeplatz ist hinter der Außenmole. Beim Einlaufen ist das Fahrwasser an Steuerbord durch eine Reihe grüner Tonnen bezeichnet, die teilweise befeuert sind.

No shallow areas in Sant Antoni bay. 4nmi west of the harbour lies eye-catching Isla Conejera with its lighthouse at the northern tip. When coming from west or southerly directions, sailors are tempted to pass the island on the south. Water depths in the passage with smaller Isla del Bosque recede to max. 4m. Therefore this passage should only be done in calm weather with good visibility.
Ferries also touch this port at a berth behind the outer pier. When entering, keep in navigable waters marked starboard by a row of green buoys, some of which are lighted.

FESTMACHEN
FIND A BERTH

A **Club Nàutic Sant Antoni**
500 Liegeplätze für Yachten bis 50 m Länge und 5 m Breite, aber nur wenige, im Hochsommer teure Gastplätze. Im Sommer eröffnet der moderne Clubhafen täglich neu eine Warteliste. *New, modern marina for 500 yachts up to 50m length and 5m width, but expensive during high season with only a few visitor berths. A waiting list is drawn up daily in summer.*

T 971 340 645

📱 UKW/VHF 09
info@esnautic.com +
reservas@esnautic.com
Reservierung über die Webseite
Reservations on the website
www.esnautic.com
🕘 Mo-Sun: 09-21 h, daily.
Winter: Mon-Fri 09-13 h + 16-20 h.
Sat 09-14 h
Marineros: 7/24 h, M 662 382 520

€ **12m:** July + August: 90,14 EUR, June + Sept.: 54,60 EUR, Inkl. Wasser, Strom, Hafengebühren und 21% MwSt. *incl. water, electr., harbour taxes and 21 % IVA*

📶 Kostenlos / *free of charge*

Fl(2)R 7s

Strom und Wasser nehmen
Power and water supply
Der Club bietet bis zu 2 Stunden die Möglichkeit, dass sich Yachten mit Strom und Wasser versorgen. Anmeldung: UKW-Kanal 12. Mon-Sun 10-18 h
A special offer of the Club Nàutic: power and water supply up to 2 hours. Registration via VHF 12. Mon-Sun 10-18 h
€ < 12m: 9 EUR, 12-20m: 12 EUR, > 20m: 50 EUR/30 min.

Wäscherei / *Laundry*
Self-Service oder Auftrag / *or by order*
UKW/VHF-Kanal 12, T 673 781 266

Sant Antoni

38° 58,6' N 001° 17,6' E

B PortsIB

Im öffentlichen Hafenteil werden im Sommer maximal 5 Liegeplätze an Gäste vergeben und für maximal drei Tage nacheinander. Büro an der Uferstraße auf Höhe des Marinazufahrt.

In the public part of this port, up to 5 visitors berths are allocated in summer where guests may stay up to three consecutive days. Office at the coastal road close to the marina entrance.

Reservierung notwendig, mind. drei Tag im Voraus über „www.portsib.es" Bezahlung per Kreditkarte. Stornierung oder Umbuchung über die Webseite.

Reservation recommended at least 3 days in advance at "www.portsib.es" Payment by credit card. For cancelation or changes please go to the webpage.

Office: T 971 340 503
portsantantoni@portsib.caib.es
🕗 8-15 h (winter), 8-20 h (summer)
€ EUR/m2: 0,60 (01/06-30/09); 0,18 (01/10-31/05) Water: 5,50 EUR; Electr.: 5,50 EUR; Alle Preise / All prices plus 21% MwSt. /VAT

Einfache Sanitäreinrichtungen neben dem Hafenbüro.

Simple sanitary facilities next to the harbour office.

BOJENFELD / *BOUY FIELD*

C Seit 2015 ist das Ankern südlich der Fahrwassertonnen offiziell nicht mehr gestattet, es wurde hier ein Bojenfeld eingerichtet. Der Club Nàutic betreibt und kassiert. Wer hier festmacht, kann u. a. die sanitären Einrichtungen des Clubs nutzen.

Die Bojenpreise sind nicht im Internet einsehbar und die Auskunft der Marina deutet auf ein gehobenes Preisniveau

Ibiza

hin: 1,12 bis 9 € pro Meter (6 bis 25m sind möglich), plus 21% MwSt.
Der Club bietet auch einen Shuttle-Service (wenn man nicht das eigene Dingi nutzen möchte). Anmeldung: siehe „Festmachen".

In 2015 the anchorage south of the buoyed channel was replaced by a buoy field. It's managed by the Club Nàutic. Those who pay for one of these buoys can, among other things, use the sanitary facilities of the club.
The buoys' prices are not available on the Internet. According to information from the marina, prices are as follows: 1,12 to 9 € per meter (6 to 25 m are possible), plus 21% VAT. The Club also offers a shuttle service (if one does not want to use one's own dinghy). Registration: see „Find a berth".

TANKEN / *FUEL*

In der Marina / *In the marina*
D+B, Verkauf von Eis / *sales ice cubes*
UKW/VHF 11, Mon-Sun 09-21 h
Winter: Mon-Sun, 09 h bis Sonnenuntergang / *09 h until sunset*

Am Ende der Aussenmole.
At the breakwater.
D+B, Mon, Wed, Fri, Sat: 8-14 h,
Tue, Thu: 8-13 + 15.30-17.30 h

TECHNISCHER SERVICE / *TECHNICAL SERVICES*

D Travellift 25 t; Bootsslip slipway Werft Shipyard: nach Anmeldung *by appointment*
varadero@esnautic.com

Tankabsaugung / *Extraction unit*
Bei der Werft gibt es eine Absauganlage für Yachten bis 1,80 m Tiefgang. Die Benutzung ist kostenlos. Muss wegen eines größeren Tiefgang die mobile Anlage zum Einsatz kommen, dann kostet diese 10 EUR pro Stunde.

In the yard there is an extraction unit for yachts up to 1.80m depth. It is free of charge. Boats with more than 1.80m are serviced by a mobile plant which costs EUR 10 per hour.

Anmeldung / *Contact*
M 673 781 266, UKW/VHF 12
coord.explotacion@esnautic.com

YACHTAUSRÜSTER / *CHANDLERIES*

E **Nautica Cosmar**
T+F 971 345 477
nauticacosmar@gmail.com
www.nauticacosmar.es

EINKAUFEN / *SHOPPING*

1 Diverse Supermärkte kleiner und mittlerer Größe in Marina-Nähe. Ebenfalls Banken, Apotheke, dazu ein breites touristisches Angebot.
Various small- to mid-sized supermarkets close to the Marina. Also banks, pharmacy, many tourist attractions.

2 Supermercado „El Marino"

3 Ein Lidl-Supermarkt in Richtung Ibiza, ca. 1 km entfernt.
One Lidl supermarket towards Ibiza, distance appr. 1 km.

RESTAURANTS & BARS

1 **La Cantina**
Am großen Platz nach Verlassen der Marina, rechter Hand. Immer gut besucht. Im alten Hotel „Portmany". Familienbetrieb. Neben mediterraner Küche auch thailändisch etc.
At the large square after leaving the marina to the right. Always well attended. Located inside the old Hotel „Portmany". In addition to Mediterranean cuisine also Thai food etc.
T 971 345 860
www.lacantinaibiza.com

Cala Compte

Café del Mar

4 **Café del Mar**
Durch sein eigenes Plattenlabel weltbekanntes Szene-Lokal an der Sunset-Seite von Sant Antoni. Es öffnet üblicherweise von Karfreitag bis zur ersten Novemberwoche und täglich ab 17 Uhr, wenn hunderte von Gäste zum Sonnenuntergang dorthin pilgern.
Made famous by its record label, Cafe del Mar is the place to be at sunset, on the west side of Sant Antoni. It usually opens from Good Friday until the first week of November and daily from 17 o'clock, when hundreds of guests flock to the sunset there.
www.cafedelmarmusic.com

Sant Antoni

Isla del Bosque
Isla Vedra
Isla del Esperto
Fl(4)20s
Isla Conejera

5 **Marina Restaurant**
T 971 341 651
restaurante@esnautic.com
www.esnauticrestaurant.com

6 Nach Verlassen der Marina ca. 100 links: / *Outside of marina, located some 100 m to the left:*
S'Avaradero, Terrasse im 1. Stock mit Blick auf die Bucht, *patio on upper floor with sea view*, T 971 401 691
info@savaradero.com

Villa Mercedes, besondere Atmosphäre, z. T. Live Music, gehobenes Preisniveau, mittags und am frühen Abend Menü-Angebote / *Villa Mercedes, spe-*cial ambiance, occasionally live music, a bit expensive, set meal offered at noon and early in the evening
www.villamercedesibiza.com

DANCING / DISCOS

Zahlreiche Bars und Clubs, in der Stadt und rund um die Bucht / *Many venues in town and around the bay*

AUSFLÜGE / EXCURSIONS

→ z. B. Nach Ibiza-Stadt
e.g. to Ibiza Town

7 Bus-Station nach Verlassen der Marina ca. 5 Min. nach rechts. Taxi-Station 100 m entferrnt. / *Bus stops outside of marina, 5 min. walk to the right. Taxi rank at 100m distance.*

Zahlreiche Fahrrad, Moped- und Autoverleihe in Marina-Nähe
Numerous bicycle, scooter and car rentals near marina

Port del Torrent – Cala Badella

ANKERPLÄTZE
ANCHORAGE AREAS

A Port del Torrent
38° 58,4' N 001° 15,9' E

🇩🇪 Wie der Name vermuten lässt, formte ein Sturzbach diese Ankerbucht, keine 2 sm westlich von Sant Antoni. Ihre Umgebung ist flach, von See ist ihre Einfahrt nicht leicht zu erkennen. Im äußeren Teil fast reiner Sandgrund bei Wassertiefen um 8 m. Hier ist die Bucht nach Norden offen. An Land Strandbars und Restaurants. Es gibt eine Landestelle für Dingis auf der Südseite beim Strand. Auch versorgen könnte man sich hier, denn die Gegend östlich der Bucht ist bis Sant Antoni bebaut, auch mit Hotels und Apartments für Urlauber. Tagsüber unruhig durch ein- und auslaufende Motorboote.

🇬🇧 *As the name suggests, a torrent created this bay that lies less than 2nmi west of Sant Antoni. Their surroundings are quite flat, so it's not easy to identify the entrance. No shallow areas. The sea floor consists mainly of sand, water depths are around 8m. No shelter with northerly winds. Restaurants and bars available. One can land by dinghy close to the beach. Provisioning is possible as the coastal area towards San Antoni is built up intensively. During the day choppy because of numerous speed and excursion boats entering and leaving.*

B Cala Bassa
38° 58,3' N 001° 14,8' E

Eine weiträumige und tiefe Bucht. Sie ist von einer flachen Steilküste umgeben und besitzt in ihrem Südwestzipfel einen Sandstrand. Obwohl nach Nordosten völlig offen, wird sie auch über Nacht zum Ankern benutzt. Ansteuerung frei von Untiefen. Ankern auf knapp 10 m vor beliebtem Badestrand mit Beachclub. Viel Seegras, einige Sandflecken.

A spacious bay 3nmi west of Sant Antoni surrounded by a low-rise cliff coast. In its southwest there is a beach with a beach club behind. Water depths are mostly 10m, bottom weed with sandy patches. Although not well protected, the bay is frequently chosen as an overnight stop.

C Cala Compte
38° 58,1' N 001° 13,4' E

Ohne die westlich vorgelagerte Isla del Bosque gäbe es diese nach Norden offene Bucht nicht. Felsen und eine Barre südlich der Insel schützen vor Seegang aus West. Sandiger Ankergrund. An Land mehrere Beachclubs, die mit der Aussicht auf den perfekten Sonnenuntergang werben. Zwischen der Isla del Bosque und der nördlich anschließenden Isla Conejera verläuft ein Felsriff. Der tiefste Punkt liegt hier bei 4 m.

Without Isla del Bosque to the west this bay would not exist. Rocks and a bar south of the island protect the bay from westerly swell. Sandy sea floor. Ashore several beach clubs that claim to be the

perfect sunset place. Between Isla del Bosque and the adjacent Isla Conejera there is a rocky shelf with a maximum depth of 4m.

D | Cala Tarida
38° 56,3' N 001° 14,1' E

Eine weite, nach Westen offene Bucht vor Feriensiedlungen. Aber gesegnet mit feinem Sandgrund und türkisem Wasser. An einem der Felsen am Strand legt ein Ausflugsschiff an. Die Ansteuerung ist frei von Untiefen. Ankerplätze auf 5-4 m. Restaurants direkt hinter dem Strand, darunter das Ses Eufabies. Diverse Geschäfte und Supermärkte in der touristischen Ansiedlung oberhalb der Steilküste.

A wide bay, not well protected to the west. Many hotels and apartment blocks in the backdrop. Cala Tarida is blessed with fine sandy bottom and turquoise waters. One of the rocks in the center of the beach is used by excursion boats from time to time. The approach is free of shoals. Drop anchor on 5-4m depth. Restaurants just behind the beach, among others Ses Eufabies. Various shops and supermarkets in the tourist village above the cliffs.

Ses Eufabies, T 971 806 328, www.eufabies.com, rte@eufabies.com

E | Cala Badella
38° 54,8' N 001° 13,0' E

An der Nordseite der Einfahrt ausreichend Abstand zur Küste wahren. Große Wassertiefen. Ankern mit Landleine. Der Grund besteht fast vollständig aus Seegras. Im inneren Teil ist die Bucht voll belegt mit Muringbojen für kleine Boote. Hier anlanden auf der Nordseite bei den alten Fischerhäusern. Restaurants, Bars und kleiner Supermarkt hinter dem Strand.

When entering the bay keep sufficient distance to the north side. One will find generous depths, most of the boats drop anchor with land line. Sea floor consists of weed. The inner part of the bay is full of mooring buoys for small boats. Landing by dinghy on the north side at the old fishermen's houses. Restaurants, bars and a small supermarket behind the beach.

Port del Torrent

Cala Bassa

Cala Tarida

Cala Badella

Cala Horts – Cala de Port Roig

ANKERPLÄTZE
ANCHORAGE AREAS

A Cala Horts
38° 53,1' N 001° 13,0' E

Ankern mit Blick auf die steil aufragende Isla Vedra, über Sandgrund vor abgetrennten Schwimmbereichen auf 7-5 m Wasser. Weiter außen auch Seegras. Bei Wind vom Meer ist es hier zu unruhig. Es liegen hier dauerhaft Mehrrumpfboote an Bojen.
Eine weitere Sonnenuntergangs-Cala. Auch auf der Steilküste südlich davon, Richtung Wachturm Torre d'es Savinar, versammeln sich allabendlich viele Menschen. Im Südteil der Bucht das Restaurant El Carmen, T 971 187 449, mit erhöhter Terrasse und längerem Blick auf den Sonnenuntergang. Im Nordteil das Restaurant Cala d'Hort, T 971 935 036, dessen Terrasse durch Palmen und Pflanzen darin und davor mehr Gemütlichkeit versprüht.

Anchorage with Isla Vedra view. Sea floor sand in front of a swimming zone, further out also weed. Water depths 7-5m. With onshore winds it becomes too choppy on the anchorage. The are permanent mooring bouys for multihull boats. Cala Horts is another bay that is famous for its sunset views. During these hours also the cliff coast south of the bay gets crowed. In the southern part of the bay, restaurant El Carmen, T 971 187 449, has an elevated terrace and an extended view of the sunset compared to restaurant Cala d'Hort, T 971 935 036, in the northern part. But here the terrace is more cozy because of some palm trees and plants.

B Cala de Port Roig
38° 52,0' N 001° 18,0' E

Die im Morgen- und Abendlicht rötlich schimmernden Steilküsten gaben den Namen. Die Bucht wird gerne zum Übernachten benutzt. Es herrscht eine friedliche Atmosphäre; viele privat ausgelegte Bojen, die nur nach Rücksprache benutzt werden dürfen.
Beim Runden der Punta de Port Roig die vorgelagerten Untiefen beachten. Weitere Unterwasserfelsen sind nicht zu beachten. In der Einfahrt liegen die Wassertiefen 12-10 m, abnehmend auf 4-3 m an den weiter innen liegenden Ankergründen.
Im Norden der Bucht findet man den besseren Ankergrund, überwiegend Sand mit Seegrasflecken. Kein abgetrennter Badebereich. Anlanden mit dem Dingi hier an einer kleinen Betonpier, sonst im südöstlichen Teil der Bucht. Es gibt keine Restaurants oder Strandbars in der Nähe der Bucht, nur das exklusive Boutique-Hotel „Las Brisas" mit Restaurant auf der Punta de Port Roig.

The reddish cliffs inspired the name. The bay is often used to stay for the night. There is a peaceful atmosphere; many private buoys that may only be used after consultation.
Round Punta de Port Roig with distance. Further in no shallow areas. Water depths are 12-10m, decreasing to 4-3m in the northern part. Here one will find the best anchorage, a mostly sandy sea floor. No separated bathing area. Landing by dinghy at a small concrete pier, otherwise in the southeastern part of the bay.
There are no restaurants or beach bars around the bay, only the exclusive boutique hotel „Las Brisas" with a restaurant on Punta de Port Roig.

www.lasbrisasibiza.com
T 971 800 801

Cala de Port Roig

Cala Horts – Cala de Port Roig

Islote Vedranell

Isla Vedra

A

Cala Horts

Ibiza

Cala Jondal – Ensenada del Canal

ANKERPLÄTZE
ANCHORAGE AREAS

A Cala Jondal
38° 51,9' N 001° 18,9' E

🇩🇪 Eine Bucht der Beachclubs. Gelbe Tonnen markieren ein Glasfaserkabel der Fa. Telefonica, das schnelles Internet nach Formentera bringt. In dem Kanal, den diese Tonnen mit einer Verschwenkung nach Westen formen, ist das Ankern für Yachten über 12 m Länge nicht erlaubt.

🇬🇧 *A bay full of beach clubs. Yellow bouys mark a fiber optic cable of company Telefonica, which connects island Formentera with fast Internet. These bouys form a channel with a deviation to the west and indicate that yachts with more than 12m in length may not drop anchor inside this area.*

Die Beachclubs von Ost nach West:
The beach clubs from east to the west:

Yemanja Ibiza
All year round, daily 13-18 h
www.yemanjaibiza.com
T 971 187 481
info@yemanjaibiza.com

Blue Marlin Ibiza
Selbstbeschreibung / *self description*:
„One of the most entertaining and avant-garde beach clubs in Ibiza."
www.bluemarlinibiza.com

Restaurant Es Savina
T 971 187 437

Tropicana Beach Club
Man kann mit dem Beiboot anlanden, es gibt einen Tonnenweg, oder sich abholen lassen. Restaurant / Bar von 12 bis 23 Uhr, täglich.
Landing by dinghy, or be picked up. Restaurant / Bar 12-23 h, every day.
www.tropicanaibiza.com; 01/04-31/10
T 971 802 640
info@tropicanaibiza.com
July / August: Res. only M 629 348 012

290 Portbook & Island Guide

Cala Jondal – Ensenada del Canal

Es Xarcu

Von Ostern bis Ende Oktober öffnet dieses kleine Lokal mit Terrassen am Meer und einem Holzsteg zum Anlanden für Dingis In der westlichen „Nachbarbucht". Beworben wird frischer Fisch und eine einfache, ursprüngliche Küche.

This small restaurant with terraces on the sea opens from easter to the end of October. There is a boardwalk for dinghies. Fresh fish and an authentic cuisine are the assets of this restaurant.

restaurante@esxarcu.com
T 971 187 867, 12–23 h
www.esxarcu.com

B Ensenada de la Canal
38° 50,2' N 001° 23,6' E

Am langen Strand ein halbes Dutzend Beach Clubs mit Strand-Disco. Hier gibt es ein Bojenfeld, das man nutzen kann, aber nicht muss. Für Yachten bis 14 m Länge wird 29,10 EUR kassiert, bis 16 m 48,50 EUR (Stand Januar 2016), es gibt keinen Tarif für kurzzeitiges Festmachen. Ankern neben dem Bojenfeld auf Sandgrund ist erlaubt, 8-4 m Wassertiefe vor einem abgetrennten Badebereich. Bei südlichen Winden läuft eine leichte Welle in die Bucht.

Behind the long beach half a dozen beach clubs. There is a buoy field that can be used, but not necessarily. The rates (January 2016): for yachts up to 14m length 29.10 EUR, up 16m 48.50 EUR. No tariff for short-term mooring. Anchoring next to the buoy field on a sandy bottom is permitted, water depth 8-4m in front of the separate swimming area. With southerly winds it gets choppy.

Res.: www.balearslifeposidonia.eu
(„Ses Salines")

Fantastic Formentera

Der Zauber Formenteras – er offenbart sich ganz besonders an der Nordspitze, Richtung Ibiza. Hier konkurrieren die Strände und Buchten mit dem Farbenrausch der Karibik.

The magic of Formentera – manifesting itself fully in this picture of its northern tip. The islands beaches and coves are a match for the Caribbean in their dazzling colours.

Formentera

Sommeranfang: Bis Juni – und auch wieder ab September – sind die Buchten so leer. Am Horizont Ibiza.
Early summer: Until June – and from September onwards – bays are not too crowded.

Formentera

Cala Torreta – Playa de Levante

🇩🇪 Formentera ist das Ziel der Begierde: An den langen weißen Stränden und karibischen Ankerplätzen kommen im Sommer hunderte Yachten zusammen.

🇬🇧 *Formentera has a magical attraction: along the endless white beaches and Caribbean-style anchorage sites, several hundreds of yachts may congregate.*

1 Cala Torreta - 38° 47,8' N 001° 25,1' E → page 301
Paradiesbucht nur für kleine Motorboote. Zufahrt aus Nord.
Paradise Bay for small power boats. Enter from the north.

2 Puerto del Espalmador - 38° 46,6' N 001° 25,3' E → page 301
Hufeisenförmige Bucht. Sehr beliebt und entsprechend voll.
Horseshoe Bay. Very popular, and correspondingly full. No services.

3 Pas de S'Espalmador - 38° 46,3' N 001° 25,8' E → page 301
Espalmador und die Nordspitze von Formentera trennt nur diese Passage.
Espalmador and the northern tip of Formentera are divided by this passage.

4 Playa de Levante - 38° 45,0' N 001° 26,4' E → page 302
Bei Westwind die Alternative zu den Ankerplätz rund um Ses Illetes …
With westerly winds a perfect alternative to the anchorage areas opposite …

5 Los Trocados / Ses Illetes - 38° 45,4' N 001° 25,8' E → page 302
Vielleicht der schönste Platz an der langen Nordspitze Formenteras.
Perhaps the most beautiful spot along the northern tip of Formentera.

6 La Savina - 38° 44,1' N 001° 25,2' E → page 296
Zwei Marinas teilen sich das Hafenbecken, hinzu kommen die Schnellfähren.
Two marinas share the port basin, which is also frequented by many fast ferries.

7 Ensenada del Cabrito - 38° 44,0' N 001° 24,3' E → page 304
Die Bucht westlich von La Savina. Es gibt hier ein Bojenfeld.
The bay west of Sa Savina. There is a buoy field to pay for.

8 Cala Sahona - 38° 41,9' N 001° 23,2' E → page 304
Im Sommer bis zu 50 Yachten. Restaurants, Auto-, Rad-, Mopedverleih.
Up to 50 yachts in summer. Restaurants and car, bike, scooter rental.

9 Cabo Barbaria - 38° 38,4' N 001° 23,4' E
An der Südwestspitze Formenteras steht dieser Leuchtturm, Fl(2)W 15s
The southwestern tip of Formentera is distinguished by a lighthouse, Fl(2)W 15s

10 Ensenada Migjorn - 38° 40,5' N 001° 27,6' E → 304
6 sm breite Bucht im Süden. Yachten ankern beim Hochland.
A 6nmi wide bay. The anchorage lies near the high plateau.

11 Faro de la Mola - 38° 38,8' N 001° 35,2' E
Am östlichen Ende Formenteras leuchtet es mit der Kennung FlW 5s.
On the eastern end of Formentera, flashing with the character FlW 5s.

12 Ensenada de Tramontana - 38° 40,6' N 001° 31,8' E → page 304
Offene Ankerplätze beim Fischerort Es Caló. Mini-Supermarkt & Restaurants.
Open anchorage areas close to fishing village Es Caló. Small shop & restaurants.

13 Cala Pujols - 38° 43,6' N 001° 28,0' E → page 305
Die Punta Prima bietet Schutz gegen Südostwind. Ankern auf ca.10 m Tiefe.
Punta Prima provides shelter against south-easterly winds.

Formentera

1. Cala Torreta
2. Puerto del Espalmador
3. Pas de S'Espalmador
4. Playa de Levante
5. Los Trocados / Ses Illetes
6. La Savina
7. Ensenada del Cabrito
8. Cala Sahona
9. Cabo Barbaria
10. Ensenada de Migjorn
11. Faro de la Mola
12. Ensenada de Tramontana
13. Cala Pujols

Isla Espardell

FORMENTERA

Portbook & Island Guide   295

Formentera

PUERTO DE LA SAVINA
PORT OF LA SAVINA

La Savina

Zona Portuaria / Harbour area	Zona ajardinada / Gardens	Parking Car Park	Casco urbano / Urban area	
Edificios / Buildings	Viales Roads	Parking Autobuses / Bus Parking area	Límite zona servicio del puerto / Limits of the port service area	
Faro / Lighthouse	Destellos aislados rojos / Isolated red flashes		Grupo 3 destellos rojos / Group of 3 red flashes	
Baliza / Landing beacon	Grupo 2 destellos rojos / Group of 2 red flashes		Grupo 4 destellos rojos / Group of 4 red flashes	
Sirena / Siren	Destellos aislados verdes / Isolated green flashes		Grupo 2 destellos verdes / Group of 2 green flashes	

Hafenplan / Harbour map – La Savina

Portbook & Island Guide 297

Formentera

La Savina

🇩🇪 Der Ort La Savina im Norden von Formentera hat den größten Hafen der Insel mit zwei Sportboothäfen. Er wird im Sommer an die 100 Mal von Schnellfähren angelaufen, denn Formentera ist auch ein Ziel von Tagestouristen von Ibiza. 20.000 Zweiräder sollen auf der Insel im Sommer vermietet werden, die meisten davon gleich in Hafennähe.

🇬🇧 *La Savina in the north of Formentera is the biggest port of the island with two marinas. Around 100 times per day high-speed ferries call at the port in summer, as Formentera is also a popular day trip destination from Ibiza. Some 20,000 scooters are said to be for hire in summer, most of them near the harbour.*

ANSTEUERUNG
APPROACHING

Man halte ausreichend Abstand zur Außenmole, weil sie von den Fähren aus- wie einlaufend üblicherweise eng gerundet wird. Rote Blinktonnen markieren den langen Strand, der beim Hafen beginnt. **Achtung:** Die Katamaran-Fähren sind gerade beim Einlaufen noch kurz vor dem Wellenbrecher mit hoher Geschwindigkeit unterwegs.

Keep distance from the breakwater, to avoid ferries entering and leaving the port. The beach is marked by red flashing buoys, beginning at the harbour. ***Caution:*** *Arriving catamaran ferries are travelling at high speed even very close to the breakwater.*

FESTMACHEN
FIND A BERTH

Zwei Marinas teilen sich das Hafenbecken, in dem auch die überaus zahlreichen Ibiza-Schnellfähren an- und ablegen. Beide haben sehr hohe Liegegebühren im Sommer und bieten im Vergleich dazu überschaubare Winter-Langzeit-Tarife.

Two marinas share the port basin, which is also frequented by countless fast ferries to and from Ibiza. Both marinas charge very high mooring fees in summer, but offer comparatively reasonable long-term rates in winter.

A **Marina de Formentera**
64 Plätze von 8-38m. Strom / electr. bis / *til* 125 A / *64 berths from 8-38 m.*
Tiefe Hafeneinfahrt / *entrance depth:* 4-3,5 m. Tiefe Hafenbecken / *harbour basin depth:* 3,5-2,5 m
€ 12-13,99 m
215 EUR (01/07-31/08)

La Savina

Esenada del Cabrito

C Office

Fl(4)W 16s

A

Fl(4)R 15s

Fl(2)G 6s

38° 44,1' N 001° 25,2' E

Fl(3)R 19 s

- Fährhafen Formenteras
- Zwei sehr teure Marinas
- Im Sommer sehr belegt
- *Formentera's ferry port*
- *Two expensive marinas*
- *Almost fully booked in summer*

150 EUR (16/06-30/06 + 01/09-15/09)
80 EUR (01/06-15/06 + 16/09-30/09)

T 971 322 346 UKW/VHF 09
reservas@marinadeformentera.com
www.marinadeformentera.com
01/07-31/08: Mon-Sun 08-21 h
June+Sept.: Mon-Sun 09-21 h
01/10-31/05: Mon-Sat 09-15 + 16-19 h

B Formentera Mar
90 Liegeplätze bis 30 m /
90 berths up to 30 m
€ 12-14,99 m
192 EUR (01/07-21/08)
119 EUR (13/07-30/07 + 22/08-18/09)
68 EUR (01/06-12/07 + 19/09-30/09 + 02/03-09/03)
31 EUR (01/01-31/05 + 01/10-31/12)

Mwst. enthalten, plus Wasser + Strom,
abhängig von Länge und Verbrauch
VAT incl., plus water + electr., charges depend on length and consumption
WiFi kostenlos / *free*

T 971 323 235 UKW/VHF 09
info@formenteramar.com
www.formenteramar.com

Portbook & Island Guide 299

Formentera — La Savina

🕐 June-Aug.: Mon-Sun 09-20 h
Sept.-May: Mon-Sun 09-14 + 16.30-19.30 h

TANKEN / *FUEL*

Marina de Formentera
D+B, 09.30-20.30 h (daily)

Formentera Mar
July+Aug.: Mon-Sun 08-20 h
June, Sept. + Oct.: Mon-Sat 10-13 + 16-19 h, Sun closed
Nov.-May: Tue + Thur 16-18 h

TECHNISCHER SERVICE / *TECHNICAL SERVICES*

Formentera Mar
Werft / *Shipyard*
Travelift 35 t, Stellfläche / *storage area*

Motonáutica Helix
Unter dem Büro von / *Below office of ...*
Marina de Formentera
Engine Service & Electric
T 971 322 373, M 639 628 092
www.nauticahelix.com

Reparaciones Navales Vidal
M 646 535 874

Servicios Náuticos Llevant
Oscar Ferrer + Juan Mayans
M 650 919 639 + 655 415 493

YACHTAUSRÜSTER / *CHANDLERIES*

Ⓒ Náutica Pins, T 971 32 26 51
info@nauticapins.com
www.nauticapins.com

EINKAUFEN / *SHOPPING*

Verschiedene kleine Supermärkte in der kleinen Ortschaft. Bankautomaten, Apotheke etc. / *Various small- to mid-sized supermarkets close to the marinas. ATMS, pharmacy, etc.*

RESTAURANTS & BARS

Reiche Auswahl an Restaurants und Bars in Hafennähe. / *Wide choice of restaurants and bars near port.*

AUSFLÜGE / *EXCURSIONS*

Beliebte Ziele sind die Leuchttürme Faro de la Mola auf dem Hochland im Westen und am Cabo de Barbaria im Südwesten von Formentera. Unterwegs bekommt man einen guten ersten Eindruck von weiten Teilen der Insel. Wer in kurzer Zeit viel von der Insel sehen möchte, sollte sich in La Savina einen Motorroller, ein Auto oder ein Rad ausleihen, Tagesmiete ab 15 €, Halbtagespreise werden nicht eingeräumt. Mehr als zwei Dutzend Anbieter mit vergleichbaren Preisen.
Popular destinations include the lighthouses Faro de la Mola on the high plateau and Cabo de Barbaria, marking the southwestern tip of Formentera. It is easy to get a first impression of the island en route. To see a lot in a short time on this island, rent a scooter, car or bike in La Savina; daily charges starts at 15 €, no short-term charges available. Some two dozen rental providers with similar pricing available.

Sant Francesc
Second-hand Markt im pittoresken Ort, *Second-hand market in the picturesque village*, sat 11-14 h.

Pilar de la Mola
Hippie-Markt im Sommer,
Mi + So, 16-21 h / *Hippie market in summer, wed + sun, 16-21 h*

Es Pujols
Der Ort mit dem meisten Rummel, Geschäften und vielen Restaurants an der Wasserlinie. Hier ist auch abends etwas los. Ausserdem jeden Abend Hippie-Markt an der Strandpromenade.
The most lively place of all, with shops and many restaurants on the waterfront. Busy until late at night. A hippie market takes place every evening at the boardwalk.

Nach Ibiza
Wenn ein Ausflug nach Ibiza gewünscht oder notwendig ist, dann sollte man sich die Fährlinie Aqua Bus anschauen. Deren Tarife liegen deutlich unter denen der Mitbewerber.
If a trip to Ibiza is desired or becomes necessary, one should hava a look at the ferry line Aqua Bus. Their rates are well below those of competitors.

> **Anchoring Service**
> **June-Sept, UKW / VHF 69**
>
> Für den Nordwesten von Formentera. / *For the north-western part of Formentera.*

Isla de Los im Norden der Durchfahrt „Freu Grande" zwischen Ibiza und Formentera
Isla de Los north of the passage „Freu Grande" between Ibiza and Formentera

Cala Torreta – Ses Illetes

ANKERPLÄTZE
ANCHORAGE AREAS

A Cala Torreta
38° 47,8' N 001° 25,1' E

🇩🇪 Paradiesbucht, exklusiv für Boote mit wenig Tiefgang. Zufahrt nur aus Nord, im Süden liegt eine knapp überspülte Barre aus Fels.

🇬🇧 *Paradise Bay for power boats with little draft only. Enter from the north, to the south there is an underwater reef.*

B Puerto del Espalmador
38° 46,6' N 001° 25,3' E

Der Hafen ist eine hufeisenförmige Bucht. Sehr beliebt und entsprechend voll. Keine Versorgung. Beim Einlaufen ausreichend Abstand zur Südwestspitze von Isla Espalmador und zur Isla del Alga halten. Es ist ein Bojenfeld ausgelegt, aber Ankern mit ausreichend Abstand dazu wurde bei starker Belegung geduldet. Reservierung:

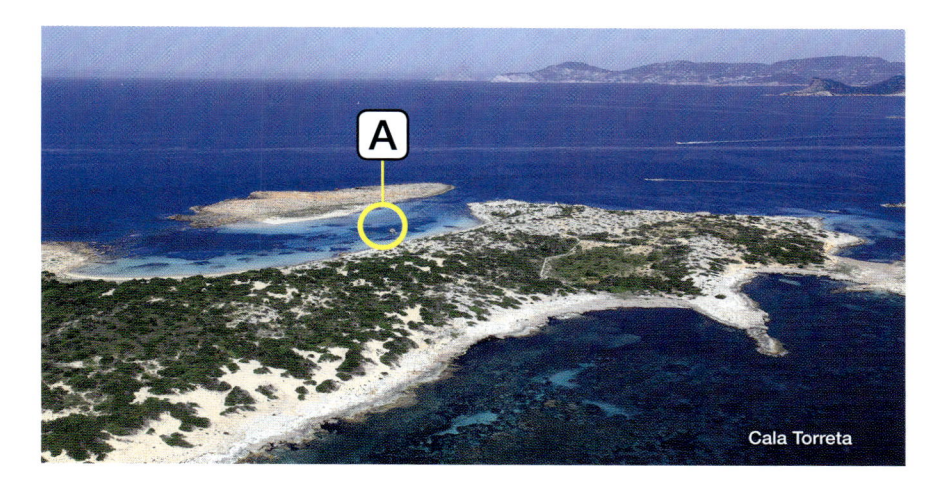

The „port" is in fact a Horseshoe Bay. Very popular, and correspondingly full. No services. When entering keep sufficient distance from the southwestern tip of Isla Espalmador and from Isla del Alga. Inside the bay a buoy field is laid out, although anchoring is tolerated if all the buoys are occupied, and a proper distance is respected. Reservation:
www.balearslifeposidonia.eu

< 14 m: 29.10 EUR, < 16 m: 48.50 EUR (January 2016); details: page 320

C Pas de S'Espalmador
38° 46,3' N 001° 25,8' E

Das Inselchen Espalmador und die Nordspitze von Formentera trennt nur diese schmale Passage, die sich mit einem Boot mit wenig Tiefgang durchfahren lässt. Die tiefste Stelle befindet

Formentera

Chriringuito „Tiburon"

sich nahe der Nordspitze von Formentera. Auf der Nordseite des Passes, bei der kleinen Isla del Alga, ist ein beliebter Ankerplatz für Kleinbootfahrer. Hier wurde die Badezone so vergrößert, dass der Platz kaum noch nutzbar ist. Ankern westlich vor dem Pas de S'Espalmador ist sehr gut möglich auf 5-3 m Wassertiefe und Sandgrund. Man muss nur auf festen Sitz des Ankers achten, da eine unterschiedlich starke Strömung durch den Pass setzt.

The islet Espalmador and the northern tip of Formentera are only divided by this narrow passage, which can be passed by dinghies. The deepest part of this passage is located near the northern tip of Formentera. On the north side of the pass is the small Isla del Alga, a popular anchorage with small boats.

In 2015 the swimming zone on Espalmador was enlarged and this anchorage area became very small.
Anchoring on the west side of Pas de S'Espalmador is possible on 5-3m water depth and sandy bottom. But the anchor has to be set carefully, as there is a current through the passage.

D **Playa de Levante**
38° 45,0' N 001° 26,4' E
Bei Westwind die perfekte Alternative zu den Ankerplätz rund um Ses Illetes.
With westerly winds the perfect alternative to the anchorage areas opposite.

Restaurante Tanga
T 971 187 905
www.restaurantetanga.com

Playa de Levante

Cala Torreta – Ses Illetes

E Los Trocados / Ses Illetes
38° 45,4' N 001° 25,8' E
Rund um die Inselchen bei der Playa des Ses Illetes liegen die beliebtesten Ankergründe. An Land nehmen sich mehrere Restaurants den Besuchern von den Stränden wie von den Booten an. Ankern auf 6-4 m über Sand. Doch kein Paradies ohne Schlange: Die ständig passierenden Fähren zwischen Formentera und Ibiza und andere Schiffe schicken regelmäßig Wellenschlag.

Perhaps the most beautiful spot along the lengthy northern tip of Formentera. Anchorage at 6-4m, very level sandy bottom. Restaurants at the beach. Frequent rocking due to swell of passing boats.

Es Moli del Sal
Schönes großes Restaurant an alter Salzmühle. Feine mediterrane Küche, Fischgerichte. / *Beautiful large restaurant at old salt mill. Refined Mediterranean cuisine, fish dishes.*
T 971 187 491
www.esmolidesal.es

Juan y Andrea, T 971 187 130
juanyandrea1971@gmail.com
www.juanyandrea.com

El Tiburon
„Haifisch-Bar" mit Robinson Crusoe-Gefühl. Nahe beim Hafen. Gut vom Boot aus zu erreichen. Von Curry-Wurst bis Champagner. Gehobenes Preisniveau. Reservierung notwendig. Dinghy-Service. / *"Shark Bar" with a Robinson Crusoe atmosphere. Near the harbour. Good access by boat. Offers everything from curry hot dogs to champagne. Elevated prices. Reservations required. Dinghy service.*
M 659 638 945
www.tiburon-formentera.com

Formentera

Ens. Cabrito – Cala Pujols

ANKERPLÄTZE
ANCHORAGE AREAS

A Ensenada del Cabrito
38° 44,0' N 001° 24,3' E

Die Bucht gleich westlich anschließend an den Hafen von La Savina. An ihrer Ostseite befindet sich die zirka 1,20 m tiefe und bepprickte Einfahrt in den Binnensee Estany des Peix. Ankern ist in der Bucht über Sandboden grundsätzlich möglich, doch dürfen weder der Anker noch die Kette dabei Seegras berühren. Einen Platz zu finden, der das ermöglicht, ist nicht leicht und zudem wird kontrolliert. Von daher sollte man sich darauf einstellen, eine Boje zu nehmen, wenn man partout hier bleiben will. Reservierung:

The bay just west to the port of La Savina. On its east side there is the entrance to the lake Estany des Peix, about 1.20m deep and marked with stakes. Anchoring inside Ensenada del Cabrito is possible in principle, but neither the anchor nor the chain may affect weed. To find such a sandy spot here is almost impossible and rangers in RIBs appear to control the boats. Therefore, if this bay is your favourite, be prepared to take a buoy. Reservation:
www.balearslifeposidonia.eu
< 14 m: 29.10 EUR, < 16 m: 48.50 EUR (January 2016); details: page 320

B Cala Sahona
38° 41,9' N 001° 23,2' E

Die Bucht ist ein Traum. Reiner Sandgrund, wohin das Auge schaut. Nur ein dunkler Fleck, aber der liegt schon innerhalb der abgeteilten Badezone und hat nur 1,80 m Wasser. Dieses Ambiente vor niedrigen Steilküsten, die einen Strand einrahmen, lockt im Sommer gut und gerne bis zu 50 Yachten. An Land Restaurants, ein Hotel und Auto, Rad-, Mopedverleih durch das Hotel und durch einen benachbarten Privatanbieter.

A georgeous bay! Pure sandy bottom, where ever you look. Only one dark spot can be identified, but that lies within the swimming zone and has only 1.80m of water. During the summer, up to 50 yachts gather along this stretch of beach. Ashore restaurants, a hotel and car, bike and motorbike rental through the hotel and a private service company.

Alquiler Cala Sahona, T 971 322 648

Ensenada Migjorn
38° 39,7' N 001° 30,7' E

6 sm breite Bucht im Süden von Formentera, aber wenig besucht von Yachten. Der schönste Ankerplatz liegt im Südosten der Bucht, wo die Hochebene beginnt. / *A 6nmi wide bay in the south of Formentera, but not very frequented by boats. The best anchorage is located in the southeastern part where Formentera's high plateau rises.*

C Ensenada de Tramontana
38° 40,6' N 001° 31,8' E

Wunderschöne, aber zum Meer hin offene Ankerplätze mit fast durchgängig sandigem Grund, die sich vom Hochland Formenteras über gut 2sm Richtung Nordwesten hinziehen. Es gibt hier den kleinen Fischerort Es Caló, mit Mini-Supermärkten, Geldautomat und Restaurants, darunter das Ca'n Rafalet.

Lovely anchorage aera with sandy sea floor and turquoise water for about 2,5nmi, although very exposed. Close to Formentera's high plateau you will find the small village Es Calo with mini supermarkets, an ATM and restaurants such as Ca'n Rafalet.
www.hostal-rafalet.com
T 971 327 016

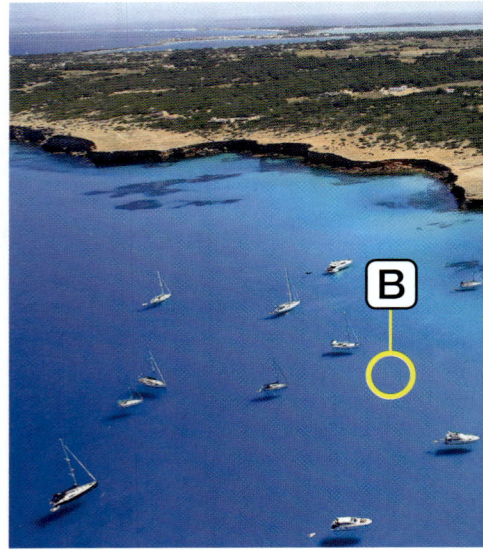

Ensenada del Cabrito – Cala Pujols

Ensenada de Tramontana

C

D Cala Pujols
38° 43,6' N 001° 28,0' E

Die Punta Prima ist eine wahrlich hervorstechende Landmarke und bietet den besten Schutz auf ihrer Nordseite. Dort ankern über Sandgrund auf zirka 10 m Tiefe. Zum Anlanden gibt es eine Betonpier in Richtung der kleinen Inseln, die den alten Fischerhafen von Es Pujols mit seinem Bootsschuppen einrahmen und schützen. Allein der Ort hat sich extrem gewandelt, ist heute ein Ableger des modernen Ibiza-Lifestyles.

Punta Prima is a truly outstanding landmark and offers the best protection on its north side. There one can drop anchor on a sandy bottom at a depth of about 10 m. To land by dinghy you will find a concrete pier in the direction of the small islands that surround and protect the old fishing port of Es Pujols with its boathouses. However, the place has seen radical change, as an offshoot of the modern Ibiza lifestyle.

Cala Sahona

Cala Pujols

D

Törn-Tipp / Cruising Tip

Palma – Cabrera – Dragonera – Palma (110 sm / nmi)

Ein Törn mit Kontrastprogramm, denn gerade 25 sm liegen zwischen der geschäftigen Hauptstadt Palma und dem Ruhepol Cabrera, ein Nationalpark, keine 10 sm vor der Südspitze Mallorcas. Hier gibt es Festmachebojen, für die kassiert wird. Verbindliche Anmeldung erforderlich!

This is a trip full of contrasts, as only 25nmi separate the bustling capital of Palma from tranquil Cabrera National Park, situated less than 10nmi from Mallorca's southern tip. Here are mooring buoys, subject to charge. Binding registration required!

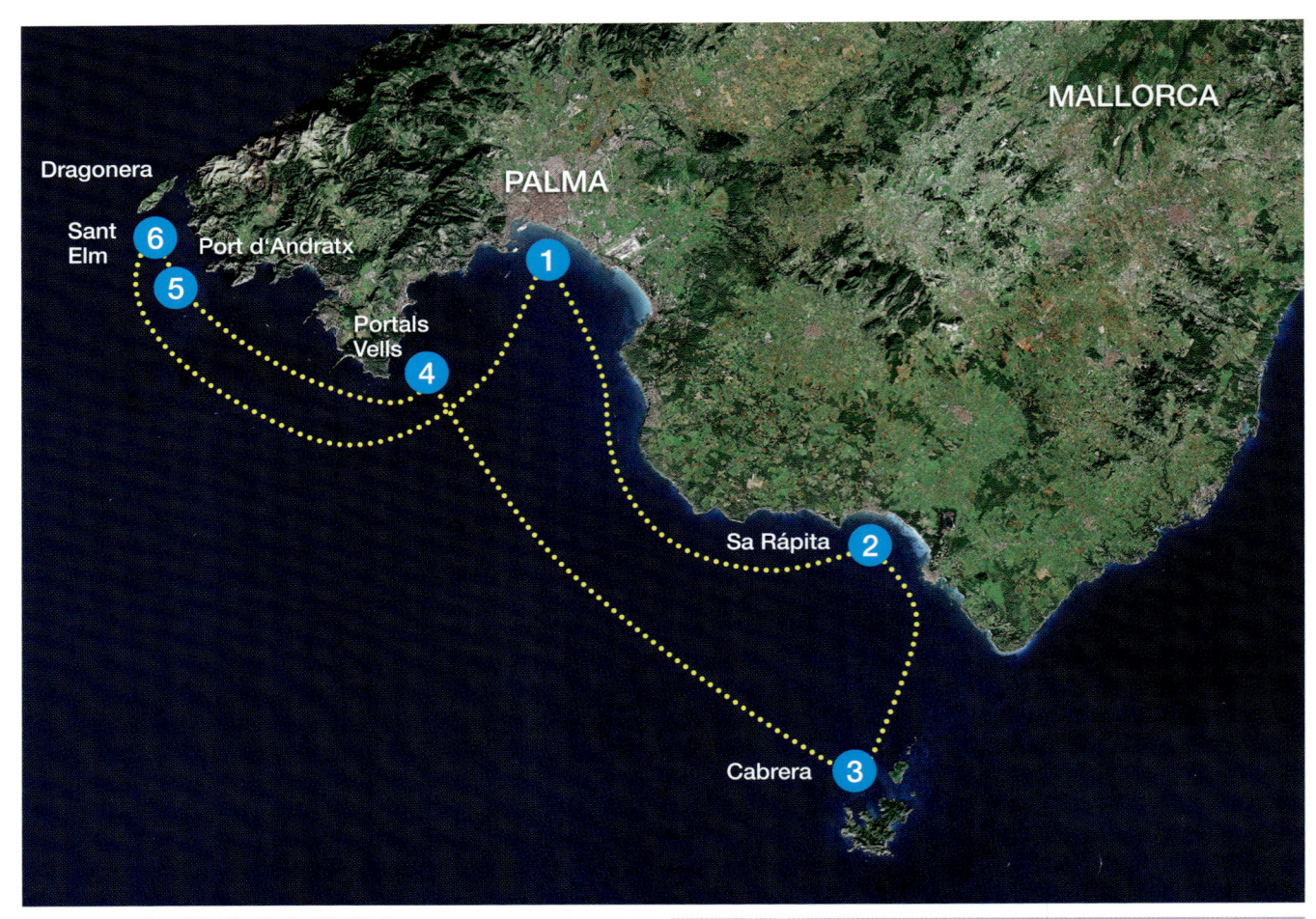

Portals Vells

Port d'Andratx

306 Portbook & Island Guide

Mallorcas Süden / The South of Mallorca

Tag 1: Palma – Sa Rápita, 25 sm

Wer noch in der Bucht von Palma zum Erfrischen im Meer stoppen möchte, steuert das Bojenfeld bei Cala Blava an. Gleich östlich von Cabo Blanco, Südkap der Bucht von Palma, liegt die kleine wie sehr bekannte Bucht Cala Pí. Von dort sind es nur noch gut 5 sm bis nach Sa Rápita, am Westrand des langen Naturstrands Es Trenc. Hier locken zahlreiche Gaststätten mit Meerblick.

Tag 2: Sa Rápita – Cabrera, 15 sm

Ankern und Baden vor dem Es Trenc bzw. südwestlich von Colònia de Sant Jordi (Puerto de Campos) in der Bucht Playa Es Carbó. Zum Abend gut verproviantiert verholen nach Cabrera, die Boje kann ab 18 Uhr belegt werden. Vorher Besuch der Blauen Grotte. Der Nachmittag ist die beste Zeit, denn dann scheint die Sonne hinein und lässt das Meer erleuchten.

Tag 3: Cabrera – Portals Vells, 30 sm

Vor dem Ablegen könnte man vom Kastell den Blick auf die Hafen-Bucht genießen, den Leuchtturm im Südwesten besuchen oder das Museum. Danach, hoffentlich ohne Aufkreuzen, bis zur Bucht Portals Vells. Dort Bar und Restaurant an den Stränden. Wenn durch östliche Winde zu viel Schwell in die Bucht läuft, dann ist die Reede von Santa Ponsa die bessere Alternative.

Tag 4: Portals Vells – Port d'Andratx, 10 sm

Das kurze Seestück lässt Zeit für eine leichte Wanderung zum Leuchtturm Cala Figuera, zirka 1 Stunde gen Süd. Man bekommt einen Eindruck davon, wie sehr die Küsten Mallorcas einst befestigt waren. Die gut zehn 10 sm nach Port d'Andratx führen vorbei an einigen beeindruckend hohen Kaps.

Tag 5: Port d'Andratx – Dragonera – Sant Elm, 10 sm

Ankern vor Dragonera für einen gebührenfreien Besuch der Insel und ihrer Leuchttürme. Über Nacht vor Sant Elm an einer Boje oder vor Anker. Zahlreiche Restaurants. Klares Wasser und viele Fische. Wer hier mehr vom Land erkunden und schöne Ausblicke auf Dragonera haben möchte, wandert zum alten Wachturm bei der Cala en Basset oder zur Klosterruine Sa Trapa und weiter.

Tag 6: Sant Elm – Palma, 20 sm

Erst Segeln, dann ein letzter Badestopp in der Bucht von Illetas, auch genannt The Anchorage, schon in Sichtweite von Palma. Immer gut besucht, geschützt durch eine kleine Insel. Bei Südwestwind wird es unruhig. Zurück in Palma haben Sie hoffentlich noch ausreichend Zeit für die Bars und Restaurants in der Hauptstadt.

Day 1: Palma – Sa Rápita, 25nmi

Those who want a stopover in Palma bay for a dip in the sea should head for Cala Blava buoy field or go straight to Cabo Blanco, the southern cape of Palma bay. Directly behind it lies small, popular Cala Pí bay. At a mere 5nmi distance from there, Sa Rapita is situated at the western fringe of sprawling natural beach Es Trenc. Numerous restaurants with sea views entice hungry guests.

Day 2: Sa Rápita – Cabrera, 15nmi

Anchoring and bathing in front of Es Trenc or southwest of Colònia de Sant Jordi (Puerto de Campos) in front of Playa Es Carbó bay. Ensure that you are well provisioned before continuing to Cabrera, where buoys can be occupied from 6 p.m. onwards. Don't forget to visit the Blue Grotto beforehand, preferably in the afternoon, when the sun shines in and renders the sea a glowing blue.

Day 3: Cabrera – Portals Vells, 30nmi

Before casting off, visitors might want to enjoy the view from the castle across the harbour bay, taking a look at the lighthouse in the southwest or the museum. Afterwards continue to Portals Vells bay, hopefully without tacking. Bar and restaurant at the beaches. If eastern winds generate too much swell, the bay of Santa Ponsa shipyard might prove the better option.

Day 4: Portals Vells – Port d'Andratx, 10nmi

This is a short stretch, so gives you time to enjoy an easy hike to lighthouse Cala Figuera, about 1 h to the south. Visitors get a good impression of how highly fortified the coasts of Mallorca were in former times. During the 10nmi to Port d'Andratx, the vessel passes along some towering capes.

Day 5: Port d'Andratx – Dragonera – Sant Elm, 10 nmi

Anchor at Dragonera for a free visit of the island and its lighthouses. Spend the night at Sant Elm catching a mooring buoy or set anchor. Many restaurants. Clear water, teeming with fish. Visitors who would like to see more of the country and enjoy the views of Dragonera hike to the old watchtower at Cala en Basset or even walk beyond the remains of Sa Trapa monastery or even longer.

Day 6: Sant Elm – Palma, 20nmi

After some sailing, take a last bathing stop at Illetas bay, also known as The Anchorage, which is already within eyeshot of Palma. Protected by a small island and often full with boats. Rather uncomfortable when south-western winds blow. After returning to Palma, you will hopefully have sufficient time to enjoy plenty of bars and restaurants.

Törn-Tipp / Cruising Tip

Palma – Portocolom – Porto Cristo – Palma (120 sm / nmi)

Der mallorquinische Genießer-Törn: von überschaubarer Distanz, dafür aber gespickt mit den schönsten Anker- und Badebuchten. Aber auch die Hafenorte sind nicht zu verachten, in erster Linie Portocolom und Cala Figuera. Ein Abstecher nach Cabrera bleibt dabei immer eine Option.

The Mallorcan connoisseur trip: with manageable distance and abundant in beautiful anchorages.. The port villages are a good choice, in particular Portocolom and Cala Figuera. And there's always room for a detour to Cabrera.

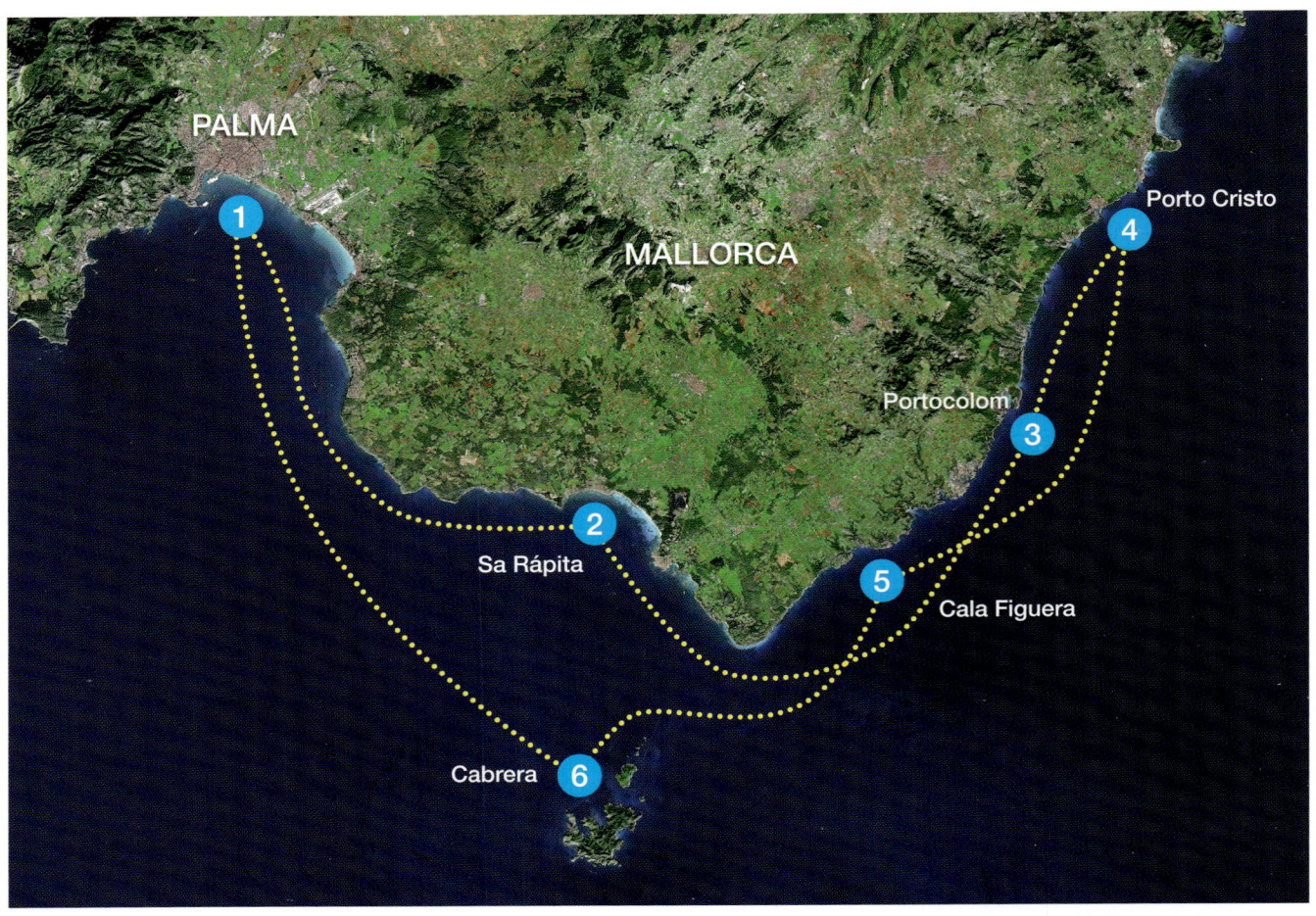

Puerto de Cabrera

Cala de sa Comuna

Mallorca Ostküste / The East Coast of Mallorca

Tag 1: Palma – Sa Rápita, 25 sm

Wer noch in der Bucht von Palma eine Erfrischung im Meer sucht, könnte ganz unkonventionell auf Entdeckungsreise gehen. Entlang der Steilküste, die zum Cabo Blanco führt. Passiert man sie nah genug, findet man hier immer wieder Ankerplätze über türkisem Wasser bei Wassertiefen um die 10 m. Sie sind natürlich sehr offen und nur bei ruhigem Wetter eine Empfehlung.

Tag 2: Sa Rápita – Portocolom, 25 sm

Nach dem Abendessen in einem der vielen Restaurants mit Meerblick passiert die Yacht tags darauf keine 10 sm später Cabo Salinas, das Südkap Mallorcas. Hier begegnet man dem schönsten Meeresblau, das Mallorca zu bieten hat und gleich danach beginnt der Buchten-Marathon. Die bekannteste Bucht hier ist die Cala Mondragó. In Portocolom warten unter anderem viele Bojen auf Gastlieger.

Tag 3: Portocolom – Porto Cristo, 10 sm

Entlang der Hafenbucht hat Portocolom mehr als ein halbes Dutzend Gaststätten, selbst zum Frühstücken könnte man dort einkehren. Denn die nächste Etappe misst nicht einmal 10 sm, und wieder einmal wird man nicht alle Buchten sehen können, aber Cala Barcas ist ein Muss. Porto Cristo ist ein netter kleiner Ort, bekannt geworden durch seine Höhlen und die nahen Strandbuchten.

Tag 4: Porto Cristo – Cala Figuera, 15 sm

Wenn man diese gut 15 sm nicht aufkreuzen muss, bleibt ausreichend Gelegenheit, eine Bucht zu besuchen, die noch auf dem Zettel stehen sollte. Für Cala Figuera muss man reserviert haben, es ist Mallorcas kleinster Yachthafen. Aber ein sehr aktiver Fischerhafen. Wie ein kleiner Fjord schneidet die Hafenbucht in die Steilküste und hat an ihrem schmalen Ende den malerischsten Teil.

Tag 5: Cala Figuera – Cabrera, 15 sm

Auch auf dem nächsten Stück folgen Buchten, die sich lohnen. So nah, dass es kaum nötig sein wird, die Segel zu setzen: Cala Santanyi, Lllombards, de sa Comuna (oder Moro), Marmols… Oder, je nach Windrichtung, die Cala Caragol schon westlich von Cabo Salinas. Die Boje für die Nacht auf Cabrera muss reserviert sein, andernfalls läuft man Gefahr, am Abend der Hafenbucht verwiesen zu werden.

Tag 6: Cabrera – Palma, 30 sm

Je nach Wind und Wetter und zu welcher Zeit die Boje verlassen wird, könnten die Buchten und Strände zu beiden Seiten von Colonia Sant Jordi das Ziel für einen letzten, schönen Ankerstopp sein. Oder aber die kleine Cala Pí nahe Cabo Blanco, im Süden der Bucht von Palma. Wer hier über Nacht bleiben will, sollte früh kommen – und diese letzte Etappe anders planen…

Day 1: Palma – Sa Rápita, 25nmi

If you're looking for a dip in the seawater in Palma bay, treat yourself to an unconventional expedition cruise along the cliff coast leading to Cabo Blanco. If you pass the coastline closely enough, you'll encounter many anchorage sites on turquoise waters with ca. 10m water depth. Of course, these are rather open and to be recommended only in calm weather conditions.

Day 2: Sa Rápita – Portocolom, 25nmi

Having enjoyed dinner in one of many restaurants with sea view, the following day your yacht will pass Cabo Salinas, Mallorca's southernmost cape, some 10nmi on. Enjoy the most beautiful marine blue of Mallorca's waters here; and then let the bay marathon begin. The most famous of these bays is Cala Mondragó. In Portocolom numerous buoys welcome anchoring visitors.

Day 3: Portocolom – Porto Cristo, 10nmi

Portocolom port bay is lined by a half-dozen restaurants. Visitors can even have their breakfast here, since the next leg of the trip does not even amount to 10nmi. Again, it is impossible to view all of the bays in one stretch, but Cala Barcas is a must-see. Porto Cristo is a cute little town, renowned for its caves which can be visited, and the nearby beaches and bays.

Day 4: Porto Cristo – Cala Figuera, 15nmi

If not forced to tack the following 15nmi, skippers should take the time to visit this bay. You need reservations for Cala Figuera as it is Mallorca's smallest yacht port. But it is also a very active fishing port. The harbour bay cuts into the cliffs like a fjord and hides its prettiest part at the very back.

Day 5: Cala Figuera – Cabrera, 15nmi

The next stage also offers some rewarding bays. They are so close, it is hardly necessary to set sails. Cala Santanyi, Lllombards, de sa Comuna (or Moro), Màrmols. Or, depending on wind direction, choose Cala Caragol to the west of Cabo Salinas. You will need to make reservations for the overnight buoy in Cabrera or you risk being sent off the port bay in evening hours.

Day 6: Cabrera – Palma, 30nmi

Depending on wind and weather conditions, and the time at which the vessel has left the buoy, the bays and beaches to both sides of Colonia Sant Jordi could be the destination for a last enjoyable stopover. Alternatively, Cala Pi near Cabo Blanco in the southern part of Palma bay, is a good option. Visitors intending to stay the night, though, should however be here on time and adjust their sailing plan accordingly.

Törn-Tipp / Cruising Tip

Palma – Port de Sóller – Port d'Alcúdia – Porto Cristo – Palma (190 sm / nmi)

In sechs Tagen machbar, aber das Wetter sollte schon ein wenig mitspielen. Viel Zeit für schöne Buchten bleibt nicht, das muss man wissen. Dafür hat man die größte Balearen-Insel einmal komplett vom Wasser gesehen und einige ihrer schönsten Häfen. Nach Möglichkeit mit der Tramuntana-Küste beginnen, weil an der Ostküste häufiger stärkerer Nord- als Südwind vorkommt.
(In Klammern sind alternative Häfen genannt.)

It is possible to sail around Mallorca in 6 days, if the weather is good. Although, this leaves little time to explore the many beautiful bays that Mallorca has to offer. You will, however, have seen the Balearic's biggest island from the sea and experience some of its most charming harbours. When possible, start with the Tramuntana coast, because on the east coast the chance of getting northerly winds is quite high.
Note: (Alternative ports in brackets)

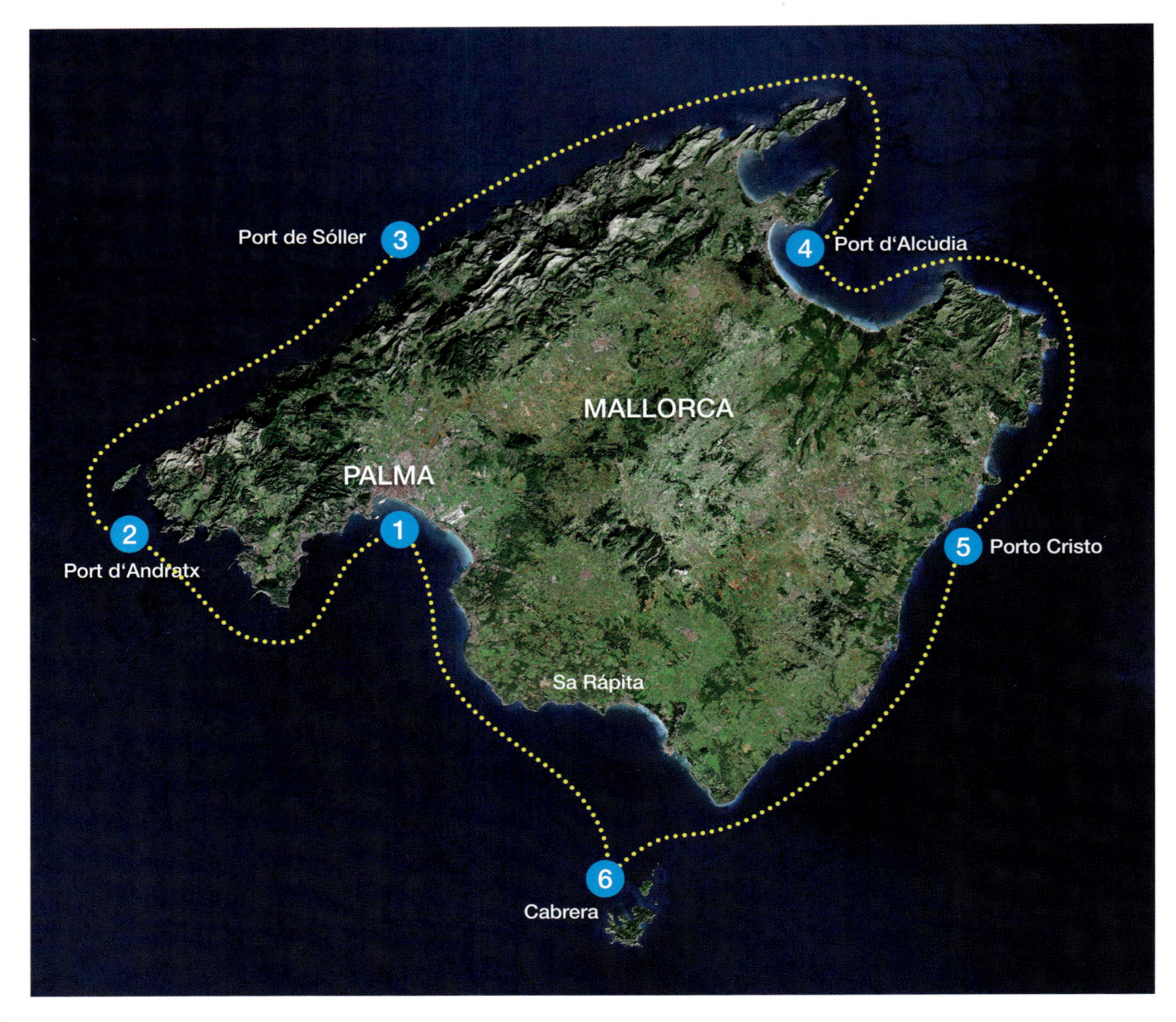

Mallorca umrunden / Cruising around Mallorca

Tag 1: Palma – Port d'Andratx (Sant Elm), 25 sm
Es geht Richtung Westspitze Mallorca, vorbei am schwarz-weißen Leuchtturm auf der Punta de Cala Figuera. Sie das markiert Ende der Bucht von Palma und nur 1sm entfernt lockt für einen kurzen Stopp die Cala Portals Vells. Auf den weiteren Meilen Richtung Port d'Andraitx passiert die Yacht mehrere große Kaps und einige Buchten. Auch das Einlaufen nach Port d'Andraitx wird von einer hohen Steilküste begleitet, La Mola genannt.

Tag 2: Port d'Andratx – Port de Sollér, 25 sm
Wer früh aufbricht, könnte in der Cala Egos oder bei Sant Elm vor der Isla Dragonera einen Badestopp einlegen. Dann folgen 20 sm Tramuntana-Küste, man passiert kleine und kleinste Fischerhäfen und – schon kurz vor dem Tagesziel – Sa Foradada, die Felsnase mit dem Loch darin. Wer einen schönen Sonnenuntergang zu schätzen weiß, sollte nicht zu spät in Port de Sollér ankommen.

Tag 3: Port de Sollér – Port d'Alcudia (P. Pollensa), 40 sm
Selten ein Baum, kaum ein Strauch – fast vegetationslos präsentiert sich der zweite Teil der Tramuntana-Küste. Ein Highlight dieser Passage ist sicherlich die Bucht von Sa Calobra, wo die Schlucht Torrent de Pareis eine Verbindung zum Meer hat. Mit dem Boot kann man vor der Schlucht ankern, auf großen Wassertiefen und im Sommer vor einer abgetrennten Badezone. Beeindruckendes Ende der Tramuntana-Küste ist das Cabo Formentor, Mallorcas nördlichster Punkt.

Tag 4: Port d'Alcudia – Porto Cristo (Portocolom), 35 sm
Der Hafenort der alten römischen Stadtgründung Pollèntia ist heute ein touristisches Zentrum, das sich über viele Kilometer an einem Strand entlang zieht. Hier gibt es eine komfortable Marina und davor einen großen Ankerplatz. Der nächste Schlag führt vorbei an Cabo Farrutx und Cabo de Pera und an Cala Rajada. Will man Cabrera nicht auslassen, sollte Port Cristo das Ziel sein.

Tag 5: Porto Cristo – Cabrera (Sa Rápita), 35 sm
Vor 18 Uhr muss man Cabrera nicht erreicht haben und da eine reservierte Boje auch danach noch freigehalten wird, kann man den Segeltag durchaus auch für Ankerstopps in einer der zahlreichen Buchten der Kliffküste im Osten Mallorca nutzen. Nur wenn man die Blaue Grotte auf Cabrera bei bestem Licht besuchen möchte, sollte man Cabrera schon am frühen Nachmittag besuchen.

Tag 6: Cabrera – Palma, 30 sm
Ein früher Aufbruch ist angesagt, will man am späten Mittag Palma erreicht haben. Von daher sollte man seine Cabrera-Ausflüge am Abend zuvor erledigt haben – oder muss sie in aller Herrgottsfrühe nachholen. Zur Not kann man Ende etwas Zeit aufholen: Die Chance, dass man in der Bucht von Palma den Wind nicht von vorne hat, ist groß.

Day 1: Palma – Port d'Andratx (Sant Elm), 25nmi
Set sail towards the western tip of Mallorca towards the black and white lighthouse at Punta de Cala Figuera. It marks the end of the Bay of Palma, and only 1nmi away Cala Portals Vells is an inviting first stop. On the following miles to Port d'Andratx one passes several large capes that divide the bays. On arrival to Port d'Andratx, you will be greeted also by a high cliff called La Mola.

Day 2: Port d'Andratx – Port de Sóller, 25nmi
For those who get up with the sun, an early morning swim at Cala Egos, or in front of Sant Elm next to Isla Dragonera, is a refreshing start to the journey. From here 20nmi stretch out along the Tramuntana coast, where you will pass many small and smaller fishing ports. Shortly before Port de Sóller, you will pass Sa Foradada, rocky outcrop with a hole in the rock. Those who love to watch beautiful sunsets, should not arrive too late in Port de Sóller.

Day 3: Port de Soller – Port d'Alcudia (P. Pollensa), 40nmi
Rarely a tree, hardly a shrub - the second part of the Tramuntana coast is almost without vegetation, but rather spectacular cliff faces plunging into the Mediterranean. A highlight of this passage is certainly the bay of Sa Calobra, where the gorge Torrent de Pareis connects to the sea. By boat, you can anchor in front of the gorge, at great water depths, and in the summer in front of a separate swimming area. An impressive end to the Tramuntana coast is Cabo Formentor, Mallorca's most northerly point.

Day 4: Port d'Alcudia – Porto Cristo (Portocolom), 35nmi
The port of the ancient Roman city Pollentia is today a tourist center that runs for many kilometers along the beach. There is a comfortable marina in front of a large anchorage area. The next sailing trip leads to Cabo Farrutx and around Cabo de Pera and Cala Rajada. If you plan to sail on towards Cabrera, then Port Cristo is your next port of call.

Day 5: Porto Cristo – Cabrera (Sa Rapita), 35nmi
You will only get access to your moorning buoy on Cabrera after 6 p.m. So there is no reason to arrive too early. Rather enjoy the many calas along Mallorca's coast before crossing over to Cabrera. Unless you want to visit the Blue Grotto on Cabrera, then you should arrive at Cabrera in the early afternoon to benefit from the best light.

Day 6: Cabrera – Palma, 30nmi
An early morning start is called for if one wants to reach Palma by late afternoon. You will therefore need to have done your excursions on Cabrera the evening before – or at the crack of dawn. You might be able to make up some time on this last stretch, as the chance of headwind in the Bay of Palma is not too big …

Törn-Tipp / Cruising Tip

Palma – Ibiza – Formentera – Ibiza – Palma (195 sm / nmi)

Die beiden südlichen Inseln der Balearen sind wegen der karibisch anmutenden Strände Formenteras und dem Ruf Ibizas als Partyinsel beliebte Ziele. Sie wurden von den Griechen Pityusen genannt wegen ihrer damals reichen Pinienwälder.

Für den Zeitraum einer Woche muss das Wetter mitspielen, am besten bei der Abfahrt schon die erste Prognose für den Schlag zurück nach Mallorca einholen. Ein Törn von Palma kann zum Auftakt nur bis Port d'Andratx führen, denn von dort hat man mit 50 sm die kürzeste Distanz. Von Palma direkt wären es knapp 65 sm. Auf der Überfahrt ist ein engerer Kontakt mit Fähren und Frachtschiffen möglich und vielleicht sieht man auch Delfine.

The two islands in the south of the Balearic Islands are popular destinations for a boat trip, because of the Caribbean-style beaches of Formentera and Ibiza's reputation as a party island. It is important to watch the weekly weather forecast, for the whole duration of your trip especially for your return to Mallorca. The first leg of your trip could be from Palma to Port d'Andratx, a total of 50nmi. From there take the stretch across to Ibiza, approx. 65nmi. On the crossing, watch out for ferries and cargo ships, and if you are lucky you may be accompanied by dolphins.

Ibiza

Ses Illetes, Formentera

312 Portbook & Island Guide

Ibiza & Formentera

Tag 1: Palma – Cala Portinatx, 65 sm
Wie der Name schon sagt, ist Cala Portinatx kein Hafen. Aber diese Bucht an der Nordspitze Ibizas hat fast alles, was auch ein Hafen bieten kann: sehr guten Schutz (außer gegen Nordwinde) und in der Saison das volle Versorgungsangebot eines touristischen Ortes. Aber es gibt kein Hafengeld. Entsprechend viele Yachten versammeln sich hier allabendlich zum gemeinsamen Ankern.

Tag 2: Cala Portinatx – Sant Antoni, 20 sm
Sant Antoni hat die einzige Marina an der Westseite Ibizas. Und eine sehr moderne dazu, die aber im Sommer nicht alle möglichen Gastyachten aufnehmen kann. Doch gibt es zahlreich Alternativen in Form von Buchten und einem Bojenfeld gleich vor der Marina. Schon auf den wenigen Meilen nach Sant Antoni laden ein halbes Dutzend Buchten zum Ankerstopp ein – oder zum Bleiben.

Tag 3: Sant Antoni – Cala Sahona, 25 sm
Bis zur Isla Vedra, Ibizas magischer Insel an ihrer Südwestecke, bieten sich wieder zahlreiche Buchten für eine Unterbrechung an. Doch die Cala Sahona im Westen Formenteras werden sie nur schwerlich toppen können. Denn topfebener Sandboden und türkisfarbenes Wasser lockt Yachtcrews sirenengleich an. Es gibt Strandrestaurants und sogar ein Inselausflug ließe sich hier beginnen.

Tag 4: Cala Sahona – Espalmador, 5 sm
Man muss sich schon losreißen von diesem Platz, aber mit der Aussicht auf die Nordspitze Formenteras mit dem Inselchen Espalmador und den langen Stränden ist das möglich. Allein, so ruhig wird man hier nicht ankern können, denn Fähren wie Perlen an einer Schnur und zahlreiche Motoryachten tragen fortwährend Schwell heran. Die Marinas von La Savina, Formenteras Hafen, wären die Rettung. Aber sie sind im Sommer sehr ausgebucht – und vor allem sehr teuer.

Tag 5: Espalmador – Ibiza-Stadt, 10 sm
Teuer ist auch das Stichwort für die Marinas in Ibiza – ergänzt um voll belegt. Ohne Reservierung im Sommer einen Liegeplatz zu finden, gleicht einem Sechser im Lotto. Ankern sollte also eingeplant werden, oder die Marina von Santa Eularia als Alternative. Auch von dort ließe sich Ibiza-Stadt besuchen, mit Taxen oder Bussen. Auf jeden Fall ist Ibiza jede Mühe wert: die von einer Festungsmauer umschlossene Altstadt und das legendäre Nachtleben will kaum einer auslassen.

Tag 6: Ibiza-Stadt – Palma de Mallorca, 70 sm

Day 1: Palma – Cala Portinatx, 65nmi
As the name implies, Cala Portinatx is not a port. But this bay at Ibiza's northern tip has almost everything a port can offer: excellent protection (except for northern winds), and catering for tourists during the high season. But since there's no port fee, many yachts meet here every evening to anchor.

Day 2: Cala Portinatx – Sant Antoni, 20nmi
Sant Antoni offers the only marina in Ibiza's west. It's quite modern, but too small to shelter all prospective visiting yachts in summer. There are numerous alternatives, however, such as bays and a bouy field right in front of the marina. The few miles towards Sant Antoni, offer many mooring possibilities, either for a short stopover, or those who have the time may be tempted to stay a little longer …

Day 3: Sant Antoni – Cala Sahona, 25nmi
Many other bays provide anchorage options during the trip to Isla Vedra, Ibiza's magic island at its south-western corner. But none surpass Cala Sahona in the west of Formentera. With pancake-flat sandy ground and turquoise water, the bay attracts yachts like a magnet. There are several beach restaurants, and you might even want to start an island excursion here.

Day 4: Cala Sahona – Espalmador, 5nmi
Though tempted to remain in this beautiful place, most visitors tend to sail on to Formentera's northern tip, in anticipation of enjoying Espalmador islet and long stretches of beach. Anchorage is less serene here, however, since ferries pass like the pearls on a string and numerous motor yachts continuously ensure heavy swells. Shelter might be found in the marinas of La Savina, the port of Formentera. But these are often fully booked in summer – and also really expensive.

Day 5: Espalmador – Ibiza-Town, 10nmi
The term „expensive" also comes to mind with Ibiza's marinas – as well as „fully occupied". To find a mooring place in summer without reservation is like winning in the lottery. Planning for anchorage beforehand is therefore recommended, or alternatively try Santa Eularia marina. From there you can continue to Ibiza city by taxi or by bus. Either way, Ibiza is well worth a visit. The historic old town embedded in fortifications and the legendary nightlife scene are unforgettable experiences.

Day 6: Ibiza-Town – Palma de Mallorca, 70nmi

Törn-Tipp / Cruising Tip

Portocolom – Ciutadella – Mahón – Portocolom (175 sm / nmi)

Vom Norden und Osten Mallorcas ist Menorca ein Ziel, das man einfach nicht auslassen will. Zu nah liegt die Nachbarinsel. Wer hier zum Chartertörn startet, hat mit etwas Wetterglück die besten Chancen, in einer Woche alle Höhepunkte zu erleben: die schönen Hafenstädte Ciutadella und Mahón, und die zauberhafte Buchten entlang der Südküste.

Starting on Mallorca's north eastern coast, Menorca is an attractive destination as it is within easy reach. Pending good weather conditions, it is possible to enjoy the highlights of Menorca in one week: beautiful harbour towns Ciutadella and Mahón, large Fornells bay in the north, and Menorca's enchanting bays on the south coast.

Menorca

Tag 1: Portocolom – Ciutadella, 45 sm
Auch wenn der Törn gerade erst anfängt, diese 45 sm direkter Kurs nach Ciutadella müssen am ersten Tag bewältigt werden. Will man in der Folge ausreichend Zeit für den Rest Menorcas haben. Die Vorfreude auf dem Zielhafen wird die Crew beflügeln, immerhin wartet die Hafenstadt, die unter all den Mitbewerbern auf den Balearen-Inseln eine Spitzenposition einnimmt – vor allem im Sommer.

Tag 2: Ciutadella – Fornells, 25sm
Wäre jetzt ein kräftiger Mistral aus dem Norden vorhergesagt, müsste der Törnplan wahrscheinlich entscheidend verändert werden. Unter anderen Bedingungen aber steht ein Segeltag auf dem Törnplan, an dem ein paar wenig frequentierte Buchten besucht werden könnten. Oder aber Skipper und Crew wollen die Zeit für das Ziel nutzen. Fornells hätte es verdient….

Tag 3: Fornells – Mahón, 25sm
Damit ausreichend Gelegenheit bleibt für die Hauptstadt Menorcas und einen Badestopp unterwegs, ist ein früher Aufbruch angesagt. Mahón belohnt seine Gäste mit einer sehr gepflegten Altstadt und einer sehr großen Auswahl an Restaurants am Naturhafen. Allein die kuschelige Atmosphäre, wie man sie im kleineren Ciutadella erleben kann, wird sich hier wahrscheinlich nicht einstellen.

Tag 4: Mahón – Cala Porté, 20 sm
Noch einmal ist Zeit für Mahóns Altstadt und andere schöne Ziele. Denn die verbleibende Distanz bis zur Cala Porté im Süden ist überschaubar. Selbst Buchten, die vorher in Frage kommen (Cala Covas oder Binibeca), könnten für die Nacht angesteuert werden ohne dass der Törnplan in Gefahr geriete. Was man auf jeden Fall beachten muss: An der Südküste gibt es keine Häfen, keine Marinas.

Tag 5: Cala Porté – Cala Macarella, 10 sm
Es ist der Tag, auf den wahrscheinlich die meisten Crewmitglieder hingefiebert haben. Die schönsten Buchten liegen nun vor dem Bug und es wäre verzeihbar, vielen die kalte Schulter zu zeigen, um gleich ihre Nr. 1 aufzusuchen. Die Cala Macarella hat einfach die schönste Kliffküste, ihr Sandgrund zaubert atemberaubende Farben ins kristallklare Wasser.

Tag 6: Cala Macarella – Portocolom, 45 sm
Ob der Segeltag schon in der Cala Macarella endete oder in der nahen Cala de Son Saura ein paar Seemeilen weiter westlich: Der Törn geht zu Ende wie er begann – mit einem längeren Tag auf dem Wasser.

Day 1: Portocolom – Ciutadella, 45nmi
Although this is just the start of your journey, these 45nmi directly towards Ciutadella have to be covered within the first day if you want to have sufficient time left to explore the whole island of Menorca. With every mile the crew will get closer to probably one of the most attractive harbour towns the Balearic Islands have to offer in summertime.

Day 2: Ciutadella – Fornells, 25nmi
If the weather forecast announces a forceful mistral from the north, the tour will have to be significantly re-planned. In fine sailing conditions, many rarely visited bays lie waiting to be explored. Alternatively, head straight for Fornells – a beautiful destination.

Day 3: Fornells – Mahón, 25nmi
To ensure sufficient time to enjoy Menorca's capital and a bathing stopover en route, you should start out early. Mahón rewards the visitor with a very well-groomed old town and a huge selection of restaurants at the natural harbour. However, do not expect to find the same cosy atmosphere as in the former capital Ciutadella.

Day 4: Mahón – Cala Porté, 20nmi
Some time is left for Mahón's Old Town and other beautiful destinations, since southern Cala Porté is only a short distance away. You might even spend the night in one of the earlier bays (Cala Covas or Binibeca) without delaying your trip schedule. Please always be aware: there are neither harbours nor marinas on the south coast (exempt Cala 'n Bosch for power boats).

Day 5: Cala Porté – Cala Macarella, 10nmi
This is probably the day most crew members have been looking forward to. The gorgeous bays lie waiting, and you may choose to sail directly to Cala Macarella – no.1 highlight. This bay simply has the most beautiful cliff coastline, and its sandy ground conjures up breathtaking colours within the crystal-clear waters.

Day 6: Cala Macarella – Portocolom, 45nmi
Whether you have finished your sailing day in Cala Macarella or in nearby Cala de Son Saura a few nautical miles to the west: the trip ends as it started, with a with a long day of sailing.

Portbook & Island Guide

Seenebel / Sea fog

Gewitter / thunderstorm

Beginn einer Wasserhose / A waterspout is developing ...

SEEWETTER
MARINE WEATHER

Das Wetter auf den Balearen besteht nicht nur aus strahlend blauem Himmel. Wenn sich gerade kein Azorenhoch über den Inseln festgesetzt hat, dann ist der Weg frei für allerlei Störungen und Frontensysteme. Die meisten machen sich von Nordwesten auf den Weg, einige kommen auch direkt aus der Sahara, die wenigsten von Ost.

Der Aufzug von Tiefs passiert natürlich außerhalb der Sommermonate am häufigsten. Im Herbst kommt erschwerend hinzu, dass dann Kaltluft und sehr warmes Meerwasser zusammen treffen, was nicht selten zu gewaltigen und zerstörerischen Unwettern führt, sogar Waterspouts (Wasserhosen, Meerestornados) treten dabei auf.

Ein Frühjahrsphänomen ist der Seenebel, wenn die schon starke Sonne das kalte Meerwasser zum Verdunsten anregt. Weil die Luft noch recht kalt ist, kondensiert die aufsteigende Luft sehr schnell und es entstehen Wolken über dem Meer, die sehr zäh und kompakt sein können.

Nicht zuletzt drohen immer wieder schwere Winterstürme vor allen an den Nordseiten der Insel, liegen die Balearen doch im Einflussbereich des Mistrals, neben Bora und Etesien eines der stärksten Windereignisse am Mittelmeer, in Europa und weltweit.

Die gute Nachricht zum Schluss: Meist ist das Wetter ideal zum Bootfahren rund um die Balearen-Inseln. Auch ohne Gradientwind stellt sich zumindest rund Mallorca an einem „normalen" Sommertag meistens ausreichend Segelwind ein, ausgelöst durch thermische Effekte. Also eine auflandige Brise, die sich ergibt, weil das Land sich schneller erwärmt als das Meer. Besonders der Bahia de Palma, in der Ensenada de Sa Rápita (Es Trenc) im Süden und in den großen Buchten des Nordens, Bahia von Alcúdia und Bahia de Pollensa wird dies spürbar.

Eine gute Wettervorhersage schadet aber nie. Hier einige Quellen.

Weather on the Balearic Islands is not just clear blue skies. Unless an Azores anticyclone has settled above the is-

Wissenswertes / Facts

lands, there is room for various disturbances and weather front systems. Most of them come from the Northwest, several arrive directly from the Sahara, only very few from the East.
This happens most frequently outside of the summer months. In autumn, the weather is aggravated by cold air meeting with warm seawater, which quite often leads to huge, destructive tempests, and even waterspouts can occur.
Sea mist is a spring phenomenon, when the strong sun forces seawater to evaporate. Since the air still remains rather cool, the ascending air condenses quickly, and tough, compact clouds form above the sea.
Finally, serious winter storms loom especially in the islands' North, since the Balearic Islands lie within the zone of influence of Mistrals, which is – with Bora and Etesien – one of the most extreme wind conditions to be met in the Mediterranean Sea, in Europe and worldwide.
And, finally, for some good news: Usually, the weather is ideal for boating and sailing around the Balearic Islands. Even without gradient wind on an equal summer day at least around Mallorca one will usually get sufficient sailing wind, caused by thermal effects. These onshore breezes arise when the land heats up faster than the sea. Thermal breezes can get strong here: Bahia de Palma, Ensenada de Sa Rápita (Es Trenc), Bahia de Alcudia and Bahia de Pollensa. But never forget to listen to the weather forecast. Some good sources follow:

SEEWETTERBERICHTE
MARINE WEATHER SOURCES

RADIO
Tägliche Seewetterberichte auf Deutsch
Daily Sea Weather Reports in German
Inselradio, 18 h + 18.30 h MESZ
UKW 95,8 Mhz, UKW 99.6 MHz für Nord-Mallorca und Menorca / *for Northern Majorca and Minorca*
Nachzulesen auch auf / *for reference* see www.inselradio.com

UKW-Sprechfunk / *VHF Voice Radio*
Über die Küstenfunkstellen, nach Ankündigung auf UKW-Kanal 16
By coastal radio stations, announcement on VHF channel 16
Palma, 07 UTC 0910-1410-2110
1755 kHz UTC 0750-1303-1950

Aussendungen der spanischen Seenotrettung / *Transmissions of the Spanish sea rescue organisation* Sociedad Estatal de Salvamento y Seguridad Marítima (SASEMAR), Station Palma
UKW/VHF 10+16 +72
Summer: 0635-0935-1435-1935 (UTC)
Winter: 0735-1035-1535-2035 (UTC)

INTERNET
www.aemet.es
Seewetter von der staatlichen Agentur für Meteorologie (Agencia Estatal de Meteorología, AEMet). Karten zu Wind und Wellenhöhe bis zu vier Tage voraus.
Weather bulletin issued by the Agency for Meteorology of the Spanish Government (Agencia Estatal de Meteorología, AEMET). Animation of wind and wave height up to four days.
Navigation: „Eltiempo" -> „Predicción" -> „Marrítima" -> „Costas" -> „Costa de Illes Baleares" -> „Parámetro" -> „Viento y mar de viento"

http://meteonav.aemet.es/MeteoNav
Routenwettervorhersage nach Eingabe von Start- und Zielhafen.
Route weather forecast provided after entering start and destination harbours.

www.passageweather.com
Animierte Vorhersagen im Drei-Stunden-Rhythmus; Achtung: Das GFS-Modell ist oft weniger genau als „COAMPS" oder „WRF" und kann bei den prognostizierten Windstärken an der unteren Grenze liegen.
Presented forecasts in three-hour intervals; Warning: The GFS model is less precise than „COAMPS" or „WRF" and may state values at the lower end of the range as regards forecasted wind speeds.

www.puertos.es
Auf der rechten Seite der Startseite „Mapas Prevision y Tiempo Real".
In großen Teilen auf Englisch bietet die Webseite für die spanischen Handelshäfen Grafisches zu Wind, Wellen etc. Für zirka drei Tage im Voraus im Dreistunden-Takt mit der Möglichkeit zum Ausdrucken.
Click on „Mapas Prevision y Tiempo Real" on the homepage. This predominantly English-language website offers graphic representations for Spanish trade ports on wind speeds, waves etc. Forecasts for three days in advance presented in 3-hour intervals with print-out option.

www.mallorcaviento.com
Verschiedene Quellen sind hier gebündelt, dazu auch Webcams.
Various weather providers are linked here, in addition web cams

www.wetterklima.de
hat unter „Seewetter" eine Linkliste parat. / *In menu item "Seewetter" you will find a list of web links according to regions.*

www.windfinder.com
www.windguru.cz/de
Viel benutzte Programme, aber eine Garantie auf die Vorhersagen gibt es auch hier nicht...
Widely used programmes, but no guarantee that the forecast is more accurate.

GRIB-Files
www.zygrib.org
www.grib.us
www.predictwind.com/grib

Beratung / *Routing*
Die Kieler Firma Wetterwelt, Inh. Dr. Meeno Schrader, bietet verschiedene personalisierte Dienste und selbstgerechnete Wetterdaten. Seit vielen Jahren am Markt, anerkannte Qualität. Die Webseite funktioniert auch auf Englisch.
The names of Dr. Meeno Schrader and his WetterWelt GmbH carry a reputation of professionalism and high quality work. Several products for sailors to choose from. The website also works in English.
www.wetterwelt.de

MEERESSTRÖMUNGEN
OCEAN CURRENTS

Oberflächenströmungen sind generell schwach ausgeprägt und treten am ehesten zwischen den Inseln (z. B. Canal de Menorca) auf und nach oder bei kräftigen Windereignissen (Mistral). Auch im Kanal zwischen Ibiza und Formentera kann der Strom spürbar werden. Strömung kann auch in Häfen und Marinas auftreten, wenn es zu plötzlichen Wasserstandsschwankungen kommt. Die werden immer wieder beobachtet, nicht nur in den schmalen Häfen, und Rissagas genannt.

Surface currents are generally weak and are most likely to occur between the islands (i. a. Canal de Menorca) and after or during strong winds (i. a. Mistral). Also in the narrow strait between Ibiza and Formentera.
Currents may occasionally occur in ports and marinas, when it comes to sudden changes in water level. These are mostly observed in narrow ports but not only and called Rissagas.

SEEKARTEN
SEA CHARTS

Elektronische Seekarten sind auch in der Sportschifffahrt Standard. Die Erfahrung zeigt aber, dass sie gerade küstennahe Untiefen manchmal nicht ausreichend genau darstellen. Die Empfehlung kann von daher nur lauten, auch gedruckte Seekarten mitzuführen, was aufgrund eines Ausfalls elektrischer und elektronischer Systeme ohnehin zu empfehlen ist.

Für die Balearen gibt es viele Anbieter, kompetent berät dazu u. a. hansenautic, ein Seekartenhändler mit jahrzehntelanger Erfahrung, der auch die Berufsschifffahrt ausstattet,
www.hansenautic.de
Sportbootkarten-Sätze (im Plastikschuber) mit einer elektronischen Seekarte als Ergänzung inklusive gibt es von Delius Klasing und dem NV. Verlag.

Electronic charts are a todays standard also on pleasure boats. However, often close to the coast they are not as accurate as they should be. Therefore, and in case of a blackout of electrical and electronic systems it is recommended to also carry printed charts.
For the Balearic Islands there are many charts to choose from, competent advice is given i. a. by HanseNautic, a leading provider for nautical charts. Equips also commercial shipping, www.hansenautic.de
Dedicated charts for pleasure boats (in plastic slipcase) with an electronic chart as a supplement included are offered by Delius Klasing and NV. Verlag.

SEENOTRETTUNG
SEA RESCUE

In verschiedenen Häfen rund um die Balearen-Inseln sind schnelle Rettungsboote der spanischen Organisation Salvamento Marítimo stationiert. Sie übernehmen auch Schleppeinsätze. Die Zentrale erteilt darüber hinaus generelle Auskünfte, auch zum Wetter.

Several ports all over the Balearic Islands shelter fast rescue boats which are operated by Spanish organisation Salvamento Marítimo. They also perform towing operations. The headquarters also issue general information, weather forecasts included.

Benachrichtigung im Notfall über / *Emergency call via*
UKW/VHF 10+16 or
T 112 or T 900 202 202

Zentrale / *Headquarter Palma*
Centro de Coordinación de Salvamento Palma
Avenida Gabriel Roca, 38- A, 1°
07014 - Palma de Mallorca
T 971 724 562, palma@sasemar.es
www.salvamentomaritimo.es

Eine Alarmierung kann auch über die Seenotleitung (MRCC) Bremen erfolgen: T+49 421 536 87 0 (24 h)

Wissenswertes / Facts

ÖFFENTLICHE HÄFEN
PUBLIC PORTS

Die Hafenverwaltung der autonomen Region Islas Baleares, **PortsIB**, bietet auch Liegeplätze für Sportboote an. Mit Langzeitverträgen, aber auch für Yachten auf der Durchreise. Die Tarife sind günstiger als in Marinas, die durch private Firmen oder Club Náuticos geführt werden. Man muss sich jedoch mit einfacheren sanitären Einrichtungen zufrieden geben. Nach einmaliger Anmeldung auf der Internetseite von PortsIB können die Liegeplätze tageweise reserviert und online bezahlt werden.
Der Quadratmeterpreis beträgt:
01/06-30/09: 0,6 EUR/m²/Tag
1/10-31/05: 0,18 EUR/m²/Tag
Wenn Wasser, Strom und Müllentsorgung angeboten werden, kommen pro Tag pauschal je 5,50 EUR für den Verbrauch von Wasser und Strom hinzu. Alles plus 21% MwSt.
Reservierung notwendig. Mindestens drei Tag im Voraus über:
www.portsib.es
Achtung: Obwohl einige Häfen Plätze über 12 m Länge anbieten, kann es sein, dass das Reservierungssystem nur Anfragen bis 12 m annimmt. Dann sollte man so verfahren …
Diese Häfen haben Platz für Gastyachten (siehe weiter unten):

*The public harbour administration Ports Islas Baleares, in short **PortsIB**, offers online booking of berths in self-administered facilities in some Balearic ports. Some of these might not offer high standard sanitary facilities, but these berths are better priced than in marinas operated by private parties or clubs.*
Currently charges are:
0.6 EUR/m²/day (1/6-30/9) or 0.18 EUR/m²/day (1/10-31/5)
If water, electricity and waste disposal are on offer there is a lump service charge of 5.50 EUR/day, each for water and electricity. All + 21% VAT.
Reservation required: at least three days in advance on www.portsib.es
***Note:** Although some ports offer berths over 12m in length, it is likely that the booking system only accepts requests up to 12m.*
These ports have berths on offer:

Mallorca
Port d'Andratx, Cala Bona, Cala Figuera, Cala Rajada, Colònia de Sant Jordi, Port de Pollença, Portocolom, Porto Cristo, Portopetro, Port de Sóller

Menorca
Ciutadella, Fornells

Ibiza
Sant Antoni de Portmany

Handelshäfen der Balearen:
Comercial ports on Balearic islands:
Palma de Mallorca, Alcúdia, Mahón, Ibiza, La Savina
Autoridad Portuaria de Balears
T 971 288 159
portsdebalears@portsdebalears.com
www.portsdebalears.com

HAFENGEBÜHREN
HARBOUR TAXES

In spanischen (und balearischen) Häfen werden Hafengebühren erhoben. Für die Sportschifffahrt relevant sind zwei, T-0 und G-5.

Tasa de ayuda a la navegación
(Leuchtturm-Steuer, auch zur Finanzierung der Seenot-Rettung) – T-0 (T Zero)

Wo diese Steuer erhoben werden muss, ist nicht bis ins Detail geklärt, aber sicher in allen Häfen und Marinas unter der Kontrolle der Hafenbehörden (im Wesentlichen die in Einzugsgebieten von Handelshäfen, hier: Palma de Mallorca, Alcúdia, Mahón, Ibiza, Sa Gavina). Für Marinas außerhalb des direkten Einflussbereichs der Autoridas Portuaria gibt es noch immer eine Grauzone.
2015 gelang der Wassersportlobby, dass diese Steuer von Yachten ohne Heimathafen in Spanien nur noch für die real verbrachten Tage erhoben wird und nicht darüber hinaus, wie zuvor praktiziert. Diese Initiative war ausgelöst worden durch eine vorangegangene Verdoppelung dieser Steuer.
Der Tagessatz für eine Yacht mit 13 m Länge und 4 m Breite beträgt etwa 1,30 EUR (Jahresgebühr geteilt durch 365). Segelboote von 12 m Länge und weniger und Motorboote von 9 m und weniger sind nicht betroffen.

Heimathafen
Wenn eine Yacht ihren permanenten Liegeplatz in einem spanischen Hafen hat (was auch nach einem dauerhaften Aufenthalt ab 6 Monaten unterstellt wird), dann muss die volle Jahresgebühr entrichtet warden.

Tasa de Embarcaciones deportivas y de recreo
(Sportbootgebühr) – G-5

In Häfen, die in Konzession betrieben werden, wird diese Steuer pro m² (Länge x Breite) und Tag berechnet. Eine einzige Nacht entspricht zwei Tagen. Bei 13x4 m ergibt sich ein Tagessatz von 1,88 EUR.
Segelboote unter 12 m Länge und Motorboote unter 9 m zahlen eine geringere Rate. Die aktuellen Preise sind wie folgt:

Besucher:
Segel ≥12m / Motor ≥ 9m
0.0484 € /m²/Tag
Segel <12m / Motor < 9m
0.0186 € /m²/Tag

Dauerlieger
(auch nach 6 Monaten am Stück)
Segel ≥12m / Motor ≥ 9m
0.0397 € /m²/Tag
Segel < 12m / Motor < 9m
0.0124 € /m²/Tag

Tasa de ayuda a la navegación
(Navigational assistance rates or the "lighthouse tax") – T-0 (T Zero)

There is a little inconsistency in where the law is applied, but all ports and marinas under the control of the Port Authorities (essentially those in basins shared by commercial ports: Palma de Mallorca, Alcúdia, Mahón, Ibiza, Sa Gavina) are strictly obliged to charge these additional rates. Non port authority-run marinas are still a grey area.

A sector-driven lobby 2015 prevented transient visitors from suffering what was universally considered to be an unfair application of the Navigational Assistance rates where in previous years, an entire year's worth of rates could be charged for what amounted to only a few days' visit. As a consequence, visiting yachts from abroad (without a home port in Spain) are now charged a daily rate. The calculation is pretty convoluted but the daily rate for a sailing (or motor) yacht with 13m LOA and 4m beam is about 1.30€. Importantly, sailing boats of 12m LOA and less and power boats of 9m LOA or less are exempt.

Home port
If a yacht is based in a Spanish port (also considered to be the case after 6 months' occupancy), the yacht will be expected to demonstrate payment of the full year's rates.

Tasa de Embarcaciones deportivas y de recreo
(Recreational vessel rates) – G-5 (T-5)

In ports operated by concession this tax is also charged by day (i. e. a single night's berthing corresponds to two days'-worth of rates) and calculated according to a yacht's m² – or LOA x Beam (m).

As a guideline, for a yacht of 13m LOA x 4m beam this corresponds to a daily rate of 1.88€. Sailing boats <12m LOA and motor boats <9m are favoured, paying a lesser rate. After 6 months, "home port" status is achieved, affording a lower daily rate.

Current rates are as follows:
Visitors:
Sail ≥12m / Motor ≥ 9m
0.0484 € /m²/day
Sail <12m / Motor < 9m
0.0186 € /m²/day
Home port
(after 6 months' occupancy)
Sail ≥12m / Motor ≥ 9m
0.0397 € /m²/day
Sail < 12m / Motor < 9m
0.0124 € /m²/day

BOJEN BUCHEN
RESERVE A BUOY

Rund um die Inseln Mallorca, Menorca, Ibiza und Formentera gibt es zwei Arten von Bojenfeldern: in der Regie von Yachtclubs und in öffentlicher Verwaltung. Beide sind seit 2012 kostenpflichtig.
Bojenfelder existieren seit 2006. Damals wurden sie mit EU-Mitteln zum Schutz der Posidonia-Seegrasfelder ausgelegt, Ihre Benutzung war zunächst kostenlos.
2012 wurden erste Bojenfelder privatisiert und in die Zuständigkeit von Yachtclubs gegeben. Auf Mallorca in Portocolom und Portopetro, wo die Vereine eigene Nutzungs-Gebühren erhoben. In Port d'Andratx erhielt der Club de Vela die Erlaubnis, in der Hafenbucht Festmachebojen zu installieren. Alle Details dazu in den jeweiligen Hafenbeschreibungen.
Seit 2013 verlangt auch die Balearen-Regierung für die verbliebenen Lifeposidonia-Bojenfelder nicht unerhebliche Gebühren für das Festmachen, nach Bootslänge gestaffelt.
bis 8 m: EUR 13,34, bis 14 m: EUR 29,10, bis 16 m: EUR 48,50
Es gibt keinen Tarif für kurzzeitiges Festmachen.

Die aktuellen Lifeposidonia-Bojenfelder liegen hier:
Mallorca: Cala Blava, Sant Elm
Menorca: Cala Fornells, Isla Colom
Ibiza/Formentera: Caló de s'Olli, Ses Salines, S'Espalmador
Die Bojen sind für den Zeitraum zwischen dem 1. Juni und 30. September ausgelegt und buchbar. Buchungen können bis 9 Uhr des Ankunftstages vorgenommen werden. Am Abfahrtstag müssen die Bojen vor 11 Uhr verlassen sein. Ankern neben den Bojenfeldern auf Sandgrund ist erlaubt.
Reservierung / Registrierung notwendig:
http://fondeos.caib.es +
www.balearslifeposidonia.eu
Kundentelefon: 971 439 779
(Mon-Fri 9-19 h)

Wissenswertes / Facts

In 2006, EU funds were used to set up 10 buoy fields around the Balearic Islands in order to protect areas with Posidonia sea grass growth. Initially, use of these buoy fields was free of charge. In 2012 the first two buoy fields were privatised and assigned to the management of yachting clubs, those in Portocolom and Portopetro on Mallorca. The clubs immediately began to charge user fees.
Since 2013, the Balearic administration also charges sizeable mooring fees for the remaining Lifeposidonia buoy fields, depending on boat length.
Up to 8 m: EUR 13.34, up to 14 m: EUR 29.10, up to 16 m: EUR 48.50
There is no short-term mooring fee.

The remaining buoy fields are located as follows:
Mallorca: Cala Blava, Sant Elm
Menorca: Cala Fornells, Isla Colom
Ibiza/Formentera: Caló de s'Olli, Ses Salines, S'Espalmador
Buoys remain installed and can be reserved between June 1st and September 30th. Reservations may be placed before 9 a.m. on the day of arrival. Buoys must be left by 11 a.m. on the date of departure. Anchoring next to a buoy field above is permitted.
Please book at:
http://fondeos.caib.es + www.balears-lifeposidonia.eu
Customer service phone: 971 439 779 (Mon-Fri 9-19 h)

SCHUTZGEBIETE AM MEER
NATURE RESERVES

Die Balearen-Regierung hat einige Küstenabschnitte als Meeresschutzgebiete ausgewiesen, so genannte „Reservas marinas". Die meisten Einschränkungen beziehen sich auf Fischen und Tauchen (nur mit Genehmigung), Ankern ist jedoch erlaubt. Wassersportler sind gehalten, in diesen Gebieten nicht auf Seegras zu ankern. Was man ohnehin vermeiden sollte, um einen festen Sitz des Ankers sicherzustellen. Nur in den Kerngebieten der Schutzgebiete (Área de Proteccíonespecial, gekennzeichnet durch jeweils zwei weiße Säulen an Land) ist Ankern, Tauchen und Fischen generell verboten. **Übrigens:** Offiziell gilt, dass Rückhaltetanks, so sie nicht abgesaugt werden (können), nur in einer Entfernung von mehr als 12 sm zur Küste entleert werden dürfen.

The government of the Balearic Islands has assigned some coastal sections the status of nature reserves, so-called „Reservas Marinas". Most limitations apply to fishing and diving (only with permit), but anchoring is allowed. Water sport enthusiasts are required to not set anchor on weed in these areas. Which should be avoided, anyway, if only to ensure a firm grip of the anchor. Only in the reserve core areas (Área de Proteccíone special, marked by two white columns on land, respectively), anchoring, diving and fishing are all prohibited. **FYI:** *holding tanks, if they cannot be extracted, should be emptied by law only at a distance of more than 12nmi away from the coast.*

Die Schutzzonen im Internet /
Nature reserves on the Internet
http://www.caib.es/sacmicrofront/contenido.do?mkey=M69&lang=ES&cont=850

YACHTCHARTER
BOAT CHARTER

Die Vermietung von Booten kann ein einträgliches Geschäft sein. Deshalb wird sie nicht nur von professionellen und zugelassenen Betrieben betrieben, sondern auch Privatleute wollen so ihr Portemonnaie füllen und versuchen über günstige Angebote ins Geschäft zu kommen. Was diesen Amateuren jedoch fehlt, sind oftmals die entsprechenden Versicherungen und ziemlich sicher die verschiedenen Papiere, die zwingend an Bord sein müssen. Sollte auch nur eines nicht vorhanden sein, kann aus dem vermeintlichen Schnäppchen ein teurer Spaß werden, denn die Polizei führt regelmäßig stichprobenartige Kontrollen durch.
Charterkunden können selber kontrollieren, ob alle geforderten Papiere vorhanden sind. Für Charterschiffe unter deutscher Flagge gilt:

Renting out a boat is good business. Which has led to the boom of unlicensed bareboat charters. It is likely that they will not have proper papers for their boats and in case of regular controls done by Guardia Civil a sailing trip can be suddenly over.
Charter customers should check for themselves whether all required documents are available. This is the list for charter vessels under a German flag:

- Despacho para embarcaciones de recreo de la Unión Europea en régimen de alquiler sin tripulación profesional
- Registro del país origen (z. B. Flaggenzertifikat)
- Certificado de Navegabilidad des país origen (z. B. Bootszeugnis)
- Declaración responsable para el arrendamiento de embarcaciones de recreo (Charter Náutico)
- Certificado de seguro de responsabilidad civil de suscripción obligatoria y de seguro de accidentes de ocupantes

Für Charterschiffe unter spanischer Flagge gilt: / *This is the list for charter vessels under a Spanish flag:*
- Permiso de Navegación
- Registro Marítimo Español
- Certificado de Navegabilidad
- Declaración responsable para el arrendamiento de embarcaciones de recreo (Charter Náutico)
- Certificado de seguro de responsabilidad civil de suscripción obligatoria y de seguro de accidentes de ocupantes

Für Nicht-Europäische-Yachten und für Yachten mit Crew an Bord gelten abweichende Bestimmungen. Kontrollen werden auch auf Yachten durchgeführt, die zum Mitsegeln angeboten werden. Wenn in diesem Fall der Skipper bei einer Kontrolle nicht über alle Lizenzen und Papiere verfügt, wird das zumindest für ihn teuer und der Törn kann schnell vorbei sein.

For non-European yachts and crewed charter other regulations apply. Checks are also carried out on yachts that are offered with captain. Again there are specific licenses and papers required by the authorities.

MALLORCAS SCHNELLSTE RUNDE
MALLORCA'S FASTEST LAP

Einmal rund Mallorca auf Zeit: Das schaffte bis heute niemand schneller als die Rennyacht „Uca" des verstorbenen Arbeitgeberpräsidenten Dr. Klaus Murmann. 17 Stunden, 14 Minuten und 39 Sekunden benötigten die Segler, um die größte Balearen-Insel mit dem 26 m langen, aus Kohlefaser gebauten Schiff und mit 12 Mann Crew am 20. April 2005 zu runden. Dafür gab es nicht einen einfach Silberpokal, sondern gleich ein ganzes Gemälde. Eines, das im Real Club Náutico Palma hängt und den alten Leuchtturm am Hafen Port Pí zeigt. Denn die so genannte „Four Stripes Challenge" wird vom Real Club Náutico vergeben.

The circumnavigation of Mallorca has never been sailed faster than on the 20th of April 2005 by the German owner of the racing yacht "Uca", Dr. Klaus Murmann. 17 hours, 14 minutes and 39 seconds was the record time on his 26 m carbon fiber slup. And because this record is something special, the reward is not just a silver trophy, but a painting, which hangs in the Real Club Nautico Palma and shows the old lighthouse at Porto Pí. The so-called "Four Stripes Challenge" is awarded by the Real Club Náutico Palma.

TOURISMUS-STEUER
TOURISM TAX

Wer zum Törn mit einer gecharterten Yacht aufbricht, fällt nicht unter die von der aktuellen Links-Regierung der Autonomen Region Islas Baleares beabsichtigten „Steuer für nachhaltigen Tourismus". Die tägliche Abgabe, die ab 2016 kommen soll, liegt laut Gesetzentwurf je nach Unterkunftsart zwischen 0,25 bis 2 EUR pro Tag. Die Yachtcharterbetriebe unterstehen dem Transportministerium, aus diesem Grund werden sie voraussichtlich anders behandelt werden als Beherbergungsbetriebe. Kreuzfahrtpassagiere sollen jedoch darunter fallen, wenn das Schiff länger als 12 Stunden festmacht.

The announced tourism tax will not apply on bareboat charter, as yacht charter companies are responsible to the Ministry of Transport. Cruise ship passengers are only excluded if the ship is going to sail after 12 hours.

DAS LEBEN IM MEER
LIFE IN THE SEA

Rund um die Balearen hat sich das Meer u. a. durch die zahlreichen Schutzgebiete eine wenig erholt. Es ziehen auch wieder mehr Thunfische in die Gewässer und in ihrer Folge auch Delfine und Haie. Selbst ein Weißer Hai, ein junges Exemplar, wurde mal wieder gesichtet und sogar fotografiert. Das war im Sommer 2014 in der Nähe von Cabo Formentor.
Pottwale sind vor allem hier anzutreffen: zwischen Mallorca und Menorca und südöstlich von Cabrera, wo der Meeresgrund auf unter 1000 m abfällt. Auch andere Walarten, darunter die großen Finnwale, ziehen von Fall zu Fall durch die Balearen-Inseln. Meeres-Schildkröten (überwiegend Caretta Caretta) sind eher selten, aber ebenfalls anzutreffen. Verletzte Tiere können an das Palma-Aquarium gemeldet werden.
T 971 746 104

Around the Balearic Islands, the sea has recovered a little due to numerous protected areas. Also more tuna fish can be found in the Balearic Sea, which is then followed by dolphins and sharks. Even a young Great White shark has been spotted and photographed in the summer of 2014 near Cabo Formentor. Sperm whales are spotted every now and then: between Mallorca and Menorca and southeast of Cabrera, where the seabed drops to below 1000 m. Other species of whales, including large fin whales, visit the waters around the islands. Sea turtles (mainly Caretta caretta) are rare, but also encountered. Injured animals can be reported to the Palma Aquarium. T 971 746 104

Wissenswertes / Facts

ÄRZTLICHE VERSORGUNG
HEALTH CARE

In vielen Küstenorten der Balearen oder in ihrer Nähe findet man ein Gesundheitszentrum, im spanischen „Centro de Salut" genannt. Hier arbeiten in der Regel Allgemeinmediziner oder Hausärzte. Eine Behandlung erfolgt für in Deutschland gesetzlich Versicherte kostenlos.

Privat Versicherte und Selbstzahler

Beeinflusst durch den jährlichen Besuch von rund 10 Millionen Touristen und einer großen Zahl von Residenten haben sich viele Ärzte aus Deutschland und anderen nordeuropäischen Ländern auf Mallorca und den anderen Balearen-Inseln angesiedelt und sich zum Teil ebenfalls zu Ärztezentren zusammen geschlossen. Eines der bekanntesten ist das Internationale Facharztzentrum in Palma de Mallorca, **Centro Medico Porto Pi**, mit zwei Standorten gegenüber vom Club de Mar. Hier sind nahezu alle Fachrichtungen vertreten und die Wartezeiten sind kurz. Die Patienten müssen meistens in Vorleistung treten, bekommen aber in der Regel die Kosten der ärztlichen Leistung durch ihre Krankenversicherung erstattet.

In many villages on the Balearic Islands or in their vicinity there are medical centres, called „Centro de Salut" in Spanish, where general practitioners work. Any treatment is free of charge for individuals who fall under the state insurance scheme in Germany.

Private insurance and self-pay patients

Attracted by annual numbers around 10 million visiting tourists as well as the many resident foreigners, quite a few doctors from Germany and other northern European countries have relocated to Mallorca or other Balearic islands, some of them joining forces by establishing their own medical centres. Among the best-known is the International Medical Centre in Palma de Mallorca, **Centro Medico Porto Pi***, with two facilities opposite to Club de Mar. Almost all medical disciplines are provided here, and waiting times are short. Patients have to pay directly, but usually the costs of medical treatments and services will be refunded by their respective insurance company.*

Centro Medico Porto Pi / Internationales Facharztzentrum
Palma de Mallorca
T 971 70 70 35 + 971 70 70 55
www.centromedicoportopi.es

KLETTERTIPPS
ROCK CLIMBING TIPS

Mallorca hat beste Bedingungen für Deep Water Soloing (DWS), eine Kletterdisziplin, bei der man über Wasser klettert, aber völlig ungesichert (Soloklettern). Vor allem im Küstenstreifen im Südosten Mallorcas zwischen Cabo Salinas und Cala Falcó gleich nördlich der Cala Barcas gibt es unzählige Routen in allen Schwierigkeitsgraden.
Petra und Rupert Kellner haben sie erkundet. Die Eigner des 20-Meter-Katamarans „Largyalo", den sie über viele Jahre mit Unterstützung von Freunden eigenhändig in Holz-Epoxy gebaut haben, sind einige Sommer hier gesegelt – und geklettert. Ihre Tipps:

*Mallorca is particularly suited for Deep Water Soloing (DWS), a climbing discipline where climbers move above the water surface, but remain completely unsecured (free solo). The entire coastal strip in Mallorca's southeast along the stretch from the north of Cabo Salinas up to Cala Falcó (right north of Cala Barcas) is offering innumerable routes in all levels of difficulty.
Petra and Rupert Kellner have tried them all. The owner of the 20-m-catamaran „Largyalo", which they brought to life on wood epoxy with their own hands and some support by friends have sailed and climbed several summers in the area. Here their recommendations:*

Cala de sa Comuna (s./p. 90):
Vor dem Eingang zur Bucht ist eine große auffällige Grotte. Innen kann man bis unter die Decke klettern und dann ins Wasser springen. Man ankert direkt vor der Grotte. / *In front of the bay entrance there is a large, conspicuous grotto. Inside, you can climb up to the ceiling and then jump into the water. Anchor right in front of the grotto.*

Cala Pilota / Cala Magraner
Der Kletterspot schlechthin. In der Cala Magraner kann man von Land aus mit Seil an zahlreichen ausgenagelten Routen entlang der markanten Felswand klettern. Dazu rund um beide Calas an den steilen Felswänden über Wasser. Beste Stellen sind in der Magraner am Westufer am Übergang zur Cala Pilota und am Südufer der Pilota.
The climbing spot par excellence. In Cala Magraner, climbers can proceed from the landside using ropes on many routes equipped with nails. Or go around both Calas alongside steep cliff banks above the water surface. The best spots are in Magraner at the western shore at the passage to Cala Pilota, and at Pilota's southern shore.

Cala Barcas
am Nordufer einige mittelschwere bis schwere Routen rund um die Grotten. *On the northern shore, some medium to difficult routes around the grottos.*

DAS NOTARZTSYSTEM AUF DEN BALEAREN FUNKTIONIERT ÜBER DIE NUMMER 112.
TO CALL AN EMERGENCY DOCTOR ON THE BALEARIC ISLANDS, DIAL 112.

Portbook & Island Guide

MALLORCA 4

Alcúdiamar 174, 184
Amarres Deportivos 29
Andraitx, Port d' 58, 72
Arenal 10, 52

Bonaire 192, 194

Cabo Blanco 92
Cabo Pera 169
Cabo Salinas 92, 109
Cabo Vermey 164
Cabrera 110
Cala Angulia 150, 155
Cala Antena 150, 152
Cala Arsenau 124, 143
Cala Barcas 150, 155
Cala Beltran 94
Cala Banyalbufar 58, 81
Cala Blanca 58, 70
Cala Blava 10, 55
Cala Boquer 192, 206
Cala Bona 150, 162
Cala Camp de Mar 58, 70
Cala Canyamel 150, 164
Cala Caragol 92, 109
Cala Castell 192, 206
Cala Deía 58, 82
Cala de Coll Baix 190, 192
Cala de sa Calobra 192, 207
Cala de sa Comuna 124, 127
Cala del Pinar 191, 192
Cala Domingos 150, 152
Cala d'es Burgit 124, 132
Cala d'Or 124, 138, 140
Cala Egos 51, 52
Cala en Gossalba 192, 204
Cala en Tugores 92, 109
Cala es Caló 174, 179
Cala es Burri 112, 118
Cala Esmeralda 124, 142
Cala Estany 150, 155
Cala Ferrera 124, 142
Cala Figuera 124, 128, 192, 204
Cala Formentor 192, 204
Cala Fornells 58, 66
Cala Gamba 10, 47
Cala Gat 167
Cala Gran 140
Cala Guya 174, 176
Cala Llamp 58, 71
Cala Llonga 140
Cala Llombards 124, 127
Cala Magraner 150, 152
Cala Marsal 124, 143
Cala Mandia 150, 155

Cala Marmols 124, 126
Cala Mata 174, 179
Cala Matsoch 174, 178
Cala Mesquida 174, 176
Cala Mitjana 174, 176
Cala Molto 6, 174, 176
Cala Mondragó 124, 132
Cala Morlanda 150, 160
Cala Murada 152
Cala Murta 192, 204
Cala Petita 150, 160
Cala Pí 92, 94
Cala Pinar 190, 192
Cala Pilota 150, 152
Cala Portals Vells 10, 12
Cala Port Salada 174, 178
Cala Rajada 150, 166
Cala San Vincente 192, 206
Cala Santanyi 124, 127
Cala s'Almunia 124, 126
Cala Serena 124, 142
Cala Torta 174, 176
Cala Tuent 192, 207
Cala Valldemossa 58, 81
Cala Veya 10, 55
Cala Virgili 150, 152
Calanova, Port 10, 20
Camp de Mar 58, 70
Ca'n Pastilla 10, 48
C'an Picafort 174, 183
Club de Mar, Palma 34
Club Maritimo San Antonio de la Playa 10, 48
Club Náutico Serranova 122
Club Nàutic S'Arenal 10, 52
Coll Baix 124, 129
Colònia de Sant Jordi 92, 104
Colònia de Sant Pere 174, 180

Deía, Cala 58, 82
Dragonera, Isla 58, 76

El Toro, Port Adriano 58, 60
Ensenada de la Porrasa 10, 13
Ensenada de sa Rápita 92, 98, 102
Ensenada de la Moreyra 150, 161
Ensenada de Santa Ponsa 58
Es Carbó 92, 108
Es Trenc 92, 102
Font de sa Cala 150, 165

Illetas 10, 18
Illoits de Can Climent 10, 55
Isla Alcanada 174, 190
Isla Conills 66
Isla Dragonera 58, 76
Isla Gabina 102
Isla Horadada 112, 117

Register

Isla Redonda 102
Islas Malgrats 66
Isla Moltana 66, 77
Islote El Toro 61, 62

Lonja Marina, Palma de Mallorca 30

Marina Naviera Balear, Palma de Mallorca 31
Marina de Bonaire 192, 194
Marina Palma Cuarentena 34
Marina Port de Mallorca 32
Moll Vell, Palma de Mallorca 29

Na Foradada 58, 82

Palma de Mallorca .... 8, 10, 24 ff.
Palmanova 10, 13
Pantalán del Mediterráneo, Palma 33
Playa de es Trenc 92, 102
Playa de sa Rápita 92, 98, 102
Playa de son Moll 167
Playa Es Carbó 92, 108
Port Adriano, El Toro 58, 60
Port Calanova 10, 20
Port d'Alcúdia 174, 184
Port d'Andraitx 58, 72
Port de Mallorca, Palma 32
Port de Sollér 58, 84
Port de Pollenca 192, 198
Port Valldemossa 58, 81
Porto Cristo 150, 156
Portocolom 124, 144
Portopetro 124, 134
Portixol 10, 47
Puerto Portals 10, 14
Puerto de Cabrera 112, 118
Puerto de Campos 92, 104
Puerto El Cocodrilo 124, 132
Punta Anciola 112, 121
Punta Avenzada 192, 200
Punta Llarga 174, 182
Punta Plana 92

Real Club Náutico, Palma de Mallorca 30

Sa Calobra 192, 207
Sa Rápita 92, 98
Santa Ponsa 58, 66
Sant Elm 58, 76
Ses Covetes 92
S'Arenal, Club Nàutic 10, 52
S'Estanyol 92, 96
Sollér, Port de 58, 84
Son Serra de Marina 174, 182
STP Shipyard Palma 29
Valldemossa, Cala + Port 58, 81

MENORCA 208

Addaya 242, 244
Cabo d'Artutx 210, 218
Cala Algaret 224, 240
Cala Algaryens 242, 252
Cala Arenal de Castell 242, 248
Cala Binibeca 224, 229
Cala Canatuells 224, 227
Cala Covas 224, 227
Cala d'es Frares 216
Cala Escorxada 210, 223
Cala Ferragut 242, 252
Cala Fornells 242, 249
Cala Degollador 210, 216
Cala de Son Saura 210, 220
Cala Macarella 210, 221
Cala Mesquida 224, 240
Cala Mitjana 210, 222
Cala Morell 242, 252
Cala 'n Bosch 210, 218
Cala Olla 242, 248
Cala Porté 224, 226
Cala Pregonda 242, 252
Cala Presili 224, 240
Cala Santandria 210, 217
Cala Galdana 210, 222
Cala Talaier 210, 220
Cala Taulera 238
Cala Trebeluja 210, 222
Cala Turqueta 210, 220
Cala Xoriguer 219
Ciutadella 210, 212
Es Grau 224, 240
Fornells 242, 249
Isla Colom 224, 240
Isla del Aire 224, 229
Mahón 224, 230
Marina Menorca, Mahón 233
Marina Port Mahón 234
Playa de Binigaus 224, 226
Playa Cavalleria 242, 252
Puerto de Addaya 242, 244
Puerto de Mahón 224, 230
Punta Prima 224, 229
Son Bou 224, 226

IBIZA 254

Cala Badella 278, 287
Cala Bassa 278, 286
Cala Blanca 256, 276
Cala Binirras 256, 277
Cala Boix 256, 272
Cala Compte 278, 286
Cala de Port Roig 278, 288

Cala Horts	278, 288
Cala Jondal	278, 290
Cala Llena	256, 272
Cala Llonga	256, 268
Cala Nova	256, 272
Cala Portinatx	256, 274
Club Náutico, Ibiza	256, 264
Cala Salada	278, 280
Cala San Vicente	256, 273
Cala Talamanca	256, 268
Cala Tarida	278, 287
Ensenada de Aubarca	278, 280
Ensenada de la Canal	278, 291
Ensenada Xarraca	256, 276
Ibiza	256, 258
Ibiza Magna	264
Isla Tagomago	256, 272
Isla Vedra	289
Islas Margaritas	278, 280
Marina Botafoch, Ibiza	263
Marina Ibiza	263
Port del Torrent	278, 286
Port Ibiza Town	264
Port Sant Miguel	256, 277
Sant Antoni de Portmany	278, 282
Santa Eularia del Rio	256, 270
Tagomago, Isla	256, 272

FORMENTERA 292

Cala Pujols	294, 305
Cala Sahona	294, 304
Cala Torreta	294, 301
Caló de s'Olli	294, 304
Cabo Barbaria	294
Ensenada de Tramontana	294, 304
Ensenada del Cabrito	294, 304
Ensenada Migjorn	294, 304
Espalmador, Puerto de	294, 301
Estanque del Peix	304
Faro de la Mola	294
Formentera Mar	299
La Savina	294, 296
Los Trocados	294, 302
Marina de Formentera	298
Pas de S'Espalmador	294, 301
Playa de Levante	294, 302
Puerto del Espalmador	294, 301
Ses Illetes	294, 302

Fotonachweis / *Photo credit*
(auch für Karten / *also for charts / maps*)

Alle Fotos | *all pictures* Martin Muth,
ausgenommen / *exempt*: .... S./P.

Satellite image by BlackBridge (www.blackbridge.com)	2
Nico Martínez	16
Claire Matches (The Superyacht Cup)	37
Port Adriano/Ocibar	60, 62, 64
IPM-Group	29, 32, 33, 263, 266
Monika Linnenbecker	50, 302
Port Calanova	20
Café del Mar	284
Marina Port de Mahón	234
J. Lehmann und H. Barholz	213
Jose Ramón García Ledesma, Ingeniero Técnico de Obras Públicas	146
Puerto de Addaya	244, 245
© caid - Fotolia.com	322
Spanisches Fremdenverkehrsamt	238
Fotolia, Lunamarina (Cala Bassa)	287
Fotolia, Sergio Formoso	235

Inserentenverzeichnis / *Advertising companies* .... S./P.

Nautor's Swan / Flensburger Yachtservice	Cover + 63
Palmawatch	Cover + 32
Marine Electric	Cover + 32
Pantaenius	Innere Umschlagseite vorne / Inner front cover
Audax	Innere Umschlagseite hinten / Inner back cover
Kreuzer-Abteilung	51 + 54
Bavaria Spain	33
Centro Medico Porto Pi / Int. Facharztzentrum	35
Dream Yacht Charter	133
Portocolom Yachting	155
Sun Charter	119
Charter del Mar	35
Sailactive	31

Vielen Dank / Acknowledgements

Vielen Dank …

… an alle, die zu diesem Buch beigetragen haben.

Zuerst an alle Personen und Firmen, die mit einer Anzeige in dieser neuen Ausgabe unseres Portbook wieder einmal oder zum ersten Mal als Partner in Erscheinung treten und dieses Buch erst möglich machen.

An die Piloten, ohne deren fliegerisches Können ich die vielen Luftaufnahmen nicht hätte realisieren können.

Ganz besonders danke ich Monika Linnenbecker für den regen inhaltlichen Austausch in der Produktionsphase dieses Buches, einige inhaltliche Ergänzungen – und natürlich für ihre gestalterische Kompetenz als Grafikerin.

Danke auch an Juanjo Lemm, Ingenieur und Hafenarchitekt aus Palma, für den regelmäßigen Informationsaustausch und den Kontakt zu seinem Kollegen José Ramón García Ledesma. Auch ihm einen Dank, nämlich für den Plan der Bojenfelder und Steganlagen in Portocolom.

Stellvertretend für viele andere, die mit Hinweisen zur Aktualität des Buches beigetragen haben, möchte ich erwähnen:
- Petra und Rupert Kellner, SY Largyalo
- Achim Weckler, SY Lazy Life, Port de Mallorca
- Dieter Brokate, SY Moorea, RCNP
- Walter Vollstädt, SY Thalatta, Club Nàutic Arenal
- Antonia und Jens Matthiesen, SY Dorette, RCNP
- Oliver Ochse, Der Segelberater
- Thomas Zehnpfenning, Kapitän, Palma
- Mickey Jarvanpaa, Kapitän, Formentera
- Johan Loch, BWA Yachting
- Beate Koebler und Christian Kaden, Adriano Yachtcharter
- Peter und Christian Winter, Yates Baleares
- Gottfried Möller, Sail & Surf Pollensa
- Thorsten Dimnik, Skipper

Entschuldigen möchte ich mich an dieser Stelle bei allen, die hier namentlich nicht genannt sind und die ebenso das Portbook unterstützen:
- durch ihre Empfehlungen
- durch eine schöne Präsentation im Handel
- durch Unterstützung bei Vertrieb und Verkauf
- durch die Ausrüstung von Charterflotten
  und und und …

Martin Muth

Acknowledgements …

… to all who have contributed to this book, thank you!

First of all, to the companies and individuals who have been partners in producing this nautical guide with their support, confidence and advertisements. You have made this book possible.

To the pilots: without their aeronautical skills I would never have been able to achieve these numerous aerial photographs.

I would particularly like to thank my graphic designer Monika Linnenbecker for an animated exchange on contents during the production phase of this book, some additional content – and of course for her creative skills.

To all those who have provided information to really help render this book up to date, I would like to mention:
- *Petra and Rupert Kellner, SY Largyalo*
- *Achim Weckler, SY Lazy Life, Port de Mallorca*
- *Dieter Brokate, SY Moorea, RCNP*
- *Walter Vollstädt, SY Thalatta, Club Nàutic Arenal*
- *Antonia and Jens Matthiesen, SY Dorette, RCNP*
- *Oliver Ochse, Der Segelberater*
- *Thomas Zehnpfenning, Captain, Palma*
- *Mickey Jarvanpaa, Captain, Formentera*
- *Johan Loch, BWA Yachting*
- *Beate Koebler und Christian Kaden, Adriano Yachtcharter*
- *Peter and Christian Winter, Yates Baleares*
- *Gottfried Möller, Sail & Surf Pollensa*
- *Thorsten Dimnik, Skipper*

There are so many I have failed to mention, who nevertheless have been vital in ensuring the success of this book.

Thank you for …
- *your recommendations*
- *retail promotion and presentation in shops*
- *distribution and sales support*
- *equipping yacht charter fleets*
- *for buying books to give on to friends, customers etc. etc…*

Martin Muth

Impressum / Imprint

Portbook & Island Guide
Mallorca Ibiza Formentera Menorca
3., stark erweiterte und aktualisierte Ausgabe, 2016
3rd updated edition, 2016
www.portbook-mallorca.com
www.bonanova-books.com

Copyright
BonaNova Books, 2016

Herausgeber, V.i.S.d.P. / *Editor*
Martin Muth
mail@bonanova-books.com
M +34 655 477 476
M +49 172 275 21 91
Louise-Schroeder-Stieg 3
22846 Norderstedt
Deutschland / *Germany* / Alemania

Gestaltung / *Graphic Design*
Monika Linnenbecker, d/vision
monika@dvision.es, T 971 701 380

Übersetzung / *Translation*
Line Hadsbjerg / Remarkable World
Martina Bühner, Dipl.-Übersetzerin
www.buehner-translation.de

Druck / *Print*
Phoenix Print GmbH, Würzburg
www.phoenixprint.de

Bibliografische Information der Deutschen Nationalbibliothek:
„Die Deutsche Nationalbibliothek verzeichnet diese Publikation in der Deutschen Nationalbibliografie; detaillierte bibliografische Daten sind im Internet über http://dnb.dnb.de abrufbar."

Ausgabe 2016 / *Printed 2016*

Hinweis
Der Nachdruck, auch nur auszugsweise, ist ohne schriftliche Genehmigung des Herausgebers nicht erlaubt. Der Portbook & Island Guide beinhaltet eine Zusammenstellung von Informationen zum Gebiet der Balearen. Eine Garantie für die Richtigkeit der Informationen kann nicht übernommen werden. Der Herausgeber ist nicht verantwortlich für falsche oder irreführende Informationen. Für etwaige Schäden kann keine Haftung übernommen werden.

Nicht zur Navigation zu verwenden
Die in diesem Buch abgedruckten Karten sind eine Navigationshilfe und ersetzen keine offiziellen amtlichen Karten. Nur offizielle amtliche Karten und die Mitteilungen für Seefahrer enthalten die für die sichere Navigation erforderlichen Informationen, und der Kapitän ist immer für ihren korrekten Einsatz verantwortlich.

Hinweis zu den Satelliten-Bildern
Die Balearen und viele andere Mittelmeerinseln sind als hochwertiger Satellitenbildkunstdruck erhältlich bei der albedo39 Satellitenbildwerkstatt, Köln, www.albedo39.de

Note
The reproduction, even partial, is prohibited without the written permission of the publisher. Portbook & Island Guide includes a compilation of information on the area of the Balearic Islands. A guarantee of the accuracy of the information cannot be assumed. The publisher is not responsible for any false or misleading information. Plans or information may not be used as a navigational aid. No liability can be accepted for any damage.

Not to be used for navigation
Charts printed in this book are an aid to navigation and do not replace official government charts. Only official government charts and notices to mariners contain all information needed for the safety of navigation and, the captain is responsible for their prudent use.

Note on satellite images
High-quality satellite image art prints of the Balearic Islands and many more islands of the Mediterranean are available at albedo39 Satellitenbildwerkstatt in Cologne, Germany. See www.albedo39.de